# AFRICAN AMERICANS

*in*

# SOUTH TEXAS HISTORY

Foreword by Cary D. Wintz

*Perspectives on South Texas*

SPONSORED BY
*Texas A&M University–Kingsville*
Timothy E. Fulbright, General Editor



A list of titles in this series is available at the end of this book.

# AFRICAN AMERICANS *in* SOUTH TEXAS HISTORY

EDITED BY

BRUCE A. GLASRUD

*Foreword by Cary D. Wintz*

TEXAS A&M UNIVERSITY PRESS • COLLEGE STATION, TEXAS

First edition

This paper meets the requirements of ANSI/NISO Z39.48-1992
(Permanence of Paper).
Binding materials have been chosen for durability.

LIBRARY OF CONGRESS CATALOGING-IN-PUBLICATION DATA

African Americans in South Texas history / edited by Bruce A. Glasrud ; foreword by Cary D. Wintz.—1st ed.
p. cm.—(Perspectives on South Texas)
Includes bibliographical references and index.
ISBN 978-1-60344-228-2 (hc-hardcover : alk. paper)—
ISBN 978-1-60344-229-9 (pb-pbk. : alk. paper)
1. African Americans—Texas, South—History. 2. Texas, South—Race relations.
I. Glasrud, Bruce A. II. Series: Perspectives on south Texas.
E185.93.T4A39 2011
305.896'0730764—dc22
2010043598

# Contents

# Foreword

## *African Americans—In South Texas?*

CARY D. WINTZ

AFRICAN AMERICAN HISTORY AND TEXAS HISTORY have been intertwined since the first Africans and Europeans arrived in this part of the world. Esteban accompanied the Cabeza de Vaca expedition, and blacks accompanied Spanish and mestizo settlers into Texas in the eighteenth century. Blacks, both slave and free, inhabited Spanish Texas and Mexican Texas. With Anglo settlement came thousands more, mostly enslaved. At the time of emancipation in June 1865, over two hundred thousand blacks called Texas home. That number swelled to over six hundred twenty thousand in 1900 and more than 2.4 million a century later. Throughout the states history the great majority of Texas blacks lived in the eastern and northeastern part of the state, especially in East Texas, the Brazos River valley, and the large cities, in particular Houston and Dallas. South Texas throughout its history has been home to relatively few African American residents.

For the purposes of this study, Bruce Glasrud defines South Texas as the more-or-less trapezoid-shaped area bounded by the Gulf of Mexico on the southeast, the Rio Grande on the southwest from the gulf to Eagle Pass, then eastward through San Antonio, continuing east on Interstate 10 to the Brazos River, and from the Brazos River back to the gulf. Today this area covers some forty-three counties with a combined population of a little over 5.1 million persons, of whom almost three hundred fifty thousand (6.8 percent) are African Americans[1]. However, three counties along the northern boundary of this region (Bexar, Fort Bend, and Brazoria counties) contain almost 78 percent of the black population of South Texas. The remaining forty counties together have fewer than seventy-eight thousand African Americans, who make up only 2.9 percent of the population. Clearly South Texas is not a center of black population. African Americans are greatly outnumbered by both Mexican Americans and whites, and they exercise neither great political nor great economic power in this region.

This demographic data is important to appreciate the significance of *African Americans in South Texas History* and the importance of the study of African American history in South Texas. First it is important to note that the study of African Americans should not, indeed, must not be confined to just those regions, cities, and states where blacks compose a large portion of the population. To understand the African American experience in all of its fullness and complexity, it is necessary to examine African American history in Seguin as well as in Harlem, and in South Texas as well as in the black belt of Mississippi, the cotton and sugar plantation areas of antebellum Texas, and the ghettos of Deep Ellum in Dallas and the Fourth Ward in Houston. The presence of African Americans in South Texas' history is unavoidable. For example, Hidalgo county, where today blacks make up less than 1 percent of the population, was the site of the 1906 Brownsville Riot, which involved an alleged attack by black soldiers on the town of Brownsville and symbolized both the high level of racial tension throughout the nation in the early twentieth century and the propensity to hold African Americans accountable for this racial strife. Less dramatic, but ultimately more noteworthy, were the experiences of individual blacks who settled in South Texas communities, raised their families, created black institutions, and struggled for dignity both during slavery and following emancipation over the past century and a half.

It is particularly important for scholars who study African American history to examine those areas with relatively small black populations in order to compare and contrast them with areas having larger black populations. How did slavery, emancipation, and Reconstruction play out in South Texas? Was Jim Crow as rigid in the Rio Grande Valley as it was in East Texas? What was the impact of the civil rights struggle in South Texas cities and small towns? How did small black communities address their needs for religion and education? These are just a few of the questions that beg attention. In addition it is important to determine what sources are available for African American history in South Texas, and what historical scholarship exists. The answers to these questions and others will deepen our understanding of the African American experience in Texas and in the Unites States. It will also serve notice that it is important to focus additional scholarship on this relatively neglected area of African American history in Texas.

*African Americans in South Texas History* remains true to the model that Glasrud developed for other regional studies of African American history in Texas. As in his volumes on East Texas and West Texas, he selected the best previously published essays on South Texas black history. The number of essays presented in this collection demonstrates the growing body of scholarship on this topic as well as the diversity of the African American experience in this part of the state. Collecting and anthologizing the scattered essays provides them a wider audience and makes them more accessible to students, scholars, and the interested public. The essays included in this collection range broadly in subject matter and in the time periods they treat. Chronologically they span the antebellum period to the late twentieth century; in theme they address slavery, Reconstruction, politics, civil rights, education, labor, the arts, and even professional sports. Among the richest essays are those that provide insight into the African Americans who settled and organized their community and institutions in the small towns and villages of South Texas.

Why a study of African Americans in South Texas? Because African Americans, though relatively small in number, built their lives, created their communities, struggled for dignity and their rights, and expressed their creativity and humanity in this area of the state. Because South Texas history is the history of African Americans.

—Texas Southern University
Houston, Texas

## NOTES

1. All population figures are taken from 2008 estimates, U.S. Census Bureau: State and County QuickFacts. Data derived from Population Estimates, Census of Population and Housing, Small Area Income and Poverty Estimates, State and County Housing Unit Estimates, County Business Patterns, Nonemployer Statistics, Economic Census, Survey of Business Owners, Building Permits, Consolidated Federal Funds Report. Last Revised: Nov. 17, 2009, 12:17:04 EST, http://quickfacts.census.gov/qfd/states/48000.html (accessed January 5, 2010).

# Acknowledgments

AT A FALL 2008 LUNCH GATHERING OF SOUTH TEXAS historians, aka the Victoria Secrets, the question raised was "Where/what is South Texas?" The essential element to this question, we determined, was "What are the boundaries of South Texas?" Upon perusing a map, and with considerable discussion, some of it knowledgeable, some from former Yankees, the conclusion—although not unanimous—was this: South Texas is that portion of the Lone Star state reaching from Eagle Pass on the Rio Grande to San Antonio, thence following a line along today's Interstate 10 to the Brazos River; the eastern border then follows the Brazos down to the coast, and includes everything between there and the Rio Grande. The southern boundary then follows the Rio Grande westward to Eagle Pass. This, then, is the South Texas described in *African Americans in South Texas History*.

*African Americans in South Texas History* was not completed without assistance and encouragement from a number of people. As noted earlier, the group of historians composing the closely knit group, the Victoria Secrets, supported and aided in the preparation of this volume. Thanks, friends. Too often do I fail to acknowledge the editorial debt I owe to my wife, Pearlene Vestal Glasrud. Thanks, Pearlene. The staff at the Seguin Public library enthusiastically and quickly filled my numerous requests for an article or a book. The late Bill Stein, director of the Nesbitt Memorial Library at Columbus, Texas, invited me to the library and kept bringing books and journals to me while at the same time asking either "Why?" or "Do you know what that means?" Prior to his questioning, I did not always know the answer. Many others listened to and answered my questions, including T. Lindsay Baker, Cary D. Wintz, Jerry D. Thompson, Ed Byerly, L. Patrick Hughes, James M. Smallwood, Tom Britten, Alwyn Barr, Cecelia Venable, and Tony Knopf.

I wish to thank the staffs at the *Journal of South Texas*, the *Journal of Southern History*, and *South Texas Studies* for granting me permission to use articles published in their respective journals. As always, the authors particularly deserve my thanks and respect, first for the effort and skill necessary to write and publish the articles, and second for allowing me to use them in this book. Janice Sumler-Edmond and Rebecca Kosary wrote articles for this project. This book would not be complete without their original work. Thanks, Janice and Rebecca. Mary Lenn Dixon, editor-in-chief at Texas A&M University Press, once more listened, encouraged, and supported; the staff at the Press brought the manuscript into book form. On the other hand, any errors or omissions remain my responsibility.

—Bruce A. Glasrud

# AFRICAN AMERICANS

*in*

# SOUTH TEXAS HISTORY

# Introduction

## *The African American Experience in South Texas*

BRUCE A. GLASRUD

THE FIRST AFRICAN AMERICANS TO ENTER SOUTH Texas came with Spanish explorers, and thousands more came later as slaves from the United States, in the tow of Anglo owners. Later still—after the Civil War—freed blacks often migrated to Texas for a better life than they could expect in their home states, especially in the deep South. In 1877 one such former slave, Solomon Melvin Coles, arrived in Corpus Christi, Texas, on a permanent assignment from the Association of the Congregationalist Church to the Freedom Congregationalist Church of Corpus Christi. For nearly twenty years Coles remained in Corpus Christi, where he became an influential religious and educational leader in the small, struggling black community of that city. Born into slavery in Virginia in 1844, Coles had received some basic education while enslaved. Soon after the Civil War, when further educational opportunities proved limited or unavailable for a young black man, he moved to Connecticut. There he attended and in 1869 graduated from Guilford Institute, the first African American to do so. Barred by his race from attending nearby Yale University, Coles moved to Pennsylvania and entered Lincoln University, where he was awarded a bachelor's degree in 1872. He delivered the salutatory address at commencement.

In the same year Coles realized an unlikely dream. He became the first African American to enroll in the Divinity School of Yale University, which had eliminated its racial restriction two years previously. He did well in the three-year course of study and graduated with a bachelor of divinity degree in 1875. During the summer Coles, like other students, was sent to small churches on behalf of the American

Missionary Association (AMA) in order to develop ministerial skills and to help the churches build their membership. A trip to Leavenworth, Kansas, the summer before he graduated left him impoverished; his church, which was small and poor, could not pay him the agreed-upon sum for his salary. After graduation Coles was unable to find a suitable position despite his degrees from Lincoln University and Yale Divinity School. As a result he continued work for the AMA, helping establish the Nazarene Congregational Church in Brooklyn. A subsequent trip to South Carolina proved difficult for his health; he asked for a leave and did not return to South Carolina.

Soon after arriving in Texas to answer the call of the Freedom Congregational Church, Coles was ordained in Goliad and set out on his new ministry. His financial prospects did not improve, at least not initially. Corpus Christi's African American community numbered about three hundred, and the Congregational Church (like the church in Leavenworth before it) lacked the wherewithal to pay his entire salary.

Coles quickly discovered that the members of the black community had almost no educational opportunities, and in the fall of 1877 he started a small private school. He taught there in addition to performing his pastoral duties. The next year he accepted a position as principal and instructor at the public school for blacks, called the Public Free School for Colored. For four years Coles both taught and preached. Then, in 1880, he resigned his pastorate to teach full time.

Coles's life was dedicated to educating black children and supporting the black community, and his influence spread. He joined and was a contributing member of the Southwest Texas Congregational Association, and in 1883 he helped establish the Colored Teachers State Association of Texas (the African American teachers' association), which sought equality for all races in educational matters. Coles served as its president, wrote articles on issues of race, education, and religion for the *Lincoln University Alumni Magazine*, and in 1892 delivered the graduation address at Prairie View State Normal School. However, a deteriorating racial climate in Corpus Christi as well as a discriminatory salary led Coles to become disenchanted with that city, and in

1894 he moved to San Antonio, where he taught for twenty years before retiring. He died in 1924 in Oberlin, Ohio.

Coles's career as a clergyman and educator spanned six decades of South Texas history after the Civil War. Born a slave, he lived through long years of poverty and racism in the late nineteenth and early twentieth centuries, yet he was able to make important contributions that are still honored today. A school was named for him in 1925, and as recently as 2000 a classroom building was dedicated to him at Del Mar College. Indeed, Solomon Melvin Coles's story is exceptional, it is centered in South Texas, and it is bound inextricably to the long struggle from slavery to education to community building.

Coles's story has been told in a short monograph entitled *Black Tracks to Texas: Solomon Melvin Coles—From Slave to Educator*, by Edna Jordan, and in two articles by Moses N. Moore Jr. and Yolanda Y. Smith that are part of a larger project, "'Been in the Storm So Long': Yale Divinity School and the Black Ministry."[1] The stories of other black South Texans remain untold. But new evidence and new stories are forthcoming each year, including those by authors writing for *South Texas Studies*, the *Journal of Southern History*, and the *Journal of South Texas*. Additionally, five folk stories useful to to historical analysis can be found in Jakie L. Pruett and Everett B. Cole, *As We Lived: Stories by Black Storytellers*.[2]

Black Americans entered what is today South Texas as early as Estevan's 1528 shipwreck and capture and his later incursion with Cabeza de Vaca in 1534–36. Other blacks accompanied Spanish explorers into the area as well. Black soldiers came with the Spanish who in 1689 founded the settlement that would become San Antonio, and later, as in 1718, black families also arrived, thus beginning the community of African Americans in South Texas. During the Spanish and Mexican periods, race and class were not necessarily inextricable, and blacks could achieve positions of wealth and influence. Felipe Eloa, for example, was one of several blacks who received land grants, and he married into a well-to-do, upper-class Spanish family. By 1790 the population of San Antonio included 862 persons of African descent. However, during the mid-nineteenth century, Anglos brought thousands of black slaves into the region, and the number and role of black Americans in South Texas expanded considerably.[3]

Free African Americans also entered and lived in South Texas. Although the U.S. Census listed fewer than four hundred free blacks in the state in 1850 and 1860, the counts were incomplete. Douglas Hales estimates that twice that many lived in the state. In South Texas the discrepancy between the real population and the census count was probably even larger; as George Woolfolk notes in *The Free Negro in Texas, 1800–1860: A Study in Cultural Compromise*, the U.S. Census did not count blacks with Spanish surnames. And these free blacks in Texas were often quite successful in a variety of economic endeavors—one Tamar Morgan Hardin, for instance, as late as 1844, during the Republic, owned four lots, additional property, and four slaves in Brazoria County. Free blacks also participated in the pre-Civil War cattle industry, especially in Jackson County. Notable among them was Harriet Reynolds, who in 1860 owned cattle assessed at $3,300.[4]

But most of the new migrants were enslaved. The extent of reliance on slavery varied in South Texas from the rather large cotton plantations in Fort Bend, Brazoria, Wharton, and Matagorda counties to the ranches and small farms to the south and west in counties such as Victoria and Goliad, and from the emerging towns and cities such as Seguin, Corpus Christi, Victoria, and San Antonio to those counties bordering the Rio Grande, such as Zapata, that registered no black slaves at all. The county that was most like the deep South in attitude, wealth, and extent of slavery was Brazoria. In 1860, for example, the population of Brazoria County included 5,110 black slaves, 2,027 whites, and 6 free blacks. Wharton County was similar; in 1858, black slaves numbered 2,181 in an entire population of 2,861. Slavery was also an essential element of the economy and lifestyle of Fort Bend County. In 1860 its slave population of 4,127 was more than double its white population. Matagorda County, with a black slave population of 2,107 in 1860, developed its wealth with cotton and cattle as the primary cash crops, although cane sugar and corn were also key staples of the economy. Slaves laboring on these crops endured a considerable range of harsh physical work and ill treatment by overbearing whites. Randolph Campbell discusses these aspects of slavery in "Slavery in Texas, 1821–1865: A Brief Overview, with Emphasis on the Lower Brazos River Valley."[5]

What distinguished the system of slavery in South Texas from that in the remainder of the state was the cattle industry. Where cattle-raising was the staple of the economy, slaves frequently worked the cattle and on the smaller farms did other chores as well. Cattle-raising frequently demanded more skills and independence than picking or hoeing crops such as cotton. Although the 1,748 slaves in Guadalupe County worked mostly on small farms, a few larger cotton plantations emerged in the 1850s. Guadalupe County's slave statistics and data are readily available in Mark Gretchen's *Slave Transactions of Guadalupe County, Texas*. In Gonzales County, which had 3,168 slaves in 1860, cotton and corn served as the chief crops. In Jackson County many of the 1,194 slaves worked as drovers or cowhands. DeWitt County's balance was remarkable; in 1860, with a total population of 5,108, the number of black slaves stood at 1,643. In that county, where grazing stock was the primary business, corn, cotton, and tobacco were also raised, with slaves engaged in all of those enterprises.[6]

Urban slavery became one more aspect of the "peculiar institution" in South Texas, particularly in Corpus Christi, Victoria, and San Antonio. Laredo, Brownsville, and Eagle Pass, on the other hand, had few black slaves, probably due in part to the number of Tejanos who did the hard work in those cities. Slavery in San Antonio is explored in Larry Knight's essay, "Defending the Unnecessary: Slavery in San Antonio in the 1850s," originally published in the *Journal of South Texas*. Knight points out that although slave-owning was not widespread in that city, the influence of slave owners and the institution of slavery were nonetheless significant. Slavery occupied a considerable amount of the time on the part of both city governance and opponents of the institution. But as Knight reminds us, "the final factor that made slavery important in San Antonio was simply the southern mentality: slavery was good, and blacks, free or slave, were inferior."[7]

Not all South Texas counties so actively supported this nefarious institution. Zapata County, as noted above, did not count any slaves in its population in 1850, and Wilson and Karnes counties reported fewer than 400 each. In the 1860 census San Patricio numbered 620 people, of whom only 95 were black slaves. On the other hand, some counties encouraged overall population growth, including its concomitant expansion of slavery. During the Civil War, Lavaca County was a haven for Confederate slave holders who wished to escape the fighting farther east; its slave population rose from 1,606 in 1860 to 2,713 in 1864 due to the large number of refugees from the war-torn South.[8]

Since African Americans did not want to be enslaved, and since they had many sympathizers, slaveholders shared a certain paranoia. Whites in South Texas feared especially that black slaves were being encouraged by Mexicans to escape, or at least that Mexicans would help them escape. In Matagorda County whites were so alarmed that in 1856 they expelled the entire Mexican population. For South Texas blacks who sought to escape slavery, Texas' proximity to Mexico offered a unique opportunity. As many as four thousand escaped slaves lived in Matamoros and other Mexican communities near the border. "After the Civil War started," former slave Jacob Branch remarked, "lots of slaves ran off to get to the Yankees. All them in this part headed for the Rio Grande River. The Mexicans rigged up flatboats out in the middle of the river, tied stakes with rope. When the colored people got to the rope they could pull themselves across the rest of the way on those boats." Felix Haywood declared, "In Mexico you could be free. They didn't care what color you was, black, white, yellow, or blue." Sallie Wroe's father hauled a load of cotton to the Rio Grande on the Mexican border; he and others then paddled a bale of it to Mexico, where he remained until the war ended.[9] That day arrived on June 19, 1865, the day of freedom celebrated among Texas blacks as Juneteenth.

The years following Juneteenth, from 1865 to 1876, are known in U.S. history as the era of Reconstruction. While historians continue to debate the successes and failures of Reconstruction, virtually all agree that it included the occupation of the southern states by the U.S. military; the federal government's use of national agents of the Freedmen's Bureau to help and protect the former slaves; the efforts of the freed people to start life anew by acquiring land, education, and the right to vote; and the often ferocious resistance to racial change by the vast majority of southern whites. In South Texas these features were present to varying degrees, frequently depending on the proportion of African Americans in the population, the presence of Mexican Americans, and the economy of a given county.

Reconstruction ushered in a period of political activity for blacks in South Texas, although it was frequently opposed by force and fraud. Blacks in politics overcame huge obstacles while at the same time arousing white disapproval. During Reconstruction blacks served as county commissioners, district clerks, members of school boards, and justices of the peace. They generally ran as Republicans and voted Republican; it was the Republican party that had brought them freedom and striven to protect their rights, while the Democratic Party represented those who had held them in slavery. Brazoria County freedmen in 1870 voted Republican for an African American from Galveston, George T. Ruby, to represent them in the Texas Legislature. Another African American, Nathan H. Haller, represented Brazoria and Matagorda counties in the Texas Legislature during the 1890s. Black voting frequently was not a matter of course. In the 1872 election in Goliad County, blacks were able to vote due in part to the presence of "nineteen armed black cowhands."[10] But blacks often were kept from voting in Jackson County through intimidation and fraud on the part of the Ku Klux Klan and through ballot-box tampering. In an interesting twist, Republican victories and political control depended upon Mexican American votes in the western counties of the region, since few blacks lived in those counties.

Reconstruction in South Texas is addressed in the second essay in this volume, Kenneth Wayne Howell's "Just Southwest of Dixie: Reconstruction in South Texas, 1865–1876." Howell looked at five South Texas counties—Nueces, Victoria, Zapata, Maverick, and Live Oak—from the perspective of politics, economics, and violence. He discovered that economic recovery in South Texas advanced due in part to the large cattle industry that had carried over from before the Civil War. Also, according to Howell, "freedmen found it easier to transition into South Texas society" after the Civil War because they had skills to help them. Further easing their social transition was the support they received from families, churches, and schools.[11]

At the same time, however, blacks faced violence and intimidation in some South Texas counties. One violent episode took place in Colorado County in an incident that demonstrated blacks' willingness to fight for their rights. During the Eagle Lake Riot in October 1873, a party of seventy-five to one hundred freedmen armed themselves to search for two missing black men. A similar number of white supremacists also took up arms. The sheriff forestalled a fight when the two men were located, dead, the next day, and the confrontation was averted. Blacks in Colorado County also demonstrated a readiness to resort to force in defense of their own. Another incident occurred in 1887 when a black settlement in Matagorda County, first known as African and later as the Vann Settlement, was attacked by armed white vigilantes from neighboring counties. Jerry Matthews, a black constable, had been killed earlier, and in the confrontation the vigilantes sought black leader Oliver Sheppard, who managed to get out of their path. However, the white marauders killed several other black residents. Antiblack violence and harassment by whites during Reconstruction is treated by Rebecca Kosary in the third article in this collection, "'Wantonly Maltreated and Slain, Simply Because They Are Free': Racial Violence during Reconstruction in South Texas." Kosary's findings provoke speculation that a race war was in fact taking place in South Texas during these early years of Reconstruction.

Antiblack violence in South Texas did not stop with the end of Reconstruction. Rather it continued well past the turn of the century. It was directed against black soldiers in Brownsville in 1906 and against other black soldiers farther east in Houston in 1917. Using violence and ultimately legal mechanisms, whites managed to force blacks out of politics; they subsequently formed White Man's Union Associations by which they kept blacks from influencing any meaningful elections. In Fort Bend County, where whites had previously been unable to overturn Republican rule, the Jaybird-Woodpecker War that culminated on August 16, 1889, finally ended it. Democrats formed the Jaybird Democratic Association, which controlled county politics for years through its exclusionary white primary.[12]

Not all occupations were open to African Americans living in South Texas. But they could wrangle cattle and they could be soldiers. Among those who registered cattle brands in Calhoun County were several blacks, including Ann Hared, "a free woman of color," who used the JD brand on her ranch.[13] Some blacks who had been cowhands as slaves continued working cattle after the Civil War. James Walker of Wilson County was taught how to break horses by his father, who had come from Alabama as a slave. James in turn taught his son, Richard "Bubba" Walker, who well into the twentieth century was known as the best cowhand in Wilson County. Robert Lemmons, a black mustanger who stalked wild horses in Dimmitt, Zavala, and Frio counties in order to tame them for riding, also worked as a freight hauler and acquired property. His ownership of property and his ability to gentle mustangs brought him respect. And women also worked with cattle. Henrietta Foster, or "Aunt Rittie," became a legend in the Texas Coastal Bend as a black woman who rode and worked cattle with the men.[14]

Black soldiers worked and operated in South Texas after the Civil War in a number of different roles, reflecting the changes that were occurring. Before the war, for instance, blacks were not permitted to own firearms. But in July 1865 a brigade of black troops from the 25th U.S. Army Corps entered Corpus Christi, where they remained for a year with apparently few incidents. Texas black militia units had been organized as part of the Texas State Police during Reconstruction and remained in a neglected, somewhat disorganized state after 1876. Three men—A. M. Gregory, Jacob Lyons, and James P. Brattan—at scattered times during the late nineteenth and early twentieth centuries invigorated the black Texas militia and brought about change and uplift. They did this by energetic recruiting, skilful leadership, and updating equipment, training, and supplies. One South Texas unit, the Seguin-based Ireland Rifles, was activated together with a white unit in 1889 to help prevent the lynching of a Mexican prisoner. Ten years earlier, African

Americans in Nueces County had established an all-black militia unit, Roberts Rifles, with Evan M. Mark as captain. The company changed its name in 1892 to the Bluff City Guards. (Mark remained as captain.) South Texas blacks also served in one of the four black regiments of the regular U.S. Army, and later they enlisted in one of the "Immune" units that fought in the Spanish American and Filipino American wars. Among the black regulars stationed in South Texas during the late nineteenth century was the first black graduate of West Point, Lt. Henry O. Flipper, who served at Fort McIntosh for a time.[15]

Black troops of the regular army stationed in South Texas at Brownsville early in the twentieth century found life filled with harassment and discrimination from whites. In 1906 a violent encounter known as the Brownsville Affair occurred when black soldiers belonging to the 25th Regiment stood accused of killing a white bartender and wounding a police officer. When the black soldiers asserted their innocence and refused to say who had committed the alleged attack, President Theodore Roosevelt dishonorably discharged over 150 troopers for engaging in a conspiracy of silence. Two first-rate books describing the affray have been published: *The Brownsville Raid* by John D. Weaver and *The Brownsville Affair: National Crisis and Black Reaction* by Ann J. Lane.[16]

The intriguing possibilities for ex-slaves with unique backgrounds and talents were evident in the emergence of the Wilson Potteries near Seguin, Texas. John Wilson, a cotton plantation owner, arrived in Seguin in the mid-1850s with slaves he had brought from Missouri, and in 1857 he set up Guadalupe Pottery. Although he had no experience with pottery (he also was a Presbyterian minister), he and his slaves established a groundhog kiln. Two slaves in particular, Hyrum and James, became especially adept at pottery making. The business remained in operation during the Civil War as there was a great demand for pottery. Wilson and his slaves remained on reasonably good terms, and after the Civil War, when freedom arrived for the slaves, they continued working for him as potters. In 1869 Wilson sold his interest to Marion J. Durham. A year or so later, Wilson's two former slaves Hyrum and James and their family members split from Durham and established their own pottery-making establishment, H. Wilson Pottery, in Capote, a small, all-black community with its own church and school, near Seguin. H. Wilson Pottery produced utilitarian, everyday pottery (mugs, pots, vases, urns); the handles were horseshoe shaped, the colors light browns. Business flourished; black men with a skill could survive in the post-Civil War period.[17]

Occasionally South Texas blacks had white help. S. A. Hackworth, a white Republican leader from Washington County and a radical Republican delegate to the 1875 Texas Constitutional Convention, bought land in Wharton, Fort Bend, and Brazoria Counties and then sold or leased it to blacks at reasonable prices during the 1870s and 1880s. After three African Americans from Washington County were lynched, Hackworth filed a complaint with the governor's office. Eventually, hundreds of African Texans moved to the Hackworth colonies.[18]

To further encourage enterprise, independence, safety, and community in the years after the Civil War, blacks in South Texas sometimes opted to establish and live in predominantly black towns such as Capote. At least one other black community, Sweet Home, was developed in Guadalupe County, and by 1876 many such communities had been established in Gonzales County. A classic example emerged in Victoria County. Originally called The Colony (later Perdido Community and, still later, Centerville), the all-black community eventually became known as Cologne. Established in 1870 by two black freedmen, Joseph Smith and George Washington, Cologne excluded white settlers during its early years. Other black families moved there, the community thrived, and it survived well into the twentieth century. Information about Cologne is available in Frederick Douglas Young (a descendent of an earlier settler), *From These Roots: Cologne—One Hundred Years*, published by Texas Southern University Press, and in Sara Massey, "After Emancipation: Cologne, Texas," originally published in the *Journal of South Texas*, and included in this volume.[19]

After the Civil War, African Americans in South Texas began leaving rural areas for towns and cities, seeking economic, social, and political opportunities as well as basic survival. In an excellent article,

"The Forging of the African American Community in Corpus Christi, Texas, 1865–1900," Rue Wood explores the topic of blacks in South Texas urban areas. Corpus Christi's black community, though small, grew through both positive and negative experiences, partly because, as Wood argues, "the development of the black community between the end of the War and the turn of the century contains elements of both a western and a southern urban experience."[20]

Railroads connected the urban centers and, toward the end of the century, linked them with the rural parts of the state. Traveling by rail was a vast improvement over traveling on horseback, in horse-drawn coaches, by water, or afoot. However, like everything else in the white-dominated society, the railroads had both good and bad effects on African Americans in South Texas. They were able to travel more readily, but only in loud, dirty, over-crowded, smoke-filled, smelly Jim Crow cars. The railroads furnished employment opportunities, but, again, at lower wages than those of whites, and usually in less satisfactory jobs. In Cologne the railroad was welcomed for the goods and services it provided. However, it came at a price: whites were now permitted to live in the previously all-black community.

Other examples exist of the mixed impact of railroad transportation on blacks in South Texas. In "Lola and Leon Houck versus the Southern Pacific Railway Company," Janice L. Sumler-Edmonds recounts the story of Lola Houck, a middle-class, pregnant African American woman who lived in Victoria. Her parents and her nine-month-old son lived in Galveston, and Houck needed to go there because the child was ill. Although she frequently traveled on the railway between the two stops, on this day she was refused admittance to the ladies' car, and she would not travel in the Jim Crow car. While attempting to enter the ladies' car, she was shoved into the brake by the white brakeman so violently that her dress ripped. She rode to Galveston on the platform between the two cars in heavy rain, and soon after reaching Galveston she collapsed. Three days later she miscarried. She and her husband sued the railroad. Although the suit was successful, it was not precedent-setting and it did not eliminate Jim Crow cars. The court ruled only that Jim Crow cars "ought" to be equal. They were not.[21]

The railroad was vital to blacks living in Kingsville; most gainfully employed black Kingsville residents worked for it even though the jobs could be dangerous. However, as Jennifer Borrer points out in "The Colored Trainmen of America: Kingsville, Black Labor, and the Railroads," the employment was unpredictable, and many black railroad employees needed a second job in order to survive. Efforts to use collective action to negotiate better working conditions were often impeded by the need to maintain separate unions, since white unions barred blacks from membership. Blacks organized the Colored Trainmen of America, went on strike in 1922, and, with trainmen in short supply, won increased wages and better working conditions. However, over the succeeding years, even into the 1960s, blacks found continued labor action necessary to protect their rights. The shrinking railroad industry reduced black potential for economic improvement in the years after the late sixties.[22]

The year 1922 was critical to black experience in South Texas in at least one other respect—opposition to the Ku Klux Klan. Prominent Texas historian Jerry Thompson, in "Hooded Bigots of Laredo" a section of his *Laredo: A Pictorial History*, describes Laredo's reaction to a Ku Klux Klan warning that the Klan was coming to town. Laredoans prepared a show of force, and the Klan did not show up. As Thompson remarked, "Laredo could take great pride and consolation that it was one of the few cities in the Lone Star state where the Ku Klux Klan never marched during the 1920s." For additional information on the unique South Texas experience of African Americans in Laredo, see Jorge O. Gonzalez's master's thesis, "The Black Experience in Laredo, 1755–1919." It offers significant insight.[23]

Access to education was even more critical to the well-being of blacks in South Texas than the railroads were. Solomon Melvin Coles realized as much when he arrived in Corpus Christi in 1877. Yet until the desegregation of the schools in the late fifties and the sixties, education for African Americans remained separate and unequal. In his article "Divided We Stand: Jim Crow Education in Victoria, Texas, 1901–1956," Edward Bylerly recounts how blacks in one community managed to avail themselves of educational instruction in spite of the inequitable system and demonstrates how the educational enterprise functioned in a hostile Jim Crow environment.[24]

In Kingsville, where African Americans enjoyed a lucrative employment with the railroad, they nevertheless faced a struggle against white supremacy in education. Even changing the name of the school became embroiled with issues of white supremacy.[25] In neither Victoria nor Kingsville nor the remainder of South Texas were blacks encouraged to attend college. Rather, they underwent training for labor-intensive employment. They were not expected to pursue scholarship or artistic, cultural, or intellectual interests. At the same time, however, South Texas did have two colleges for African Americans, St. Philip's College in San Antonio and Guadalupe College in Seguin.

St. Philip's College, founded by the Episcopal Church in 1898 for black women, and initially named St. Philip's Normal and Industrial School, expanded and in 1926 became a junior college for the black community. In 1942 it became a public institution, and in 1955 it admitted its first white students. (At the same time San Antonio College was admitting its first black students.) From 1902 until 1954, a remarkable black woman named Artemisia Bowden headed the college. Born in Georgia, she arrived in San Antonio in 1902 as principal of St. Philip's Normal and Industrial School. In 1926, when the institution became a junior college, Artemisia Bowden became president, undoubtedly the first African American woman to serve as president of a Texas college. She died in 1969 after accomplishing much for the school, for blacks in San Antonio, and for interracial adjustments in San Antonio and Texas. She received numerous awards, including a listing by the National Council of Negro Women as one of the ten most outstanding women educators in the country. In 2000 a growing St. Philip's College numbered over eight thousand students.[26]

Founded in 1884 by Texas Baptists, Guadalupe College opened in 1887 as a school for African Americans. The driving force behind its formation was a black Civil War veteran, William B. Ball, who in the twentieth century was to serve as the school's president for eight years. The first president of the college, who held that post until 1905, was

David Abner Jr., who in 1881 had become the first African American to graduate from a Texas school of higher education, Bishop College. Although much of the instruction at Guadalupe College was, like that in both white and black schools throughout the state, below college level, the institution enrolled an average of two hundred students per year until 1907, when enrollment jumped to 450. After Abner left, turmoil over the policies of a new president, and the necessity for building improvements, plagued the campus until the 1920s, when San Antonio philanthropist George Brackenridge stepped in to provide financial assistance as well as leadership support. The state gave the school junior college accreditation in 1926 and four-year college accreditation in 1929. The impact of the Great Depression of the 1930s was particularly severe on the fledgling institution. The fatal blow occurred in 1936, when fire destroyed its main building; although there were some efforts to rebuild and start over, none proved successful.[27]

Blacks in South Texas, whether pursuing education, the vote, employment, or just plain survival, found their efforts restricted by a savage Jim Crow environment implemented by an unsympathetic white society and enforced too often by a racist police force. Segregation in Texas traces its roots to the antebellum period but expanded in the latter half of the nineteenth century, when whites virtually prevented blacks from voting or holding office.

In San Antonio, black leader Charles Bellinger exerted his influence and power to counteract Jim Crow. At the same time, it was this segregated system that had allowed Bellinger's political career to thrive, because he provided services for blacks that whites refused to provide. Born in Lockhart, Bellinger had become a successful gambler and had taken his skills to San Antonio. As his wealth grew, he branched out into the community. He built a political machine with the help of black ministers who could deliver a significant percentage of the vote. Ironically, it was black voting in San Antonio that led the Texas Legislature to enact a statute establishing a white primary in the early 1920s. Bellinger's efforts and political acumen undoubtedly reduced the sway of Jim Crow in San Antonio: no segregation statutes were enacted there, and more services were found in black San Antonio than in comparable Texas cities. Convicted of income tax violation and pardoned by Franklin Roosevelt, Bellinger died in 1937.[28]

One of the politicians affected by the political strength of Charles Bellinger and his son Valmo was Maury Maverick, a southern liberal and the mayor of San Antonio. As Judith Kaaz Doyle reports in "Maury Maverick and Racial Politics in San Antonio, Texas, 1938–1941," Maverick collided with the Bellinger machine, partially as a result of his white southern upbringing and views. Maverick, on the national scene a staunch civil rights advocate, even defended the white primary. Nonetheless Maverick ultimately broke with his tradition-bound southern past, attracted black voters, encouraged and supported African American voting as well as civil rights, and made peace with San Antonio black leader Valmo Bellinger.[29]

Alongside black men in South Texas, black women were establishing themselves as well. Among the many black women of note in South Texas were Christia Adair, Madame Blackley, Jennie Belle Covington, Maud Anna Berry Fuller, and the aforementioned Artemisia Bowden. Born in Victoria, Christia Daniels Adair taught school in Edna before marrying. In 1918 she and her husband moved to Kingsville, where Adair became an advocate for woman's suffrage and civil rights. In 1920, while teaching, she took black children to see Republican Warren Harding, who was campaigning for the presidency. She and the children watched as Harding reached over the heads of the black children to shake hands with white ones. More determined than ever to open up voting for black Texans, Adair left the Republican Party. She took her South Texas spirit and determination with her, and spent much of her remaining life in Houston, working for both civil and voting rights as a leading member of the city's National Association for the Advancement of Colored People (NAACP).[30]

Other black women contributed to the growth of African American communities in South Texas in different ways. African American seers, also called fortunetellers, clairvoyants, and "finders," were usually women and served as valuable adjuncts to the black community. Madame Blackley, the so-called "Seer of South Texas," lived in Victoria and used her gifts for the benefit of the whole community, both black and white.[31]

Although she spent most of her adult life east of South Texas in Houston, Jennie Belle Covington was born in DeWitt County and attended Guadalupe College in Seguin, where she worked her way through school as a seamstress for the college president's wife. In 1902 she married a doctor, Benjamin Jesse Covington, and a year later the couple moved to Houston. During her years in Houston, Covington enhanced the image of the black community with her cultural and social endeavors, including hosting prominent visitors—the Covington house served as a "hotel" for distinguished blacks who visited Houston during the era of Jim Crow.

Born in Lockhart, Maud Fuller attended Guadalupe College and taught in Texas public schools in Seguin and elsewhere. A Baptist leader and youth organizer, Fuller gained national stature as a speaker. After her marriage in 1914, she and her husband engaged in the funeral and insurance business in Austin. Maud Fuller died in 1972 at the age of 103.[32]

Another particularly interesting South Texan was J. Mason Brewer, born in Goliad in 1896. Brewer was a folklorist. His family background was rich in stories and lore, especially of the west. Brewer's father had led a varied life and followed a number of occupations—he was wagoner, mail carrier, postmaster, grocer, and barber. He told his son stories about his days as a drover making trail drives to Kansas and as a trail boss in Hidalgo County. Brewer's grandfathers had been freight haulers who transported goods from Goliad to Victoria in the 1880s; they too were avid storytellers. Brewer graduated from high school in Austin, Texas, received a BA degree from Wiley College in Marshall, and during World War I served in France with the American Expeditionary Forces. After the war, he taught school in Fort Worth and worked for an oil company (part of the time in Colorado) and published poetry and short stories, including a small book, *Glimpses of Life*, in 1923. By 1926 he had assumed a teaching position at Samuel Huston College in Austin. Although in the late thirties he pursued an advanced degree in Indiana, Brewer returned to Austin in 1943 without having finished it; he received his master's degree from Indiana University in 1950. He taught at the renamed Huston-Tillotson College until 1959, when he moved to Livingston College in North Carolina. Brewer became one of the two greatest black folklorists of the twentieth century (Zora Neale Hurston was the other). He returned to Texas to become a visiting professor at East Texas State University in 1969.[33]

Life for African Americans in South Texas was not all work. One pastime they particularly enjoyed was playing and watching baseball. It was a game appreciated by black and white alike, and many teams and leagues formed, some independent, some amateur, some high school and college, some semiprofessional, and a few, professional. Texas then and now contributed great black ball players to the professional leagues, including Rube Foster and Willie Wells to the Negro Leagues and, later, Joe Morgan to the integrated Major League Baseball. Joe Morgan played for the integrated Texas League team in San Antonio before being called to the majors. Other South Texans played, and sometimes starred, for black baseball teams. "Smokey" (originally known as "Cyclone") Joe Williams, born in Seguin, pitched for the black San Antonio Bronchos from 1905 to 1909 before becoming a stalwart pitcher for numerous teams of the Negro Baseball League. He was later inducted into the Baseball Hall of Fame. Ty Cobb, after watching and facing Williams, said that if Williams were white, he could win thirty games a season in the white majors.[34]

By the end of the period, after Jackie Robinson broke the color line in major league baseball, a Negro League team originally from Newark arrived in Houston. But it was too late. The all-black Houston Eagles struggled for two years, from 1949 to 1950, with poor attendance, inadequate finances, lack of respect from the local black community, and a less-than-impressive record. What this failure really signaled was that the integration of major league baseball, generally considered a positive development, had hastened the end of professional black baseball teams for African Americans by depleting the black league of its best talent. Rob Fink, in "The Houston Eagles and the End of the Negro Leagues," does a skilled job of delineating these changes and their historical background.[35]

Music for listening and dancing provided another means of recreation in the South Texas black community. Constructed in 1950, the Galvan Ballroom, owned and operated by Tejano leader Rafael Galvan, became a popular venue for public and private dances and other social events for Mexicans, blacks, and whites in Corpus Christi. Although the ballroom was "home" to the Galvan Orchestra, it also hosted a broad array of local and nationally prominent musicians, such as Tommy Dorsey and Duke Ellington and their bands. As David Louzon notes in "Corpus Christi's Galvan Ballroom: Music and Multiculturalism in the 1950s," the Galvan Orchestra's repertoire of jazz, swing, and popular big band music, along with the Galvan family's desire to bring the best jazz and swing bands to South Texas—regardless of their racial or ethnic composition—made the Galvan Ballroom a harbinger of multiculturalism. Even so, the trappings of segregation held. African Americans could not dance or listen while whites used the ballroom, even when black musicians such as Ellington performed.[36]

With the Supreme Court's 1944 decision in *Smith v. Allwright*, black Texans achieved what Darlene Clark Hine terms a "black victory."[37] This time the arena was politics. The Court's decision outlawed the statewide white primary of the Democratic Party in Texas. The decades-long struggle against the white primary was nearly over. In some Texas counties white associations held their own preprimary before the Democratic primary, insuring that the black vote in the Democratic primary would not matter. This subterfuge was overturned by the Supreme Court in *Terry v. Adams* (1953), since it made the primary and general elections moot. The specific case arose as a challenge from Fort Bend County. As with *Smith v. Allwright*, the *Terry* decision was initiated by the NAACP. Two black leaders and activists from the county, Arizona Fleming and Willie Melton, fought the preprimary with money, disdain for Jim Crow, and dedicated effort. Fleming, who used up most of her money in the effort, was proprietor of the Fort Bend Fraternal Undertaking Company, while Melton was a prosperous farmer.[38]

Other African Americans living in South Texas contributed to black community development. Matt Thomas, a bellboy, worked from the late 1920s into the 1950s at hotels in Corpus Christi and at the El

Jardin Hotel in Brownsville. In his book *Hopping on the Border: The Life Story of a Bellboy*, Thomas emphasized using his skills and knowledge to accomplish his goals.

Another person who helped bring about racial change in South Texas was Charles Andrews, who led the quiet and peaceful effort to integrate facilities in Kingsville. Andrews, born in 1922, likely in Cuero, moved from Cuero to Kingsville in 1939, served in World War II, and returned to Kingsville in 1946. He married, and then built Andrews Barbershop, which soon prospered, as did Kingsville's growing black middle class. As a successful barber, Andrews was an important part of that community. He was a member of the Human Relations Committee that developed a plan for the integration of what is now Texas A&M University–Kingsville and worked to desegregate public accommodations in Kingsville. Andrews and the Human Relations Committee were successful, and Kingsville's restaurants, theater, and bowling alley agreed to admit African Americans. Andrews died in an unfortunate accident in 1978.[39] But his efforts, and those of others like him, helped pave the way for the *Brown v. Board of Education of Topeka* decision and hastened desegregation. African Americans in South Texas began attending formerly all-white colleges; both Victoria College and Del Mar College in Corpus Christi admitted blacks by the fall of 1954.

While violence and police action captured the nation's attention in the wake of the southern civil rights movement of the 1960s, South Texas cities, particularly the region's largest, San Antonio, moved toward integration largely without fanfare. Nationally, the southern civil rights movement received considerable attention, especially the violent efforts to resist integration and the stance of charismatic black leaders such as Martin Luther King Jr. In Texas, however, civil rights activities did not appear as dramatic, even though the results were accomplished sooner and more thoroughly. San Antonio, for example, captured national attention only briefly, but desegregation continued apace. In 1960, San Antonio became the first southern city to begin integrating its lunch counters, and by 1963 most places of public accommodation had been integrated. In 1965, in an inconspicuous action barely noticed outside the city, the San Antonio City Council, with one black member, passed an ordinance integrating all public accommodations; businesses that ignored the law were fined.

A moderate racial atmosphere existed in the Alamo city—the city had never enacted a segregation law, even though the police enforced de facto segregation. San Antonio whites largely pursued a policy of gradual progress rather than resistance. In the late 1950s blacks became more aggressive, but city leaders stole some of their militant thunder by acquiescing. According to Robert Goldberg's study, "Racial Change on the Southern Periphery," in San Antonio, at least, "civil rights had been granted, not won." This pattern of voluntary desegregation—the "Texas Way"—was duplicated in most other Texas cities (such as Kingsville). San Antonio showed the way, and the rest of the region, rejecting the example of the deep South, followed.[40] One black San Antonio leader of the movement toward integration of the city was the Reverend Claude W. Black Jr., who later published a poignant book entitled *Grandpa Was a Preacher: A Letter to My Grandson*. Black, who worked tirelessly as a civil rights leader, died in March, 2009.[41]

In "A Pearl of Great Price: Socio-Literary Activism in the Life and Writings of Olga Samples Davis," Jeanette Nyda Passty discusses the poet Olga Samples Davis, another San Antonio native. Davis juxtaposed her writings, her art, and her community responsibilities. She pursued, as Darlene Clark Hine puts it, "making community." Davis's expressive poems, published in *A Time to be Born*, refuse to go out of print. Davis also published a volume entitled *Things My Mama Told Me*, which includes her mother's maxims, witticisms, and rules for living, among them the observation that "Your rules are your life tools." Born in 1949, Davis attended Hampton Institute and graduated with a bachelor's degree from the University of Texas at Austin in 1973. She earned a master's degree from the University of Texas at San Antonio in 1976 and shortly thereafter began to teach at St. Philip's College, where she is today professor emeritus. Among her works is a one-act play entitled *Artemisia*, honoring the former leader of St. Philip's College, Artemisia Bowden.[42]

Antoinette V. Franklin is another contemporary black poet of San Antonio. Her volume *In the Mist of Struggle Stands a Woman* pays homage to African American women. The gist of her work is contained in the last stanza of a poem dedicated to Zora Neale Hurston:

*The woman gathered her tattered dreams,*
*Remembered her disappointments.*
*The woman veiled her soul*
*And sought the unknown.*

Franklin graduated from Incarnate Word College in 1978 and received master's degrees from both Webster University and the University of the Incarnate Word. She published at least six other volumes of poetry, including *An Untouched Song* and *A New Beginning*; she now teaches English as a second language at Lackland Air Force Base.43

The African American experience in South Texas has been rich and varied. The region bred and attracted astute, hard working, and courageous individuals who left an imprint on the area, and in the process avoided much of the bloody history of other states. Their status has changed over the years, thanks in part to civil rights laws and activities, increased access to education, the growth of cities, and, of course, the right to vote. Blacks in South Texas have weathered the trials of white supremacy, though problems still exist from time to time. During the lengthy journey from slavery, segregation, and second-class treatment to freedom, integration, and equality, South Texas blacks have persevered.

Ironically, in this area of Texas less inimical than others to its black citizens, the African American percentage of the population has declined significantly during the twentieth century. In Gonzales County in 1990 blacks numbered only 10 percent of the population; in DeWitt County in 2000, 11 percent; in Wharton County in 1980, 17 percent. In Guadalupe County, the black population declined from 34 percent in 1870 to 6 percent in 1980. How will such demographic changes affect black Texans of the twenty-first century? Perhaps a forthcoming article in the *Journal of South Texas* or *South Texas Studies* will look at the decline in black population. Whatever the cause, South Texas' black Americans continue to contribute mightily to the region in many, many ways, as they did in the past.

## NOTES

1. Edna Jordan, *Black Tracks to Texas: Solomon Melvin Coles, From Slave to Educator* (Corpus Christi: Golden Banner Press, 1977); Moses N. Moore Jr. and Yolanda Y. Smith, "Solomon M. Coles: The First Black Student Officially Enrolled in Yale Divinity School," *Spectrum*, Winter 2007, 6–7, http://www.yale.edu/divinity/publications/spectrum/spectrum_wint_07.shtml; Moore and Smith, "Solomon M. Coles: Preacher, Teacher, and Former Slave: The First Black Student Officially Enrolled in Yale Divinity School, http://www.yale.edu/divinity/storm.

2. Jakie L. Pruett and Everett B. Cole, eds., *As We Lived: Stories by Black Storytellers* (Burnet, Texas: Eakin Press, 1982).

3. Kenneth Mason, *African Americans and Race Relations in San Antonio, Texas, 1867–1937* (New York: Garland, 1998), 3–22. Mason's book is the most thorough exposition of black life in San Antonio.

4. Douglas Hales, "Free Blacks," *Handbook of Texas Online*, http://www.tshaonline.org/handbook; George Ruble Woolfolk, *The Free Negro in Texas, 1800–1860: A Study in Cultural Compromise* (Ann Arbor: University Microfilms International, 1976), 180–86; Sherilyn Brandenstein, "Morgan, Tamar," *Handbook of Texas Online*.

5. Diana J. Kleiner, "Brazoria County," Merle R. Hudgins, "Wharton County," Virginia Lair Ott, "Fort Bend County," and Kleiner, "Matagorda County," *Handbook of Texas Online*; Randolph B. Campbell, "Slavery in Texas, 1821–1865: A Brief Overview, with Emphasis on the Lower Brazos River Valley," in *Viewing the Past through Different Lenses: The African American Legacy in the Lower Brazos Valley*, ed. Barry Hutcheson (Austin, Texas: Texas Parks and Wildlife, 2002), 17–23. See also Reba W. Palm, "Slavery in Microcosm: Matagorda County, Texas" (master's thesis, Texas A&I University, 1971) and Palm, "Protestant Churches and Slavery in Matagorda County," *East Texas Historical Journal* 14, no. 1 (1976): 3–8.

6. Vivian Elizabeth Smyrl, "Guadalupe County," Dorcas Huff Baumgartner and Genevieve B. Vollentine, "Gonzales County," Stephen L. Hardin, "Jackson County," and Craig H. Roell, "DeWitt County," *Handbook* of Texas Online.

7. Larry P. Knight, "Defending the Unnecessary: Slavery in San Antonio in the 1850s," *Journal of South Texas* 15, no. 1 (2002): 57–72 (quotation, 63). For comparison with other cities, see Paul D. Lack, "Urban Slavery in the Southwest," in *The African American Experience in Texas*, ed. Bruce A. Glasrud and James M. Smallwood (Lubbock: Texas Tech University Press, 2007), 31–56. Documents containing important insights of former South Texas slaves into slavery and life after slavery can be located in the U.S. Works Progress Administration, Federal Writers' Project, *Slave Narratives, Texas*, Part 1, Box A390 (for Monroe Brackins and Julia Blanks) and Part 2, Box A931 (for Ben Kinchlow), Manuscript Division, Library of Congress, Washington, D.C. I wish to thank Dr. T. Lindsay Baker, historian, archivist, and museum director at Tarleton State University for bringing these to my attention and for sending copies to me. Baker authored a helpful tool for using the slave narratives; see T. Lindsay Baker, "How to Use the W.P.A. Slave Narratives in Museum/Historic Site Interpretation," in Hutcheson, *Viewing the Past through Different Lenses*, 59–64.

8. Christopher Long, "Lavaca County," *Handbook of Texas Online.*

9. Ronald E. Goodwin and Bruce A. Glasrud, "On the Edge of First Freedoms: Black Texans and the Civil War," in *The Seventh Star of the Confederacy: Texas and the Civil War*, ed. Kenneth W. Howell (College Station: Texas A&M University Press, 2009), 268–86.

10. Diana J. Kleiner, "Brazoria County," and Craig H. Roell, "Goliad County," *Handbook of Texas Online.*

11. Kenneth W. Howell, "Just Southwest of Dixie: Reconstruction in South Texas, 1865–1876," *Journal of South Texas* 16, no. 1 (2003): 45–64; Alwyn Barr, "African American Reconstruction in Brazoria County," in Hutcheson, *Viewing the Past through Different Lenses.*

12. Rachel Jenkins, "Vann Settlement, Texas," Diana J. Kleiner, "Matagorda County," and Pauline Yelderman, "Jaybird-Woodpecker War," *Handbook of Texas Online*; Yelderman, *The Jay Birds of Fort Bend County: A White Man's Union* (Waco: Texian Press, 1979).

13. Diana J. Kleiner, "Calhoun County," *Handbook of Texas Online*.

14. See Lee N. Coffee Jr., "Richard 'Bubba' Walker: Best Cowhand Wilson County Ever Had," 273–82, Allan O. Kownslar, "Robert Lemmons: A Black Texan Mustanger," 49–66, and Louise S. O'Connor, "Henrietta Williams Foster, 'Aunt Rittie': A Cowgirl of the Texas Coastal Bend," in Sara R. Massey, ed., *Black Cowboys of Texas* (College Station: Texas A&M University Press, 2000), 67–72.

15. Randolph B. Campbell, "Reconstruction in Nueces County, 1865–1876," *Houston Review* 16 (Fall 1994): 3–26; Alwyn Barr, "The Black Militia of the New South: Texas as a Case Study," *Journal of Negro History* 63 (July 1978): 209–19; Frank Wagner, "Roberts Rifles," *Handbook of Texas Online*; Roger D. Cunningham, "'A Lot of Fine, Sturdy Black Warriors': Texas's African American 'Immunes' in the Spanish-American War," *Southwestern Historical Quarterly* 108, no. 3 (2005): 345–67. On Flipper see Charles M. Robinson III, *The Fall of a Black Army Officer: Racism and the Myth of Henry O. Flipper* (Norman: University of Oklahoma Press, 2008) and Bruce A. Glasrud, "Henry Ossian Flipper," in *Encyclopedia of African American History*, ed. Joe W. Trotter, Stephanie Shaw, and Daniel Littlefield, vol. 2 (New York: Facts on File, 2010).

16. John D. Weaver, *The Brownsville Raid* (New York: W. W. Norton, 1970); Ann J. Lane, *The Brownsville Affair: National Crisis and Black Reaction* (Port Washington, New York: Kennikat Press, 1971).

17. Michael K. Brown, The Wilson Potters: *An African-American Enterprise in 19th Century Texas* (Houston: Museum of Fine Arts, 2002); Joey Brackner, "Wilson Potteries," *Handbook of Texas Online*; Elmer Joe Brackner, "The Wilson Potteries" (master's thesis, University of Texas at Austin, 1981).

18. Diana J. Kleiner, "Brazoria County," *Handbook of Texas Online*.

19. Frederick Douglas Young, *From These Roots: Cologne—One Hundred Years, 1870–1970* (Houston: Texas Southern University Press, 1973); Sarah R. Massey, "After Emancipation: Cologne, Texas," *Journal of South Texas* 20, no. 2 (Fall 2007): 184–96.

20. Rue Wood, "The Forging of the African American Community in Corpus Christi, Texas, 1865–1900," *Journal of South Texas* 12 (1999): 34–75; the quotation is from p. 63.

21. Janice Sumler-Edmonds, "Lola and Leon Houck v. the Southern Pacific Railway Company." The paper is in the editor's possession.

22. Jennifer Borrer, "The Colored Trainmen of America: Kingsville Black Labor and the Railroads," *Journal of South Texas* 11 (1998): 74–103.

23. Jerry Thompson, *Laredo: A Pictorial History* (Norfolk: Donning, 1986), chap. 26; Jorge O. Gonzalez, "The Black Experience in Laredo: 1755–1919" (master's thesis, Laredo State University, 1986).

24. Edward Byerly, "Divided We Stand: Jim Crow Education in Victoria, Texas, 1901–1966," *South Texas Studies* 19 (2009): 1–32.

25. Bradly C. Harper, "The Frederick Douglass School and Early Black Education in Kingsville, Texas (1909–1969)," *Journal of South Texas* 6 (1993): 80–88.

26. Clarence Windzell Norris Jr., "St. Philip's College: A Case Study of a Historically Black Two Year College" (PhD diss., University of Southern California, 1975); John S. Gray III, "St. Philip's College," and Judith N. McArthur, "Artemisia Bowden," *Handbook of Texas Online.*

27. Anne Brawner, "Guadalupe College: A Case History in Negro Higher Education, 1884–1936" (master's thesis, Southwest Texas State University, 1980); Anne Brawner, "Guadalupe College," Diana J. Kleiner, "Abner, David, Jr.," and Nolan Thompson, "Ball, William B.," *Handbook of Texas Online.*

28. Bruce A. Glasrud, "Jim Crow's Emergence in Texas," *American Studies* 15 (1974): 47–60; Herbert J. Bailey, "Charles Bellinger and Jim Crow in San Antonio, Texas, 1905–1937," *South Texas Studies* 4 (1993): 75–88; Alwyn Barr, "Charles Bellinger," *Handbook of Texas Online.*

29. Judith Kaaz Doyle, "Maury Maverick and Racial Politics in San Antonio, Texas, 1938–1941," *Journal of Southern History* 53 (May 1987): 194–224.

30. Bruce A. Glasrud, "Time of Transition: Black Women in Early Twentieth-Century Texas, 1900–1930," in *Black Women in Texas History*, ed. Bruce A. Glasrud and Merline Pitre (College Station: Texas A&M University Press, 2008): 99–128; Nancy Baker Jones, "Adair, Christia V. Daniels," *Handbook of Texas Online.*

31. Henry Wolff Jr., "Madame Blackley: Seer of South Texas," in *Folklore: In All of Us, In All We Do*, ed. Kenneth L. Untiedt, TFS 63 (Denton: University of North Texas Press, 2006), 95–105.

32. Mary M. Standifer, "Covington, Jennie Belle Murphy," and Algerene Akins Craig, "Fuller, Maud Anna Berry," *Handbook of Texas Online*; Andrew Webster Jackson, "Maud Anna Fuller," *A Sure Foundation and a Sketch of Negro Life in Texas* (Houston: A. W. Jackson, 1940): 205–207.

33. James W. Byrd, *J. Mason Brewer: Negro Folklorist* (Austin: Steck-Vaughn, 1967); James W. Byrd, "J. Mason Brewer," *Handbook of Texas Online*; Bruce A. Glasrud, "From Griggs to Brewer: A Review of Black Texas Artists, 1899–1940," *Journal of Big Bend Studies* 15 (2003): 195–212; Bruce A. Glasrud, "John Mason Brewer," *BlackPast Online Encyclopedia*, http://www.blackpast.org.

34. Bob Luke, *Willie Wells: 'El Diablo' of the Negro Leagues* (Austin: University of Texas Press, 2007); Joe Morgan, *Joe Morgan: My Life in Baseball* (New York: W. W. Norton, 1993); Paul M. Lucko, "Williams, Joe," *Handbook of Texas Online*.

35. Rob Fink, "The Houston Eagles and the End of the Negro Leagues," *South Texas Studies* 14 (2003): 98–113; Rob Fink, "Houston Eagles," *Handbook of Texas Online*. On Texas' African American baseball see also Robert Fink, "African-American Baseball in Texas: 1900–1950" (master's thesis, Texas Tech University, 1999); Robert C. Fink, "Semi-Professional African American Baseball in Texas before the Great Depression," in *The African American Experience in Texas*, ed. Bruce A. Glasrud and James M. Smallwood (Lubbock: Texas Tech University Press, 2007), 218–30.

36. David Louzon, "Corpus Christi's Galvan Ballroom: Music and Multiculturalism in the 1950s," *Journal of South Texas* 20, no. 2 (2007): 213–35.

37. Darlene Clark Hine, *Black Victory: The Rise and Fall of the Democratic White Primary in Texas* (Milwood, New York: KTO Press, 1979).

38. Pauline Yelderman, *The Jay Bird Democratic Association of Fort Bend County: A White Man's Union* (Waco, Texas: Texian Press, 1979); Nina Benware Margraves, "The Jaybird Democratic Association of Fort Bend County: A White Man's Union" (master's thesis, University of Houston, 1955); Bonni C. Hayes, "Fleming, Arizona," and Christopher Long, "White Man's Union Associations," *Handbook of Texas Online*.

39. Matt Thomas, *Hopping on the Border: The Life Story of a Bellboy* (San Antonio: Naylor, 1951); Mary Jean Rives, "Charles Andrews, Barber and Civic Leader," *Journal of South Texas* 9 (1996): 102–108.

40. Robert A. Goldberg, "Racial Change on the Southern Periphery: The Case of San Antonio, Texas 1960–1965," *Journal of Southern History* 49 (1983): 349–74; the quotation is from p. 373.

41. Claude W. Black Jr., *Grandpa Was a Preacher: A Letter to My Grandson* (Bloomington, Indiana: AuthorHouse, 2007); *San Antonio Express-News*, March 14, 2009.

42. Jeanette Nyda Passty, "'A Pearl of Great Price': Socio-Literary Activism in the Life and Writings of Olga Samples Davis," *South Texas Studies* 11 (2000): 65–82; Olga Samples Davis, *Things My Mama Told Me* (Colorado Springs, Colorado: WaterBrook Press, 2004); Davis, *A Time To Be Born* (San Antonio, Texas: Pecan Grove Press, 1991).

43. Antoinette V. Franklin, *In the Mist of Struggle Stands a Woman* (Bloomington, Indiana: AuthorHouse, 2005).

# Defending the Unnecessary

## *Slavery in San Antonio in the 1850s*

LARRY P. KNIGHT

THOUGH SAN ANTONIO IS USUALLY PERCEIVED AS A Mexican or Mexican American city, from 1845–61 it was an antebellum southern city. Its location and the domination of the city's government by Anglos caused the city to embrace that most distinctive of all southern institutions, slavery[1]—which, though neither numerically large nor economically significant, was important in San Antonio. This fact raises two questions: Why was slavery important in San Antonio? And what did slavery look like there?

The importance of slavery in San Antonio was due in part to the status of the slaveholders. Although a small minority in the city, they were generally wealthy and powerful people and their ideas about slavery carried great weight. Gross wealth (in real and personal estate) given in the 1860 census for the seventy-nine identified slaveholders was $2,969,469, or $37,588 each. Nonslaveholders averaged only $1,548. So while slavery was of little economic importance, slaveholders in the city had great economic importance.[2]

Another important aspect of slavery in San Antonio (though difficult to prove) was that immigrants from the free states were listed among the slaveholders, and by becoming slaveholders they seemed to admit that the South, in its most controversial difference with the North, was correct. While it is true that not many nonsouthern natives owned slaves, the percentage of nonsouthern heads of household who owned slaves was slightly greater in San Antonio than the percentage of southern heads of household who did, and the percentage grew during the 1850s. Nonsoutherners in 1850 composed 57.6 percent of slaveholders, and in 1860 they composed 58.3 percent.[3] The *San*

*Antonio Herald* interpreted these numbers, initially proclaiming the impossibility of Yankees becoming southerners: "It is useless to say that Northern men become Southernized after their removal. It is impossible for them to feel as we do. They are not to the manor born. They cannot feel hostile to their old homes, to their relatives and friends. They must always be strangers to that sectional, Southern love and enthusiasm which would constitute the all-important element in the great crises."

However, the writer left the door open by admitting that there were "some worthy exceptions to these rules." By the next year the door was wide open. J. H. French, who later become mayor and was a Yankee immigrant, remarked that most northerners were ignorant about life in the South. The editor of the *Herald* now agreed and believed that if Yankees ever came to Texas, they would never leave: "If they would come among our people and see the freedom of thought and action, the general intelligence and thrift characteristic of our giant young State, the scales would fall from their eyes, and they would bid adieu forever to the land of flint rocks, freezing winds, and 'free negroes' and end their days among the beautiful savannas of Texas."

In another article the *Herald* writer noted that "the great majority of Northern men who have come among us, and have made the South their permanent home, have become the advocates of slave labor, and many of them among the largest slave holders." The *Herald*'s assessment was that immigrants from free states had been transformed into slaveholders and advocates of slavery. It was not a far stretch, then, to assume that since the South was correct concerning the greatest difference between the sections—as evidenced by the Yankee slaveholders themselves—it was also correct in all other differences between the sections.[4]

Though not noted with the same interest, immigrants of foreign birth were also numerous among the slaveholders. They hailed from such diverse countries as Scotland, England, Ireland, Nova Scotia, Italy, France, Poland, Mexico, and Germany. Among the groups most associated with animosity to slavery, the Hispanics and the Germans, six slaveholders from each were found in the 1860 census. Included among the German slaveholders was state senator Gustav Schleicher.[5]

Further evidence of slavery's importance was the inordinate amount of time and effort given to slavery by the city government. Beginning in 1850 and continuing until 1860, numerous slave codes were enacted to control the city's few slaves.

The first city ordinance aimed at the slaves, passed in 1850, actually placed few restrictions on them; it was merely a curfew, which could be avoided if the slave had a pass from the master.[6] Slaves had to be in their homes by 9:30 P.M. from October 1 until April 1 and by 10:15 P.M. from April 1to October 1, although the term "home" was not defined. To insure that slaves were not caught unaware, a warning bell was rung fifteen minutes prior to the curfew bell. The fifteen minutes was no great imposition since there was no point in San Antonio that could not be reached from any other point on foot within fifteen minutes. Slaves caught outside after curfew were to be kept "in the calaboose" until their master paid a $5 fine. If the fine was not paid, the slave would be worked by the city as payment. The clause was not stringent, especially since a slave need not obey it if the master allowed an exception.[7]

This ordinance was followed a few months later by one that defined "home." Home was the place so designated for the slave by the master. However, even this restriction allowed the slave to sleep outside the home if the slave's master provided a pass designating the place and duration of residence away from home. The punishment for violating the first part of the code was a fine of $5 to be paid by the master, or the slave would pay for the infringement by being whipped. The second section of the ordinance prohibited, without exception, the right of a slave to rent his own place. In case of a violation of this section, punishment, a fine of from $10 to $50, was assigned to the master. The third section of the ordinance prohibited slaves and free blacks from opening eating or rooming establishments unless given express consent to do so by the city council, an event so unlikely that no instance of it was recorded in the city council minutes in the entire decade of the 1850s. Violations of this section of the ordinance were punishable by a $10 fine to be paid by the master.[8]

No further slave ordinances were passed for more than a year, when the city added three further restrictions to the lives of the slaves. No one was allowed to sell them liquor, they were not allowed to sell anything, and they could not carry weapons in town—all with the exception that these things could be done with permission from their master. Punishment for violations was a fine of $5 to $20 for anyone selling liquor to the slave, $5 to $25 for buying from the slave, and $1 to $10 levied against the master of the slave carrying a weapon without permission, or a thirty-day incarceration for the slave.[9]

The slave codes of San Antonio remained unchanged for the balance of the 1850s, good evidence that the citizens of San Antonio saw no need to change them. And, in fact, nothing within the confines of the city occurred that warranted changing them. Yet, changed they were, and severely, when the tension-filled decade of the 1850s gave way to the 1860s. The 1850s, which opened with a compromise designed to solve all past, present, and future problems of slavery, saw the publication of *Uncle Tom's Cabin*, the Kansas-Nebraska Act, the "Bleeding Kansas" conflict, the Dred Scott decision, and John Brown's raid. These events were followed by the presidential election of 1860, which kindled fears of a black Republican's attaining the presidency of the United States. Though all these events affected Texas, what caused the leaders of San Antonio to create a more severe slave code was the "Texas troubles." These consisted of a number of fires presumed to be acts of arson, and a number of well poisonings in the summer of 1860. All were attributed to slaves acting under the influence of abolitionists.[10]

Because of these troubles, a new slave ordinance was enacted that year. It lengthened the number of hours when slaves had to be off the city's streets. The curfew now began at 8:15 P.M. instead of 10:15 P.M. from April to October and at 7:15 P.M. instead of 9:30 P.M from October to April. Any slave outdoors after that time was to be arrested, and the master was to be fined $2.50 per day from the time of the slave's arrest. If the owner refused to pay the fine, the slave was to receive up to twenty lashes with a whip or to provide labor for the city for up to five days. If the master arrived and wanted the slave whipped, the fine was dropped, but the master had to pay $1 for the whipping. The only exception was that a slave could be out during the hours of curfew if he had a pass from the master. Unlike the 1850 ordinance, however, the pass was good for only one day and had to state the purpose of the slave's outing.

The lives of the slaves of San Antonio became more severely restricted in other ways as well.[11] Slaves could not live separately from their masters, and no provision was made for the owner to give consent for an exception. Nor could a slave visit or even "hang around" a liquor-selling business. Both of these offenses were punishable by fines of up to $50 for the master, and the slave could also receive up to thirty-nine lashes.[12]

Other provisions were focused on the master, though the slave might still bear the punishment. A slave was not allowed to "hire his or her time, or to go at large and trade as a free person." The master of a slave caught in such action was to be fined up to $50. Although a slave could not hire himself out, he could be employed by other than his master, but only with the master's written permission, and the permit was valid for no more than a week. Those wanting to employ a slave had to do so through the master or an agent, but if through an agent, permission in writing from the master had to be obtained.[13]

Previously there had been no restrictions on slaves' assembling, but under the new ordinance no more than five slaves could gather, except with the permission of the owner or at worship services. For a dance to be held, the owner not only had to be present but also had to secure written permission from the mayor. Punishment for a violation of the proscription against assembly could be as much as $20 for an owner or twenty lashes for the slave.[14]

Two sections of the ordinance included free blacks as well as slaves. No one from either group could keep a weapon; nor could he or she play cards. The punishment for carrying a weapon was thirty-nine lashes or a fine of $10. The punishment for card- playing was twenty lashes or $10. More severe monetary punishment was reserved for a white person who played cards with a black person; the fine could be as high as $75. One section of the ordinance remained the same as the previous ones—the city would provide the service of administering a whipping that consisted of up to thirty-nine lashes for only one dollar.[15]

Not only were the slave ordinances made stricter, the city council also established a night watch for the city, and citizens were warned to secure their property at night.[16] A night watch had been established once before, during the political conflict of 1856 between the Know-Nothings and the Democrats, but it had met with such opposition that it was repealed. The fear of fires and poisonings, however, insured that there was no such opposition this time.

Only two of the eight councilmen owned slaves, and nothing had occurred in San Antonio to warrant the new slave codes. No fires had been set, no wells poisoned, no secret slave societies uncovered, and no abolitionists unearthed. Such extreme action with so little provocation in itself suggests the fundamental significance of slavery to the city leaders.

Further evidence of the importance of slavery in San Antonio was its frequent discussion in the city's newspapers; regular reading about slavery made it an important aspect of the lives of the citizens despite the fact that few of them owned slaves. Shortly after the firing on Ft. Sumter, the editor of the *Ledger and Texan* noted that the "question of slavery is the only question between us, all others are incidental and subsidiary. . . . It is the negro and the negro alone that underlies our undying hostility." His statement was merely the culmination of years of articles about slavery in the newspapers. In the mid-1850s the papers had noted the runaway slave scare that swept through Texas, reported the formation of a Vigilante Committee of ten of the city's leading citizens, and reported the notice of a reward offered by three of the city's slaveholders "for the apprehension and conviction of any free person who may be guilty of enticing away or stealing any slave from the County of Bexar." The runaway scare—that produced no runaways in San Antonio—was followed closely by the political fight between Know-Nothings and Democrats previously mentioned. Though both parties had the same stand on slavery, each flailed away at the other on the issue. The Democrats accused the Know-Nothings of softness on slavery, and the Know-Nothings tried to prove that the Democrats were abolitionists by linking them to the Germans while linking the Germans to abolitionist newspaper editor Adolf Douai. Throughout the decade the *San Antonio Zeitung* also carried advertisements by owners seeking runaway slaves, and the Texas troubles were also widely carried in the papers. Thus slavery as a topic was seldom absent from the city press.[17]

Another aspect of slavery that enhanced its importance was the opposition to it, though that opposition was more perceived than real. The most outspoken opponent of slavery in San Antonio was Douai. His importance was due not so much to his opposition to slavery as to the assumption that he represented many other Germans who, though too afraid to speak openly against slavery, were nevertheless ready if the opportunity arose to help in a slave escape or join a slave revolt, and who might quietly increase in numbers until they were powerful enough to establish a free state of Western Texas.

In 1852, Douai moved to San Antonio and became the editor of the *San Antonio Zeitung*, which was the city's first German-language newspaper. In 1854, he used a *Sangerfest* (singing festival) held in the city as his launching pad for an abolitionist campaign. The campaign was a failure from its inception. Only fifty-four of the one thousand *Sangerfest* attendees were present at the antislavery meeting. Despite the poor showing, the meeting convinced many San Antonians that the German citizens of the city were abolitionists, a belief that maintained its currency throughout the decade despite the paucity of evidence. The attention paid to this event and to Douai, who left San Antonio in 1856, attests further to the significance of slavery in San Antonio.

Allied to the Germans in their opposition to slavery were, it was believed, the majority of Hispanic citizens. Though they did nothing overt to help the slaves, they wanted to see slavery end and would support the Germans in establishing a free state with San Antonio as its major city; at least, that was the belief. It was enforced by the Hispanics' penchant for making no distinction based on race. Abolitionist Benjamin Lundy noted this in the 1830s. In speaking to a free black in San Antonio who was a blacksmith, Lundy learned that the Hispanics gave him "the same respect as to other laboring people, there being no difference made here on account of color." Frederick Law Olmsted, also an abolitionist, observed the same thing in the 1850s. He noted that the Hispanics of San Antonio "consort[ed] freely with the negroes, making no distinction from pride of race." Their "intimacy with the slaves" caused the slaveholders to hold them in "great contempt and suspicion." That few Germans or Hispanics opposed slavery strongly enough to take any action against it, and may have not opposed it at all, was of little importance. The perception of opposition made slavery, and the need to protect it, more important.[18]

The final factor that made slavery important in San Antonio was simply the southern mentality: slavery was good and blacks, free or slave, were inferior. The *Herald* demonstrated this mentality in its attitude toward the disposition of Africans aboard the ships of slave runners that had been captured by the U.S. Navy. Though opposed to the reopening of the slave trade, the paper nevertheless disapproved of the government's policy of sending the Africans back to Africa. The question was not one of economics but of morality. What was best for the Africans? Returned to Africa, the slaves would be condemned to a life of subsistence and savagery whose end then led to a worse existence in the fires of hell. Life in the South, which the *Herald* thought should be the destination of the captured Africans, would, however, provide material well-being and civilization, which would be followed by the eternal bliss of heaven for the Christianized slaves. Why was this course not followed by the federal government? Because those in charge of the government were opposed to slavery; but their misguided opposition did not alter the goodness of the institution of slavery.[19]

The primary factor that made slavery good was that it gave an inferior race a place in American society. But while slavery was the greatest evidence of inferiority, free blacks were also considered inferior. Although free blacks in San Antonio were regulated far less strictly than the slaves, they were still more circumscribed in their affairs than any other "free" inhabitants of the city. The ordinance mentioned above that excluded slaves and any "free person of Color" from opening eating and rooming establishments without consent of the city council, excluded blacks only. Even the first city ordinance aimed at slaves carried with it a sense of African American inferiority; it was initially termed "An Ordinance Concerning Negroes," while what was meant was slaves. The error showed the unconscious mindset of the city's leaders: blacks, free or slave, were considered on an equal footing, a footing far inferior to that of white citizens.[20]

Wealthy slaveowners, the attention of city leaders, space in the local newspapers, opposition (real or imagined) to slavery, and a belief in the rightness of the institution and the inferiority of blacks all demonstrate the importance of slavery in San Antonio. However, what was the reality of slavery in San Antonio? What effect on and what place in the economy did it have? Were the slaves of San Antonio prone to run away as suggested in the city's papers from time to time? Did Germans or Hispanics entice the slaves to run away or help them in their quest for freedom? How did the citizens of San Antonio perceive the slaves?

That slavery had little effect on the economy was shown by the 1850 and 1860 censuses. In 1850 the total free population of the city was 3,168; the slave population was 220, only 6.49 percent of the total population. By 1860 the free population had grown to 7,683 and the number of slaves to 514; however, this was a relative drop in the slave population to 6.27 percent. Not only had the percentage of slaves dropped, but the percentage of slaveholders dropped more dramatically, from 6.34 percent of the city's heads of households in 1850 to 4.24 percent in 1860.[21]

The age and gender of the slave population also demonstrate that slavery was economically unimportant in the city. Of the 167 slaves listed with owners in the San Antonio census in 1850, 100 were females and 67 were males, a sex ratio of 1.49. The sex ratio increased according to the 1860 census to 1.58. Also, of the 352 slaves whose owners could be identified in the manuscript census of 1860, an equal number, 176, were adults and children. Thus, in 1860 adult male slaves in San Antonio composed only 19.3 percent of the slaves. This figure reveals that the slaves in San Antonio were primarily used as house servants—a group not known to produce great economic gain in a society. The figure also hints that white women were primarily responsible for the management of the slaves in San Antonio.[22]

Further evidence that slavery was not economically important in San Antonio lies in the 1850 and 1860 product-of-industry censuses. In 1850 the city reported thirteen industries; by 1860 that number had risen to twenty-eight. Neither census reported slave labor in any of these industries. This is not to imply that slaves did not work in the businesses of San Antonio. Rice and Childress, saddle makers in San Antonio, jointly owned a slave, and W. A. Menger, prominent hotelier, used six slaves, four of whom were not yet teenagers, in his hotel. Slaves were even sold at auction in San Antonio; but even here the evidence showed the unimportance of slavery in the city. In side-by-side advertisements J. M. Carolan and Frank Paschal advertised their auction houses. Carolan included slaves as one of the properties he auctioned; Paschal—a slave owner—did not. The low number of slaveholders and slaves, the gender and age of the slaves, and their economic contribution to San Antonio showed that slavery in the city was economically of little importance.[23]

Slavery caused few problems in San Antonio, despite the runaway slave scare in 1854, the often-stated belief that the Germans and Hispanics of San Antonio opposed slavery, and fear caused by the Texas troubles that abolitionists would influence slaves in San Antonio. In fact, one of the greatest forms of slave rebellion, running away, seldom occurred in San Antonio.

While it is doubtful whether any slaves were content with their lot, the slaves in San Antonio apparently did not see running away as a solution. Felix Haywood, the only San Antonio slave interviewed in the *Slave Narratives*, stated that he and his father spoke of fleeing to Mexico, but "we didn't have no idea of running and escaping. We were happy." The *Ledger* noted the same fact during the days of slavery. Despite the proximity of San Antonio to Mexico, the slaves in San Antonio "being all well treated are happy and contented [and] evince no disposition to leave their owners." "Happy" is no doubt a huge stretch, and it should be noted that Felix Haywood was interviewed decades after slavery ended, and that the author of the *Ledger* article was white. A more balanced picture of San Antonio is available in the papers of a slave-owning couple in San Antonio, Sam and Mary Maverick. Included in their papers was a receipt paid by Sam Maverick to the sheriff of the city for whipping one of Sam's slaves, Granwell. Apparently Granwell was guilty of gambling. Granwell was later sold to Ira Hewitt, a sale that was afterwards nullified at the request of Mary. However, another slave, Jack, was so troublesome to Mary that Sam wanted to send him to New Orleans and sell him there. Certainly slavery was not as benign as the *Ledger* painted it. Nevertheless, the slaves of San Antonio almost never ran away. In fact, the 1860 Census of Bexar County reported only one runaway from San Antonio.[24]

Further evidence that runaways were few was provided by the papers of San Antonio, which carried information and advertisements concerning runaway slaves. The paid notices found in the city's newspapers of owners seeking runaways revealed that runaway slaves were not a problem in San Antonio. A search of the San Antonio newspapers for the period 1857–59 proved that point. The first notice advertising a runaway slave in the San Antonio newspapers occurred in the July 11, 1857, *Ledger*. The notice concerned a fourteen-year-old who was apparently abducted from San Antonio to East Texas or Louisiana—hardly the place a runaway searching for freedom or an abolitionist-assisted runaway would head. The boy spoke English, Spanish, and French and was apparently coerced or coaxed away from San Antonio for that reason. In October of that year two runaways were captured on two stolen horses on Culebra Creek, but they were not from San Antonio.

The next runaway report in the San Antonio papers concerned two slaves who murdered their master in Ft. Bend County in February 1858. No other runaways were reported until July when two slaves belonging to General Waul of Gonzales ran away and were found near Houston; a further report that same month told of a runaway slave from near Richmond, Texas, 150 miles to the east of San Antonio. Two weeks later the *Ledger* ran another advertisement for three runaways from two owners in Freestone County. But Freestone County was over 200 miles to the northeast of San Antonio; the advertisement was in the San Antonio paper because it was assumed that the runaways' destination was either Mexico or the Indian Nation, either one of which might bring them through the area of circulation of the San Antonio papers.

Another runaway was reported in November 1859, but he, too, was from far away, this time Brazoria. An indicator of the scarceness of the problem of runaway slaves in San Antonio was the number of advertisements and notices of strayed and runaway horses and mules compared to the number of advertisements and notices of runaway slaves. The newspaper reported strays in almost every issue. Not only were reports of strayed or stolen horses and mules more numerous than reports of runaway slaves, the reports of the horses and mules were from San Antonio and its surrounding area while those of the slaves were from areas far from San Antonio. Regardless of what had been printed in the city's papers during a time of stress or hysteria, the slaves of San Antonio were not prone to run away.[25]

Neither is there any indication that anyone in San Antonio ever attempted to help or encourage a slave to escape. The only incident reported in the city's papers even remotely akin to helping slaves escape occurred when three Hispanics, Doloros Salinas, Romana Montes, and Juana Ydalgo, were fined $20 each for trading with slaves. Certainly the infrequency with which slaves ran away from their masters in San Antonio was evidence that neither the Germans nor the Hispanics of the city were enticing them to do so, or at least that they saw no success from their efforts.[26]

Although slaves in San Antonio were at least satisfied enough with their lot in life not to run away, as people they were viewed somewhat ambiguously by the citizens of San Antonio. Sometimes they were seen as children who never grew up, sometimes as a people whose place at the bottom of society gave them a gift of wisdom, and sometimes as immortal beings whose souls needed to be saved.

Since slaves were viewed as children they were often seen as foolish and were made the butt of jokes. Two examples from the *Herald* demonstrate this.

> COLORED LADIES, SAYS AN EXCHANGE, MAY BE COMPARED TO MANY ROSES BECAUSE THEY WERE 'BORN TO BLUSH UNSEEN.' IT IS THE FRAGRANCE RATHER THAN THE HUE THAT MAKES

THE ROSE, AND IF COLORED WOMEN ARE 'BORN TO BLUSH UNSEEN' THEY ARE NOT BORN TO BLUSH UNSMELT. A FACT WE KNOW.[27]

LOOK HERE, CLEM, CAN YOU TELL DIS NIGGER WHY DAT WOOLY HEAD OB YOURS AND DE MOON AM ALIKE?
WELL, SAMBO, I GUESS ITS KASE DEY AM BOF ROUND!
NO, DAT AM NOT IT; IT IS KASE DAY AM BOF SPOSED TO BE INHABITED.[28]

Slaves were not always portrayed as the butt of jokes; they were at times portrayed as endowed with great wisdom. Even the joke about Sambo and Clem shows the intelligence of Sambo, but there is better evidence from the aftermath of John Brown's raid on Harper's Ferry. During the raid a slave boy was captured with his master. The boy was given a pike and told that he was now free and should fight the whites. He replied, "I don't know anything about [freedom], I was free enough before you took me. I'm not going to fight until I see Massa Washington is fighting, and then I will fight for him," which showed, at least to white southerners, that slaves were wiser than those who attempted their "emancipation." Another newspaper entry, entitled "Bound to Come," strengthened the argument about slave wisdom. In that article slaves were praised for their wisdom and insight—this time into the workings of the South. The article reported on a group of slaves working on a railroad in one of the seceded states. In this report on the slaves' wisdom they were referred to as Negroes, and were asked why the flags that they hoisted on their work cars had eight stars since only seven states had as yet seceded. The reply of the wise slaves was, "Old Wirginny's bound to come."[29]

While it was believed that the teachings of the church would help maintain order among the slaves, it was just as true that the care of the souls of the slaves was a primary interest. Slaves had souls that needed to be nurtured. Francois Guilbeau, a leading citizen of San Antonio, had the son of one of his slaves, Pauly, baptized at San Fernando Church in 1856. The child was not only baptized but was given the surname Guilbeau, and had as his godparents James Callaghan, one of Francois' friends, and Anita Guilbeau, Francois' eldest child. The local churches also accepted slaves into their congregations. The Baptists of the area organized in 1858 as the San Antonio River Baptist Association, and their membership of 362 included forty-two African Americans. The Methodists too accepted slaves in large numbers. By 1861 the Paine Church, the local Methodist church, had 127 members, of whom sixty were blacks.[30]

Another indication of the belief that slaves had souls was the report in the *Ledger* concerning the execution by hanging of two slaves in Fort Bend County. The two had, according to the newspaper report, murdered their master. Planters from around the area brought their slaves to witness the execution, certainly hoping that the spectacle would act as a deterrent. Numerous clergymen were at the assembly and spoke to the gathered crowds, yet the only one mentioned by name in the article was Bill Lone, "a colored preacher," who led a hymn and then went up on the scaffold to talk with the condemned men. The condemned were also allowed to bid farewell to their families and friends. It was reported that "both seemed penitent, and warned others against their fate." Had the report ended there, the whole affair could be written off as an attempt by owners to impress upon their slaves the futility of murder and of running away. Better results of that sort would have been obtained, however, had both men been reported as howling in fear for their eternal souls in their last moments. Such was not the case. The *Ledger* reported that although both men expressed sorrow over their deeds, both were also ready to die because they "were both prepared for a better world."[31]

Slavery in San Antonio presented a somewhat confusing picture. Though there were few slaveholders there, slaves lived in the city and were visible to its citizens every day, and were thus an integral part of life. However little economic impact slavery had on the city, it left its mark psychologically and historically. That mark can be traced through the city ordinances, the newspapers, and in fact the entire heritage of

San Antonio. The institution of slavery, if not the reality of slaveholding, figured prominently in the imagination of San Antonians. They spent time, effort, and money on it, although its practical influence was small enough to demonstrate that slavery was not necessary to the life of at least one urban area in the South.

## NOTES

1. "Anglo" as used here simply means one who was a native-born white citizen of the United States.

2. United States Eighth Census, 1860 (cited hereafter as census of 1860), Bexar County, Texas, population schedules and slave schedules. Only slaveholders shown as San Antonio residents in both the population and the slave schedules were included. The wealth of nonslaveholders was taken from a random sampling of the 1860 population schedules.

3. United States Seventh Census, 1850 (cited hereafter as census of 1850), Bexar County, Texas, population schedules and slave schedules.

4. *San Antonio Herald*, February 7 (first and second quotations) and May 15, 1858 (third and fourth quotations).

5. Censuses of 1850 and 1860, population and slave schedules.

6. The term "master" is used in this article to denote owner, agent, employer, or other person responsible for the slave.

7. "An Ordinance Concerning Negroes," San Antonio Ordinance Books 1850–2001 (cited hereafter as Ordinance Books), 01–3, October 2, 1850 (quotation), Office of the City Clerk, San Antonio Municipal Archives. "Negroes" was later amended to "Slaves."

8. "An Ordinance relating to slaves, etc.," Ordinance Books, 01–6, February 26, 1851.

9. "An Ordinance Concerning Slaves," Ordinance Books, 01–25, April 16, 1852.

10. Walter Buenger, *Secession and the Union in Texas* (Austin: University of Texas Press, 1984), 55–58.

11. "An Ordinance to Regulate the Conduct of Slaves and Free

Persons of Color in the City of San Antonio," Ordinance Books, 01–6, sections 1–3, August 25, 1860.

12. Ibid., sections 4, 5, and 7 (quotation).

13. Ibid., sections 9 and 10 (quotation).

14. Ibid., sections 14 and 15.

15. Ibid., sections 13, 16, 17, and 18.

16. San Antonio, Council Journal, Book C, August 8, 1860, 260; "An Ordinance to Provide for the Appointment of City Patrols and to Prescribe Their Duties and Powers," Ordinance Books, 01–46, April 14, 1856; *San Antonio Herald*, April 26, 1856.

17. *San Antonio Ledger and Texan*, July 28, 1860, July 13, 1861 (first quotation); *San Antonio Alamo Star*, September 2, 16, 1854; *San Antonio Ledger*, January 25 (second quotation), July 14, 21, 1855; *San Antonio Herald*, June 12, July 10, 1855.

18. *San Antonio Zeitung*, February 10, 1855; Thomas Earle, ed., *The Life, Travels and Opinions of Benjamin Lundy, including His Travels to Texas and Mexico* . . . (n.p., 1847; repr., New York: Augustus M. Kelley, 1971), 48 (first quotation); Frederick Law Olmsted, *A Journey through Texas: A Saddle-Trip on the Southwestern Frontier* (New York: Dix, Edwards, 1857; repr., Austin: University of Texas Press, 1978), 141–42, 163 (second and third quotations).

19. *San Antonio Herald*, September 18, 1858.

20. "An Ordinance relating to slaves, etc.," Ordinance Books, 01–6, February 26, 1851; "An Ordinance Concerning Negroes," Ordinance Books, 01–3, October 2, 1850.

21. Censuses of 1850 and 1860, population and slave schedules. The figures used for population in this essay are a sampling of every fifth head of household from the 1850 population schedule and a random sampling of the heads of households from the 1860 population schedules.

22. Ibid. Only the slaveholders identifiable in both the population and slave schedules were included.

23. Ibid., product of industry schedules; *San Antonio Ledger and Texan*, November 10, 1859.

24. Ronnie C. Taylor and Lawrence R. Murphy, eds., *The Slave Narratives of Texas* (Austin: Encino Press, 1974), 69 (first quotation), 132; *San Antonio Ledger*, May 22, 1859 (second quotation); receipt from the City of San Antonio to Sam Maverick, October 30, 1857, and letter from Sam Maverick to Mary Maverick, November 9, 1857, in the Maverick Family Papers, Center for American History, University of Texas at Austin; census of 1860, slave schedules.

25. *San Antonio Ledger*, July 11, October 24, November 7, 14, December 5, 1857, February 20, 27, April 24, May 22, June 26, July 24, August 7, October 9, 1858; *San Antonio Ledger and Texan*, November 16, 1859.

26. *San Antonio Ledger*, October 9, 1858.

27. *San Antonio Herald*, September 18, 1855.

28. Ibid., January 31, 1857.

29. *San Antonio Ledger and Texan*, November 22, 1859 (first quotation), March 18, 1861 (second quotation).

30. John Ogden Leal, *San Fernando Church Baptismals*, 1851–1858 (San Antonio: privately printed, 1977), 277; Mrs. George L. Houston, *In the Shadow of His Hand* (San Antonio: privately printed, 1961), 21; Josephine Forman, *We Finish to Begin: A History of Travis Park United Methodist Church, San Antonio, Texas, 1846–1991* (San Antonio: privately printed, 1991), 13a.

31. *San Antonio Ledger*, February 20, 1858.

# Just Southwest of Dixie

## *Reconstruction in South Texas, 1865–1876*

KENNETH WAYNE HOWELL

SCHOLARS HAVE PRODUCED NUMEROUS STUDIES on Reconstruction in Texas since the mid-twentieth century, but they have generally focused on regions in East Texas where African American populations were concentrated. This was natural considering that federal officials between 1865 and 1876 devoted most of their time to protecting the newly freed slaves and white Unionists from the attacks of white ex-Confederates. Nevertheless, scholars seemingly have forgotten that South Texas was also part of the state during the period and therefore an integral part of the story of Reconstruction in Texas.

Because of this lack of attention, one could assume that Reconstruction in South Texas is still basically an untold story. Such an assumption would not, however, be completely accurate. The history of South Texas during this complex era is hidden among the pages of numerous dissertations, published scholarly works, and scattered primary sources. With the exception of Randolph B. Campbell's work on Nueces County, the history of South Texas between 1865 and 1876 is primarily discussed within the context of South Texas itself, as if the region were not part of the Lone Star State.[1] For example, the rise of the cattle industry is often studied within the confines of a mythical period known as the "Cattle Kingdom"; rarely do those discussions deal with how the industry influenced the development of Reconstruction in the southern part of the state. Likewise, scholars have written numerous accounts of the violence that occurred in South Texas between 1865 and 1876, but their narratives are usually placed in the context of economic studies, local histories, and the biographies of various men such as Juan Cortina, the infamous Mexican raider of the Lower Rio Grande.[2] Scholars have not deemed it necessary to place the violence of the region in the broader setting of Reconstruction in Texas. Perhaps the story of Reconstruction in South Texas is more properly defined as a "hidden" history than as an untold story in Texas' past.

In an effort to understand how South Texas residents experienced Reconstruction, this paper looks at three distinct aspects of human activity—politics, economics, and violence—in five geographically diverse counties: Nueces, Victoria, Zapata, Maverick, and Live Oak. Each county provides a unique perspective on South Texas. Nueces County, located along the Gulf Coast, reveals how residents in coastal communities reacted to the changes taking place in their world in the post-Civil War years. Victoria County, also located near the Texas coast but further inland, represented something of a transition county between East and South Texas. During this period Victoria County was the gateway to South Texas. Zapata County, located in deep South Texas along the Rio Grande, illustrates the concerns and hardships that residents living on the Texas-Mexico border confronted daily. Likewise, Maverick County, also located on the Texas-Mexico border, reveals the isolation and dangers of living on the outer edge of the Texas frontier. Finally, Live Oak County, in central South Texas, represents a crossroads between the western and eastern portions of the region. As was true throughout the state, the residents of each county experienced Reconstruction on their own terms. Some people probably gave little thought to the events taking place in their county or their state while others were greatly affected by both local and statewide issues.

Politically, Reconstruction in Texas went through six stages of development. The initial stage began when President Andrew Johnson appointed Andrew Jackson Hamilton as provisional governor of Texas in June 1865. Facing the immense task of reorganizing the local and state governments, Hamilton immediately established a temporary government and began to fill county offices with men who were believed to be loyal to the Union and willing to support President Johnson's plan for reconstructing the state. Within a month Hamilton restored civil rule in eighty counties. The provisional governor also called for the election of delegates to the 1866 state constitutional convention. The convention met from February 7 to April 2, 1866, and created a constitution that fulfilled the minimal standards for readmittance into the Union. Abolishing slavery was the most important of the new standards adopted at the convention.[3]

The second stage of Reconstruction began in June 1866 when the voters of the state approved the 1866 Texas Constitution and elected state and local officeholders according to its provisions. Many of the men elected to the new government were former Confederates, and their electoral victory dampened the hopes of the newly freed slaves, especially when the new legislature enacted the infamous Black Codes, laws designed to reduce the freedmen to semi-slavery. However, the reign of the newly elected government was short-lived. Radical Republicans took control of the United States Congress in the spring of 1867 and replaced all major state officials, as well as many local officeholders, with men loyal to the Union and supportive of congressional policies. In addition, the United States military took a more active role in supervising the registration of loyal voters. The actions of the Radical Republicans constituted the third stage of Reconstruction in Texas.[4]

The fourth stage of Reconstruction in the state began in December 1869 when voters approved yet another new constitution and elected a new slate of local and state officials. Radical Republicans were in control of the state, as Edmund J. Davis's election to the governorship revealed, but results at the local level were somewhat more divided. At the county level, Democrats made inroads into Republican support and eventually regained control of the state legislature in 1872.[5]

The fifth and sixth stages of Reconstruction in Texas centered on the success of the Democratic "Redeemers" in regaining control of the state government. The fifth stage was initiated on December 2, 1873, when the Democratic candidate for governor, Richard Coke, defeated Davis and effectively ended Republican control of the state government. Democrats wasted no time in writing yet another "new" state constitution that was more favorable to their party. The sixth stage of Texas Reconstruction began in February 1876, when voters approved the 1875 constitution and elected local and state officials according to its provisions.[6]

It must have been difficult for the citizens of Texas to keep pace with the numerous constitutional changes taking place during this ten-year period. Local offices were defined and redefined each time the state constitution was revised. Before the 1866 constitution the most significant officials at the local level were the county judges, county commissioners, and county sheriffs. Each county in Texas in the immediate postwar period had a four-man commissioners' court chaired by the chief justice of the county. The commissioners' court was responsible for selecting grand juries, making a list of petit jurors, establishing election precincts and polling places, and appointing election officials—along with maintaining and constructing the transportation network in the county, assigning property taxes according to state guidelines, and providing police protection for local citizens. Additionally, the chief justice was charged with presiding over the probate court. The county sheriff was responsible for enforcing the decisions of the chief justice and commissioners' court, carrying out the laws of the state, and overseeing the daily operations of the county jail.[7]

The constitution of 1866, which was constructed under the auspices of Presidential Reconstruction, maintained and further strengthened the powers of local officials. Chief justices, known simply as county judges under the new constitution, still presided over the commissioners' court, but the judges were assigned greater judicial authority that allowed them to hear probate and misdemeanor cases as well as civil cases involving amounts less than five hundred dollars.[8]

When the constitution was once again revamped in 1869, the position of county judge was eliminated along with the county court's judicial authority, and the duties of the county commissioners' court were handed over to justices of the peace who were elected by districts or precincts. The 1869 constitution also enhanced the powers of county sheriffs by making them tax collectors. The Redeemers' constitution of 1876 reversed the changes of the 1869 constitution. The offices of county judges and county commissioners were restored to their 1866 status and the powers of the sheriffs were left intact. Sheriffs even remained tax collectors in counties with populations of less than ten thousand.[9]

In addition to political reorganization, Texans had to cope with the military occupation of their state. Federal troops began entering the state in May 1865 and remained until March 1870. Military commanders of U.S. forces undertook the daunting tasks of providing protection for the newly emancipated slaves and ensuring that the state government remained loyal to the Union. The U.S. Army's insistence upon loyalty to the federal government and equality for the freedmen naturally meant that the military authorities would suffer the indignation of ex-Confederates. While not always successful, the military did its best to prevent the ex-rebels from holding political offices that would have given them a greater opportunity to obstruct the rights of the freedmen. Several factors prohibited military commanders from effectively accomplishing their tasks, one of which was the rapid demobilization of troops serving in the state during the early years of federal occupation. Troop strength fell from a high of fifty-one thousand to a low of three thousand. This reduction of federal soldiers guaranteed that the military would face difficulties in providing protection to the freed people and in maintaining general law and order in the state. Even though the federal forces stationed in Texas were undermanned, military commanders still attempted to intervene in local and state politics. Their efforts to establish and sustain any type of lasting policy in the state were greatly thwarted by a high turnover rate among the army's top commanders. From May 1865 to March 1870, command of federal troops in Texas was transferred eight times. Despite these frequent changes, the military was successful in protecting many freedmen and white Unionists from the abuses of ex-Confederates. The military's success, however, caused ex-rebels to become more determined in their defense of antebellum social and political customs and resulted in further violence against the freed people.[10]

The Bureau of Refugees, Freedmen, and Abandoned Lands, commonly referred to as the Freedmen's Bureau, was also in operation in the state between 1865 and 1872.[11] The bureau was charged with overseeing the transition of the newly freed people from slavery to freedom. Even though the bureau was underfunded and inadequately manned, bureau agents did achieve limited success in curbing ex-Confederate abuses against former slaves and white Unionists. As with the military, the bureau's successes made ex-Confederates even more determined to prevent blacks from peacefully coexisting in white society.[12]

Politics in Nueces County has been examined in greater detail than the other four counties considered in this study. As in other South Texas counties, Nueces County residents, at least those who cast ballots, strongly supported secession in 1861, giving the impression that citizens of the county favored the southern cause. However, the secession referendum by itself is misleading. Other election returns revealed that the county was more divided than the secession vote might otherwise suggest. For example, in the 1859 gubernatorial election that pitted Sam Houston against proslavery candidate Hardin R. Runnels, voters overwhelmingly cast ballots in favor of Houston. Divided loyalties in the county between former secessionists and Unionists continued to exist in the Reconstruction era. Some of the more notable figures in the Unionist camp were E. J. Davis and John Dix. Prominent ex-Confederates included William Maltby, Richard King, Mifflin Kenedy, and Felix Blucher.[13]

In July 1865 a brigade of black troops from the 25th U.S. Army Corps entered Corpus Christi. While Union officers in charge of the occupation forces began to parole ex-Confederates, Presidential Reconstruction under the direction of President Andrew Johnson was beginning to take shape. In Nueces County, Governor Hamilton appointed local loyalists as new officials in the county's provisional government: John J. Dix became the county judge; Henry W. Berry became sheriff; James Bryden, Matthew Cody, and John McLane became commissioners; and Miles R. Polk assumed the duties of tax assessor and collector. Unionists in the county seemingly approved of the Hamilton appointees, and the ex-Confederates, who probably objected to the slate of new officials, remained quiet on the issue.[14]

In Nueces County during this period the only controversy concerning a Hamilton appointee focused on District Judge E. P. Upton. Apparently, Upton was too sympathetic to former Confederates in his courtroom, a development that led Unionists in the county to demand his removal. On January 1, 1866, Hamilton obliged the Unionists' request and replaced Upton with Benjamin F. Neal. This was a move that should have infuriated the Unionists because Neal was an ex-Confederate. A native Virginian, Neal had served in both houses of the Texas Legislature during the war, defended Corpus Christi in 1862–1863 against federal invasions, earned a rank of major, and served as a district judge in the final days of the Confederacy. Neal was clearly not a Unionist and his acceptance in Nueces County can only be explained in that the citizens of the county trusted him because he was a longtime resident of the region.[15]

The new county officials immediately went to work assessing and levying new state and local taxes and discussing ways to improve transportation into and out of the county, especially the city of Corpus Christi. More importantly, they implemented Governor Hamilton's plan for registering loyal voters and electing delegates to the constitutional convention that was scheduled to convene in February 1866. Any delegate sent to represent the county was supposed to be a "loyal" citizen who would take the oath of allegiance mandated by President Johnson. Nueces County voters sent E. J. Davis, the county's most prominent Unionist, to Austin to serve as their constitutional delegate.[16]

With Texas readmitted to the Union under a new state constitution, general elections were held, and local voters elected new officials to replace the ones serving in the state's provisional government. Unionists continued to hold key offices in Nueces County: Dix remained county judge; Berry was sheriff; and Cody, Bryden, and McLane were commissioners. The fourth seat on the commissioners' court went to John Kellett, a native of Florida who was also a Unionist and later a member of the Republican party. Benjamin Neal, though not a Unionist, retained his judgeship in the Fourteenth District Court. Because the newly elected officials had previously served as provisional appointees, the 1866 elections in Nueces County and the transfer of local offices passed with only minor disputes. Once secure in their offices, officials began concentrating on the economic recovery of the county and curbing the general lawlessness that prevailed in the region.[17]

At the same time that counties were experiencing Reconstruction, municipal governments were also being reformed. In Nueces County city officials for Corpus Christi were elected on June 6, 1866. The Corpus Christi municipal government primarily became concerned with how to revitalize their town's economic prosperity and how to control the crime in the streets. In fighting general disorder, the city council took a firm stand against one of the more light-hearted dilemmas facing the townspeople. Apparently, Corpus Christians maintained a certain affection for nude bathing in the bay during daylight hours. This practice did not set well with some of the fathers of the city and they attempted to thwart the pastime by passing a city ordinance that prohibited bathing "without proper apparel" during daylight hours. No restrictions, however, were placed on those who chose to engage in nighttime bathing. In all, the city governments of South Texas, like the county governments, witnessed a relatively smooth transition from provisional status to elected government.[18]

In the fall of 1866 the Radical Republicans gained control of the U.S. Congress. Shortly after Congress convened in March of 1867 it revoked the status of Texas as a reconstructed state. The Lone Star State was placed within the newly created Fifth Military District, which included Louisiana and was assigned to the command of General Philip Sheridan. Congress also passed the Reconstruction Acts of 1867 requiring southern states, including Texas, to register voters again and to have elected officials take the iron-clad oath or face removal from office. General Charles Griffin, who was named commander of the Texas district and who was stationed in Galveston, issued an executive order authorizing that the freedmen be placed on juries and that all jurors regardless of color should take the ironclad oath before allowing to serve.[19]

Nueces County officials, especially John Dix, were pleased with this turn of events in Texas politics. The county began the process of voter registration on June 18, 1867, but the local registrar's efforts were temporarily disrupted by a severe outbreak of yellow fever that took the lives of many Nueces County citizens. The registration process was not completed until January of the next year. At this point the registration list included 261 names representing 133 voters of European descent, 80 of Mexican descent, and 48 freedmen. All populations in the county were adequately represented except southern-born whites.[20]

Despite actions that favored Unionists, they still worried about the ultimate outcome of Congressional Reconstruction. Dix was especially suspicious of Judge B. F. Neal, whom he viewed as no better than his predecessor, E. P. Upton, in enforcing the laws broken by ex-Confederates. Additionally, Dix believed that the number of ex-Confederates disenfranchised by the Reconstruction Acts was not sufficient to ensure that loyal delegates would be sent to Austin to participate in the creation of the 1869 constitution. Dix's fear about Judge Neal did not go unnoticed; General Joseph J. Reynolds, who had to replace Charles Griffin as commander of the Texas district upon the latter's untimely death from yellow fever, replaced Judge Neal with George Scott, a staunch Unionist. Dix's concerns regarding the disfranchisement of ex-Confederates, however, proved unwarranted, because in February of 1868 the voters overwhelmingly approved the call for a constitutional convention and chose E. J. Davis as their delegate.[21]

In a four-day election beginning November 30, 1869, voters in the state elected Davis to the governorship over A. J. Hamilton. Nueces County voters strongly supported Davis, but local elections produced mixed results. Locally, Nueces County voters supported both Radical Republicans and moderates. Radicals won several key races, including the one where Dennis Kelly defeated moderate Henry Berry for the sheriff's office, and the one in which Joseph Fitzsimmons won the race for district clerk. However, Radicals were surely disappointed when Miles R. Polk, a native North Carolinian, defeated John Dix as presiding officer in the county court. Of the other four positions on the county court, only two were contested and Radicals Samuel Miller and Norman Collins won both. Those justices who were not up for reelection, Richard Schubert and John Greer, soon joined the Democrats. The mixed results of this election proved that Republicans still had enough votes to control the local governments, but unlike in regions of East Texas, the Radicals' victories depended on Mexican American votes rather than African American votes. Thus the Radicals could not depend on a single bloc of voters in upcoming elections. This promised mixed results in future political contests.[22]

The mixed results in local politics continued throughout the rest of the Reconstruction era, even during the so-called period of "redemption." In fact, once the Davis administration ended, local politics seems to have been less partisan and less concerned with Reconstruction issues. Republicans and Democrats still confronted each other at the polls, but they tended to focus more on the performance of local officials than on their partisan qualifications. Thus the mixed results of Nueces County reveal that citizens in the county did not witness the same types of political struggles that characterized other regions in Texas between 1865 and 1876.[23]

Nueces County was reflective of the political trends occurring in Victoria and Live Oak counties during the Reconstruction era. Republicans and Democrats in these counties went through the various phases of Reconstruction attempting to gain political control of the local government.[24] Radical Republicans were less favored in Victoria County where ex-Confederates characterized the Davis administration as having a "total disregard for the interest of any but Republican partisans, high taxes, and the summary executions of [criminals] at the hands of the state police."[25] One of Victoria's discontented citizens later claimed that "Texas was an incipient hell, with promise of full, and intense development." The Victoria resident continued, "Four years of this misrule [referring to the Davis Administration] was born, when the aroused people, at the succeeding election [1873], bore Richard Coke to the gubernatorial succession by a majority too great to be ignored, and he had the manhood to seize the reins in spite of the threatened resistance of the retiring governor."[26] The moderate and conservative voters' reaction against Radical Reconstruction probably hinged upon the fact that African Americans and mulattos made up more than 30 percent of the county's population.[27]

In Zapata and Maverick counties the political circumstances were somewhat different from those present in the more settled area of South Texas. Located on the Texas frontier, these counties were dominated by a handful of prominent landowners and ranchers who handed out their own brand of justice. Reconstruction politics, it seems, mattered little to these individuals. There were few blacks present in Zapata and Maverick counties and thus the political leaders were not agitated by ex-Confederate propaganda relating to issues such as "Negro rule" or "Radical Republicanism." These western settlers were primarily concerned with two issues, frontier defense and internal improvements.[28]

Despite the fact that the majority of the populations in these counties were Mexican Americans, Anglos tended to dominate the affairs of the counties in western South Texas. Mexican Americans who had served faithfully in the U.S. Army during the Civil War were greatly disappointed in the outcome of Reconstruction in this region. With the exception of Clemente Zapata, who became a justice of the peace in Zapata County, the loyal Tejanos of the region did not achieve any real measure of political power.[29] Those counties fell under the system of "boss rule." Men such as J. King Fisher in Maverick County and Stephen Powers in Zapata County ruled over the citizens as they saw fit. Backed by private ranging companies and sizable financial resources, these men in essence were the unofficial law of the regions.[30]

Throughout Reconstruction Texas the state's economy was stagnant, recovering only slowly from the financial devastation caused by the Civil War. However, South Texas seemed to be spared many of the economic hardships experienced in other regions of the state. One of the most significant reasons behind South Texas' advanced economic recovery was the rise of the cattle industry. Many men such as Richard King and Mifflin Kenedy in Nueces County made fortunes in the cattle industry. Edward King, an eye witness to the rise of the cattle industry in South Texas, characterized cattle ranching as "one of the most remarkable industries of the southwest . . . nearly all the immense region from the Colorado to the Rio Grande is given up to stock-raising."[31]

The extent to which the cattle industry became important to the South Texas economy is evident from the rising number of cattle present in the five counties examined here. Local tax rolls showed 218,969 cattle worth $942,000 in Nueces County in 1871, a figure more than four times the value recorded in 1860. Additionally, during the early 1870s, ten slaughter houses operated in the same county. People such as William Franklin Burks and his family moved into Nueces County to enter into the stock-raising business in 1866. In two wagons, the Burks moved into the county with $2,200 in gold and some thirty-five horses. They bought enough land to support a small-scale cattle operation and raised cattle to sell at markets outside the state. The Burks maintained their cattle ranch until the family relocated in La Salle County in 1876. The Burks' business adventure paled in comparison to large-scale cattle ranches such as the ones owned by Kenedy and King. In Victoria County, at a time when cotton production was in decline, the number of cattle in 1870 grew to 61,651 head, making Victoria seventh among Texas counties engaged in cattle ranching. Live Oak County had 63,000 cattle in 1870, a number triple that of the count in 1860. Maverick County had a long-standing ranching heritage which could be traced back to 1765 when twenty-five leagues of land were granted to Don Antonio Rivas by the Spanish government. This was a tradition that was maintained throughout the 1800s, and in the 1870s several new ranches were developed by Mike Wipff, Frank Lehmann, Patrick Thomson, and John Towns. Zapata County, while heavily engaged in sheep ranching, also witnessed a growth in the number of cattle in the county—from 6,957 in 1870 to 9,202 in 1880. It is probable that Zapata County's close proximity to the Texas-Mexico boundary retarded the county's involvement in the cattle industry, especially given the numerous outlaws who moved freely across the border stealing and butchering cattle in South Texas.[32]

It seems obvious that the cattle industry promoted economic recovery in the five counties examined here. This recovery improved the quality of life in these counties and softened racial animosities between whites and blacks, which were commonplace in other regions of Texas. In counties such as Nueces and Victoria, which had larger slave populations in 1860 than most South Texas counties, cattle ranching provided an alternative to cotton production and other agricultural pursuits that used slave labor. Also, it provided people who incurred financial loss due to the emancipation of slaves an opportunity to recover their losses more quickly. It is therefore reasonable to assume that economic recovery made it easier for whites in South Texas to accept emancipation. This is not to say that racism was absent in South Texas, because it was clearly present and many African Americans and Mexican Americans suffered at the hands of Anglo residents. However, the freedmen found it easier to transition into South Texas society.

While it was easier for freed people to make the transition to freedom, economic recovery did not mean an absence of violence in South Texas. Violence was actually widespread and pervasive in the region. The motives behind the violence were multifaceted. Certainly, white violence was waged against the freed people in counties that had larger African American populations. White-on-black violence was clearly evident in Nueces and Victoria counties. Even though the violence against the freedmen in these counties was relatively mild when compared with other areas in Texas, African Americans in Nueces County were treated badly enough to make Judge John Dix repeatedly ask for a Freedmen's Bureau agent to be stationed in the county. His requests must have had some merit, because he was eventually appointed the Bureau's subassistant agent for his county. Evidence of violence against African Americans in Victoria County was clearly present in the Black Codes found in the minutes of the County Court of Victoria. The county court attempted to throttle the rights of black citizens in Victoria by passing vagrancy and convict-lease laws. If convicted of being a vagrant, a black man was to be sentenced to labor on the public works for a three-week period. Only the presence of the military in Nueces and Victoria counties kept white violence against the freedmen under control.[33]

More common was the violence waged among Mexican Americans, Native Americans, and Anglos. Scholars have well documented the conflicts that occurred among these groups in South Texas. However, the historical literature does not tie the violence to the larger picture of Reconstruction in Texas. In simple terms, the federal authorities were unable to curb the violence in South Texas because they were forced to use many federal resources to protect freedmen from Anglo violence in other regions of the state. In addition, because state troops posed potential problems for military authorities in charge of reconstructing the state, Texas officials were not allowed to muster state militias for the protection of frontier counties until the Davis administration was elected to the governorship in 1869. To complicate matters further, many of the miscreant outlaws who raided homes and ranches in South Texas effectively used the Mexican border to escape legal prosecution. Neither federal nor state troops had the authority to pursue these bandits across the border. For the most part, the citizens of South Texas were forced to form private ranging companies or vigilante mobs that meted out their own brand of frontier justice. Violence was commonplace in all five counties examined in this paper.[34]

In conclusion, South Texas experienced Reconstruction differently than other regions of Texas. Politically, geographical proximity to the frontier produced varied results in South Texas counties. Those counties located in well-established areas such as Nueces and Victoria struggled with the rapid changes and with directives associated with Reconstruction policies being employed in the state. Counties such as Zapata and Maverick, which were less populated and inhabited by fewer African American residents, seemingly cared little about Reconstruction policies and devoted greater time to combating outlawry in their region. Here boss rule was commonplace.

The cattle industry was vital to economic recovery of South Texas since it brought a great deal of money into the region from other regions in Texas as well as from areas outside the state. The cattle industry gave the people of South Texas an alternative to labor-intensive agricultural pursuits and provided the freedmen greater opportunities for acceptance into white society—a chance not readily available in other regions of the state.

Finally, violence was pervasive throughout South Texas during the Reconstruction era. This violence involved all ethnic and racial groups in the region but centered primarily on long-standing animosities that existed between Anglos and Mexican Americans. Because the freedmen and white Unionists needed protection from ex-Confederate abuses in other regions of Texas, federal and state authorities provided minimal assistance in curbing the violence permeating South Texas. Local residents of South Texas were forced to protect themselves against the general outlawry present in their region of the state.

This study represents a synthesis of the historical literature that includes information on South Texas during the Reconstruction era. Given the limited number of studies specifically covering Reconstruction in South Texas, there is vast potential for future research projects focusing on this period. Such research is paramount if scholars are going to fully understand how this region fits into the story of Reconstruction Texas. Perhaps this work will serve as a first step toward completing this consequential task.

## NOTES

1. Randolph Campbell, "Reconstruction in Nueces County, 1865–1876," *Houston Review* 16 (1994), 3–26. This work is an excellent example of the type of research that still needs to be done for other south Texas counties.

2. A definitive biography of Juan Cortina has yet to be written, but two informative works on Cortina's life are Lyman Woodman, *Cortina: Rogue of the Rio Grande* (San Antonio: Naylor, 1950) and Jerry D. Thompson, ed., *Juan Cortina and the Texas-Mexico Frontier*, 1859–1876 (EI Paso: Texas Western Press, 1994).

3. Randolph B. Campbell, "Grass Roots Reconstruction: The Personnel of County Government in Texas, 1865–1876," *Journal of Southern History* 58 (February 1992), 99–116; Robert A. Calvert, Arnoldo De Leon, and Gregg Cantrell, *The History of Texas* (Wheeling, Illinois: Harlan Davidson, 1990, repr. 2002), 150–53.

4. Calvert, De Leon, and Cantrell, *History of Texas*, 153–54; Campbell, "Grass Roots Reconstruction," 100–101.

5. Campbell, "Grass Roots Reconstruction," 101; Calvert, De Leon and Cantrell, *History of Texas*, 155–68.

6. Calvert, De Leon, and Cantrell, *History of Texas*, 168–72; Campbell, "Grass Roots Reconstruction," 101.

7. Campbell, "Grass Roots Reconstruction," 102.

8. Ibid.

9. Ibid.

10. For an excellent article examining the military's participation in the reconstruction of Texas, see William Richter's "Devil Take Them All: Military Rule in Texas, 1862–1870," *Southern Studies: An Interdisciplinary Journal of the South*, 25 (Spring 1986), 5–30. See also Carl H. Moneyhon, "Reconstruction," *Handbook of Texas Online*, http://www.tshaonline.org/handbook/online/articles/RR/mzr1.html (accessed January 13, 2003), also published in Ron C. Tyler et al., eds., *The New Handbook of Texas* (Austin: Texas State Historical Association, 1996), 5:474–81.

11. Moneyhon, "Reconstruction," *Handbook of Texas Online*; Barry Crouch, *The Freedmen's Bureau and Black Texans* (Austin: University of Texas Press, 1992), 37; Calvert, De Leon, and Cantrell, *The History of Texas*, 160–61.

12. Crouch, The Freedmen's Bureau and Black Texans, 12–40; Moneyhon," "Reconstruction," *Handbook of Texas Online.*

13. Campbell, "Reconstruction in Nueces County," 5; Eugenia Reynolds Briscoe, "A Narrative History of Corpus Christi, Texas" (PhD diss., University of Denver, 1972), 464.

14. Ibid., 464–65; Campbell, "Reconstruction in Nueces County," 7.

15. Campbell, "Reconstruction in Nueces County," 8.

16. Briscoe, "A Narrative History of Corpus Christi," 465–69.

17. Ibid., 475–78; Campbell, "Reconstruction in Nueces County," 9.

18. Briscoe, "A Narrative History of Corpus Christi," 469–70.

19. Ibid., 482–86.

20. Ibid., 481–83; Campbell, "Reconstruction in Nueces County," 12.

21. Campbell, "Reconstruction in Nueces County," 10–13.

22. Ibid, 16–17.

23. Ibid., 21–26.

24. Craig H. Roell, "Victoria County," *Handbook of Texas Online*, http://www.tshaonline.org/handbook/online/articles/VV/hcv3.html (accessed Nov. 14, 2002); Roy Grimes, ed., 300 *Years in Victoria County* (Victoria, Texas: Victoria Advocate, 1968), 329; Sharon Smith, "Victoria County, Texas, 1824–1870: Mexican Colonization to Reconstruction" (master's thesis, Southwest Texas State University, 1998), 77–78; "Live Oak County," *Handbook of Texas Online*, http://www.tshaonline.org/handbook/online/articles/LL/hc111.html (accessed November 14, 2002).

25. Victor Rose, *Victor Rose's History of Victoria*, ed. J. W. Petty Jr. (San Antonio: Lone Star Printing, 1961), 64.

26. Ibid.

27. Smith, "Victoria County, Texas, 1824–1870," 82–83.

28. Jorita Gonzales, "Social Life in Cameron, Starr, and Zapata Counties" (master's thesis, University of Texas, 1930), 48–50, 83–84.

29. Jerry Thompson, *Mexican Texans in the Union Army* (El Paso: Texas Western Press, 1986), 36.

30. Gonzales, "Social Life in Cameron, Starr, and Zapata Counties," 84–85; Ruben E. Ochoa, "Maverick County," *Handbook of Texas Online*, http://www.tshaonline.org/handbook/online/articles/MM/hcm6.html (accessed November 14, 2002); Vera L. Dugas, "A Social and Economic History of Texas in the Civil War and Reconstruction Periods" (PhD diss., University of Texas, 1963), 430.

31. Larry Adams, "Economic Development in Texas During Reconstruction, 1865–1875" (PhD diss., North Texas State University, 1980), 171–91; Dugas, "A Social and Economic History of Texas," 483–96; Edward King, Texas: 1874: *An Eyewitness Account of Conditions in Post-Reconstruction Texas*, ed. Robert Gray (Houston: Cordovan Press, 1974), 123–24; Briscoe, "A Narrative History of Corpus Christi, Texas," 480–81; David Robinson, *A Little Corner of Texas* (Tulsa: John Hadden, 1991), 69. Robinson reminds scholars that sheep ranching was also important in the South Texas region.

32. "Nueces County," *Handbook of Texas Online*, http://www.tshaonline.org/handbook/online/articles/NN/hcn5.html (accessed August 27, 2002); Dugas, "A Social and Economic History of Texas," 441–46; Johnye C. Sturcken, "Amanda and William Franklin Burks: A Nueces County Partnership," *East Texas Historical Journal* (1992), 45–49; *The Handbook of*

*Victoria County* (Austin: Texas State Historical Association, 1990), 129; Smith, "Victoria County, Texas, 1824–1870," 89; Roell, "Victoria County," *Handbook of Texas Online*; Live Oak County Historical Commission, *The History of the People of Live Oak* (privately published by Live Oak County Historical Commission, 1982), 12–13; Kurt House, "An Early History of Live Oak County, Texas," *West Texas Historical Associated Year Book* (1981), 92; John Leffler, "Live Oak County," *Handbook of Texas Online*, http://www.tshaonline.org/handbook/online/articles/LL/hc111.html (accessed November 14, 2002); J. Frank Dobie, "The Cowman Who Was My Father," *Southwest Review* (1967), 313; Ben E. Pingenot, *Historical Highlights of Eagle Pass and Maverick County* (Eagle Pass, Texas: privately printed, 1971), 6–7; "Zapata County," *Handbook of Texas Online*, http://www.tshaonline/handbook/online/articles/ZZ/hczl.html (accessed August 27, 2002).

33. Dugas, "A Social and Economic History of Texas," 331; Barry Crouch and L. J. Schultz, "A Crisis in Color: Racial Separation in Texas during Reconstruction," *Civil War History* (March 1970), 38–44; Briscoe, "A Narrative History of Corpus Christi," 458–472; Campbell, "Reconstruction in Nueces County, 1865–1876," 9–18; William Richter, *Overreached on All Sides: The Freedmen's Bureau Administration in Texas, 1865–1868* (College Station: Texas A&M University Press, 1991), 185–86; Christopher Long, "Nueces County," *Handbook of Texas Online*, http://www.tshaonline.org/handbook/online/articles/NN/hcn5.html; Rose, *Victor Rose's History of Victoria*, 54–58; Grimes, *300 Years in Victoria County*, 324–25; Richter, "Devil Take Them All," 13; Charles W. Ramsdell, *Reconstruction in Texas* (New York: Columbia University Press, 1910; repr. 1970); Minutes of County Court of Victoria, Victoria County, Texas, vol. 2; Smith, "Victoria County, Texas, 1824–1870," 91–92.

34. Arnoldo De Leon, *They Called Them Greasers: Anglo Attitudes toward Mexicans in Texas, 1821–1900* (Austin: University of Texas Press, 1983), 87–102; Briscoe, "A Narrative History of Corpus Christi, Texas," 458–519; George Blackburn and Sherman Ricards, "A Demographic History of the West: Nueces County, Texas, 1850," *Prologue: The Journal of the National Archives* 4, no. 1 (1972): 3, 7; Woodman, *Cortina: Rogue of the Rio Grande*, 99; Dugas, "A Social and Economic History of Texas," 365–66, 567; King, *Texas: 1874*, 125–29; Thompson, *Juan Cortina and the Texas-Mexico Frontier*, 71–72;

Maria Augusta von Blucher, *Letters From the South Texas Frontier, 1849–1879*, ed. Bruce Cheeseman (College Station: Texas A&M University Press, 2002), 234, 239; Live Oak County Historical Commission, *The History of the People of Live Oak*, 287; Robinson, *A Little Corner of Texas*, 20–21, 32, 207–208; Pingenot, *Historical Highlights*, 7; Gonzales, "Social Life In Cameron, Starr, and Zapata Counties," 47; Zapata County District Court Minutes, 1874–1881 (microfilm), 23–24; "Maverick County," *Handbook of Texas Online*; "Zapata County," *Handbook of Texas Online*.

# "Wantonly Maltreated and Slain, Simply Because They Are Free"

## *Racial Violence during Reconstruction in South Texas*

REBECCA A. KOSARY

THE *SAN ANTONIO EXPRESS-NEWS* WARNED in February of 1894 that colonizing African Americans in Liberia to alleviate the "race problem" in Texas was a risky proposition. Not because the state of Texas or the southern region of the United States might lose a large proportion of agricultural laborers, and certainly not because most African Americans did not consider themselves necessarily "African." According to this concerned *Express-News* writer, even if black Americans were "wafted to the choicest portion of Africa and furnished with everything necessary to the enjoyment of civilized life," they would "rapidly retrograde" into savages like their ancestors. The writer further justified his position, explaining, "wherever the Negro has been removed from the influence of the white man he has rapidly drifted back to barbarism."[1] The next month antilynching activist Ida B. Wells toured England to inform European audiences of the frequency with which the barbaric practice of extralegal justice against African Americans was carried out in the United States. At a gathering in Manchester on March 21, a school principal informed Wells of a front-page article in the afternoon paper that described the lynching of a black woman in San Antonio, Texas, who was "boxed up in a barrel with nails driven through the sides and rolled down a hill until she was dead." Having not heard of the specific case until that very moment, Wells sat "as if turned to stone, with tears rolling down [her] cheeks at this new evidence of outrage and the apathy of the American white people."[2]

The juxtaposition of these two stories demonstrates the extreme chasm that existed between the perceptions of whites and the realities of life for blacks at the turn of the century in Texas. By the 1890s many white Texans, it seems, believed the only way to control the alleged "savagery" of blacks was through savagery itself. But this attitude was nothing new. On the contrary, whites in Texas used extremely brutal forms of violence against African Americans immediately following emancipation in 1865, not only to control their alleged bestiality, but to create a climate of fear in order to subjugate all black Texans.

This essay examines the general atmosphere of violence during the Reconstruction conflict in South Texas, particularly the years 1865–68, when the Freedmen's Bureau kept detailed records of white abuses perpetrated against the former slaves. Bureau records indicate that even before the advent of Congressional Reconstruction, when white Texans bitterly opposed federal "occupation" forces and used violence and intimidation to limit black male voting, Texas was in the midst of a racial conflict that dramatically affected African Americans of both genders. Freed people were abused and killed in disproportionately large numbers during the period, and the brutality of the violence perpetrated against them rarely fit the alleged provocations. Violence was used to keep blacks economically and socially subordinate, to keep them from gaining an education, and to keep black men, in particular, from participating in the political system. The extremely violent atmosphere that existed in Texas during the early years of Reconstruction was more than a manifestation of racism and bitterness toward blacks. Rather, the period may be viewed as an extension of the Civil War; a race war in which violence perpetrated against black men, women, and children was a central component in the overall strategy of racial dominance and control.

Over the last quarter of a century scholars have demonstrated clearly that violence was a major component of race relations in Texas and throughout the former Confederacy during Reconstruction. Texas historians, including James Smallwood, Gregg Cantrell, and the late Barry A. Crouch, among others, have determined that violence against blacks during Reconstruction was far-reaching and frequent. Arguing that it was either socially, economically, or politically motivated, these Texas historians successfully advanced the view that violence was a major component of race relations in the state during Reconstruction. Yet few recent works have focused on the southernmost counties in the state, an area with a rich history and, unfortunately, rampant racial violence. This essay attempts to fill this void in the literature.[3]

On June 19, 1865, when federal troops arrived in Galveston, Texas, General Gordon Granger read a statement that dramatically changed the lives of African Americans: all slaves were now free. Although Granger did not specifically define "freedom," former slaves clearly realized that they were no longer to be the property of others. Most white Texans, whether or not they were slaveholders, refused to heed the order and attempted to hold African Americans in a condition of virtual slavery through the use of quasi-legal means. A substantial number of white Texans, however, also employed violence. As both blacks and whites struggled in an atmosphere of frustration and resentment to redefine their social, economic, and political roles, even the presence of the military could not suppress the violence. Former slaveholders, having previously exerted complete control over their human chattel, were now forced to acknowledge the freedom and independence of those who had never known it. While white resistance in some form was perhaps inevitable, the amount and brutality of the violence perpetrated by white Texans against African Americans during Reconstruction was of extraordinary proportions.[4]

The Texas Reconstruction Convention, which met in Austin in 1868, recognized after an extensive study by the "Committee on Lawlessness and Violence" that an alleged "war of the races" existed throughout the state of Texas, and acknowledged that it was "all on the part of the whites against the blacks." The report concluded,

"When we come to examine the persecutions suffered by the freed people, the mass of testimony is so overwhelming that no man of candor can for a moment question the statement that they are, in very many parts of the state, wantonly maltreated and slain, simply because they are free, and claim to exercise the rights of free men."[5]

Violence, long associated with the control of slaves, escalated immediately after emancipation to become the predominant method of controlling the lives of freed people during the postwar years in Texas. Groups and individuals, including men, women, children, and the elderly and infirm, were all potential victims of abuse. According to Freedmen's Bureau records, the types of violence perpetrated against blacks ranged from serious assault to homicide and from relatively minor assault to robbery and property damage, and included various types of threats and intimidation.[6] Although these statistics also indicate that nonblacks were injured during the period, the fact that former slaves made up the overwhelming majority of reported victims is significant. It demonstrates that, even though many crimes against them probably went unreported for fear of retaliation, blacks were injured or killed in disproportionately large numbers in Texas during Reconstruction.

African Americans in Texas received brutal treatment after emancipation, many times for practically no identifiable reason. The Bureau reported numerous instances where the severest kind of vigilante justice was meted out by whites for seemingly trivial offenses committed by blacks. This criminality reveals deep-seated feelings of natural superiority and the belief of some white Texans in their right to be judge, jury, and even executioner for no reason other than that the "deserving" party was black and, thus, considered inferior.

The violence perpetrated against freed people in South Texas took many forms, as it did throughout the state. Individuals were very frequently brutalized for such "offenses" as simply asking for their earned wages or asserting that they had been emancipated. Reasons cited for the majority of these and other violent acts vary in the extreme. On one hand were those few assaults that, not surprisingly, stemmed from the Texas frontier mentality. For example, parties involved were drinking heavily while gambling or fighting over a woman and a shoot-out or barroom brawl ensued. These incidents, however, typically involved whites as both perpetrators and victims. On the other hand, in the majority of incidents involving black victims and white perpetrators, the severity of the assault rarely fit the alleged provocation, demonstrating white hostility toward the concept of black freedom in any form.[7]

Violence was most often used to keep black Texans in a white-defined role of subordination, particularly with regard to their economic activities. Evidence makes clear that, according to many white employers, the words "employee" and "slave" were synonymous. This is seen clearly in the many cases in which black men and women were assaulted or murdered for asking for their wages, or for the "crime" of simply desiring to leave their white employers.[8] For example, when a freedman in Brazoria County asked his boss, one Mr. Taylor, for his pay and expressed a desire to quit his job, Taylor beat him over the head with a monkey wrench. Similarly, Brazoria County resident James Tankesly used the butt end of a pistol to answer Robert Jones' request for his earned wages. Jones suffered a knocked-out tooth and bruised face as a result of the altercation, but did not receive his pay. In Fort Bend County, a freedman listed as "Leton" was whipped, chained, and threatened because he would not remain in the employ of a Dr. Phillips. In this case, Leton arrived at the Bureau office in Houston with the chain still attached to his body.[9]

It is understandable that after emancipation former slaves would be reluctant to engage in work that undermined their newly gained independence. Because most planters did not have the resources to pay workers in cash after the war, contractual labor, where labor was exchanged for crops, became the usual arrangement between former slaves and former masters, with Bureau officials serving as negotiators in many instances. The contractual relationships that developed between ex-master and ex-slave, however, served mostly to keep blacks tied to the land and under the control of white landowners. As the Bureau attempted to regulate contracts and hiring practices, agents found themselves constantly adjudicating conflicts between white employers and black laborers. Landlords regularly held "court" and freely imposed fines upon workers they found guilty of insolence, disobedience, and, particularly, losing work time for unapproved absences.[10] Competition for agricultural hands was intense in postwar South Texas and planters often attempted to lure black laborers from other plantations to their own. Whites often quarreled among themselves over who had the earliest-dated contract for a black worker, and as such, the right to his labor. When blacks unknowingly signed more than one contract, however, they often found themselves caught between feuding landlords and suffered beatings as a result.[11]

A majority of southerners believed that African Americans were inherently lazy and therefore would not work, even for wages, without physical coercion. Bureau records are filled with examples of physical violence perpetrated upon former slaves for such "offenses" as working too slowly or being lazy. For example, an unnamed freedman in Guadalupe County told Bureau agents in Seguin that he had been whipped repeatedly to "make him pick cotton." Bureau agent Craig described the freedman being covered with "scabs and scars" and "many marks made by a strap buckle."[12]

The fact that many former slaves desired to work less after emancipation only confirmed whites' fears that freed labor would destroy the plantation system and their way of life. To help ease their fears, in some instances planters held their former slaves in bondage far beyond the date of emancipation in Texas. Where this practice occurred, the bondage often was enforced with violence. In Nueces County, a white landowner whom we only know as "Bass" held several children in slavery and "treated them in a very brutal manner . . . had them clothed in rags and covered with scabs." A white family in Seguin held a freed boy named Levy Jenkins in bondage until 1867, when the local Bureau agent discovered the outrage. Likewise in 1867, the Littlefield family of Seguin held Ann Dougherty as a slave until the Bureau made the shocking discovery.[13] To many Texas planters, it seems, the new system of "freed" labor was simply a form of modified racial slavery—one of coercion, intimidation, and violence.

Since landowners had been used to relying on the discipline of slavery to ensure their own economic welfare, during Reconstruction they were obviously concerned over the independence exerted by their former bondsmen. From their perspective, black social and economic independence severely weakened the discipline necessary to control a newly freed labor force. Thus, many landowners resorted to violence to ensure that former slaves remembered their subordinate place in society. But freedom of movement was a new concept for most black Texans. Having the ability to come and go became not only an assertion of autonomy, but more importantly, it was psychologically liberating.[14] In response, many white landowners or their hired, extralegal enforcers threatened laborers and their families, and evicted them after the harvest with no compensation. Because reasons for this conduct were often not spelled out in the records, it seems reasonable to assume that landowners did it simply to reap the full profit of the crop as they had under slavery. In the majority of such cases, it appears that white employers had no intention of paying freed people for their work, and their unwillingness to accept their former slaves as actual employees is strikingly clear.[15] For example, Jacob Carroll of Guadalupe County threatened an entire family of freed people as he drove them off his property without pay. Likewise, in the same county, a white man known as "Phillips" threatened one of his black employees with a six-shooter before chasing him off the property permanently.[16] In many cases, landowners used the most trivial excuses to resort to eviction. William Freeman threatened his former slave, Charles, before driving him off his property in Fort Bend County for "disputing the price of a turkey." Freeman shot another former slave named Abe for a similar "offense" before running him off the land as well.[17]

The Ku Klux Klan appears to have helped many Texas property owners control their former slaves through terrorism and coercion. Although evidence connecting the Klan with individual landowners is sparse, Bureau records do indicate many incidents of Klan and Klan-like mobs throughout Texas robbing freedmen and driving them off their employers' land.[18] Allen Trelease defined any group practicing physical or psychological terrorism (or terroristic measures) during Reconstruction as the Klan. In addition, whites who either aided the Klan outright or failed to report acts of intimidation and violence were part of the "Klan Conspiracy" although they may not have been actual members of a klavern. From this perspective, the Klan was extremely active in Texas between 1865 and 1868. By the end of 1868, over 50 percent of the counties in Texas had "suffered disruption characterized by Klan methodology and tactics." By that time, the Klan began using violence primarily to keep black and white Union men from voting freely. However, circumstances surrounding some of the earlier outrages by the group and its imitators reveal the underlying purpose of keeping blacks economically inferior while reinforcing the notion of their subordinate place in society. By 1868, klaverns had formed in the South Texas counties of Bexar, Goliad, Victoria, Nueces, Colorado, Wharton, Matagorda, Fort Bend, and Brazoria. However, Bureau records for these counties fail to mention Klan activity specifically.[19]

After the Civil War, many whites sought to sustain antebellum racial deference—blacks catering to whites—and used violence to do so. Not only did white men and women of every social class expect humble obedience from blacks, they regularly responded with brutal violence when confronted with what they observed to be insolence, disrespectful language, or acting out of place. Surprisingly, black women appear to have been especially vulnerable to these kinds of attacks by whites of both genders during Reconstruction, and although records reveal fewer incidents perpetrated against them than their male counterparts, women frequently endured extremely brutal violence for seemingly trivial "offenses."[20] A black woman in Brazoria County was beaten on her shoulders and face and was threatened with her life by a man who claimed she spoke disrespectfully to his wife.[21] For a similar offense, a group of white men severely beat another Brazoria County woman, inflicting blows on her head with the iron butt of a whip. After the beating, they tied her hands together, "bucked" her, and then gave her nearly 200 lashes. Bucking was a form of corporeal punishment used primarily during the antebellum period but which continued throughout Reconstruction in Texas. After being totally or partially stripped, a victim was forced into a squatting position with both hands tied together in front of the shins; a log or sturdy branch would then be placed through the opening above the elbows and below the knees, serving to hold the victim in the squatting position, bent over forward, while being whipped or beaten over the bare back.[22] For this particular woman, the bucking was in retaliation for the insulting noises she allegedly made as the wife of one of the group passed. In contrast, when a black woman scolded a white man for using vulgar language in her presence, she was brutally beaten for *her* insolence. The Bureau reported that civil authorities failed to take action in these cases. Their inaction not only reinforced the notion that whites dictated acceptable behavior for both races, it also suggests more significantly, the unwillingness of southern white society to expand its prewar definition of womanhood to include former slaves.[23]

The sexual exploitation and rape of black women and girls, considered the most significant basis of white male power during slavery, was just as widespread, if not more so, after emancipation.[24] Because freedom from slavery meant that black women were no longer the legal property of a particular white man, they became, to a great degree, "sexually available to all white men."[25] Most white Texans, both civilians and law enforcement officials, rejected the idea that a black woman could actually be raped. As was the case in most of the violent incidents perpetrated against black women, charges and convictions against white perpetrators were rare; neither were black men likely to be charged with nor convicted of raping black women.[26] In Colorado County after an "Irishman" was accused of the attempted rape of a black child, he was briefly arrested and released. In DeWitt County, a group of men came into the home of Mille Andrews, beat her over the head with a revolver, and attempted to rape her daughter, in the process beating Ms. Andrews over the head with a revolver. The District Court refused to charge the criminals in this case.[27]

In complete contrast to incidents involving black women, alleged rapes of white women by black men inspired white supremacy in its extreme. In response to white fears of innate black male lustfulness, the Texas Legislature in 1866 amended the penal code so that black men who violated whites could be easily incarcerated, while white men who violated blacks remained free. Of particular importance was Article 529, which was amended to ensure that rapists, insinuated to all be black, were given the severest punishments. The amended article read, "Whoever shall be guilty of rape, shall be punished by death, or by confinement in the penitentiary for life, or for any term of years not less than five, in the discretion of the jury."[28] Although the wording appears nondiscriminatory, Bureau records indicate that this outwardly color-blind law was not applied equally when the rape victim was black. The selective application of Texas law demonstrates that, in cases of rape, the law was designed strictly for the protection of a white woman's "prized possession."[29]

Black men suspected of rape were regularly charged for the offense but rarely served the sanctioned prison terms because they were typically turned over to extralegal entities rather than given a day in court. The lynching of black men for the alleged rape of white women is typically thought to have been a phenomenon that started after Reconstruction. Yet there is an abundance of evidence in Texas indicating that whites during the period clearly associated the granting of black rights with the rape of white women. Because emancipation also allegedly released black men from the sexual restraints of slavery, many whites believed newly freed black men thought that their rights extended over white women's bodies.[30]

Although laws had been amended in 1866 so that it was relatively easy to use legal means to convict and incarcerate alleged black rapists, in the majority of cases, legal justice was not immediate enough to suit white Texans. While the rape of black women reasserted white male dominance in "the private arena," the lynching of black men accused of rape "reasserted hierarchical arrangements in the public transactions of men."[31] Further, because most white men believed so firmly that only direct and swift violence could keep black male bestiality in check, it was often carried out immediately following accusations and arrest. For example, an unnamed freedman, having been arrested on the charge of attempted rape, was taken out of jail by a mob and hanged in clear view of citizens and law enforcement in Fort Bend County. The alleged rapist was denied an opportunity to defend himself in court, and it appears that civil authorities failed to take action against the perpetrators.[32] In another particularly brutal incident, Judge Thomas Ford, along with a minister and two medical doctors, took it upon himself to castrate a teenage boy in San Antonio who had allegedly attempted to rape a white girl. Although the boy had not been officially charged or arrested for his alleged crime, castration was decided upon as his punishment after the three perpetrators declared the suspected rapist guilty but too young for hanging.[33] Alleged inappropriate social behavior (whether consensual or not) between black men and white women was so frequently met with swift and violent retribution that it clearly demonstrates white attitudes toward black men (as bestial rapists), but it also reveals the general lack of value placed on the lives and bodies of black women.[34]

Many violent acts against blacks were extremely brutal, characterized by apparent frustration and suggesting the intense hostility of the white population toward the former bondsmen. Bureau records indicate that most of these incidents were perpetrated without provocation, or, perhaps, the sheer savagery of the incident left recorders perplexed as to a reason. Descriptions reveal numerous "grisly episodes of psychotic and sadistic violence." From 1865 through 1868, whites dragged, castrated, hanged, dismembered, and otherwise gruesomely treated black men, women, and children in Texas by the hundreds, very often with impunity.[35]

Various forms of mutilation commonly accompanied white attacks on blacks. Mutilation not only prolonged suffering before death, it also allowed whites to reassert the social control to which, they believed, they were inherently entitled. Cutting off ears, burning body parts, eye gouging, disembowelment, and castration had been legally sanctioned forms of punishment for slaves and lower-class freed men as far back as ancient Greece and Rome. Historically, torture was justified on grounds that slaves, who owned nothing, paid with their bodies, while property owners saw their holdings diminished. These notions were transplanted to the United States, and, as Bureau records reveal, were inflicted all too frequently upon former slaves immediately after the Civil War.[36] For example, an unidentified freedman's body was found in Clear Creek in Columbus, Texas, with "his bowels all taken out and the body filled with stones." Also in Columbus, a man named Lem was murdered by a group of white men for no apparent reason. His head and genitals were cut off and his mutilated body thrown into the Brazos River. In nearby Wharton, a freedman was murdered by a white mob, his body found to be "shockingly mutilated." Records do not indicate that any of these victims had been charged with or even accused of having committed crimes, and the perpetrators faced no immediate legal consequences for their actions.[37]

Many of the murders and other outrages described in Bureau records have no stated reason. In many more incidents, where a justification is given, the reasons seem completely irrational and absurd, perhaps motivated by nothing more than hatred and bitterness toward African Americans. One such incident occurred in Fort Bend County when Dan Davis shot and killed John Picket "for fun." When he succeeded in his attempt, he declared, "I have shot one at last." Likewise, in Nueces County, D. W. Pickle boasted that he "had killed a damned nigger" after fatally stabbing freedman William Forbus. These incidents demonstrate that many whites placed little if any value on the lives of African Americans, and that it was clearly acceptable behavior to kill them indiscriminately for no reason whatsoever.[38] Although racism cannot be ruled out as the prime motivation for these and similar crimes, it is also likely that these perpetrators were well aware, as the records indicate most citizens were, that the chance of facing a conviction for violent crimes perpetrated against blacks was unlikely in postwar Texas.[39] This condition certainly helps explain why black Texans often faced extremely brutal treatment at the hands of whites.

Black Texans did retaliate, albeit infrequently, against their attackers. Usually, however, retaliation could be met with even more severe violence and, in many cases, resistance could likely lead to death. Instead of risking the physical fallout from retaliation, many black Texans sought justice by taking their cases of abuse to local authorities. But public apathy combined with prejudice among officials made it virtually impossible to secure convictions against whites for crimes against blacks during Reconstruction in Texas. Civil authorities contributed to the violence against former slaves by their outright failure to protect them.

In general, then, because civil authorities regularly failed to successfully prosecute and convict whites, black Texans looked to the underfunded Bureau, which tried but could do little.[40] Clearly, frustrated and disappointed local Bureau agents were unable to protect African Americans from white violence in the majority of cases. Because so few civil authorities, it seems, were willing to enforce the law, federal troops were frequently the local agents' only recourse. In that regard, however, the shortage of available military personnel and the enormity of the state magnified the problems. Inspector W. H. Sinclair summed up the situation in Texas when he reported that with only "an isolated agent" responsible for a huge area "and troops farther apart . . . the freed people hardly know what an agent of the Bureau is for."[41]

Change in command in 1867 added to the problems agents faced. When Major General Winfield Scott Hancock replaced General Philip Sheridan as commander of the Fifth Military District, which included Texas and Louisiana, Hancock decided to subordinate military, and thus Bureau, authority to state and local power. In so doing, he in many ways undermined the agency's already limited ability to deal with corrupt and noncompliant civil entities. In late 1868, with the termination of Bureau activity in Texas on the horizon, disappointed agent A. H. Cox wrote that "he never had any troops and it would be useless anyway," since civil authorities "will never deal with the freed people as they should, so therefore, we had as well let the colored people learn now as later."[42]

The Freedmen's Bureau was the only government agency specifically created to help former slaves in their transition to freedom. In South Texas, as in the rest of the state, the Bureau was understaffed, spread thinly across a huge area, and not supported by the overwhelming majority of local citizens and civil authorities. As a result, the Bureau was unable to perform its job effectively, although most agents probably did the best they could. They found themselves in a difficult position; most were threatened on a daily basis and some even murdered in the line of duty.[43] It is reasonable to suspect, therefore, that many agents may have wondered if protecting their charges was worth the risk. Although there is some disagreement about whether the Bureau's performance was adequate, an analysis of the numerous and often brutal acts of violence inflicted upon freed people in South Texas make it clear that they would most likely have suffered considerably more without it.

## NOTES

1. "The State Press—What the Papers throughout Texas Are Talking About," *Dallas Morning News*, February 20, 1894.

2. Ida B. Wells, *Crusade for Justice: The Autobiography of Ida B. Wells*, ed. Alfreda M. Duster (Chicago: University of Chicago Press, 1970), 149.

3. For the purposes of the current essay, South Texas is defined broadly to include Bexar County eastward to Fort Bend County, southward to Brazoria County, south-westward along the Gulf Coast to Nueces County, then northward to Bexar County. Barry A. Crouch, "A Spirit of Lawlessness: White Violence, Texas Blacks, 1865–1868," *Journal of Social History* 18 (Winter 1984): 217–32; James Smallwood, *Time of Hope, Time of Despair: Black Texans during Reconstruction* (New York: Kennekat Press, 1981); Gregg Cantrell, "Racial Violence and Reconstruction Politics in Texas, 1867–68," *Southwestern Historical Quarterly* 93 (January 1990): 333–55. See also Randolph B. Campbell, *Grass-Roots Reconstruction in Texas*, 1865–1880 (Baton Rouge: Louisiana State University Press, 1997). Although quite limited on the violent conditions that existed in the state, Campbell's is the most thorough study of Texas Reconstruction at the county level. See also Kenneth Wayne Howell, "Just Southwest of Dixie: Reconstruction in South Texas, 1865–1876" (reprinted here); James M. Smallwood, Barry A. Crouch, and Larry Peacock, *Murder and Mayhem: The War of Reconstruction in Texas* (College Station: Texas A&M University Press, 2003).

4. Barry A. Crouch, "Hidden Sources of Black History: The Texas Freedmen's Bureau Records as a Case Study," *Southwestern Historical Quarterly* 83 (January 1990): 217.

5. *Journal of the Texas Reconstruction Convention Which Met in Austin, Texas, 1 June 1868* (Austin, Texas: Tracy, Siemering, 1870), 194–96. See also Douglas Hales, "Violence Perpetrated against African Americans by Whites in Texas during Reconstruction, 1865–1868" (master's thesis, Texas Tech University, 1994) and LaVonne Roberts Jackson, "Freedom and Family: The Freedmen's Bureau and African American Women in Texas in the Reconstruction Era, 1865–1872" (PhD diss., Howard University, 1996).

6. Blacks were objects of these types of offenses in 77 percent of cases reported to the Texas Bureau between 1865 and 1868. The Bureau listed

blacks as perpetrators in 10 percent of the incidents, and nonblacks were victims as well. Whites were listed as injured parties in 20 percent of the cases and Mexicans, Germans, Portuguese, and Scots made up approximately 1 percent of the victims. In less than 1 percent of cases, the race of the injured party was either not reported or not listed. Previous scholars have indicated that the total number of incidents recorded by the Bureau was 2,316, but the recorders of the original records skipped from 909 to 1,000, from 1,111 to 1,120, from 1,232 to 1,234, from 1,266 to 1,277, from 1,765 to 1,767, and from 2,132 to 2,134. In addition, several numbers were used twice, including 452, 682, 752, 860, 1,021, 1,165, 1,170, 1,690, and 2,170, making the official incident count 2,214. All tabulations by the author are from Records of Criminal Offenses Committed in the State of Texas (cited hereafter as Records of Criminal Offenses followed by incident numbers), Assistant Commissioner (AC), Texas, vols. 11–13 (T), Bureau of Refugees, Freedmen, and Abandoned Lands (BRFAL), Record Group (RG) 105, roll 32, National Archives (NA).

7. See for example, Records of Criminal Offenses 36, 454, 1,580.

8. See Section 9 of the contract law, part of the Texas Black Code, in H. P. N. Gammel, *The Laws of Texas*, 1822–1897 (Austin: Gammel Book Company, 1898), 5:995–96, which describes in detail the "governance" of laborers. Sean Michael Kelley describes the diversity of work contracts between former slaves and former masters in "Plantation Frontiers: Race, Ethnicity, and Family along the Brazos River of Texas," 1821–1886 (PhD diss., University of Texas, 2000), 315–16.

9. Records of Criminal Offenses 1,775, 213, 203.

10. Smallwood, "Charles E. Culver, A Reconstruction Agent in Texas: The Work of Local Freedmen's Bureau Agents and the Black Community," *Civil War History* 27 (1981): 350–61.

11. William L. Richter, "'The Revolver Rules the Day': Colonel DeWitt C. Brown and the Freedmen's Bureau in Paris, Texas, 1867–1868," *Southwestern Historical Quarterly* 93, no. 3 (1991): 303–32; see 307. See also Crouch, "Hidden Sources of Black History," 216, 217.

12. Records of Criminal Offenses 141, 222.

13. Phillip Howard to L.K. Morton, September 25, 1866, Letters Received (LR), Sub-assistant Commissioner (SAC), Meridian, Texas; and Craig

to Henry A. Ellis, September 6, 1866, LR, SAC, Austin, Texas, BRFAL, RG 105, NA; Records of Criminal Offenses 904, 1,017, 1,023.

14. Colin Palmer, *Passageways: An Interpretive History of Black America, 1863–1965* (Fort Worth: Harcourt Brace, 1998), 5.

15. See for example Records of Criminal Offenses 1,147, 1,305, 2,170, 1,797, 741.

16. See Records of Criminal Offenses 1,731. SAC Thomas C. Griffen commented on this state of affairs' being rampant throughout Texas after learning that a freedman in Kaufman County was forced to flee his home after the harvest, leaving his children behind while local whites burned his property. According to Griffen, the freedman's willingness to leave everything behind so quickly, even his family, showed "how great his terror must have been" (Records of Criminal Offenses 1,024, 730).

17. Records of Criminal Offenses 211, 212.

18. See Roy F. Baumeister, *Evil: Inside Human Cruelty and Violence* (New York: W. H. Freeman, 1997), 251–54, for a description of the Klan's transformation from a fraternal group into "perpetrators of murder, rape and violent assault."

19. Allen Trelease, *White Terror: The Ku Klux Conspiracy and Southern Reconstruction* (1971; repr., Baton Rouge: Louisiana State University Press, 1995), xi–xii. While many incidents in the Bureau records for South Texas attribute violence to groups of two or more white men, no incidents in the "Outrages" specify the Klan or other organized groups. For South Texas, see Records of Criminal Offenses 62, 153, 154, 188, 198, 199, 626, 710, 732, 733, 873, 1,019, 1,020, 1,021, 1,036, 1,232, 1,756, 1,849, 1,870, 1,871, 1,872, 1,873, 1,874, 1,889, 1,890, 2,204. According to Everette Swinney (*Suppressing the Ku Klux Klan: The Enforcement of the Reconstruction Amendments, 1870–1874* [New York: Garland 1987]), "since there is no practical way to distinguish between the Klan and imitators like the Knights of the White Camelia, the White Brotherhood, the White Line, The Seventy-Six Association, or any other group, organized or spontaneous, which donned sheets and hoods, all such terroristic societies must be treated together as part of a generic Ku Klux movement" (46–47). See also Barbara Leah Clayton, "The Lone Star Conspiracy: Racial Violence and Ku Klux Klan Terror in Post-Civil War Texas, 1865–1877" (master's thesis, Oklahoma State University, July 1986).

20. See Rebecca A. Kosary, "To Degrade and Control: White Violence and the Maintenance of Racial and Gender Boundaries in Reconstruction Texas, 1865–1868" (PhD diss., Texas A&M University, 2006). Many important works address violence against women during the post-war period in the former Confederacy, especially Jacquelyn Dowd Hall, "The Mind That Burns in Each Body: Women, Rape, and Racial Violence," *Southern Exposure* 12 (1984): 61–71, and Catherine Clinton, "Bloody Terrain: Freedwomen, Sexuality, and Violence during Reconstruction," in *Half Sisters of History: Southern Women and the American Past*, ed. Catherine Clinton (Durham: Duke University Press, 1994).

21. Records of Criminal Offenses 241.

22. Records of Criminal Offenses 199. "Bucking" was a common form of punishment used during the antebellum and Reconstruction periods. For more information on bucking and other forms of sexualized violence perpetrated on both men and women, see Kosary, "To Degrade and Control" (PhD diss., Texas A&M University Press, 2006), 108–38. Although she does not cover incidents in Texas, see also Lisa Cardyn, "Sexualized Racism/Gendered Violence: Trauma and the Body Politic in the Reconstruction South" (PhD diss., Yale University, 2003).

23. Records of Criminal Offenses 902; Catherine Clinton, "Reconstructing Freedwomen," in *Divided Houses: Gender and the Civil War*, ed. Catherine Clinton and Nina Silber (New York: Oxford University Press, 1992), 310.

24. Many historians have posited that black women were, in fact, more vulnerable to rape and other forms of sexual abuse after emancipation. According to Laura F. Edwards, *Gendered Strife and Confusion: The Political Culture of Reconstruction* (Chicago: University of Illinois Press, 1997), "emancipation heightened the vulnerability of African-American women to violence at the hands of white men, who used rape and other ritualized forms of sexual abuse to limit black women's freedom and to reinscribe antebellum racial hierarchies" (199). See also Hazel V. Carby, *Reconstructing Womanhood: The Emergence of the Afro-American Woman Novelist* (New York: Oxford University Press, 1987), 39; Clinton, "Bloody Terrain," 331.

25. John D'Emilio and Estelle B. Freedman, *Intimate Matters: A History of Sexuality in America*, 2nd ed. (Chicago: University of Chicago Press, 1997), 107.

26. The Bureau's "Record of Criminal Offenses" does not list black men as perpetrators of rape or attempted rape of black women—although one incident describes the "constant ravishing of a favorite black man" (497). This is a surprising oversight in the Bureau's compilation of violence, as some black women did report such crimes to agents who then in many cases alerted civil authorities. See, for example, L. H. Warren, a Bureau agent in Houston, to Mayor De Daligethy, June 13, 1867, Vol. 102, 27, and Warren to Judge B. P. Fuller, June 27, 1867, 57–58, AC, T, BRFAL, RG 105, NA. Unfortunately, there is no record of charges being filed in these specific cases. Jacquelyn Dowd Hall speaks to the prevalence of black-on-black rape and its near inevitability during the period: "In a society that defines manhood in terms of power and possessions, black men are denied the resources to fulfill their expected roles. . . . Inevitably, they turn to domination of women, the one means of asserting traditional manhood within their control" (Hall, "The Mind that Burns," 70).

27. Records of Criminal Offenses 1,589 and 497.

28. Gammel, *The Laws of Texas*, 161.

29. Victoria Bynum, *Unruly Women: The Politics of Social and Sexual Control in the Old South* (Chapel Hill: University of North Carolina Press, 1992). According to Bynum, throughout the nineteenth century rape was regarded as "the theft of a woman's prized possession—a body reserved exclusively for her future or present husband" (109).

30. For Reconstruction-era Klan rhetoric specifically acknowledging fear of alleged black rapists, see Cardyn, "Sexualized Racism / Gendered Violence," 46–49. For the myth of the black rapist and lynching specifically during the Reconstruction period, see, for example, Richard Maxwell Brown, "Legal and Behavioral Perspectives on American Vigilantism," *Perspectives in American History* 5 (1971): 95–144; W. Fitzhugh Brundage, *Lynching in the New South: Georgia and Virgina, 1880–1930* (Urbana: University of North Carolina Press, 1997), 6–7; Hall, "The Mind That Burns," 64–67; Dianne Miller Sommerville, "The Rape Myth in the Old South Reconsidered," *Journal of Southern History* 61 (1995): 481–518; Christopher Waldrep, "Word and Deed: The Language of Lynching, 1820–1953," in *Lethal Imagination: Violence and Brutality in American History*, ed. Michael A. Bellesiles (New York: New York University Press, 1999), 229–260; Joel Williamson, *The Crucible of Race: Black-*

*White Relations in the American South Since Emancipation* (New York: Oxford University Press, 1984), 183.

31. Hall, "The Mind that Burns," 63.

32. Records of Criminal Offenses 252.

33. Phillip Howard to L. K. Morton, September 25, 1866, LR, and Testimony of Freedman, SAC, Meridian, Texas, BRFAL, RG 105, NA.

34. Alleged rape was hardly the only crime for which black men could be lynched during Reconstruction. In Brazos County, Gary Holt was "taken out of his bed by a party of whites, about 30 or 40 of them in all and hung [sic]" for killing and saving the meat of an injured steer, and agents in Falls County found the bodies of three black men hanging from a tree in the woods. Many other incidents allude to lynchings (that is, perpetrators are referred to as members of a "mob" or a "gang of desperados"); see Records of Criminal Offenses 1,745, 1,746, 1,747, 1,965, 1,966, 1,535, 2,034, 2,035, 2,036. Although its attention to the Reconstruction era is limited, for an in-depth examination of a "lynching culture" that developed in Central Texas see William D. Carrigan, *The Making of a Lynching Culture: Violence and Vigilantism in Central Texas, 1836–1916* (Chicago: University of Illinois Press, 2004), 112–130.

35. George C. Rable, *But There Was No Peace: The Role of Violence in the Politics of Reconstruction* (Athens: University of Georgia Press, 1984), 22.

36. J. Thorsten Sellin, *Slavery and the Penal System* (Westport, Connecticut: Greenwood Press, 1976), 177.

37. Harris to Kirkman, March 19, 1867, LR, SAC, Columbus, Texas, BRFAL, RG 105, NA; Records of Criminal Offenses 62, 1,890.

38. Frank Holinger to W.H. Sinclair, March 19, 1866, LR, SAC, Beaumont, Texas, BRFAL, RG 105, NA; Records of Criminal Offenses 727, 454.

39. Records of Criminal Offenses 446. Christopher Waldrep, *Roots of Disorder: Race and Criminal Justice in the American South, 1817–1880* (Urbana: University of Illinois Press, 1998) has made a similar assertion about how the law, or lack of its enforcement, "plays a role in shaping the attitudes that encourage or discourage vigilantism," 2.

40. See Records of Criminal Offenses 138 and 139 for two similar incidents in Guadalupe County.

41. W. H. Sinclair, August 18, 1868, Inspection Tour, BRFAL, RG 105, NA.

42. A. H. Cox to Charles Vernou, November 30, 1868, LR, SAC, Liberty, Texas, BRFAL, RG 105, NA.

43. For the most thorough study of the Texas Bureau and its agents to date, see Crouch, *The Freedmen's Bureau and Black Texans* (Austin: University of Texas Press, 1992).

# After Emancipation

## *Cologne, Texas*

SARA R. MASSEY

LOCATED ON U.S. HIGHWAY 59 NEAR THE VICTORIA County line in eastern Goliad County, about two hours south of San Antonio, is a highway sign for Cologne, a town that has a unique place in Texas history. Today, there is no town, only three collapsed homes, but in 1877, a small village blossomed that was home to freed slaves of Victoria County and that excluded white inhabitants until the railroad came in 1889.

Joseph Smith and George Washington were both slaves born in Virginia and after emancipation, both lived in the town of Victoria.[1] In 1850, Victoria County registered 1,396 whites, 52 free blacks, and 571 slaves for a total of 2,019 people. In the town of Victoria 806 people, including 157 slaves, lived. By 1860, Victoria's population had expanded to 1,986 residents, including 521 slaves and one free black man.[2]

Five years later, after the Union's victory in the Civil War, General Gordon Granger landed on Galveston Island. On June 19, 1865, he issued a proclamation freeing all slaves in Texas. Along with their new freedom, however, African Americans experienced pure, unadulterated fear for their lives. From 1865 to 1868 white Texans committed over 1,500 acts of violence against blacks, including more than 350 murders. Only intervention by the U.S. Congress and the imposition of military rule in the state brought a modicum of safety to African Americans. The era of Reconstruction had arrived.

The use of the political and legal system to regulate the behavior of African Americans was accompanied by a reign of terror in the state. Fifty thousand federal troops (including black soldiers) marched into Texas occupying all sections of the state. Despite the influx of troops, lawlessness and chaos prevailed. In Victoria the troops rebuilt the railroad but also committed numerous criminal acts. Black troops reportedly stormed the jail claiming that civil courts had no jurisdiction over the military and released two African American prisoners, one a horse thief and the other a Union soldier convicted of robbery. The troops then proceeded to lynch a white man in the jail, who awaited trial for killing an African American.[3]

For the newly freed slaves Smith and Washington, though, it was a time of new civil rights. In the midst of the turmoil, Smith and Washington created new lives for themselves and their families by opening a freight and passenger business with mule-drawn wagons that hauled goods from Indianola on the Gulf Coast inland to Victoria, Goliad, and Beeville. With their newly acquired income, in March 1866, Washington bought lot three in block 140 in Victoria for $45 from Martha Leonard.[4] Within five years, Washington's home was valued at $300 and he had two horses valued at $70 and six mules valued at $180 plus miscellaneous property valued at $50 for a total taxable wealth of $600. Smith, meanwhile, lived in town on lot four in block 41. He was even better off with his home valued at $500, nine horses valued at $270, three cows valued at $20, and miscellaneous property valued at $145 for a total taxable value of $935. Both men paid their state and county taxes.[5]

Over the next few years, disenfranchised whites sought ways to regain control of the political system and the Klu Klux Klan arrived in Texas. Evidence of the Klan was first noted in March 1868, and by May the Klan began to resort to murder and acts of intimidation directed at freedmen and white Republicans.

In 1869, a Congressional Reconstruction Plan replaced military rule in Texas, giving control of both the state and local governments to loyal radical Republicans appointed by the military governor. With the support of President Ulysses S. Grant and the U.S. Congress, those who came to power by appointments were the freed African Americans, businessmen from the North (sometimes referred to as "carpetbaggers"), agents of the Freedmen's Bureau, and Texans who had supported the Union cause.[6] In 1870 with the new coalition of voting African Americans, the Republican government gained a majority. More blacks than whites paid their state and county poll taxes in Victoria. Both Smith and Washington registered to vote and paid their poll taxes, thus enabling them to exercise their new right to vote in county and state elections.[7]

In 1870, Smith, age forty-seven, lived at his Victoria home with his Alabama-born wife Diana, age forty. Two of their three children (Harriet, age sixteen, and Van, age nine) were attending school, which was a new right granted African Americans. Their son Harry was only four, so he stayed at home with his mother.[8] Washington was seven years younger than Smith, but his wife Elizabeth (Lizzie), born in Tennessee was forty-five, and they had one son at the time, Nathan, age thirteen, who also attended school.[9] Among their friends were Jim (James) Hall and his wife Barbara. Like Smith and Washington, Hall worked as a drayman driving loaded wagons from the shipping port at Indianola. He also had a home in Victoria where his son, Monroe, age fourteen, attended school. Hall was registered to vote as well.[10]

With the three men traveling their route for extended periods of time, they quickly became acquainted with other African Americans in the area. John Hall, forty-one, was a farmer, who also came from Virginia, as did his wife Jane. It is possible that John came to Texas as a slave along with Smith and Washington. The Halls had a family of six children but only two of them were old enough to attend school.[11] Also known to the men was the family of Jack (Jackson) Patterson—a forty-five-year-old laborer who supported his wife Martha, age twenty-one, and their three children, Sally, Julie, and Nora.[12]

In 1870, although Smith, Washington, and their friends worked hard to provide for their families and carve out a new life as freed men and women, their lives were frequently endangered. After Edmund J. Davis (who as part of the Union Army had led the invasion of the lower Rio Grande in 1863) won the Texas governorship in 1869, state legislators ratified the Fourteenth and Fifteenth Amendments and in March 1870, Texas regained admittance into the Union. The subsequent withdrawal of federal troops from Texas contributed to widespread lawlessness and vigilantism. One of Davis's first acts was to push passage of a controversial Police and Militia Bill through the Texas Legislature. The bill established a state police to restore order in Texas, but the new organization's employment of substantial numbers of African American officers sparked widespread disaffection among many Texas residents. Democrats, in particular, disapproved of the state's deployment of police officers at polls during election time and charged that the police were simply political tools of the Republican administration.[13]

In 1873, the Democrats returned to power. Former secessionist Richard Coke defeated Edmund Davis in a heated—and at times volatile—election. The new regime disbanded the state police, some of whom became Texas Rangers. In the next election in 1876, the last of the Republicans were voted out of office and the era of Reconstruction, along with its nascent civil rights for African Americans, ended.[14] The heretofore quiet and relatively prosperous lives of Smith, Washington, and his friends and the black community of Victoria were soon to change as the Democrats, some of whom had relied economically on slave labor, returned to power. Smith and Washington, concerned about the safety of themselves and their families, decided it would be better to live with other African Americans some distance from town.

In 1877, with knowledge of the local area acquired from their long freight hauls, Smith and Washington purchased land along the road between the towns Victoria and Goliad. It was on Perdido Creek in the L. Ward survey and the Juan Reñee and Sons grant of Goliad County. Washington purchased 510 acres for $693 on April 5, 1877, from George W. May of Lavaca County. He paid $110 in cash and made his marks before witnesses on two promissory notes. The first promissory note for $200 was due December 25, 1877. The second note for $380 was due December 25, 1878, plus 10 percent interest from December 25, 1877, to December 25, 1878.[15]

While no record exists for Smith's land purchase, the Goliad County Courthouse records indicate he went to the courthouse on September 3, 1877, to record with the Goliad county clerk a transfer of all his possessions to his wife Diana Smith, including two hundred acres in the W. L. Hunter survey, which they occupied as a homestead.[16]

The reason Smith gave for the deed transfer is recorded as follows: "Knowing the uncertainty of life and being desirous of Securing to my beloved wife Diana Smith so far as in me lies a competency in the event of my death and in consideration of the natural love and affection for my said wife Diana Smith have this day and by these presents do give grant."[17]

Smith, understandably, was concerned for his life and during these troubled times he made a prudent decision to secure his assets for his family. In addition to the land, he transferred seven mules, one six-horse wagon and harness, one two-horse hack and harness, and all the household and kitchen furniture.

After acquiring their land, Smith and Washington sold parcels to their friends and families from Victoria while other African American families made adjoining land purchases. Giving birth to a new colony, the first settlers, along with their children, arrived in oxcarts or mule-driven wagons. They included

JOE (JOSEPH) AND DANIAH (DIANA) SMITH
GEORGE AND LIZZIE WASHINGTON
JIM AND BARBARA HALL
JOHN AND JANE HALL
JACK (JACKSON) AND MARTHA PATTERSON
HENRY AND MARTHA LOTT
MILTON AND SALLY WALLS
JIM (JAMES) R. AND LUCY YOUNG FROM DEWITT COUNTY
SPOTSAVILLE (SPOTSWOOD) AND MARIAH SMITH FROM CALHOUN COUNTY[18]

Before the Civil War, Goliad County recorded a population of 2,541 whites and 843 slaves. With the land purchased by Smith, Washington, and the other families a village emerged that they simply referred to as the "Colony," located on the eastern edge of the county.[19] As the population increased, the settlers started calling their village "Perdido" after the nearby creek. They soon established a thriving community.[20]

In the 1870s and 1880s, longhorn cattle ran wild on the grass and brush plains of the area. Until the cattle drives got under way, the Perdido settlers hauled hides and tallow for making candles into Victoria and sold them since they were worth more than the cattle. During the difficult times of drought and harsh winters cattle succumbed in large numbers with bones bleaching in the sun. The Perdido families gathered the bones in their mule-driven wagons and hauled their load to Victoria to keep the families going through the rough times.

When the cattle drives started, the cattlemen from ranches around Goliad began herding stock up the feeder trails out of Refugio through Goliad and into Lockhart where they met up with the Chisholm Trail, which headed toward Red River Station and Kansas. Black cowboys hired on with the various drovers for these drives. Joe Smith's son, Henry, George Washington's son, Nathan, and Milton Wall's son, Jim, were among the young men who left homes in Perdido and hired out for several months driving the longhorns up the trail to market.[21]

Before the coming of the railroad, Smith and Washington's freight and passenger service was the most lucrative business in the community, and this started the business of raising mules to sell. Of course, when the wild mules reached maturity they had to be broken and trained to work, which led to the need for "mule skinners."[22]

During the community's first few years, residents built a Methodist church on land given by Moses Johnson of Victoria, who bought fifty acres in the community but never lived on it. Smith also gave a portion of his land, up Perdido Creek about two miles from the village, where local men erected the Mt. Carmel Baptist Church. The hurricane of 1886 destroyed both structures but churchgoers soon rebuilt them. The new Baptist church was erected closer to the community so it would be more accessible to its members.

While the census indicates that none of the original Perdido settlers could read or write, the education of their children was definitely a priority, as they soon had a one-room school built on a one-acre tract donated by Washington. William T. Howell, a schoolteacher from Kentucky, assumed the teaching duties.[23] In 1884, the state passed legislation requiring counties to develop a plan of organization for education and permitted the collection of local taxes to further that effort. The residents of Goliad County established seven districts, including the Perdido district. One of the early schoolteachers, unfortunately, ran into some difficulty.

Dave Rowden came to the community from North Carolina to stay with his brother, W. M. Green. He taught at the school for one year, and then made a trip into Goliad to take an examination for a second-grade teaching certificate. The exam apparently did not go well; Rowden was accused of trying to bribe the examiners and was arrested. He was tried and sentenced to two years in the state penitentiary.[24]

The residents worked their farms and ranches, sent their children to school, attended church and enjoyed life safely in their town. By the 1880s, the school served as a recreational center for the area where spelling bees and socials were regularly scheduled events. Women hosted Saturday night suppers with lots of frolicking children that continued until the music started. As one resident recounted, "The high point of the evening was when the food was all consumed, the tables were pushed back against the walls and the guitars and accordions were being tuned up. That was when the 'marching' started. We didn't dance in those days. The church frowned on it. But, marching two-by-two a fellow could 'cut a pretty fancy figure' and get a little 'sparking' (courting) done at the same time."[25] Along with all the construction in town, the name of the community was changed. Jim Hall noted that their community of Perdido was located midway between Goliad and Victoria, so they changed the name to Centerville. During the 1880s, the Centerville residents got their mail a short distance away at the Old Rock Store operated by Benson (Bence) Goff.[26]

Not all went smoothly, though, for one of the town founders, George Washington. On October 4, 1881, he was an absentee defendant in a suit brought by George May for defaulting on his promissory notes for the purchase of 510 acres in the L. Ward survey and the Juan Reñee and Sons grant. The court awarded May \$207.15 plus 10 percent interest from the December 2, 1877, due date of the note. The county sheriff received orders to seize and sell the land for the amount due plus trial costs. Some of Washington's land was sold to pay the debt;

on August 27, 1888, the county clerk received of G. W. Bell, sheriff of Goliad County, $213.07 for payment in full of the principal and interest in the judgment against Washington.[27] Undaunted, a week after the trial in 1881, Washington was busy trying to help the community prosper by transferring some of his remaining land in the Juan Reñee and Sons grant to the New York, Texas and Mexican Railroad that proposed to build a rail line through the area to the Rio Grande.[28] This effort failed when the projected line stopped at Victoria, but seven years later in 1888, successful land transfers did bring a railroad to town.

The Gulf, Western Texas and Pacific Railway (the GWT&P Railway, which later became the Southern Pacific Railroad) in March 1888 proposed building a branch line from Victoria to Beeville through Centerville and Goliad.[29] The railroad company asked all landowners in Goliad and Bee Counties to sign notes making contributions for building the line through their counties.[30] People in the area donated over $60,000 to the railroad for the extension of the line and numerous Centerville/Perdido/Colony residents gave land in exchange for one dollar with the expectation that the value of their remaining land would increase. According to the county deed records, these are some of the land donors:

1. George Washington & Harriet (Washington) German (his daughter) gave a 100' width for $1.00, July 8, 1888,
2. John and Martha Patterson also gave 100' width, July 1888,
3. Charles and Lizzie Willemin (of Victoria County) received $20 for their 100' width, August 1888,
4. James F. and Barbara Hall gave 100' for the building of a railroad station, August, 1888,
5. Monroe J. and Emma A. Hall gave 100,' August 1, 1888,
6. Joseph Smith gave some of his land from the Juan Reñee and Sons grant, August 8, 1888,
7. Chas. Williams also gave part of the Juan Reñee and Sons grant, August 17, 1888, and
8. Frank and Fannie Lott gave 50,' August 17, 1888.[31]

Railroad workers constructed a depot and station stop on the land at Centerville that James Hall had donated in return for a lifetime job for himself as station agent and a guarantee that the railroad would not abandon the station. As part of the railroad transactions the town name changed again. When the gravel platform, depot, and cattle pens were completed, the first train arrived in the summer of 1889 and Centerville became known as Ira Station, or Ira.

Hall got his job as stationmaster—along with a new agent's cap. His job in the two-room depot was to keep the waiting room clean and the freight room locked and to drive cattle off the tracks when it was about time for one of the two daily trains to arrive. All passengers, including the German families living across the creek, were welcome to wait for trains at the new depot. For about ten years, the village had the only integrated railroad depot in Texas.

When the railroad arrived, Goff closed his business, the Old Rock Store, and built a large two-story building further north of Perdido Creek, which started the community of Fannin.[32]

The building of the railroad brought numerous men to the community, some of whom stayed, married, or brought their families. But it also ended the lucrative freight business of Smith and Washington. And it put an end to the long cattle drives since cowboys could simply move cattle to the cattle pens for shipment north. The newly named town of Ira became a center for slaughtering cattle and pigs as well as being center for shipping.

Many of the landowners were farmers who worked hard to make a living. Along with raising cattle and pigs, some of them grew cotton. After harvesting the cotton and hauling the bales to town for shipping, some of the young men hired out to pick cotton. In addition to growing and shipping cotton, area residents raised watermelons, which grew well in the soil of the county. They also shipped wood from the new railroad station—thousands of cords cut each year from the nearby timberland.

The town's hog-slaughtering plant may have led to its final name, Cologne. Many farmers raised hogs, letting them roam in the fall of the year to fatten on the acorns and nuts. When the animals reached sufficient weight, the farmers hauled them to the slaughter and rendering plant in town, creating a grand stink. When resident William M. Young submitted an application requesting a post office building for the town he proposed the name of Cologne because he thought it was time for a more sweet-smelling fragrance in town as opposed to the stench emanating from the slaughtering businesses.[33] The U.S. Postal Service approved Young's application in 1898 for the town of Cologne, the town's fifth and final name.

When accidents occurred or doctors were needed it was twelve to fifteen miles by horseback into Goliad or Victoria, so area residents relied on local medical experts. One of them was Sue Noble. For a while, the Nobles were the only white family in Cologne and each spring "she would make pills out of what she called 'blue mass' and send them to all the neighbors. Nobody knew what was in them, but we took them."[34] "Dr. Roach," another local, got bark, roots, and herbs from wood that he then pounded into pulp and boiled. He drained off the liquid and put his tonic into jugs, which he sold house-to-house. Other home remedies included horehound weeds, sage, quinine weeds, red root, and milkweed.[35]

There were many good times in Cologne. Young men formed baseball teams and, for a while, Smith had a drill club with drums and fifes heard all around the town. Smith also had a pasture where folks raced ponies and sometimes thoroughbred horses. There was a tournament track where men raced their horses and tried to pick rings off hooks. In the summer, there were religious revivals when people would come from all over to hear the preaching, and there was always lots of singing.

Land transactions over the years seem rather muddled for the residents of Cologne. In 1898, Joseph Smith, now seventy-five years old, had a home on land owned by his old friend, George Washington, so they made a trade. In exchange for the one-acre land parcel where Smith's home stood, he traded Washington a "brown gotch ear horse branded on the front shoulder" worth $14.[36]

As the nation entered the twentieth century in rural towns across the country, the urban migration got underway. In Cologne, the children and grandchildren of the original settlers left to attend colleges and universities across the country, to fight in World War I, or to find employment. Then they married, got jobs, and returned home only to visit family and friends. The railroad discontinued its passenger service to Cologne and William Young's post office closed in 1925. By 1940, the town population had dropped to just twenty-five people.[37]

While no town of Cologne is now evident, there is a cemetery, which ironically is on the land reserved by George W. May from the original land sale to Washington in 1877. In the deed to Washington, May withheld "one acre known as the grave yard which two said portions are herein reserved from this sale and not conveyed."[38] This graveyard remains and recent interments are evident. Stone markings have eroded and many stones are buried in the dirt or gone, but the metal headstone of Joseph Smith still stands.

> JOSEPH SMITH
> JANUARY 18, 18__
> OCTOBER 10, 18__

It is assumed Smith died a few months after the transfer of the horse to Washington in December 1898. That would make him seventy-six years old.[39] While no stone is now evident for Washington, his son, Nathan Washington, 1848–1910, and his wife Lora, 1863–1954, had a very large stone in a concrete-lined plot that included their nine children, of whom the last, Nodine, died in 1994. Headstones of founders J. R. Young, February 19, 1843–March 22, 1917, and his wife, Lucy Young, who was born in Missouri in 1842 and died in 1911, were also present along with headstones for numerous members of the Lott family. From freedom to death, the African American founders of Cologne resided together.

Given Texas' turbulent history with respect to slavery and reconstruction, one wonders at the absence of any historical marker noting the remarkable achievements of Joseph Smith and George Washington, who began their lives as the property of white masters in Virginia and ended their lives in a community that they founded in the brush country of Texas, along Perdido Creek in the county of Goliad.

## NOTES

1. U.S. Census, 1870, Victoria County, Texas, Precinct 1, 256B, 361B, microfilm roll 1607, Public Library, Victoria, Texas. Stories passed down through Cologne families tell of slaves' being bred in Virginia for sale in Alabama and Louisiana, where they were again sold, some possibly to Preston Robinson Rose of the Rose Plantation, located thirteen miles south of Victoria on the east side of the Guadalupe River. Rose came to Victoria in 1845 and died in 1860, leaving a widow with three young children to rear on the plantation. Jeanie Tavitas-Williams, "Life Project Takes Root," *San Antonio Express News*, June 18, 2002, 1D; J. W. Petty Jr., *Victoria Rose's History of Victoria* (Victoria, Texas: Book Mart, 1961), 185.

2. Robert W. Shook, "Victoria, Texas," *Handbook of Texas Online*, http://www.tshaonline.org/index.html (accessed December 20, 2006).

3. Jack Jackson, *Lost Cause* (Amherst, Massachusetts: Kitchen Sink, 1998), 62.

4. Deed Record, Book 9, County Clerk, Victoria County Courthouse Annex, 185.

6. Donald D. Hoffman, *South of the Guadalupe: A History of Nixon and Southern Gonzales County* (n.p.: Donald D. Hoffman, 2006), 137.

7. Voters' Registration Index, 1867, Victoria County Courthouse; Assessment Roll of County of Victoria, 1870.

8. U.S. Census, 1870, Precinct 1, 256B. All members of the family were listed in the census as Mexicans and the three children were born in Texas.

9. Ibid., Precinct 2, 361B. George Washington was listed as black, but his wife Lizzie and son were listed as Mexican, and Nathan was born in Texas. Lizzie Washington's age is unclear; it was possibly forty-eight rather than forty-five.

10. Ibid., Precinct 1, 252A; Voters' Registration Index, 1867. Jim Hall was forty years old and born in Tennessee, while Barbara was born in

Alabama. She was listed as thirteen years old, which is obviously an error as their son was fourteen years old. All members of the family are listed in the census as Mexican.

11. U.S. census, 1870, Precinct 1, 256B. While Jane Hall is listed as a black, all the children and John are listed as Mexican.

12. Ibid., 245A. Jack and his wife Martha were born in Mississippi; their three children were born in Texas. All family members were listed as black.

13. Shook, "Victoria, Texas," *Handbook of Texas Online*, http://www.tshaonline.org/handbook/online/articles/VV/hdv1.html (accessed August 24, 2007).

14. Hoffman, *South of the Guadalupe*, 146.

15. Deed Records, Book N, Part 1, County Clerk, Goliad County Courthouse, 335. This land was originally part of the very large Juan Reñee and Sons grant in Goliad and Victoria counties that became part of the William L. Hunter survey, which Hunter sold to William Noble in 1853. Noble in turn sold a portion of it to George W. May in 1874.

16. Ibid., Book M, Part 1, Goliad County, 264–65.

17. Ibid., 264.

18. Frederick Douglas Young, *From These Roots: Cologne—One Hundred Years, 1870–1970* (Houston: Texas Southern University Press, 1973), 5.

19. The Voters' Registration Index of Victoria County, 1867, notes that the following residents registered to vote: Joseph Smith, #190, June 26, 1867, Precinct 1; George Washington, #181, June 26, 1867, Precinct 1; John Hall, #184, June 26, 1867, Precinct 1; Jack Patterson, #255, June 28, 1867, Precinct 1; Frank Lott, #852, November 26, 1869, Precinct 2.

20. Confusion exists in the local records as it seems the village of Fannin, which was located a short distance west of Cologne and got its start when the railroad arrived, was also known as Perdido for several years. The inhabitants of Fannin were primarily Germans (like Benson Goff) and other Anglo-Americans.

21. Young, *From These Roots*, 2. A review of the Marks and Brands ledger at the Goliad County Courthouse indicates that of the original settlers, only Harry Lott registered a cattle brand. The owner of the Old Rock Store, Benson Goff, registered his brand on June 6, 1879, and his father, Charles Goff, registered his on September 2, 1870.

22. Young, *From These Roots*, 40–41.

23. Sidney R. Weisiger, "Cologne Settlement," *Sidney's Journal*, comp. Hilda Weisiger and Robert W. Shook (Victoria, Texas: University of Houston–Victoria, 1976), 58. This short article is from *The Victoria Advocate*.

24. Young, *From These Roots*, 23.

25. Ibid., 44; Goliad County Historical Commission, *The History and Heritage of Goliad County*, ed. Jakie L. Pruett and Everett B. Cole (Austin, Texas: Eakin, 1983), 54.

26. Goff built the large two-story store north of the railroad tracks, where the Fannin community grew up around it.

27. Deed Records, Book T, Part 1, Goliad County, 313–14. Attorneys Lane and Payne represented the note-holder, George W. May.

28. Ibid., Book O, 752. The date for this transfer was October 13, 1881.

29. Elizabeth Lee Bass, "Gulf, Western Texas and Pacific Railway," *Handbook of Texas Online* (accessed December 13, 2006).

30. Goliad County Historical Commission, *History and Heritage*, 106.

31. Deed Records, Book S, Part 2, Goliad County, 492–501.

32. Goliad County Historical Commission, *History and Heritage*, 110.

33. See Craig H. Roell, "Cologne, Texas," *Handbook of Texas Online* ( accessed November 19, 2006).

34. Young, *From These Roots*, 40.

35. Ibid., 40–41.

36. Deed Records, Book 29, Goliad County, 93. This transaction occurred on December 28, 1898.

37. For an online magazine about Cologne, see http://www.texasescapes.com/SouthTexasTowns/Cologne-Texas.html (accessed November, 2006).

38. Deed Records, Book N, Part 1, Goliad County, 335.

39. Sidney R. Weisiger, handwritten notes from an interview with Elliott Washington, December 20, 1971, Weisiger Collection, Box 7, File 122A, Item 28, University of Houston–Victoria Campus Library, Local History Room, Victoria, Texas. Elliott Washington, grandson of founder George Washington, visited the cemetery in 1969 and reported that the metal headstone gave Smith's date of birth as January 18, 1818 and his date of death as October 11, 1891. But given the land transfer deed recorded at the Goliad County courthouse, Smith was still alive in December 1898.

# The Forging of the African American Community in Corpus Christi, Texas, 1865–1900

RUE WOOD

UNTIL RECENTLY, THE AFRICAN AMERICAN EXPERIENCE in Texas had not been as thoroughly studied as in other southern states. This can partly be attributed to the fact that slavery in the state became a significant and visible institution only during the thirty years before the Civil War. In addition, Texas is commonly associated with the West, not the South, making regional identity an issue that continues to perplex historians.[1] Texas provides a unique backdrop for African American history since it was the only member of the Confederacy to remain a frontier state after the war. Yet there is no comprehensive study of blacks in Texas between the end of the Civil War and the turn of the twentieth century that encompasses both western and southern perspectives.[2]

Corpus Christi during this period was a Texas frontier town and growing seaport at the confluence of diverse cultural and economic streams. To the northeast lay the cotton and sugar producing region of East Texas, and beyond that the deep South. African Americans composed a majority of the population in many of the counties in these regions. To the southwest stretched vast semiarid ranchlands dotted with Mexican communities. These geographic, economic, and cultural realities produced an African American community in Corpus Christi that was a hybrid of sorts. The small size of the black community and its economic ties to the ranching industry are indicative of a frontier experience.[3] Development of black religious and educational institutions in the city, however, parallels the development of similar institutions in the urban South. The role of the New England-based American

Missionary Association (AMA) in the founding of both a church and a school for blacks in Corpus Christi along with segregation in education are experiences repeated throughout southern cities.[4] In essence, the African American experience in Corpus Christi during this era was typically southern with a western flair.

James Weldon Johnson, the national secretary of the National Association for the Advancement of Colored People (NAACP), wrote in the *Denver Post* in 1925, "Your west is giving the Negro a better deal than any other section of the country. I cannot attempt to analyze the reasons for this, but the fact remains that there is more opportunity for my race, and less prejudice against it in this section of the country than anywhere else in the United States."[5] Indeed, blacks moved westward in search of expanded economic opportunity and to escape the restrictions of the South. In general, they found more opportunity and less discrimination, but they encountered legal restrictions, commonly in the form of antimiscegenation laws and school segregation. Whites in western states appear to have accepted the "doctrine of parallel development," that is, the idea that blacks should be accorded equal protection under the law and equal opportunity in the marketplace but not "social equality" in the form of intermarriage or racial integration of clubs, fraternal societies, churches, and entertainment facilities.[6]

Blacks were too few in number in the West to challenge whites for economic and political resources and power. This was not true of the South where they composed a significant proportion of the total population and posed a serious threat to the political power and dominant economic position of whites. Consequently, in the West race relations formed a patchwork of various levels of discrimination, segregation, and exclusion. Legislation to segregate the races, limit economic opportunities, or curtail the political rights of African Americans was more common in western cities, territories, and states with higher concentrations of blacks than it was in those with lower concentrations.[7]

After the Civil War there was an exodus of southern blacks to western states, notably Kansas and Nebraska. The peak of this migration occurred in 1879 when blacks, responding to false promises of free land, made their way from Texas, Louisiana, Mississippi, and Tennessee to Kansas.[8] The lure of the mining industry brought an influx of African Americans to California and Colorado. By 1900 these two states had the largest black populations in the Far West.[9] Western cities did not have high concentrations of blacks; percentages for major cities ranged from 1 to 12 percent of the total population.

Employment opportunities in the West were greater than in the South. African Americans worked mainly in the fur, mining, and cattle industries with varying amounts of success. Mining attracted black capital. Thus, by the end of the Civil War the Convention for Colored Citizens of California reported that blacks owned three mining companies in the state.[10] A significant number of blacks bound for California during the gold rush of the late 1840s and early 1850s established roots in San Francisco and opened businesses. By 1865 San Francisco County reported four black-owned tobacco factories, two soap factories, one tallow processing plant, two salvage stores, and two laundries; it also had two black real estate agents and two newspaper editors.[11]

In his study of black San Francisco, Douglas Henry Daniels, professor of Black Studies at the University of California, Santa Barbara, found that nineteenth-century African American residents of the city were "much like frontiersmen: they were robust mature adults, predominantly single male workers with few dependents." He goes on to assert that they were also "unmistakably urbanites" with urban origins and high literacy rates. In addition, black San Franciscans came from diverse geographic regions. Daniels reports that in 1860, on the eve of the Civil War, roughly equal numbers hailed from northern and southern states. He goes as far as to state that "illiterate Blacks with large families and few marketable skills stayed in the north or in Dixie."[12]

As the population of San Francisco grew in the late nineteenth century, the ratio of males to females equalized and families were established although economic opportunities diminished. Daniels claims that the windows of opportunity for African Americans were limited to the mid-nineteenth century and the period between the two world wars, and that the city "offered economic opportunities for only a few—those with physical mobility, ties with leading [white] citizens, and considerable independence, versatility, and perseverance."[13] This appears to be a pattern repeated in many western urban areas. African Americans were often mature males who initially enjoyed expanded opportunities in frontier towns. However, the growth of the cities, the establishment of families, and the expansion of "culture" and "civilization" meant that blacks were relegated to familiar roles prevalent in both northern and southern cities.

The cattle industry was perhaps the least discriminatory of all the western industries. This has been attributed to the demanding nature of the jobs entailed in raising stock and driving them north along trails to railheads in the Midwest. Life on the trail was rugged and often dangerous and the success of a trail drive depended, to a large extent, on each cowhand performing his assigned tasks. The interdependent nature of the work, the long hours spent in one another's company, and the rough living conditions left little room for racial prejudice to be a defining aspect of relationships.[14]

It is estimated that about one-quarter of the men who drove cattle northwards up the trails from Texas between the end of the Civil War and 1895 were African American. Blacks were hired on as cooks, broncobusters, and cowhands. Some rose to the position of remuda, the overseer of the extra horses on a trail drive. Few became trail bosses or foremen, but there was usually no discrimination in wages for white and black cowboys. Numerous black cowboys achieved fame, wealth, or both. "Eighty John" Wallace, an ex-slave from Victoria, Texas, worked for several cattle barons before investing in his own enterprise in the 1880s. By 1929 he owned twelve hundred acres of unmortgaged land in Mitchell County.[15]

Educational opportunity in the West was more limited than economic opportunity. After the Civil War several western states and territories passed laws to segregate the races in public schools or to exclude blacks altogether. California legislation in 1866 prohibited non-white students from attending public schools. The law was not strictly enforced, however, and in 1870 the state provided for separate public schools. Many communities had few blacks, and problems with the financing of these schools arose. The state devolved admission and financing authority to the counties and districts. Most school districts found separate schools to be impractical and their schools were integrated. However, some districts maintained segregated systems well into the next century.[16]

Segregated education was impractical in areas with few African Americans. Consequently Wyoming, Washington, New Mexico, Idaho, Utah, North Dakota, South Dakota, Minnesota, Wisconsin, and Nebraska generally escaped protracted struggles generated by the segregation issue. Experiments in segregation were attempted in Montana, Oregon, Nevada, Kansas, Iowa, and Colorado. With the exception of Kansas, these states had statewide integrated school systems by the early 1880s. Overall, separate schools did not become as institutionalized in the West as they did in the South, but African Americans nevertheless had to fight legal battles for their educational rights in several western states.[17]

Black churches were as integral to the formation of African American communities in the West as they were in the North and South. There have been few studies of black churches in the region, but is clear that the African Methodist Episcopal (AME) church was the leading denomination.[18] An African Methodist church was organized in San Francisco in 1852, and by 1865 there were enough AME members in California to hold a statewide conference. By 1900 AME churches were established in most black communities in the West. The Presbyterian and Episcopal churches attempted to attract black members but were not successful to any significant degree. This has been attributed to the fact that they were more ritualistic and frontiersmen preferred practicality over formality in religion.[19]

The South faced enormous challenges at the end of the Civil War. Emancipation necessitated that both African Americans and whites adapt to changing labor systems and social relationships. In addition, freedmen had to somehow be incorporated into political life. After the war, southern urban populations swelled. The migration of blacks to the cities resulted in black urban populations' averaging one-fourth to one-third of the total population in most southern cities by the turn of the twentieth century.[20] The cities were unprepared for this influx and initially dealt with their problems by excluding blacks from public services and social institutions. During both Reconstruction and the period of Redemptionist rule, exclusion or segregation was often de facto, that is, it was not based on law but on custom and practice.[21] This elaborate system of de facto segregation became de jure with the passage of the Jim Crow laws of the late nineteenth and early twentieth centuries. Jim Crow legalized a system of segregation that had evolved since the end of the war.

Segregation was spawned from prevalent racial attitudes in the postbellum years and was supported by large segments of both the black and white communities. Most southern whites believed African Americans were inferior by nature and harbored the inherent vices of "indolence, theft, and sensuality."[22] Even many Radical Republicans, Northerners, agents of the Freedmen's Bureau, and southern whites who favored equality before the law believed that blacks as a race were limited in their abilities. Their common mission was to safeguard the black under general laws so that he would "somewhere find, and [would] maintain, his own appropriate social position."[23] African Americans fought legal battles against segregation, but in the face of defeat, they came to believe the message of black educator Booker T. Washington—that their greatest hope lay in self-help and the building of strong, self-sufficient communities.

At the center of African American communities throughout the South were the black churches and schools. These two institutions were the hub of urban life and the primary vehicles for progress in the years after the war. Black Baptists and Methodists began their own churches, and northern missionaries of the AMA founded black Congregational churches in most major southern cities. Churches not only provided for spiritual needs but also served as school classrooms and meeting places for political and social activities.

The AMA and the American Freedmen's and Union Commission played leading roles in establishing black schools and universities in the South. Reconstruction governments in most southern states established public financing for equal but separate schools for blacks. The AMA and Freedmen's schools were absorbed into the public systems. The Civil Rights Act of 1875 did not forbid segregation in schools and thus most southern states had separate school systems by the late 1870s. In theory these schools were to be equal, but in fact, a widening gap in financing and teachers' salaries opened between the black and white systems.[24]

Economic opportunity was limited in the South for most blacks. By 1890 a small black middle class of skilled workers, professionals, and business owners had emerged. However, the majority of African Americans were unskilled laborers or were engaged in domestic or personal services. The two most common black-owned businesses in the 1870s and 1880s were barber shops and livery stables. Although whites disdained these businesses, blacks who engaged in them made a good living and occasionally accumulated a good deal of wealth.[25]

In general, African Americans in the urban South enjoyed less economic opportunity, faced greater restrictions, and encountered more discrimination than their counterparts in the western states. Black churches perhaps served a more vital role in southern communities than they did out West. Black southerners generally received an inferior education in segregated schools. With this in mind we turn our attention to the black community in Corpus Christi, a small port on the southern Gulf Coast of Texas, in 1865.

Between the years after the end of the Civil War and the turn of the twentieth century, the town of Corpus Christi grew at a modest rate. In 1870 the total population stood at 2,140; thirty years later the city boasted 4,703 residents. African Americans composed 7.3 percent of the total population of Corpus Christi in 1870 and 9.8 percent in 1900.[26] While most southern cities had burgeoning numbers of African Americans by the turn of the twentieth century, Corpus Christi's black population remained small and was more in line with black populations in urban areas of the West. Yet during these years, Corpus Christi's African American community experienced a pattern of economic development similar to that found in other southern cities. This pattern was characterized by the loss of skilled black labor, the movement of blacks in greater numbers to domestic and personal service jobs, and the emergence of a small professional class comprised mainly of ministers and teachers.

Corpus Christi was established as a trading post in the fall of 1839 by Henry Lawrence Kinney. The town's economy developed around sea commerce and the ranching business. Ranchers in what later became Nueces County raised sheep and cattle. By the outbreak of the Civil War the port was the embarkation point for wool and hides going to other ports, most notably Galveston. In addition, the city engaged in a brisk oxcart trade with Mexico. Union forces blockaded the port during the war and there were two engagements between Union and Confederate forces on the beaches. The federal occupation force in the city after the war was comprised of two black regiments of the Twenty-fifth U.S. Army Corps, commanded by white officers.[27]

The African American population of Corpus Christi before the Civil War was small. Slavery did not take a firm hold in Nueces County largely because the land was used for raising stock and not for intensive staples agriculture. The city was also perhaps too close to Mexico to make the ownership of slaves practical. After Mexico abolished slavery in 1829, South and West Texas became escape routes for runaways. Census figures for 1850 report 650 freed people in Nueces County, 1 free woman of color, and 47 slaves (19 males and 28 females). The census also indicates that the free black woman, Jane Bias, lived in town and was literate. None of the slaves residing in the county lived in the town itself.[28]

Both the population and the economy of Corpus Christi boomed in the years immediately after the war despite a yellow fever epidemic in 1867 that claimed nearly 300 of the city's 1,000 residents.[29] Wool exports continued in large volumes, and several factories for the processing of hides and tallow were constructed. By 1870, the African American community of Corpus Christi was comprised of 254 individuals (7.3 percent of the total population).[30] The majority of these blacks were natives of other southern states. The largest number had been born in Alabama, followed by Louisiana, Virginia, Mississippi, Georgia, Kentucky, North Carolina, Missouri, South Carolina, and Florida, in that order. Only three blacks were born in northern states (two in New York and one in Pennsylvania). Eighty-one percent of the black adults were illiterate. This was consistent with the overall rate for blacks in Texas in 1870.[31]

Records indicate that most African Americans in Corpus Christi in 1870 were employed either in domestic service as house servants, cooks, laundresses, and dressmakers, or as unskilled laborers. Many of the domestic workers were single women with children. The livery business was predominately black with black draymen outnumbering whites two to one.[32] In all likelihood some of these individuals were engaged in the oxcart trade with Mexico. The livery business must have been a good livelihood because six of the black draymen listed property worth $300 or more. In addition, theirs was usually the only income brought into the house; spouses or other live-in relatives did not work outside the home. In fact, a sizable number of families must have fared relatively well since thirty-seven black women were listed as "keeping house" in their own homes.

Blacks were represented in Corpus Christi's skilled labor force in 1870. Ten were listed in the census as butchers, carpenters, brick masons, or blacksmiths. However, there was a marked difference in the net wealth of these men and their white counterparts. Each of the black skilled workers owned property worth, on average, $300, with the exception of Alfred Bailey, a blacksmith who reported $1,200. Peter Dunn, a white blacksmith, reported real estate and personal property worth $1,900. Net wealth for white skilled workers varied to a considerable degree. The most affluent held property that ranged from $1,200 to $4,420, amounts considerably higher than those of their black counterparts.[33]

The cattle industry gave Corpus Christi's economic profile a western character. Eight African American city residents were employed in the ranching industry. Undoubtedly there were more black ranch hands who lived in the rural areas of the county. The most notable black cowpuncher was William Harrison Mays. Mays was a brickmason by trade but went to work after 1870 on the King Ranch. He later worked for Mifflin Kenedy and was eventually put in charge of cattle shipments. In 1869, Mays married Alice Sinclair, the daughter of Clara Sinclair, who was one of the two black women in Corpus Christi listed as property owners in the 1870 census. The Sinclairs were prominent in the black community. Alice's brother, Moses Sinclair, was a carpenter by trade. He became the second pastor of St. Matthew Baptist Church, the first black Baptist church in the city. Alice became the church's organist and first music director.[34]

Descendants of William Harrison Mays and Alice Sinclair Mays continue to live in Corpus Christi. Alclair Mays Pleasant, age 92 at this writing, is the granddaughter of the couple. She was named after her paternal grandmother Alice Sinclair. Alclair Pleasant has in her possession the deed for land bought by her great-grandmother Clara. The land, designated as "Lot 8, BL 12 on-the beach," was acquired in 1854 for $150 by James Gallagher from Henry Lawrence Kinney, whose signature appears on the document.[35] Apparently Gallagher sold the lot to Clara and turned the deed over to her before 1870.

William Harrison Mays worked a good number of years dealing in cattle shipments. He named his son (Alclair's father) James Mifflin Mays after Mifflin Kenedy.[36] Alclair also retains a handwritten letter from George J. Reynolds, a prominent rancher from the Lone Ranch near Realitos, Duval County, dated May 22, 1899. The letter is addressed to Alclair's father and inquires, "Dear Sir: When will your papa [William Harrison Mays] leave with the stock of Mr. Horatio for here? about when will he get up here with them. how are the cattle doing are they getting fat[?]" The letter is a very warm one, and Reynolds goes on to inquire about James's mother and sister. He also asks James how his (Reynolds's) roan horse is doing, how the corn is doing, and "have you plenty of water in water holes[?]"[37] The intimate nature of the letter perhaps gives credence to the assertion that black cowhands faced less discrimination than did blacks in other occupations.

Corpus Christi's economy in 1900 was firmly tied to the cattle industry, although the nature of the industry had changed. Gone were the days of the unfenced range, the "long drive" of cattle to railheads in Kansas, and the cowboy. In 1875 Uriah Lott, a native of New York, began construction on a railroad that would link Corpus Christi and Laredo. Lott attracted investment from ranching magnates Richard King and Mifflin Kenedy, and in 1881 the Corpus Christi, San Diego, and Rio Grande Narrow Gauge Railroad was completed. This venture and a railway connecting Corpus Christi with San Antonio in 1886 ended both the "long drive" and the Mexican oxcart trade.

Cattle became "big business," run by an army of professional breeders, ranch hands, and managers. Corpus Christi became a service and social center for the ranchers.[38]

Another contributing factor to the decline of the oxcart trade was a plague that decimated the local sheep population in the early 1890s. Between the mid-1800s and 1893, the area between Corpus Christi and Laredo was populated with more sheep than any other region in the United States. In the wake of the plague, sheep ranchers moved herds further inland away from the wet coastal areas that harbored the sheep parasite.[39] These changes in the local economy are perhaps responsible for the decline in the percentage of blacks engaged in the transportation industry. The extent to which blacks were employed in the new railroad ventures is a topic for further study, but at least one black, James Reed, worked for the railroads in 1900 as a brakeman.[40] By the late nineteenth century a small number of African Americans in southern cities experienced economic advancement through proprietorships of businesses or through the professions, mainly as clergymen or teachers. The majority of blacks remained in unskilled jobs in industry and domestic service. The situation for black skilled workers between the end of the Civil War and the turn of the century worsened. They were often excluded from unions, harming earning potential and quashing hopes for the future since apprenticeships were denied. Their numbers became concentrated in the lower-level skills such as barbering and brickmaking instead of more lucrative fields such as carpentry, machine operation, printing, plumbing, and furniture making.[41]

These patterns are mirrored in the economic profile of Corpus Christi in 1900. The black professional class consisted of six people—four clergymen and two teachers.[42] There was a slight increase between 1870 and 1900 in the proportion of workers engaged in unskilled labor or domestic services, while the number engaged in the livery business or in transportation declined. Those who provided domestic service or unskilled labor were often cooks, washerwomen, waiters, or day laborers.

There is a noticeable trend in the decline in the number of highly skilled workers. Not a single black carpenter, butcher, or machinist is listed as residing in the city in 1900. Of the skilled workers listed in the census there were four blacksmiths, one brick mason, one wagoner, two painters, two musicians, one water cistern builder, and seven barbers. Barbers dominated the small black business community in Corpus Christi at the turn of the century as the city directory for 1907 lists only three black-owned businesses—two barbershops and one garment-cleaning enterprise.[43] The 1900 census indicates that two men, D. N. Leathers and Preston Mead, dealt in dry goods and groceries. James Howard was a fish and oyster salesman, and Mollie Anderson was engaged in business, although the type is indiscernible from the records.[44] Leathers must have remained in the grocery business for a long period of time as Alclair Pleasant recalls visiting his store during her youth in the 1910s.[45]

The small number of blacks in the total population and the preeminence of the cattle industry in Corpus Christi's development after the Civil War undoubtedly reflect the experiences of western urban areas. Despite these facts, the overall economic profile of the African American community during this period resembles that of other southern cities like Raleigh, Atlanta, Richmond, and Nashville.[46] The end of both slavery and the Civil War provided blacks hope for new opportunities; however, the three decades after the war failed to provide most blacks with any significant upward economic mobility. While a small black business and professional class emerged, the majority of southern urban blacks found themselves on the bottom rungs of the economic ladder in unskilled or domestic service jobs.

The social and cultural experiences of African Americans in Corpus Christi after the war, especially in regard to religion and education, are distinctly southern in character. Throughout the South before emancipation blacks attended religious services with whites, although they commonly sat in segregated sections of churches. This practice allowed for a degree of white control over black religion and blunted the fear of insurrection that may have been born out of any gathering of slaves. After emancipation blacks continued to attend white churches for a short while, but they withdrew when it was apparent they would not achieve equal recognition or status. Their own churches were a symbol of their freedom and pride. The construction of a black church demonstrated material and spiritual growth to an entire community. Initially, black congregations typically were pastored by white ministers or white northern missionaries, but this rapidly changed as more black ministers were trained.[47]

This typical southern pattern is illustrated in the founding of Corpus Christi's first black church. In 1866 Aaron Rowe, a white chaplain assigned to the black regiments stationed in Corpus Christi after the Civil War, founded the Freedom Congregational Church. Blacks had worshiped previously with white Methodists at a small, shell, concrete church on Mann Street or at interdenominational services at various sites in the city. Although the Freedom Congregational Church was open to all denominations and races, the membership became predominantly black. Services were held in a small frame house near Twiggs Street and Broadway.[48]

Apparently Rowe left the city but returned in 1870 to rebuild the church with the help of the American Missionary Association. The AMA was a branch of the northern-based Congregational Church; it was dedicated to establishing schools, colleges, and churches for blacks in both the North and South. In 1870 the Twiggs Street house was also being used by the Missionary Baptists. Rowe set out to find a permanent home for the Congregational Church. He attempted to hold services at the Methodist Church but was unsuccessful in this endeavor, so he sought to avail himself of the new Presbyterian church. The incensed Presbyterian minister, Reverend Sproull, wrote in his diary, "I still believe that it was an insidious plan to get the use of our church until he, Rowe, could strengthen his party by drawing off as many as possible from us, when he would retire with the spoils."[49] Reverend Rowe was not to be deterred and in February 1871, he began to advertise in the Nueces Valley Weekly that services would be held at the County Courthouse.[50] It is not clear whether services continued at the courthouse or resumed at the property on Twiggs Street, but advertisements in the Corpus Christi Gazette in February 1873 show that the Reverend preached at 11 A.M. and 7:30 P.M. on the Sabbath.[51]

The Reverend Rowe left Corpus Christi in 1873 for missionary work in Georgia, where he died two years later. The white superintendent of the Sabbath School, W. B. Lacy, became the second pastor of the Congregational Church and served the church through 1874. The church sold its property on Twiggs in November of 1874 to the Missionary Baptists and moved to 909 Broadway on the Bluff.[52] The history of the church went unrecorded until 1877, when Solomon Melvin Coles arrived to assume pastoral care of the church.[53]

Solomon Coles was an exceptional black minister and educator. Born a slave in Virginia in 1844, he trained as a coachman for a wealthy tobacco planter. Taught how to read and write by the local sheriff, he moved north after the Civil War, where he attended preparatory school in Connecticut and a black college in Pennsylvania, Lincoln University. After earning a master of arts degree at Lincoln, Coles entered the Yale University Divinity School, the first black to do so and the first to earn a divinity degree there. It was at Yale that Coles became involved with the Congregational Church and the AMA. Coles was unusual within the association since most missionaries were white.[54]

Coles took temporary assignments in South Carolina, Kansas, and Massachusetts before embarking for Texas in January 1877. When he arrived in Corpus Christi he found a congregation of six males and fourteen females. He received a kind reception from the church members but wrote and asked the AMA to pray for him, as the "state of religion in Corpus is low, low!" The congregation of the church grew, and in November 1877, the members gave a supper to raise money for fencing the property upon which the church stood. Coles's correspondence with the AMA reveals that financial problems plagued the church. He received only $56 for his first year's service even though the congregation had initially pledged a yearly salary of $225.[55]

During his first year in Corpus Christi Coles realized the poor state of education for black students in the city. He had been interested in teaching before coming to Texas, but the AMA had discouraged this and requested that he focus on his ministry. Between the fall of 1877 and the fall of 1880 Coles satisfied both longings by serving the church part-time and teaching. He opened a private black school in the fall of 1877 that enrolled fifty students. In 1878 Coles closed his private school and was hired to teach in the public school for blacks. In 1880 he resigned as minister of the Congregational Church to devote himself solely to teaching. He was replaced by a new black pastor, J. W. Strong.[56]

The Reverend Strong was a graduate of Talladega College, an AMA school in Alabama. He pastored the church for at least nine years, perhaps longer. In 1889 he was elected alderman for the city from the fifth ward. He suffered a disappointment in April 1890 when he resigned his position as alderman to apply for the principalship of the black public school. Coles was principal at the time and Reverend Strong's wife taught third and fourth grade there. When Coles was retained as principal, Reverend Strong applied for assistant principal but was denied when Adelaide Moore Schwein became assistant.[57]

The Congregational Church was closely linked with the Colored Public School. Students performed in a program held at the church at the end of the school year. A note at the end of the program for the closing exhibition on July 1, 1884, announced that "Rev. J. W. Strong will address the people and school Monday night, at the close of examination, on the 'Advance of the Negro since the War.'"[58] It is evident that the Reverend Strong, Principal Coles, and the members of the black community held their church and school in high esteem and viewed them as avenues for progress.

The second and eventually most successful black church to assemble in Corpus Christi was St. Matthew Baptist Church. Groups of Baptists had assembled in the city for informal prayer meetings since 1863. After the war, Missionary Baptists worshiped with the Congregationalists but wanted to become a separate, autonomous congregation. When the Congregational Church moved to the Bluff in 1874, the Baptists bought the old church from them. At the time of the sale the church was called the Freedman's Baptist Church, but the name was changed to St. Matthew Missionary Baptist Church in 1879. Joseph Whitlock, a carpenter, became the first minister. Women were instrumental in the founding and development of the church; of the sixteen charter members, ten were women. Alice Sinclair Mays served as the first organist and music director.[59]

Little is known of the early history of St. Matthew's as the hurricane of 1919 destroyed the building and church records. The membership of the church increased in 1875 and the next year, after residents of Indianola fled to Corpus Christi in the wake of two severe storms. An influx of families from Jamaica in 1882 further swelled the ranks of the faithful. County records show that the church moved to a property on Waco Street near the Colored Public School in 1910.[60] Although the devastating winds from the 1919 hurricane swept the church away, it was rebuilt and has remained at the Waco Street location, in various forms, to the present day.

By the early twentieth century, Corpus Christi's African American community was represented in five black churches—the First Congregational Church, St. Matthew Missionary Baptist, Free Mission Baptist, African Methodist Episcopal, and Methodist Episcopal.[61] Services at Baptist and African Methodist churches had a reputation for being emotional, and the membership was often swept up in religious fervor. Congregational sects founded by the AMA were generally more sedate and disciplined.[62] This seemed to hold true in Corpus Christi as well, according to Mary Sutherland, who observed in her 1916 memoirs, "The members of the present day [Congregational Church] are a very orderly, quiet people, not given to holding all night sessions as are their more tuneful Methodist and Baptist brethren, who have been brought out and moved out of sounding distance."[63]

The educational system established for blacks in Texas in the last three decades of the nineteenth century was similar but slightly superior to the systems of other southern states. Until 1880 Texas led the southern states in reducing black illiteracy but had slipped in the rankings by the turn of the century.[64] Throughout the South the evolution of black education between 1865 and 1900 was accomplished in four phases: (1) the establishment of private schools supported by the Freedman's Bureau or missionary efforts, (2) the acceptance of a state-supported educational system, (3) the demand for separate but equal schools for blacks and whites, and (4) the acknowledgment that blacks should teach and govern black schools. Education for blacks as it emerged in Texas in general and in Corpus Christi specifically, can be viewed within this framework.

The foundation of black education in Texas immediately after the Civil War was laid by the Freedmen's Bureau.[65] Bureau schools were limited to the area around Galveston and Houston. By 1870 the Bureau discontinued its work in education since the state, by this time, had provided for a public system of schools. The Texas Legislature made no effective provision for the education of black children until the Radical Republicans gained control of state government in 1869. The Republicans instituted a system of free public schools for all children regardless of race, made attendance compulsory, and centralized the system under a powerful state superintendent of schools. There was public dissatisfaction, however, with the idea of public funding of education in general, and the Democrats dismantled parts of the system when they regained control of the legislature in 1872.[66]

The Democrats formulated a "community plan" of education which, in effect, institutionalized a segregated system of schools in Texas that provided inadequately for blacks and whites alike.[67] Blacks, however, maintained some control over their schools in those cases where they could act as trustees on the local level. This control was eroded when the state replaced the community system with a permanent district system in 1884. Most districts had white majorities and blacks were squeezed out of trusteeships. Local levying of taxes was now sanctioned by the state. However, in predominantly white districts voters failed to embrace this option since revenues were to be divided equally among black and white schools. The initial drive for the education of black children in Texas was reined in by the 1880s and the state's efforts declined in this endeavor as compared with several other southern states. Despite the setbacks, African Americans made major achievements in education between 1865 and 1900 and the black illiteracy rate in Texas during this period dropped from 95 percent to 38 percent.[68]

Black education in Corpus Christi during this era operated within the framework of Texas law and developed along the lines of black education in other southern states. Until the opening of a "colored" public school in 1873, blacks in Corpus Christi either went without any education or attended one of the private schools in town. Several private schools operated in the city and a few accepted black students. Father Gonard, a Catholic priest, taught both black and white students in a small frame house, and Mary Eliza Hayes Dix (the wife of John Dix, the county judge in 1865) taught in her home. Annie Moore Schwein, the daughter of one of the first slaves brought to Corpus Christi, recalled in her memoirs that Eliza Dix "taught school at her home here, colored girls in the morning and white girls in the afternoon."[69] By 1871, the Republican legislature mandated public schools for all children between the ages of six and eighteen. Although segregation was not required, white students in Corpus Christi assembled upstairs in the First Methodist Church and black students received lessons at the Virginia House, a store owned by William Mann.[70] The next year Captain and Mrs. Richard King donated property in the 500 block of North Carancahua for the construction of two one-room public school houses—one for black students and one for whites.[71] W. B. Lacy, the white pastor of the Congregational Church, was hired to teach the black students, and classes began in 1873. The city council assumed control of the public schools in 1875 under the community plan laws passed by the legislature. The state provided funds for a four-month term only. To extend the term to six months, the city council collected subscriptions of between $2 and $3 from individuals.[72] The enrollment at the school for blacks at this time was ninety-two.[73]

It closed in 1876. The reasons for its closure are not entirely clear, but financial problems and circumstances surrounding Lacy may have been contributing factors. In January 1877 two black members of the Congregational Church, George Guilmenot and Henry Reed, wrote to the AMA to request a new pastor for the church. They also suggested that the new minister might open a school since they had no teacher. Solomon Coles was dispatched to Corpus Christi in response to their request.[74]

In his first year as pastor of the Congregational Church, Solomon Coles operated a private black school that enrolled fifty students. As noted earlier, he became increasingly absorbed with his role as an educator and applied for a job as teacher at the Colored Public School. The school reopened in 1878 with Solomon Coles serving as both a teacher and principal. His monthly salary was $42.88. The city council rehired Coles the next year but cut his monthly pay to $30, an amount significantly lower than that earned by teachers in the white school. His request for parity in salaries was not met. Nevertheless, Coles decided to devote all his energies to teaching, and in 1880 he resigned his ministry and severed his formal ties with the AMA.[75]

Solomon Coles's tenure as principal of the public black school ran from 1878 to 1893. Enrollment increased rapidly in the first years of his principalship. In 1887 he reported to the Corpus Christi Free Public School Board that 108 of 162 potential black students were enrolled in the school. Overcrowding at the school prompted a move in 1893 to a property at 924 Winnebago Street. The school board purchased an old broom factory and moved it onto the site to serve as the new schoolhouse. By September 1893 the factory was converted into four rooms, and the new school opened with Coles as principal and teacher of the fifth through the eighth grades. The wife of the Reverend Strong, the minister of the Congregational Church, taught grades three and four and Adelaide Schwein taught first and second grades.[76]

Discipline at the school was strict. Also, Coles had a penchant for keeping the materials and building in order and in good repair. Years later a former student, Beulah Crockett, said that Principal Coles "would make you feel so good when you did right, and spank your hands when you didn't."[77] In an editorial in the *Corpus Christi Caller* that appeared in May 1883, Professor Coles lauded the reforms in Texas that lengthened the school year from five to eight months. He also reported that the city's public schools had been repaired and repainted and thanked the school board and the mayor for leaving "little undone that lay in their power to make these schools attractive, efficient and popular."[78] In an appeal that seems to echo down to our time, Principal Coles implored parents to "manifest more interest in the public schools, by frequent visits."[79] Coles was obviously dedicated to his profession, because in 1887 he wrote a letter to the Corpus Christi Board of Education requesting the use of the building for a private summer school that he planned to conduct. He apparently felt some students required additional tutelage or had some "catching up" to do. He promised that "It [the school] shall be kept in good order."[80]

The Colored Public School appears to have offered a solid educational experience. The fundamental "three r's" were stressed, but beyond this Coles taught Latin, history, geography, natural science, and orthography. Select students performed music or recited dialogue in a "closing exhibition" at the end of each school year. A surviving program for the 1884 closing exhibition indicates that religion, moral lessons, and the value of education were emphasized at the school. Selections from the program include "Truth and Falsehood," "Value of Education," and "Disobedience of Adam," along with more innocuous titles such as "Sunshine," "Rain-bow," and "Hand and Heart."[81] In addition, Fannie Washington gave a piano performance that was well received.[82] The school program for blacks was similar in content to the program for the 1893 commencement of the white high school, which featured piano, vocal, and instrumental solos along with the recitation of essays such as "Necessity of Labor" and "Influence of Music."[83]

In keeping with intellectual trends among black leaders of the late nineteenth century, Solomon Coles and the pastor of the Congregational Church, J. W. Strong, tirelessly espoused education as the vehicle for freedom and betterment of the individual and the black community. Although Reverend Strong extended "heartfelt thanks to the board of education, and white friends generally, for the impartial treatment which our educational interest has ever had from them," equal pay for teachers was, in fact, not a reality. After the move to the new school in 1893, Solomon Coles once again requested a $5 per month increase in pay and once again was refused. He then decided to accept a position in the public schools in San Antonio for the 1894–95 school year.[84]

Coles continued to teach in San Antonio until 1914, when he retired to Oberlin, Ohio, to live with his daughter. He died in Oberlin in 1924 and is buried there. A brick high school, dedicated to Coles, was constructed on the Winnebago Street property in 1925. Solomon M. Coles High School continued to serve the African American community as Corpus Christi's only public black high school until the city's schools integrated in 1967. The school was converted to a junior high school in 1968, and in the 1970s it became an elementary school. The school continues to serve the needs of children in Corpus Christi as the Solomon Coles Special Emphasis School. It is a tribute to the ex-slave and educator who claimed in 1875, "My desire is that my lot be cast where I—with my peculiar advantages—may render the greatest service to my people . . . so that my influence and labor may be thrown both in the line of education and of saving souls."[85]

In race relations and the social milieu for blacks, Corpus Christi resembled other southern cities in the second half of the nineteenth century. Howard Rabinowitz, a scholar of urban history, contends that de facto segregation replaced exclusion of blacks throughout the South after the Civil War. Complicit in this shift from exclusion to segregation were "white Republicans, who initiated it; blacks, who supported and at times requested it; and Redeemers, who accepted and expanded the new policy once they came to power."[86] Segregation also existed to some extent in the West, but integrated schools and public facilities were far more common than in the South.[87] The development of black churches and education in Corpus Christi reflects a southern pattern. Furthermore, social life was entirely segregated as black residents of the city struggled to become respectable citizens within its confines.

Although white Corpus Christians saw themselves as frontier people, many considered themselves southerners. The majority of white residents of the city in 1870 was native Texans or had been born in other southern states. A substantial portion of residents were foreign-born, with Mexico and Ireland representing the two major sources of immigrants. Fewer than one hundred residents in 1870 claimed northern states as their birthplace.[88]

During Reconstruction Corpus Christi residents appear to have directed a good deal of ire toward Mexicans. Perhaps this was the manifestation of the bitterness some Anglo-Americans harbored against Texas Mexicans in South Texas who had generally sided with the Union during the Civil War. Heightening the tension was the "Cattle War" that lasted from the end of the Civil War to the late 1870s. During this period Mexican nationals raided the herds of unbranded cattle that roamed between the Nueces and the Rio Grande.[89] Several articles in the local newspaper, the *Corpus Christi Gazette*, lamented the problems of unprotected borders with bands of robbers and "the very dregs of civilization" who stole cattle and crossed the Rio Grande. "Once there, they [the cattle] are past all redemption. They are sold for a mere song." Washington was made aware of the problem and a commission was appointed to investigate it. Mexico also appointed a commission, and the newspaper asserted that this was "to try and prove to the world they are the most abused of the two nations."[90] News about Mexican individuals was often reported without providing names, as in a notice in the February 1, 1873, edition that stated, "A Mexican died on the bluff last Tuesday."[91] Incidents of domestic violence or disorderly conduct involving Mexicans were frequent fodder for the press.

News about blacks was reported in a similar vein. African Americans were often referred to not by name, but as "a colored man" or "a colored woman." On June 13, 1874, the *Corpus Christi Weekly Gazette* reported: "A rather demonstrative darkey was several times admonished, at the court house last Thursday, that silence was wanted, but not until he had been confined in the cage and a fine imposed by Judge Borden did he seem to realize the situation and understand the peculiarity of his position relative to the law. In the future we believe he will maintain a respectful silence when requested."[92]

Many Corpus Christians viewed themselves as southerners and undoubtedly held the prevalent racial views of that region. The *Gazette's* reporting on the Civil Rights Bill of 1875, which made it illegal to discriminate between black and white patrons in places of entertainment and public accommodation, lends support to this proposition. The newspaper closely followed the progress of the bill through the United States House of Representatives and the Senate in late 1874 and the first part of 1875. The paper lambasted a northern white minister who expressed the view that all humans are equal and that the political rights of Negroes had been eroded in the South. The newspaper accused the minister of "calumny and slander to injure the character of the South," denounced him as no friend to blacks and branded him as having a "warped mind" and a "soul as black as hell."[93] The article asserted that southerners "do not refuse to the Negro any of the rights accorded to him by Congress but only see to prevent, if possible, the enactment of laws that must prove detrimental to the welfare of the race."[94] It continued by stating that separate provisions for whites and blacks were in the best interests of both races and were desired by both races.

When the legislation passed the upper house of Congress and was signed into law by President Ulysses S. Grant in early 1875, the *Gazette* responded vociferously. The newspaper claimed the bill would "result in nothing but harm to the Negro," and would be moot in Texas, since "the Negroes of the State are as a whole, orderly and well disposed, and there are no bad men to foment bad feelings between the races." The editorial ends on a more ominous note by stating: "There are certain natural laws regulating such things, and no matter what the penalty enacted for the violation of the Civil Rights bill may be, the deluded Negro who may have the temerity to presume upon it to force himself into the society of white men will, in ninety-nine cases out of a hundred, come to sudden grief."[95] The view that nature dictated that colored races were inferior and that, consequently, they should be kept segregated was a prevalent one throughout America in the nineteenth century but was most strongly embraced in the southern states.

It is difficult to determine how seriously Corpus Christians, both black and white, took the Civil Rights Bill. Only a month after the law was enacted, James O. Luby, a merchant and shipper in San Diego, Texas, and justice of the peace for Precinct 3, delivered a young African American man, Joe Johnson, to Peter Benson of Corpus Christi. The bill of lading, dated April 10, 1875, states:

> Marks. Black One Culled boy Joe Johnson no allowance made for the XVth amendment or for the usual wear and tear of the Civil Rights bill NB No relation to Br) Andy Johnson . . .
> —P. Benson Esq Dear Sir Dona Anastasia Escamilla the woman that had the boy says her charges are for keeping him which you can pay to Don Alejo.[96]

Since James Luby was a justice of the peace, it is possible that Joe Johnson was a prisoner being transferred from San Diego to the jail in Corpus Christi.

De facto segregation developed in Corpus Christi after the Civil War. Blacks attended separate churches and schools and formed their own societies. Their social life was apparently quite rich. There was at least one secret fraternal organization, the "UBF" which was apparently a black freemason's organization with a ladies' auxiliary (the "SMT").[97] In May 1883 the organization held a parade along with a public installation of officers, a supper, and a ball. The black Excelsior brass band headed the parade.[98] The brass band also performed at memorial services and Juneteenth celebrations.[99] In 1893 the band went to San Antonio to participate in Juneteenth celebrations there, and the Mexican String band filled in to provide music for the Corpus Christi festivities.[100] The Roberts Rifles, a black military company, and the Juvenile Soldier company also were a mainstay of Juneteenth celebrations in the mid-1880s.[101]

Juneteenth celebrations and the closing programs for the school for blacks at the end of each academic year were the events in the African American community most thoroughly covered by the local newspaper. Juneteenth festivities were elaborate with parades of decorated horse-drawn carts. The 1884 parade contained nine carts that visually unfolded the "History of the Negro from the Auction Block to the Treasurer's Office, 1884."[102] The celebration lasted all day, with a picnic at Headen's wharf, speeches by William Leonard, William Mead, Thomas Wilson, and Felix Thompson, a banner presentation by the ladies, baseball and croquet games, and a grand ball at Market Hall in the evening.[103]

White Corpus Christians apparently took a paternalistic attitude toward the black residents of the city. Newspaper coverage of black social events usually included comments upon the orderly conduct of the people and the lack of dissension or strife at the affairs. The article about the 1884 Juneteenth celebration ends, "Our colored people are deserving of great credit."[104] The black community apparently valued orderly conduct. They viewed it as a measure of their progress and worth. At a meeting held at the Congregational Church in the fall of 1884, William Leonard noted that a black person had not been confined to the county jail nor convicted for any offense during the previous two years. The participants at the meeting then voted on a resolution to challenge any county in Texas to "make as good a showing." If any county in the state could do so, Nueces County blacks would "acknowledge it the 'Banner County' for the colored people of Texas."[105]

Corpus Christi's black residents were involved in ventures to promote and improve their city, and their efforts and accomplishments were apparently appreciated by the white community. In 1884 white city leaders headed by Dr. William DeRyee formed a committee to organize an exhibit for Nueces County at the World's Fair. Blacks met at the Congregational Church to discuss whether they would also assemble an exhibit. Dr. DeRyee attended the meeting to attempt to convince them to unite with the county effort instead of sending their exhibit through Senator Blanche K. Bruce, the commissioner for blacks.[106] A year later, when Corpus Christi raised subscriptions for bringing a branch of the San Antonio railroad to the city, black residents heartily supported the venture. By September they had raised $1,530. The *Caller* lauded their enterprise and noted that they had been, in their contributions, "far more liberal than the white population."[107]

African Americans faced the challenge of building communities and adjusting to new economic circumstances after emancipation. They were successful to varying degrees in different regions of the country and in individual localities. The West afforded blacks a slightly greater degree of economic opportunity and generally presented fewer legal obstacles for educational and personal advancement than did the South. In the latter blacks moved in large numbers to urban areas, where an elaborate system of segregation developed. It was in these towns and cities that blacks built strong communities around their own social and cultural institutions, namely their schools and churches.

Corpus Christi was a small gulf port on the edge of the Texas frontier at the end of the Civil War. As such, it was at the confluence of several cultural streams—those of the South, the western frontier, and Mexico. The development of the black community between the end of the war and the turn of the twentieth century contains elements of both a western and a southern urban experience.

The small size of the community and its economic ties to the cattle industry, along with the presence of a significant number of skilled black workers in the 1870s, are indicative of a western experience. The development of black churches and schools in Corpus Christi along with the city's racial relations and shaping of the black community are distinctly southern in character. Occupation of the city by black federal regiments after the war, the active role of the American Missionary Association in the establishment of the black Congregational Church and early black private education, the links between the black public school and black churches, and the development of a firmly entrenched segregated school system are all elements of patterns that unfolded in numerous southern cities during this era.

The evidence presented in this paper points to the likelihood that the experience of blacks on the western frontier was not homogeneous but depended on local factors such as the nativity of both white and black residents, the local economy, and the proximity to southern or midwestern states. Corpus Christi was a growing frontier ranching community. As such, it provided some blacks with the expanded economic opportunity of working in the cattle business. And yet the city skirted the fringe of the southern "Black Belt," which meant that many residents had southern roots. This can perhaps explain why a system of segregation in education and social life emerged in the city. A more detailed investigation of Corpus Christi's black community during this period would provide further validation for the conclusions of this study. In addition, a more comprehensive study might reveal information on areas not covered here, such as political participation, welfare services, and public accommodations. Nevertheless, one thing is clear—African Americans in Corpus Christi met colossal challenges after the Civil War. They did so with vigor by forging a thriving community that was prepared to meet the challenges of a new and very different century.

## NOTES

1. Alwyn Barr, "African Americans in Texas: From Stereotypes to Diverse Roles," in *Texas through Time: Evolving Interpretations*, ed. Walter L. Buenger and Robert A. Calvert (College Station: Texas A&M University Press, 1991), 51.

2. Lawrence D. Rice, *The Negro in Texas 1874–1900* (Baton Rouge: Louisiana State University Press, 1971); Alwyn Barr, *Black Texans: A History of Negroes in Texas 1528–1971* (Austin: Pemberton Press, 1973); James M. Smallwood, *Time of Hope, Time of Despair: Black Texans During Reconstruction* (Port Washington, New York: Kennikat Press, 1981). All three works focus on eastern and central Texas, especially the sixteen eastern counties whose black population exceeded 50 percent, the so-called "Black Belt."

3. Philip Durham and Everett L. Jones, *The Negro Cowboy* (New York: Dodd, Mead, 1965); William Lorenz Katz, *The Black West* (Garden City, New York: Doubleday, 1971); William Sherman Savage, *Blacks in the West* (Westport, Connecticut: Greenwood Press, 1976); Jesse T. Moore Jr., "Seeking a New Life: Blacks in Post-Civil War Colorado," *Journal of Negro History* 78, no. 3 (Summer 1993): 166–87; Randall B. Woods, "Integration, Exclusion, or Segregation? The 'Color Line' in Kansas, 1878–1900," *Western Historical Quarterly* 14, no. 2 (April 1983): 181–98; James L. Hill, "Migration of Blacks to Iowa 1820–1960," *Journal of Negro History* 66, no. 4 (Winter 1981): 289–303; Quintard Taylor, "The Emergence of Black Communities in the Pacific Northwest: 1865–1910," *Journal of Negro History* 64, no. 4 (Fall 1979): 342–54; C. Robert Haywood, "'No Less a Man': Blacks in Cow Town Dodge City, 1876–1886," *Western Historical Quarterly* 19, no. 2 (May 1988): 161–82; Douglas Henry Daniels, *Pioneer Urbanites: A Social and Cultural History of Black San Francisco* (Philadelphia: Temple University Press, 1980); Lawrence B. de Graaf, "The City of Black Angels: Emergence of the Los Angeles Ghetto, 1880–1930," *Pacific Historical Review* 39 (August 1970): 323–70; Bradford Luckingham, *Minorities in Phoenix: A Profile of Mexican American, Chinese American, and African American Communities, 1860–1992* (Tucson: University of Arizona Press, 1994); Lynda F. Dickson, "African-American Women's Clubs in Denver, 1880s–1920s," in *Peoples of Color in the American West*, ed. Sucheng Chan et al. (Lexington, Massachusetts: D. C. Heath, 1994), 224–34.

4. Howard Rabinowitz, *Race Relations in the Urban South, 1865–1890* (New York: Oxford University Press, 1978); Howard Beeth and Cary D. Wintz, eds., *Black Dixie: Afro-Texan History and Culture in Houston* (College Station: Texas A&M University Press, 1992); Kenneth W. Goings and Raymond A. Mohl, "Toward a New African American Urban History," *Journal of Urban History* 21, no. 3 (March 1995): 283–95; Elsa Barkley Brown and Gregg D. Kimball, "Mapping the Terrain of Black Richmond," *Journal of Urban History* 21, no. 3 (March 1995): 296–324; and Kenneth W. Goings and Gerald L. Smith, "'Unhidden' Transcripts: Memphis and African American Agency, 1862–1920," *Journal of Urban History* 21, no. 3 (March 1995): 372–94.

5. James Weldon Johnson, *Denver Post*, June 24, 1925, in Katz, Black West, 282.

6. The state legislature of Oregon, for instance, passed an antimiscegenation law in 1866, one year after the Civil War ended. A movement to repeal the law was organized in 1893 by Portland blacks. See Taylor, "Emergence of Black Communities," 350. For a discussion of the "doctrine of parallel development" specifically as it applies to Kansas, see Randall B. Woods, "Integration, Exclusion, or Segregation," 181–98.

7. Moore, "Seeking New Life," 167.

8. A thorough account of this movement is related by Nell Irvin Painter, *Exodusters* (New York: Alfred A. Knopf, 1977).

9. Kansas and Oklahoma Territory had African American populations of 52,003 and 55,000 respectively; California had 11,045 black residents, and Colorado had 8,570. "The Growth of the Black Population in the Western States," *United States Bureau of the Census*, reprinted in Savage, *Blacks in the West*, appendix, 201.

10. Savage, *Blacks in the West*, 83.

11. Ibid., 128.

12. Douglas Henry Daniels, *Pioneer Urbanites*, 12 (1st and 2nd quotations), 22 (3rd quotation); for an analysis of the origins of San Francisco's black populations, see 17–19.

13. Ibid., 17.

14. Kenneth W. Porter, "African Americans in the Cattle Industry, 1860s–1880s," in *Peoples of Color in the American West*, ed. Sucheng Chan et al., 164–67; and Haywood, "No Less a Man," 161.

15. Porter, "African Americans in the Cattle Industry," 159; Savage, *Blacks in the West*, 91.

16. Savage, *Blacks in the West*, 168–75.

17. Savage, *Blacks in the West*, 175–82; Taylor, "Emergence of Black Communities," 350–51; Randall B. Woods, "Integration, Exclusion or Segregation," 186–89.

18. The African Methodist Episcopal Church was organized by free blacks in the North in response to the stifling influence of white-controlled Methodist Episcopal churches. The founding of the church can be traced to the severance of ties between black and white members of St. George's Methodist Episcopal Church in Philadelphia in 1787. Missionary work was an important element of the organization, and the AME (African Methodist Episcopal) Church sent missionaries into both the western frontier and the South during and after the Civil War. For a history of African American Methodism, see C. Eric Lincoln and Lawrence H. Mamiya, *The Black Church in the African American Experience* (Durham, North Carolina: Duke University Press, 1990), 47–75.

19. Savage, *Blacks in the West*, 185–86.

20. Richard C. Wade, foreword to *Race Relations in the Urban South, 1865–1890*, by Howard N. Rabinowitz, ix.

21. Reconstruction was the period after the Civil War when the South was rebuilt and reintegrated into the Union. The political party associated with the Union, the Republican Party, dominated politics in the South during Reconstruction. Redeemers were southern Democrats who wrested control from the Republicans after Reconstruction. For a history of this period see Eric Foner, *A Short History of Reconstruction, 1863–1877* (New York: Harper and Row, 1990).

22. Rabinowitz, *Race Relations*, 27.

23. George M. Fredrickson, *The Black Image in the White Mind: The Debate on Afro-American Character and Destiny, 1817–1914* (New York: Harper Torchbooks, 1971), 175.

24. Rabinowitz, *Race Relations*, 153, 169–81.

25. Ibid., 61–63, 85–86.

26. U.S. Bureau of the Census, *Population Schedules of the Ninth Census of the United States, 1870, Nueces County, Texas*, vol. 15 (Washington, D.C.: National Archives and Records Service [cited hereafter as NARS], 1965);

*Twelfth Census of the United States, 1900*, vol. 1 (Washington, D.C.: U.S. Census Office, 1901), 643. The 1870 census designates individuals as either "black," "mulatto," or "white." Mexicans or Americans of Mexican descent are listed as "white." For the purpose of this study, blacks and mulattos are combined and considered "black."

27. Rosalie B. Hart Priour, *Autobiography: Adventures of a Family of Emigrants*, ed. Frank Wagner, undated typescript, 191, La Retama Local History Room, Corpus Christi Central Public Library, Corpus Christi, Texas (cited hereafter as La Retama); Eugenia Reynolds Briscoe, *City by the Sea* (New York: Vantage Press, 1978), 246.

28. U.S. Bureau of the Census, *Seventh Census of the United States, 1850*, "Population by Counties—Ages, Colors, and Condition," Table I (Washington, D.C.: Robert Armstrong, Public Printer, 1853), 504.

29. Briscoe, *City by the Sea*, 257, 281.

30. U.S. Bureau of the Census, *Population Schedules of the Ninth Census of the United States, 1870, Nueces County, Texas* (NARS, 1965).

31. Alwyn Barr, *Black Texans*, 64.

32. Population schedules for the 1870 census list fifteen blacks and seven whites as draymen.

33. U.S. Bureau of the Census, *Population Schedules of the Ninth Census of the United States, 1870, Nueces County, Texas* (NARS, 1965).

34. Thurma Hilton, "They Built Corpus Christi," *Corpus Christi Caller-Times*, July 4, 1976, 6M; Bessie M. Johnson et al., *Centennial History 1874–1974: Saint Matthew Baptist Church, Corpus Christi, Texas*, 2, La Retama; *Population Schedules of the Ninth Census of the United States, 1870, Nueces County, Texas* (NARS, 1965).

35. Manuscript deed, 1854, personal papers of Alclair Mays Pleasant, Corpus Christi, Texas.

36. Alclair Mays Pleasant, interviewed by the author, audiocassette, Texas A&M University–Kingsville, South Texas Oral History and Folklore Collection, February 26, 1998 (cited hereafter as Pleasant interview).

37. Reynolds to Mays, Realitos, Texas, May 22, 1899, personal papers of Alclair Mays Pleasant. Pleasant indicated that she believes "Mr. Horatio" might be Horatio Gussett.

38. Bill Walraven, *Corpus Christi: The History of a Texas Seaport* (Sun Valley,

California: American Historical Press, 1997): 61–62; Nueces County Historical Society, *The History of Nueces County* (Austin: Jenkins, 1972), 150–51.

39. Walraven, *Corpus Christi*, 61–62.

40. U.S. Bureau of the Census, *Population Schedules of the Twelfth Census of the United Slates, 1900, Nueces County, Texas* (NARS, 1965).

41. Rabinowitz, *Race Relations*, 69–71; and Barr, *Black Texans*, 92–94.

42. Interestingly, in the manuscript census records, R. E. Brown is listed as a "clergyman" while D. Sapp, George Webb, and the Reverend Donaldson are listed as "preachers." R. E. Brown lived on Mesquite Street in ward 1 of the city, an area inhabited by many of the wealthy and influential white families, while the three "preachers" lived in ward 5, the ward with the highest concentration of black residents. The two teachers were a married couple, the Nollowells, who lived on Tancahua in ward 5 with their four children. U.S. Bureau of the Census, *Population Schedules of the Twelfth Census of the United States, 1900, Nueces County, Texas* (NARS, 1965).

43. *Corpus Christi City Directory*, 1907, n. pag., La Retama.

44. U.S. Bureau of the Census, *Population Schedules of the Twelfth Census of the United States, 1900, Nueces County, Texas* (NARS, 1965).

45. Pleasant interview.

46. Rabinowitz, *Racial Relations*, 61–96.

47. Rabinowitz, *Racial Relations*, 199–203; Smallwood, *Time of Hope*, 97–98.

48. Elizabeth Camp Pritchett, *A Short History of the First Methodist Church, Corpus Christi, Texas*, 2, La Retama; Edna Jordan, *Black Tracks to Texas: Solomon Melvin Coles, From Slave to Educator* (Corpus Christi, Texas: Golden Banner Press), 11–12; Johnson et al., *Centennial History*, 1–3.

49. Margaret Lasater Clark, *On This Bluff . . . Centennial History 1867–1967, First Presbyterian Church, Corpus Christi, Texas* (Corpus Christi: Renfrow, 1967), 26.

50. Ibid., 27.

51. *Corpus Christi Weekly Gazette*, February 8, 1873, 3.

52. Jordan, *Black Tracks*, 12; Johnson et al., *Centennial History*.

53. Jordan, *Black Tracks*, 12.

54. Ibid., 3–7.

55. Ibid., 8–10, 12 (quotation), 13.

56. Ibid., 14–18.

57. Hilton, "They Built Corpus Christi," 6M.

58. *Program for the Closing Exhibition of Corpus Christi Colored Public School, July 1, 1884* (Texas A&M University–Corpus Christi Archives and Special Collections [cited hereafter as TAMU–CC Archives]), collection 24, folder 1.16, 3.

59. Johnson et al., *Centennial History*, 1–3; Elizabeth King, "A Historical Sketch of St. Matthew Baptist Church," *Echoes of St. Matthew Baptist Church, Corpus Christi, Texas, 1874–1954* (TAMU–CC Archives), 6.

60. Johnson et al., *Centennial History*, 5.

61. *Corpus Christi City Directory*, 1907.

62. Rabinowitz, *Race Relations*, 206–207.

63. Mary A. Sutherland, *The Story of Corpus Christi* (Corpus Christi: Corpus Christi Chapter, Daughters of the Confederacy, 1916), 34.

64. Rice, *The Negro in Texas*, 209.

65. The Freedman's Bureau was a federal agency charged with helping former slaves in the South make the transition from slavery to freedom. The Bureau worked to help blacks secure political rights, establish educational institutions, and arrange new forms of labor agreements. For a study of the Freedman's Bureau in Texas, see Barry Crouch, *The Freedman's Bureau and Black Texans* (Austin: University of Texas Press, 1992).

66. Rice, *The Negro in Texas*, 209–14.

67. The "community plan" provided for state financing of public schools but placed administration into the hands of county judges and local trustees. Local taxes were not to be used for financing schools, and integrated schools could not receive state funds. For a discussion of the development of black education in Texas during the latter half of the nineteenth century, see Rice, *The Negro in Texas*, 209–39.

68. Barr, *Black Texans,* 64; Rice, *The Negro in Texas*, 209.

69. Annie Moore Schwien, *When Corpus Christi Was Young*, typescript memoirs, 1941, 10, La Retama.

70. Nueces County Historical Society, *History of Nueces County*, 118.

71. Jordan et al., *Centennial History*, 18.

72. Edna Weedon Tobias, "The History of Education in Nueces County" (master's thesis, Sul Ross State College, 1936), 24.

73. Nueces County Historical Society, *History of Nueces County*, 119.

74. Jordan, *Black Tracks to Texas*, 14.

75. Ibid., 18.

76. Ibid., 21, 23.

77. Ibid., 23.

78. Solomon M. Coles, "City Free Public Schools," *Corpus Christi Caller*, May 27, 1883, 2.

79. Ibid.

80. Jordan, *Black Tracks to Texas*, 19.

81. *Program for the Closing Exhibition of Corpus Christi Colored Public School*, 2–3.

82. J. W. Strong, "Closing Exhibition of the Colored School," *Corpus Christi Caller*, July 6, 1884, 4.

83. "Entertaining Affair: First Commencement of the Corpus Christi High School—Three Graduate," *Corpus Christi Weekly Caller*, June 2, 1893, 3.

84. J. W. Strong, *Corpus Christi Caller*, July 6, 1884 (quotation); Jordan, *Black Tracks to Texas*, 24.

85. From a letter by Coles to the American Missionary Association, March 23, 1875, cited in Jordan, *Black Tracks to Texas*, 26.

86. Rabinowitz, *Race Relations*, 332.

87. Few hotels, bars, and restaurants in Dodge City, Kansas, in the 1870s and 1880s, for instance, were segregated; even the skating rink was not. See Haywood, "Blacks in Cow Town Dodge City," 167–70.

88. U.S. Bureau of the Census, *Population Schedules of the Ninth Census of the United States, 1870, Nueces County, Texas* (NARS, 1965).

89. Arnoldo De León, *They Called Them Greasers: Anglo Attitudes toward Mexicans in Texas, 1821–1900* (Austin: University of Texas Press, 1983), 55–56.

90. *Corpus Christi Weekly Gazette*, January 11, 1873, 2.

91. *Corpus Christi Weekly Gazette*, February 1, 1873, 3.

92. *Corpus Christi Weekly Gazette*, June 13, 1874, 3.

93. *Corpus Christi Weekly Gazette*, October 17, 1874, 2.

94. Ibid.

95. *Corpus Christi Weekly Gazette*, March 6, 1875, 2.

96. James O. Luby to Peter Benson, bill of lading, April 10, 1875, TAMU–CC Archives.

97. According to Alclair Pleasant, her mother, Annie Cox Garcia, belonged to the Household of Ruth, the women's auxiliary of the Odd Fellows, a black fraternal organization that was active during her childhood in the 1910s and 1920s. There was a chapter of the Odd Fellows operating in Corpus Christi in 1893, but it is not clear whether this was a white or a black chapter. See "Societies and Organizations," *Corpus Christi Weekly Caller*, June 23, 1893, 8.

98. *Corpus Christi Caller*, May 13, 1883, 5.

99. Juneteenth is celebrated to commemorate the freeing of the slaves in Texas on June 19, 1865. Technically, slaves in states in rebellion against the Union were freed by Lincoln's Emancipation Proclamation of 1863; however, freedom did not actually come to slaves in Texas until Union forces landed at Galveston on June 19, 1865.

100. "Emancipation Day: It Is Celebrated in Appropriate Style by Corpus' Colored People," *Corpus Christi Weekly Caller*, June 16, 1893, 6.

101. "The Colored People's Day," *Corpus Christi Caller*, June 22, 1884, 5; "The Colored People Celebrate," *Corpus Christi Caller*, June 21, 1885, 5.

102. *Corpus Christi Caller*, June 22, 1884, 5.

103. The city had a white baseball team that played teams from surrounding towns and cities. The results of the games were published in the newspaper. Blacks did not play on the team, but on at least one occasion a black was asked to umpire. "Baseball at Aransas Harbor," *Corpus Christi Weekly Caller*, June 2, 1893, 6.

104. *Corpus Christi Caller*, June 22, 1884, 5.

105. "Good Colored People," *Corpus Christi Caller*, October 5, 1884, 5.

106. "An Exhibit by the Colored People," *Corpus Christi Caller*, September 28, 1884, 5.

107. "Enterprise of Our Colored Citizens," *Corpus Christi Caller*, September 20, 1885, 5.

# Lola and Leon Houck versus the Southern Pacific Railway Company

JANICE L. SUMLER-EDMOND

AT THE END OF THE NINETEENTH CENTURY, MANY of the nearly eight million African Americans then living in the United States bore witness to deteriorating race relations. The situations they faced provided a bitter reminder of their second-class citizenship in a self-proclaimed democratic republic.[1] Black people, especially those living in the former Confederate states, encountered numerous obstacles in their quest for citizenship and equal opportunities. Although the Thirteenth Amendment to the United States Constitution had abolished slavery, it had done precious little to eradicate racial prejudice. In the relatively short time span between the end of the Civil War in 1865 and the dismantlement of Reconstruction in 1876, African Americans experienced both a rise and a decline in their expectations for inclusion into the mainstream of American life.

Optimism ran high among African Americans with the ratification of the Fourteenth Amendment that granted citizenship to blacks in 1868 and the Fifteenth Amendment that removed race as a barrier to voting in 1870. But those high expectations began to decline in the increasingly racially charged atmosphere. Jim Crow practices segregated the races in everyday life and often found support in legislation and judicial opinions. African Americans also experienced widespread disfranchisement, racial animosity, and even violence. Such antiblack actions and attitudes characterized plummeting race relations during the waning years of the nineteenth century.[2]

American racism had no regional limitations during that era, and the state of Texas mirrored other former Confederate states in having laws that restricted African Americans to a subordinate status. Many white Texans held racially biased attitudes and acquiesced in the discriminatory treatment directed toward black people. Texas newspapers often articulated the prevailing views about race. In its April 13, 1889, editorial the *Victoria Advocate* offered both an opinion and a possible solution regarding an issue of significant concern to its readers in Victoria, Texas. In a piece entitled "The Local Negro Problem" the *Advocate* posed two important questions: First, what was to be done with the growing black population and, second, what level of social, political, and economic involvement was most suitable for these newest citizens to assume? The *Advocate*'s answer: stop listening to all the philosophy, especially the so-called Negro philosophy espoused by northerners and other self-labeled race experts. For the most part, the newspaper considered those pundits to be ill-advised. "This class of writers," the *Advocate* contended, "generally get themselves too high above the negro [sic] and lose sight of some important facts while settling his status as a man, as a citizen and as a part of the public economy." Yet the *Advocate* did not wholeheartedly condone the thinking of those who would condemn all hard working black people to a permanent lowly status in society. "It is too late," the *Advocate* advised, "to go back, as some of our republican friends are doing, and ask if it were not a mistake to enfranchise him. He is enfranchised." At the same time, the *Advocate* was reluctant to concede that in the future the two races might be looked upon as equals. The newspaper called the prospect of racial equality "an idle dream." The *Advocate* concluded its editorial with a predication that so long as black people remained employed, primarily as agricultural laborers, and accepted a subordinate place in American society the races could live in harmony.[3]

While the *Advocate* may have espoused the white community's view of the so-called Negro problem, many African Americans did not share the same opinion. The historical record reveals that a considerable segment of the black community strongly objected to the Jim Crow system and other discriminatory practices prevalent during the post-Reconstruction era. Instead, through their hard work, education, and political involvement, African Americans sought avenues to experience all the rights, privileges, and responsibilities of citizenship.

Such was the case with the Houcks of Victoria, Texas. Although Lola and Leon Houck did not record their reaction to the *Advocate* editorial, we can speculate that this African American couple would have vigorously rejected the newspaper's promise of racial harmony in exchange for the subordination of African American ambition and relegation to second-class citizenship. In fact, by the spring of 1889 when the *Advocate* article appeared, the Houcks were already celebrating their legal victory over the Southern Pacific Railway Company. Instead of accepting racial discrimination as a matter of course, the Houcks had hired legal counsel and filed a lawsuit.[4]

This research profiles the Houcks and their legal case against the Southern Pacific Railway Company. The Houcks were a fascinating couple. In many ways they characterized the gifted and progressive "Talented Tenth" of the black race that pioneering African American sociologist and philosopher W. E. B. DuBois would soon memorialize in his insightful collection of essays entitled, *Souls of Black Folk*. In the flower of their youth, educated, entrepreneurially minded, and family-oriented, Lola and Leon Houck embodied many of the hopes and dreams of the African American community at the end of the nineteenth century. Texas born and reared, Lola hailed from Galveston, Texas, where she had lived with her parents, George and Eliza Ennis. Recognizing that their daughter needed an education to take her place in society, Lola's parents sent her to the Prairie View State Normal School for black youth in Hempstead, Texas. Lola graduated from that school and would have applied for a teaching position had it not been for her courtship with and subsequent marriage to Leon L. Houck of Victoria.[5]

In a modest ceremony held on February 18, 1885, at Riedy Chapel African Methodist Episcopal Church in Galveston, Lola Ennis married Leon Houck. The Reverend J. E. Edwards, Riedy's assistant minister, officiated. After their nuptials, the couple set up housekeeping in Victoria where Leon, an educator by profession, operated a school. In short order, the Houcks gained a reputation as respectable black people in that small south Texas community. In January of 1886 the couple had a son. By the early fall of the next year, Lola announced to her husband that she was pregnant with their second child. The Houcks frequently made the ninety-mile train trip from Victoria to Galveston to visit Lola's parents. On occasion, the Houcks allowed their son to stay with his grandparents.[6]

This was the situation on September 21, 1886. The Houcks's nine-month-old son was in Galveston visiting his grandparents when he suddenly became very ill. When the child's condition took a turn for the worst, his grandparents telegraphed their daughter Lola and urged her to come to Galveston without delay. It is very likely that before she headed to the Victoria train, the nearly frantic Lola hurriedly sent a telegraph to her husband who was traveling in New York on business. Somewhat distracted and anxious about the well-being of her son, Lola had no way of knowing that the journey to reach her child would involve harrowing incidents aboard the train and serious injury to herself. She also had no way of knowing that her journey that fateful day would serve as the impetus for a lawsuit against the Southern Pacific Railway Company. Following the typical pattern for her frequent trips to Galveston, Lola bought a first-class ticket for $4.75 at the train depot and proceeded to board the train. In order to reach her final destination, Lola was obliged to ride on two trains that afternoon. The first leg of her journey would begin on a train leaving Victoria and traveling to the town of Rosenburg with intermediate stops in Inez and in Edna. Once she arrived at the Rosenburg station, Lola would transfer to a second train for the last leg of the trip to the city of Galveston.[7]

The train that was ready to depart the Victoria station for Rosenburg that September afternoon included an engine car and two passenger cars. The rear passenger car with padded seats and other first-class features was commonly known as the "ladies' car" and was typically set aside for the use of white passengers in accordance with the company's unwritten rule. The forward car, also known as the "Jim Crow car," was located closest to the engine car. This forward car had inferior seating and was designed to accommodate African American passengers and smoking passengers of either race. Having purchased her first-class ticket, Lola proceeded to the rear ladies' car, but she was not permitted to enter. This was an unusual situation for Lola who had ridden in the ladies' car without incident on at least seven or eight different occasions during the preceding twelve months. Although she was an African American woman, Lola Houck could pass for white. It is likely that during her previous train trips, the railroad personnel had assumed Lola was a white woman.[8]

On this particular occasion, the young bootblack working at the railway station spotted Lola as she purchased her ticket at the Victoria station, and took it upon himself to inform the train's brakeman that Lola was an African American. Armed with this new information, the brakeman and the train conductor spent the bulk of the afternoon making Lola's life miserable aboard their train. As the train departed the station, these two white employees began tormenting Lola by locking her out of the first-class car while permitting white passengers to enter through the rear door. For the duration of Lola's journey on the train to Rosenburg, the brakeman taunted her with crude remarks. He called her a nigger, he shut the train door in her face, and he ridiculed her. At one of the intermediate stops in the journey, when Lola tried to enter the ladies' car through the rear door, the brakeman ran ahead of her and locked the door in her face. In his haste to prevent Lola from entering the ladies' car, the brakeman used all his strength and pulled Lola back from the door, ripping her dress at the waistline. The force made Lola fall backward and hard against the wheel of the brake. If she had not managed to hold on to the brake wheel, she would have fallen from the train. Besides his rough treatment of her person, the brakeman also tossed Lola's potted plant off the train.[9]

When they testified at trial a year later during the Houcks's lawsuit, both the brakeman and the conductor denied tormenting Lola. Under oath, the men assured the jury that at any time during her journey Lola could have taken a comfortable seat in the forward Jim Crow passenger car. The two railway employees seemed baffled that Lola had refused the seat offered to her. But from Lola's vantage point entering the Jim Crow car, filled with loud and boisterous passengers of both races some of whom were drinking and smoking, was simply not an option she was willing to entertain. Described as demur and very ladylike, "a refined and delicate, educated lady" in manners and dress, Lola did not want to subject herself to the atmosphere of the Jim Crow car. To further aggravate Lola's predicament, the brakeman had repeatedly ridiculed and pointed to Lola as she stood helpless on the train's platform situated between the two passenger cars. The noise from the commotion on the platform drew attention and the other passengers knew she was riding there. Some sympathized with Lola's predicament and urged the brakeman to treat her with respect, but other passengers laughed and made fun of her. Apprehensive and humiliated, Lola felt she had no other choice but to remain during the entire trip on the platform where she got soaking wet in a rainstorm. Later that day when she finally reached her parents' home in Galveston, a physician was summoned to examine Lola, who had fallen into a semi-unconscious state. In spite of the medical care, Lola suffered a miscarriage three days after the train incident, and she was confined to her bed for over a month. Over the succeeding weeks as Lola slowly regained her health, she and her husband Leon made plans to sue the Southern Pacific Railway alleging the company's discriminatory treatment had caused Lola's injuries.[10]

The compelling facts of the train incident undoubtedly aided the Houcks in retaining legal counsel to litigate their case. They hired the law firm of Labatt and Nobles of Galveston to represent their interests. The distinguished legal team of H. J. Labatt and S. B. Nobles was well known and maintained a lucrative legal practice throughout the greater Galveston area. Their office was located at 24 Strand Avenue between Twenty-fourth and Twenty-fifth Streets in downtown Galveston. Four years earlier, these two lawyers were among a select group of white men who called for the creation of the Texas Bar Association. On the first day of the organizational session, held in Galveston on July 15, 1882, Labatt had called the meeting of his legal brethren to order. Over the next several days, Labatt played a key role in laying a foundation for what would become a statewide organization of lawyers.

While Labatt and Nobles championed the side of the Houcks, the firm of Waul and Walker defended the Southern Pacific Railway Company. Like their opposing counsel, Thomas Neville Waul and John C. Walker were also prominent Galveston attorneys. Their law office was located on the northwest corner of Mechanic Avenue and Twenty-second Street. Mirroring their opposing counsel in the Houck lawsuit, attorneys Waul and Walker were also founding members of the Texas Bar Association. Waul, the more famous member of the two-person firm, had served as a Confederate officer. After the Civil War, he amassed a considerable fortune representing corporate clients, and he acquired extensive land holdings in Galveston and in Greenville. During his representation of the Southern Pacific Railway Company in the Houck litigation, Waul also served as the president of the Galveston Bar Association.[11]

As the lawyer for the Houck couple, H. J. Labatt advised his clients to seek justice in the federal district court. When Lola was well enough to travel from Galveston back to her home in Victoria, Labatt accompanied her aboard the train. In an attempt to test the level of treatment she would receive on the return trip, Labatt and Lola entered the first-class accommodations of the ladies' car where they rode undisturbed for the entire journey. Railway personnel, including the same brakeman who had tormented her a month earlier, duly noted Lola's presence aboard the train but did not approach her or her attorney. If the railroad employees suspected that a lawsuit was brewing, they were correct in that assumption. In March of 1887, Labatt filed petition number 1439 in the United States District Court for the Eastern District of Texas at Galveston. The Houcks claimed damages in the amount of $7,500 against the railroad company. The petition alleged that the wrongful actions of the Southern Pacific employees had caused Lola's illness and miscarriage. In its reply to the complaint, the railway company denied all the allegations and argued that the petition should be summarily dismissed as insufficient in law. The railway company also argued that its obligation to Lola Houck and all other paying passengers extended only to providing safe and comfortable passage to their destinations. It contended that Lola had caused her own injuries by remaining on the train's platform and refusing to take a seat in the forward car.[12]

The court docket must have been crowded with cases because it took twenty-one months from the filing of the Houck petition to the selection of a jury panel to hear the case. Finally on December 12, 1888, the jury began to hear sworn testimony in the case of *Houck* v. *Southern Pacific Railway Company*. The litigants called a host of witnesses. Lola Houck made an appearance as the lead plaintiff in the case. Under direct examination by attorney Labatt, Lola recounted her frightening experiences aboard the train. In one of the more dramatic segments of her sworn testimony, she described a confrontation with the brakeman as follows:

> I thought if I could get in the rear door I would go with them (white passengers), and I started around with them. The brakeman seemed to know I was going around there, and just before I got to the door at the rear of the car, he made a break to get there first, and he caught hold of me and pulled me back and threw me against the brake, which was all I had to hold to, or to catch hold of, and if it hadn't been for that I would have been thrown off the car. He stepped on my dress and tore it from my waist. I sat down on the steps to pin my dress up. I was ashamed to stand there with my dress like that.[13]

To support Lola's testimony, attorney Labatt summoned additional witnesses. Surviving court records reveal that George Ennis, Lola's father, gave sworn testimony although the transcript of his statements has been lost. It is likely that Ennis's statement verified his daughter's prolonged illness following the September 1886 train incident. Others who appeared on behalf of the Houcks included J. J. Shannon, Roger Duffy, and Charles J. W. Johnson. Johnson, a white passenger who rode on the same train with Lola on the day of the incident, took the witness stand and verified many portions of Lola's testimony. Johnson also offered sworn testimony that the two passenger cars varied significantly in terms of the comfort of their seating and their overall accommodations. Johnson observed that the rear ladies' car was "a very nice car" while the forward car was used primarily for smoking. Johnson's testimony corroborated Lola's reasoning for refusing to take a seat in the forward car. When he was asked by the Houcks's attorney about the type of people who were occupying the smoking car, Johnson explained, "There were some pretty rough cases there. There were two near the door next to the first-class car, and they were telling some boisterous stories among themselves; and talking rough, and smoking and chewing tobacco."[14] Johnson also recollected that he had seen "colored ladies" riding in both the forward and rear passenger cars. When asked, was there anything particular about a Jim Crow car, Johnson replied that "it is the car that carries all sorts of rough people and [a] rough class of men."[15]

The last two witnesses for the plaintiffs were Leon Houck and attorney Labatt. Leon testified that he had traveled several times on the train to Galveston, occasionally taking time to smoke in the Jim Crow car. Most illuminating was his testimony detailing previous conversations with his wife about his observations of the smoking car. Having seen women insulted in the smoking car, Leon had specifically warned his wife to avoid the Jim Crow car. Attorney Labatt took the witness stand and gave sworn testimony about his experiences aboard the railroad line. Labatt, who had been a frequent traveler on the Southern Pacific Railway over the previous three years, testified that the forward car was partitioned and contained two kinds of seating, wooden slats for seats in the front portion of the car and rattan seats in the rear portion of the car.[16] The forward car contained none of the more comfortable padded seating found in the rear car.

Witnesses for the Southern Pacific Railway Company included some of their employees as well as passengers. The first defense witness was Charles Oaks, the brakeman who had denied Lola entry to the ladies' car. Oaks testified about the company's rules about black passengers and the verbal instructions he had received from his supervisor. On direct examination, Oaks explained, "At the time we didn't allow the colored people to ride in the rear coach; and had orders from the superintendent; and I used to lock the doors at the stations to keep them from going to the rear coach to ride. We wanted them to go in the second-class coach."[17]

To refute Lola's testimony that he had mistreated her, Oaks swore that he never touched Lola Houck nor did he call her any derogatory names. According to brakeman Oaks, he merely directed her to take a seat in the Jim Crow car. He told the jury, "She came up on the platform of the rear car to go in; and I told her she could go in the other car; but she said she wouldn't go in there; and I walked off and left her there, and she said she would ride on the platform before she would ride in that car in front. I walked away and left her then.[18]

After the brakeman's testimony, the company called Fester Farnsworth, the train conductor who had also been on duty the day of Lola's journey to Galveston. Farnsworth corroborated the brakeman's testimony. Farnsworth told the jury that he had repeatedly asked Lola to take a seat in the forward car. Concerning the physical condition of the forward car, Farnsworth conceded that it contained a partition to permit smoking by passengers, but he insisted that the passenger cars were equal in comfort.[19]

Before Farnsworth was excused from the witness stand, the trial judge took it upon himself to ask the defense witness a question. Having established that the Southern Pacific Company had a standing rule against permitting passengers to ride on the platforms, the judge asked why conductor Farnsworth had failed to insure that Lola Houck was not standing on the platform of a moving train. In his response, Farnsworth admitted he had seen Lola riding on the platform but that he had taken no action to prevent her from remaining there for the duration of her journey.[20]

Another witness, B. B. Creary, also testified for the Southern Pacific Railway Company. Creary, a white ranch manager from Wharton County, had been a passenger on the train bound for Galveston. He explained that he had conversed with Lola as they rode on the platform between the two passenger cars. Creary asked Lola to go into the Jim Crow car, but she refused. He testified that he heard no rude comments spoken to Lola by the railroad employees. According to him, the two railway company employees were respectful to her.[21]

After the presentation of evidence, the trial judge placed the case in the hands of the jury for a decision. The jury had to tackle two key issues, both of which were ultimately decided in the Houcks's favor. The first issue was whether the railway had satisfied its duty under the law of public carriers to provide substantially equal accommodations to passengers whom it elected to separate. Lola prevailed on this issue. Very likely crucial to her winning argument was the fact that the company sold her a first-class ticket at the Victoria depot station but then failed to provide her with first-class accommodations. Trial testimony established that, on the day of the incident, Lola had repeatedly attempted to enter the first-class ladies' car, but was denied entry by the brakeman and the conductor. Unsuccessfully, the railway attempted to prove that the two cars were essentially comparable and that the company had satisfied their duty to Lola by offering her a seat in the forward Jim Crow car. The company failed in its attempt to prove that the car into which Lola Houck was directed to go by Conductor Farnsworth was as safe and substantially as comfortable in its overall condition as the ladies' car.

The Houcks presented evidence that the Jim Crow car was inferior to the rear ladies' car in terms of passenger seating, comfort, and safety. When describing the conditions in the forward car, Lola testified that the seats "were just plain wooden seats" and "rough looking."[22] Yet for Lola the lack of comfort was secondary in importance to the type of crowd occupying the forward Jim Crow car. On that September day, it had been Lola's goal to avoid going into the forward car. From the witness stand, she explained to the jury that she had never ridden in the front car before and did not intend to ride there because in her opinion, "it was not a fit place for a woman to go in. Because I would have been insulted."[23] As stated above, the Houcks's legal team convincingly used the testimony of Charles J. W. Johnson, a white passenger, to corroborate their version of the case. Johnson concurred with her statements about the disparity in seating accommodations between the forward and rear passenger cars. He also verified the rough crowd of smoking and drinking passengers Lola would have encountered if she had been forced to enter the Jim Crow car. The cumulative impact of the testimony convinced the jury that the railway company had failed to satisfy its duty to provide substantially equal accommodations to Lola, who had paid for first-class accommodations aboard the train.

The second issue the jury had to consider was whether the injuries Lola sustained were caused by the rude and wrongful actions of the brakeman. The judge had instructed the jury that Lola could not prevail on the second issue if the factual evidence suggested that her injuries resulted from her own negligence in refusing to take a seat. As a matter of law, the railway company could not be held liable for any sickness or injury sustained by Lola Houck from her decision to remain on the platform in the rain when she might have easily sought shelter from the weather within the train. Conversely, the company would be held responsible if the jury, in its review of the evidence, found that Lola's injuries were the result of the "mental irritation, humiliation, annoyances, and rude acts caused by the faults and wrongs of the brakeman" [24] In what amounted to a stunning victory for the Houcks, the jury determined that the brakeman's actions had caused Lola's injuries.

While the Houcks claimed damages in the amount of $7,500, the jury awarded them a total of $5,000. The monetary award consisted of $2,000 in punitive damages to punish the Southern Pacific Company and another $3,000 to compensate Lola for her injuries, including the miscarriage she had suffered. The railroad company immediately appealed the jury's verdict and asked for a new trial.

Judge Aleck Boarman of the Fifth Circuit Court of Appeals reviewed the Southern Pacific Railway Company's request. The judge carefully examined the trial court proceedings and confirmed the lion's share of the jury's findings. Judge Boarman concurred with the verdict that Lola had been wrongfully denied first-class accommodations because she was a black person. Boarman acknowledged that Lola, having purchased a first-class ticket, was directed to ride in a car that was occupied by "boisterous passengers" who were smoking and drinking. The car that the brakeman and conductor had assigned Lola to ride in was in the judge's review of the trial evidence "nothing like as comfortable to ride in as the car kept exclusively for white people."[25]

The trial evidence also convinced Judge Boarman that Lola had been mistreated by the railway employees. The judge affirmed the jury's decision that the railway company was culpable for causing harm to Lola Houck aboard the train on September 21, 1886. "I thought," the judge wrote in his opinion, "the evidence unquestionably showed, that the brakeman treated plaintiff, who 'acted all the time in a lady-like manner,' rudely, wrongfully, and in some degree, maliciously."[26] Judge Boarman denied the railway company's motion for a new trial. Further, the judge agreed with the jury's findings and monetary award, except for the compensatory damages award, which he reduced from $3,000 to $500. While the judge felt there was sufficient evidence to hold the railway company liable for a substantial portion of Lola's injuries incurred aboard the train, the judge was not convinced that Lola's miscarriage had been the result of the actions of the brakeman and conductor in denying her admission to the rear ladies' car. The judge allowed Lola the sum of $500 in damages to compensate her for the ill treatment she suffered by the actions of the railway employees. The jury's award to punish the railway company remained untouched; Judge Boarman permitted the punitive damage award of $2,000 to stand. The judge noted his annoyance that brakeman Oaks had not been dismissed from his job because of his rude actions toward Lola Houck. Instead, the railway company rewarded Oaks with a promotion to baggage manager and express man.[27]

In addition to denying the railroad company's request for a new trial, Judge Boarman's 1889 opinion also set forth guidelines for transportation companies offering services to the general public. Using language that seems to anticipate the historic *Plessy* v. *Ferguson* case that would be decided by the United States Supreme Court seven years later (in 1896), Boarman's opinion championed the separate but equal doctrine. While he recognized that transportation companies were entitled to formulate reasonable rules separating the races, the judge noted that the lawful enforcement of such rules depended on the existence of certain contingencies. Essentially, companies were obliged to furnish cars "to the colored passenger who pays first-class fare over the line a car to ride in as safe and substantially as inviting, to travel in, as it [the management] furnishes to white passengers."[28]

In support of his ruling in the *Houck* case, Boarman cited the precedent set forth in *McGuinn* v. *Forbes*, a case litigated in the United States District Court for the District of Maryland during the winter of

1888. Robert A. McGuinn, a respected African American Baptist minister, sued the captain and the owners of the steamer *Mason L. Weems* for $2000 in damages. McGuinn, a first-class paying customer on the steamer, claimed he had been insulted by passengers and crew members, including the captain, when he answered the dinner bell and sat down at a table where several white passengers were already seated. When the white passengers complained that a black man was sitting at their table, the captain asked McGuinn if the waiters could seat him elsewhere in the dining room. In response to Reverend McGuinn's refusal to move, the steamboat captain immediately arranged for the white passengers to be served at another table. Waiters served McGuinn his dinner, but he felt humiliated and insulted by being forced to dine alone after being shunned by the white passengers. Reverend McGuinn's torment did not end with the dinner meal. McGuinn reported that later that evening he was assaulted by several passengers and crew members. Fearing that the angry threats to throw him overboard might be carried out, McGuinn elected to disembark the steamer before reaching his intended destination. Although McGuinn had paid for first-class accommodations, he was forced to sit in a segregated dinning arrangement. In his subsequent lawsuit McGuinn alleged that the steamboat company had discriminated against him because of his race.[29]

In his written opinion that decided the outcome in the *McGuinn* v. *Forbes* litigation, Judge Thomas J. Morris had relied on the prevailing law of common carriers. According to that law, all persons who paid for the first-class tickets must be allowed to enjoy the same accommodations, or in the alternative, the establishment must make a bona fide effort to furnish separate but equal accommodations. Lola Houck prevailed in her lawsuit by presenting convincing evidence that she had paid for but did not receive first-class accommodations. Reverend McGuinn made no such showing, and he lost his lawsuit against the steamboat company. Judge Morris determined that although McGuinn may have suffered some discomfort and humiliation, he had been permitted to remain at a first-class dinner table, and he was served his meal.[30]

Although the *Houck* and *McGuinn* cases resulted in different outcomes, the underlying rule that determined both cases was identical.

Separate but equal accommodations that segregated passengers according to race were acceptable to the courts. The American judicial system beginning in the late Reconstruction era bowed to racial prejudice. As the judge in the McGuinn case explained, "[w]hen public sentiment demands a separation of passengers; it must be gratified to some extent."[31] Similarly, in the Houck case, the court remarked that the railway company had made a sufficient showing that the kind and character of the black clientele residing along the train route and most likely to be passengers warranted the railway's management to require by its rules a rear car for the exclusive use of white passengers. While separation of the races could be authorized by law, first-class passengers of both races had to be offered first-class accommodations. In discrimination lawsuits, like the Houck and McGuinn cases, the plaintiff's factual scenario would figure prominently in determining the outcome.

Even though Lola and Leon Houck successfully confronted racial discrimination, their legal victory was primarily personal with limited implications for improving race relations and conditions for African Americans in Victoria, Texas. Trial testimony revealed that following that incident in 1886, the Southern Pacific Railroad Company began allowing African American women to sit in the ladies' car, but still the very existence of a Jim Crow car negatively stigmatized the black race. Judge Boarman's opinion in the Houck case advised railroad companies that while they could separate African American passengers, those separate accommodations had to be commensurate with the accommodations available to white passengers. Yet, at the same time, the Houcks and many other African Americans rejected the notion of separate but equal accommodations aboard public transportation and in all other spheres of public life. In asserting their citizenship rights, Lola and Leon Houck had responded to discriminatory treatment aboard the Southern Pacific train by filing a lawsuit against the company. Their ultimate goal was an extension of first-class citizenship rights in the form of open seating to all persons irrespective of race. As the historical record reveals, it would take nearly another half century—well into the modern civil rights era—before that goal would be realized.[32]

## NOTES

1. According to census data, the African American population in 1880 was 6,581,000. By 1900, it had increased to 8,834,000. See Darlene Clark Hine and William Hine, *The African American Odyssey* (Upper Saddle River, New Jersey: Prentice Hall, 2003), appendix 31.

2. David Delaney, *Race, Place and the Law: 1836–1948* (Austin: University of Texas Press, 1998), 98–99; Janice Sumler-Edmond, "The Quest for Justice: African American Women Litigants, 1867–1890," 100–119, in *African American Women and the Vote, 1837–1965*, ed. Anne D. Gordon et al. (Amherst: University of Massachusetts Press, 1997).

3. Editorial, *Victoria Advocate*, April 13, 1890; John Hope Franklin and Alfred A. Moss Jr., *From Slavery to Freedom*, 7th edition (New York: Alfred A. Knopf, 1994), 259–63. For a discussion of slavery in Texas and its impact on the postbellum era, see Randolph Campbell, *An Empire for Slavery: The Peculiar Institution in Texas, 1821–1865* (Baton Rouge: Louisiana State University Press, 1989), 258–59.

4. See *Houck v. Southern Pacific Railway Company*, 38 Federal Reporter 226 (1888).

5. See W. E. B. DuBois, *The Souls of Black Folk: Essays and Sketches* (New York: Library of America, 1903). The members of the Ennis family were listed in the U.S. Census records for Galveston County for 1870 and 1880. The census records may be viewed at the Texas State Library and Archives Commission in Austin, Texas.

6. *Houck* case testimony in the Circuit Court of the United States for the Fifth Circuit, Eastern District of Texas at Galveston, March term 1887, National Archives, Fort Worth, Texas; testimony of Lola Houck, pp. 1, 6, and 13; testimony of Leon Houck, 57–58. Leon L. Houck appeared on the tax rolls for Victoria County, Texas, in 1890 (Tax Rolls for 1846–1893, Reel 12–3501, Texas State Library and Archives Commission). He paid a total of $6.03 in state and county taxes that year. For marriage, see Marriage Records for Galveston County, Texas, February 18, 1885, microfilm reels 1008863 and 1008867, Texas Local History Department, Houston Public Library. The Houcks are listed in *Fourny's General Directory for the City of*

*Galveston*, 1884–1885 and 1886–1887 (Galveston, Texas: M. Strickland and Company, 1885, 1887). Cited hereafter as Galveston *General Directory*).

7. *Houck*, testimony of Lola Houck, 1–2, 4, 6, 10; Leon Houck, 57.

8. See *Houck*.

9. *Houck*: testimony of Lola Houck, 2–5. The law firms were listed in the Galveston *General Directory* for 1884–1885.

10. *Houck*, testimony of Lola Houck, 9; Charles Oaks, 28–33; Fester Farnsworth, 42–43.

11. Ron Tyler, ed., *The New Handbook of Texas* (Austin: Texas State Historical Association, 1996), 852; James D. Lynch, *The Bench and Bar of Texas* (Nixon-Jones: St. Louis, Missouri, 1885), 404, 408–409; Charles S. Morse, ed., *Proceedings of the Texas Bar Association at Its Organization Session* (Galveston, Texas: Printed by Order of the Association, 1882), 1–3, 21–24, State Bar of Texas, Governor Bill and Vara Daniel Center for Legal History, Austin, Texas. See also holdings at the Texas State Law Library, Tom C. Clark Building, Austin. The addresses for the law offices of Labatt & Noble and Waul & Walker *were listed in the Galveston* General Directory.

12. *Houck* case records, Petition of Leon L. Houck and Lola Houck; *Houck*, testimony of Oaks, 37–38.

13. *Houck*, testimony of Lola Houck, 3.

14. *Houck*, direct examination of Charles J. W. Johnson, 21–22.

15. Ibid., 23–25.

16. *Houck*, testimony of Johnson, 22; Leon Houck, 57–58; H. J. Labatt, 60–61.

17. *Houck*, testimony of Oaks, 28.

18. Ibid.

19. Ibid., 28–30; testimony of Farnsworth, 40–42.

20. *Houck*, re-direct examination by the court; and testimony of Farnsworth, 48–49.

21. *Houck*, testimony of B. B. Creary, 50–51.

22. *Houck*, testimony of Lola Houck, 12.

23. Ibid., 16.

24. *Houck*, 229.

25. Ibid.

26. Ibid.

27. *Houck*, testimony of Oaks, 32; jury verdict on December 11, 1888 (J. S. Brown, foreman); *Houck*, 229.

28. *Houck*; *Plessy v. Ferguson*, 163 U.S. 537 (1896).

29. *McGuinn v. Forbes et al.*, 37 Federal Reporter 639 (1888).

30. *McGuinn*, 641.

31. Ibid.

32. *Houck*, testimony of Lola Houck, 15–17; Leon Houck, 57–58. See also Janice Sumler-Edmond, "Quest for Justice," 101, 108–111.

# The Colored Trainmen of America

## *Kingsville Black Labor and the Railroads*

JENNIFER BORRER

SOUTH TEXAS URBANIZED LATER THAN MANY parts of the state due to geographical conditions such as the lack of an available water source and sparse vegetation. Technological advances of the day such as barbed wire and windmills closed the open range and aided the area's cattle ranches. The availability of water and the flourishing cattle and farming industries attracted settlers to the area. But there were more reasons for urbanization in South Texas. Settlers needed a method of transportation to move their goods to a market. It was the railroad that created many South Texas towns, one of which was Kingsville. In 1900, B. F. Yoakum, general manager of the San Francisco Railway, and Uriah Lott, South Texas transport industry entrepreneur, united to build a railroad in the Rio Grande Valley. At the same time, the King Ranch needed a way to transport cattle to markets in other areas of the United States. Robert Justus Kleberg Sr., son-in-law of Henrietta King, owner of the King Ranch, joined Yoakum in 1902 and planned to build the St. Louis, Brownsville and Mexico Railway (SLB&M). It was chartered January 12, 1903.[1] In June of the same year, the construction plans were finalized in a contract.[2] Landowners between Corpus Christi and Brownsville supplied the land on which the track was laid. Henrietta King granted 76,675.[4] acres, more than any other donor.[3] After the completion of the railroad Jeff N. Miller, general manager of the SLB&M, brought the first train to Kingsville July 4, 1904.4

In giving his account of the arrival of the first train Marcus Phillips, an early resident of Kingsville, stated, "The principle signs of civilization at Kingsville were the tents of [railroad] construction crews."

He also remembered that a crowd of about 300 people gathered at the depot to witness the arrival of that initial run.[5] With the railway came hundreds of railroad employees who would work on the trains themselves, in the repair shops, and in the general offices that were to be constructed in Kingsville.

Due to the large tract of land donated by the King Ranch and the involvement of her son-in-law, Robert Kleberg, Henrietta King exercised tremendous influence on the development of the town of Kingsville. King gave 853 acres of land upon which to plan and build the townsite of Kingsville.[6] King also supplied land to churches, established the Kingsville Publishing Company, financed the Kingsville Power Company, and dispensed funds for construction of a school for the community.[7] She was involved extensively in almost every aspect of the development of infrastructure in the town. Her philanthropic nature even sparked rumors in "The Quarters," the black community in Kingsville, that she had demanded that the SLB&M employ only black brakemen and shop workers to work on the railroad.[8] No concrete evidence exists that King actually made this demand, but her legendary status and importance to the community supported this rumor.

Kingsville's black community drew its lifeblood from the SLB&M railway. There were few jobs available for African Americans, and most that did exist were manual labor jobs. Of those, the most lucrative was work on the railroad. This was the vocation of most of the men living in The Quarters of Kingsville. Brakeman Woodie Horn said, "Mostly all the jobs blacks had in Kingsville were railroad jobs. Practically all Negroes worked there, and this is the reason why the railroad made such a big impact on our community. . . . Even the school teachers didn't make the kind of money we did on the railroad."[9] Employment by the railroad made it easier for African Americans living in The Quarters to combat the poverty that threatened most blacks in the South, who often had neither the education, connections, nor opportunities for upward mobility. Railroad employment was also more stable than other occupations accessible by African Americans, and these jobs led to better housing, improved education, and higher status within the black community.[10]

Working for the railroad was comparatively lucrative for Kingsville's black citizens, but it was also often dangerous and unpredictable. When the SLB&M filed its yearly report with the Texas Railroad Commission, reports of accidents were included. In 1918, black brakemen were injured in thirteen of twenty-one train accidents. In 1919, brakemen were injured in four of fifteen train accidents, but in 1920 and 1921, more than half of the train injuries involved brakemen. One black brakeman, William Moseley, lost the tips of his third through fifth fingers on one hand, and all of the fourth and fifth fingers on the other hand. In addition, he dislocated his wrist. Trainmen also suffered concussions and scalding by steam and eye injuries caused by hot sand and gravel, and they had cargo dropped on them while unloading cars.[11] Life as a railway brakeman was dangerous.

The neighborhood these men lived in did not offer the peace of geographical distance from life on the railroad. The Quarters was located on twenty city blocks in the southwest corner of the original townsite in close proximity to the railroad and its shops.[12] In 1913 the King Ranch built shotgun houses there for the families of black railworkers and the SLB&M allowed purchase of the homes through payroll deduction.[13]

The railroad did not always provide consistent work for Kingsville's black employees. Many were forced to find second jobs to supplement their income. A small business district within The Quarters existed at the intersection of Huisache and Second Street.[14] Some people whose income came mainly from the railroad also opened grocery stores, bars, and taxi companies.[15] This segregated community, along with its churches and businesses, thrived as long as the railroad prospered.

The SLB&M and all other rail carriers were drastically affected by the onset of World War I. Railroad unions, which had organized in the 1860s and 1870s, eventually became entrenched in the industry. They were powerful, and they excluded blacks from their membership.[16] Left unprotected, blacks had little choice but to comply with whims of the carrier if they wished to keep the only profitable jobs available to them.

The Bureau of Census indicated that in 1910, 93.4 percent of black railworkers in Texas (9,070), were employed as laborers.[17] African American men did most of the heavy labor on Texas railroads. Until World War I it was not uncommon to find a black fireman working in the same car with a white engineer. Railway companies used black firemen and trainmen (brakemen, switchmen, or flagmen) on 25 to 90 percent of train runs across the South.[18] African Americans worked in these areas primarily because it was dirty work and whites did not wish to do it.

World War I prompted a migration that led to better conditions and pay for blacks working in the railway industry. Many blacks migrated north to work in war industries, such as shipyards, for better pay. Some even went north for better compensation working for other railway carriers. There were many black farmworkers in the South who were recruited by northern railroads. One officer of the Illinois Central Railroad said, "We took black labor out of the South until it hurt." The result was that the tracks in the South fell into disrepair because of the shortage of experienced labor.[19] This situation created the potential for a serious problem on Kingsville's railroad. There was a threat that their pliable black labor force might also leave the area. This, in combination with the fact that there were few blacks in all of South Texas, must have alarmed the SLB&M executives.

Because of economic, military, and political necessities, the United States government had to keep the railroads operating in wartime. Therefore, due to labor shortages, the government took over operation of the entire American railroad industry. Furthermore, in 1918, provisions were made nationally that made the industry more attractive to blacks. On May 25, 1918, Director General William G. McAdoo of the United States Railroad Administration issued General Order 27 equalizing wages for blacks and whites doing comparable railway work. He referred to this order as "an act of simple justice."[20] It was more like an act of preservation considering that this was never attempted before the labor shortage. Wages for Texas blacks overall increased 20 to 25 percent due to the migration of blacks to the northern part of the United States.[21] So African Americans made significant economic gains due to demands for their labor during wartime.

Black trainmen used the opportunity of the wartime situation and the scarcity of labor to improve their working conditions. Many times a white engineer would choose to have a black fireman work with him rather than a white fireman. Engineers often demanded extra labor from these men that white firemen would not do, such as shining shoes, chopping wood, or carrying groceries. Due to their restricted options outside the railroad industry, black firemen felt that their jobs would be in danger if they refused these tasks. African Americans tolerated these duties until 1918 when, due to their newfound value to the war-time economy, they felt they had the opportunity to object. Blacks lodged angry complaints with the United States Railroad Administration claiming these practices abridged the right to equal treatment given them by wartime regulations.[22]

In 1918, black railworkers in Texas were in short supply and high demand. They had a window of opportunity through which they could possibly influence future working conditions. They could make demands on the rail carriers that would legally provide them leverage—they could unionize. But what would happen if Kingsville brakemen did so? They could not join the existing railroad labor organization in Kingsville. The Brotherhood of Railway Trainmen (BRT) was a white union that had a formal race bar. Blacks were not allowed to join. Residual animosity toward blacks in the South meant that most unions established in the late 1800s, like the BRT, were not integrated.[23] Black competition for jobs that whites wanted meant that the white brotherhoods would adopt a strategy to preserve their interests.

This was complicated because, after World War I, unions grew and demanded that seniority rights on the railroad govern promotions and job placement. This assured that blacks, who could not be promoted to higher positions, would have seniority for manual jobs such as firemen. Engineers needed experience as firemen before they could be promoted but, since they were white, they had less seniority than blacks who had always done this work.

The white brotherhoods had to make a choice. They could do away with the seniority system, promote blacks, or attempt to have blacks removed from the railroad completely. They chose the latter.[24]

Not only did blacks in Kingsville not have the option to join the BRT, it was likely that the Brotherhood would act to remove them when and if whites wanted their jobs. Furthermore, if Kingsville blacks organized their own labor union, they would certainly face opposition from both the carrier and the BRT.

Still another complication involved the lack of consensus among black railway workers as to the wisdom of unionizing. For example, some black workers argued that union membership would strengthen their bargaining power and help them circumvent white trickery.[25] But some conservative national black leaders opposed unionization.[26] One such leader visited Kingsville and attempted to discourage the move to unions by stressing the real possibility of job loss.[27]

Even so, other groups of blacks who organized independent labor unions experienced some success. In 1870, a longshoremen's black local in Galveston came to represent all longshoremen. Apparently the white local went out on strike demanding that no black labor be used on the wharf at all. They were replaced by blacks leaving the black local as sole representative of longshoremen there.[28] But, in another labor conflict, when forty black truck drivers went out on strike in 1919, they were replaced by whites.[29] Despite the mixed record, Kingsville's black brakemen made the choice to organize a union to represent themselves.

In 1918, the black railworkers of the SLB&M formed the Colored Trainmen of America (CTA). Their charter was filed with the secretary of state, George F. Howard, June 13, 1918. This document stated that their purpose was "to promote the condition and welfare of colored trainmen and to elevate their social, moral, and intellectual standing and welfare."[30] They composed a constitution establishing a grand lodge to lead the organization and make provisions for local lodges upon their development. The full membership elected grand lodge officers, and local members elected local officers. The constitution outlined financial, grievance, and election procedures in detail.[31] The two most active local lodges were Local 1 in Kingsville and Local 2 in DeQuincy, Louisiana.

The activities of rail carriers and external events impacted the success of the CTA. Often the mitigating factor guiding labor policies of the rail carriers was the existence of either a labor shortage or a labor surplus. A labor shortage in the railroad industry occurred during and shortly after World War I, and a more brief and less important shortage marked the World War II era. But a significant labor surplus plagued the railroad industry in the 1930s and the introduction of the diesel locomotive exacerbated the surplus by causing a decrease in the workforce after World War II.

In 1925, the Missouri Pacific Railroad (MoPac) bought the Gulf Coastal Lines of which the SLB&M was a part.[32] At this time, the railroad industry was prospering due to the lack of competition it had enjoyed up to this point, but as the trucking and bus transport industries developed, the railroads began to lose business. This, in combination with the Great Depression, meant less business for rail carriers. During this era in Kingsville, operations in the companies' repair shops were reduced due to national economic conditions.[33] Evidence of more pervasive cutbacks exists in the fact that after this time, the number of railworkers throughout Texas decreased dramatically. This decrease disproportionately affected white railworkers.[34] Consequently, tension grew where white railroad unions observed their numbers dwindling disproportionately in comparison to their black counterparts.

The community of Kingsville witnessed some of this tension. By the turn of the century most all of the brakemen on the Gulf Coastal Lines, of which Kingsville was a part, were black.[35] Railworkers across the nation formed labor unions to protect their employment. Meanwhile, even though black railworkers sought the same protection, they were denied membership in those organizations, particularly in the unions that originated in the South. Railway labor unions chartered in the South were not only fraternal but social organizations.[36] These men were friends whose families formed a social community. But this was not a community that accepted blacks as social equals; therefore blacks were not allowed entry to the unions.

One of these white brotherhoods was the BRT, which had a local lodge located in Kingsville. Several of its members also belonged to the Davy Crockett Lodge #10 of the Ku Klux Klan. Between 1919 and 1920, there were special KKK trains that ran from Kingsville twice a year on which only members of Kingsville's KKK were allowed. Black brakemen were not permitted to work on these special train runs, which normally had four or five carloads of Klan members.[37] The extent to which racial tension affected events on SLB&M is difficult to discern. It is important to note that negative racial attitudes not only hampered black membership in labor unions, but also altered railroad operations. The existence of these special trains by the rail carrier resulted in a loss of income for black brakemen who could not work on KKK trains. This example suggested the possibility that race played a part in other decisions made by SLB&M management and other employees.

Race also played an unusual role on the outcome of a CTA repair shop strike in 1922. Traditionally, the philosophy of labor unions required solidarity of all workers to facilitate bargaining success with a company. If workers were not united, a company could use one group of its workers to undermine the efforts of another group making demands. Eric Arnesen, one student of black railroad unions, concluded that white union officials knew that their employers wanted to use black labor to prevent labor disputes by operating an alternating scheme—supporting one at times, and then the other.[38] Strangely, in this case, the separation of workers based upon race on the SLB&M worked to the advantage of the CTA in its efforts to gain better pay and working conditions.

In the early twenties, CTA brakemen and shopmen worked for less pay than their white counterparts and labored in terrible working conditions. Ed Erard, a white citizen of Kingsville, recalled that black brakemen were receiving about two dollars per day and were living away from home at least half of the time.[39] Brakemen were also forced to purchase special fifty-dollar watches, with their own money, to use on the job. They also received no pay for deadhead time (on empty trains returning to Kingsville after a train run).[40] In 1922, railroad business was booming and the SLB&M highly valued the cheap labor of these black brakemen and shopmen. Being aware of this, the CTA chose to strike to obtain better pay and working conditions.

The members of the CTA knew exactly when to go out on strike because national union leaders sent a telegram to them saying, "The sun shall not rise tomorrow."[41] Once the strike began, the carrier asked the BRT to send its men to do the work of the striking brakemen and shopmen. The white workers refused because the work done by black trainmen was considered by whites to be a "black job."[42] Whites in the BRT did not want to set a precedent that they would be willing to do this work. Whites wanted to begin work as conductors, not shopmen, and agreeing to do the work of shopmen would have reduced their potential earnings.[43]

During the strike one conductor even told two other white railworkers, "You can't couple an air hose or read a signal"—both duties of black railworkers in Kingsville. The BRT would not do the work of either brakemen or shopmen. Someone had to do this work, so the auditors sent its clerks to do the work. Ed Erard recalled that this, "tied up everything but the mail."[44]

Erard aided in ending this strike. He met with the CTA and convinced their leaders to meet with the carrier's superintendent to appeal for better pay and working conditions. This appeal took place just as two of the inexperienced clerks tied up a passenger train at the Kingsville depot.[45] Jerry Morrison, a porter, was a spokesman for blacks during the strike. The CTA successfully negotiated a raise in pay from sixty dollars per month to one hundred dollars per month.[46]

The rail carrier in Kingsville needed these men and had little choice but to succumb to their demands. When the SLB&M's superintendent signed the agreement ending the strike, one CTA member asked, "Are you sure you're authorized to sign this for the company? Is you sure you're qualified to write your name on this paper?"[47] Horace Cayton and George Mitchell, scholars of black unionism, stated, "Appealing to road officials on a grievance is dangerous. It involves the probability of incurring the displeasure of local officials and white craftsmen, with a consequent possibility of physical violence being used against any Negro who attempts it."[48] Apparently, the CTA knew how valuable blacks were to the industry and were willing to risk angering their employees.

There were more workers in the railroad industry in the early 1920s than at any other time in its history.[49] Consequently, white railroad employees were able to choose which jobs they wanted to do, and blacks dominated the jobs that required heavy labor and for which whites did not apply. These were essential occupations on the railroad. The CTA used its dominance in these occupations, and its awareness that whites would not do this work, to its advantage. The attitudes of the BRT, a high demand and short supply of labor, and the cohesiveness of the CTA as an organization, made this strike against the SLB&M a success for black brakemen and shopmen.

The economic success for the SLB&M between 1918, the year the CTA originated, and 1922, the year of the strike, is documented in the growth of payroll figures. In 1912 the total for monthly payroll figures was $26,000; in 1917 it was $40,000, and in 1922 it bulged to a staggering $194,288.[50] During this period of growth the CTA bargained with the rail carrier on numerous occasions and negotiated at least four working agreements for better working conditions and pay. The most important of these was finalized January 1, 1929, the same year that the CTA added a new local lodge, located in DeQuincy, Louisiana, to its membership.[51]

Enforcement of this 1929 agreement with the SLB&M was guaranteed for one year. The agreement guaranteed rates of pay, based on mileage, at about five dollars per day. It also promised pay for deadheading, which these brakemen had never before received. Brakemen with the highest levels of seniority chose the train runs they wished to work before brakemen with less seniority. It gave CTA members rights to work in the yard and established a procedure for brakemen who wished to file grievances with the company.[52]

One of the more important aspects of the 1929 agreement was Article 15 outlining the makeup of crews (the number of CTA brakemen who would always be assigned to work on each train). It guaranteed that three specified types of trains would be furnished with two black brakemen. The yard crews would consist of one CTA engine foreman and two helpers. Consequently, as long as the agreement was in effect, the Colored Trainmen of America would be guaranteed work. The only way the carrier could deny them work was if the railroad abolished their positions completely due to natural attrition.[53]

There were, however, several problems with the 1929 agreement. The brakemen of the CTA could only eat lunch if the rest of the crew decided to do so. The SLB&M provided no regular lunch break to CTA members. Also, the carrier only provided twenty minutes for a lunch break when other workers on a train decided to eat lunch. In previous agreements black trainmen had received thirty minutes. The carrier also reserved the right to ignore seniority and select from the ranks any brakemen to work on "special trains such as Director's Specials, other inspection trains, and trains for lodge members.[54] The KKK trains were one example of special trains. This could have been problematic for blacks if the carrier decided to designate a large portion of trains as "special." The SLB&M could use this clause to eliminate blacks from service completely.[55]

Another problem existed in a clause in Article 11 concerning reductions and increases in forces: "Reductions and increases to the extra board, (those who stand by to fill in as brakemen on train runs on an as-needed basis), will be made by the company as business demands always eliminating the man with least seniority first." Many CTA brakemen worked the extra board and could be fired by the carrier easily without explanation. This meant that the agreement did not secure the employment of many CTA brakemen. Finally, in Article 25, members of this extra board were forced to provide themselves with proper uniforms, but the company would not pay for them. This meant that members of the extra board had little job security, and if they worked they were penalized further by being required to pay for their own uniforms.[56]

This agreement between the CTA and the SLB&M reflected the time period in which it was reached. It was an accomplishment for both the black trainmen and the rail carrier. Both received guarantees they later used to force change on the other. The ambiguous nature of this agreement highlighted a turning point in the life of the SLB&M of which both negotiating parties may have been aware.

Blacks made tremendous employment gains from 1910 to 1930. During that period they more than doubled their share of jobs in the railroad shops.[57] This prosperity dwindled quickly in the 1930s during the Great Depression. The black man went from a highly valued employee on the railroad to begging for work. This changed the relationship between the CTA and its rail carrier.

The fact that the CTA existed as an organized labor union in 1930s was remarkable. According to historian Alwyn Barr, black laborers in all fields remained mostly unorganized due to the opposition from both employers and white-controlled unions.[58] Between 1930 and 1940 employment of white railworkers in Texas decreased much more than employment of blacks.[59] Due to this fact, the CTA faced not only job reductions in a depressed economy but the resentment and opposition of white brotherhoods like the BRT whose members were collectively losing more jobs than their black counterparts. Further employment reductions occurred in the 1930s due to new competition for railroads from the infant trucking and bus transport companies that provided both passenger and freight services.[60] Knowing their limited value to an employer who expected them to work cheaply and that their economy was waning, the CTA tried to help its members keep their jobs. It did so by attempting to force the SLB&M, which became the Missouri Pacific Railroad (MoPac) in the early 1930s, to honor its 1929 agreement.

In the 1930s, one area of employment in Kingsville's railway industry that stood the least chance of job reductions was the repair shops. The railcars at this time were being equipped with air conditioning. This work, some of which was done in the Kingsville shops, was of such a high quality that MoPac officers from other states transferred their cars to Kingsville for outfitting and repairs.[61] The security of these jobs, as other railway jobs became more scarce, meant fierce competition from whites. Research concerning the repair shops of Alabama in the same time period reveals that many black shopworkers there were laid off during the 1930s while whites with less seniority were retained.[62] In light of this, it is no surprise to learn that C. O. Barney, a CTA member, recalled that in 1932 or 1933 over 135 blacks were fired in one day.[63] Willie Keno, a black woman in Kingsville, remembered that most blacks lost their jobs during the depression years. She also noted that the King Ranch provided meat every week or two for the unemployed, and that many African Americans found employment with the Works Progress Administration. They were paid fifty cents per day to dig ditches, trim bushes, build sidewalks, and build highways.[64]

Even though Kingsville's black railworkers were trapped by a bad economy that was getting worse, they continued to demand employment from the Missouri Pacific as well as the rights that had been guaranteed in their 1929 agreement. CTA Grand Chairman W. H. Jefferson wrote a letter to MoPac January 5, 1936, citing several concerns of black union members. He claimed that there were brakemen switching engines in the yard who were not being paid to do so.[65] This duty was the work of a class of service that received higher pay. Article 16 of the 1929 agreement specified that "Brakemen performing more than one class of service on a day or trip will be paid for the entire service at the highest rate of pay applicable to any service performed."[66] MoPac's reply on January 13, 1936, claimed that when the two duties performed were one yard and one road duty, this article did not apply.[67] Here the brakemen were denied higher pay by a stipulation that was not set forth in the 1929 working agreement.

Grand Chairman Jefferson again complained, but this time the topic was seniority rights for brakemen. MoPac violated these rights by allowing the names of the same white rail workers to be present on seniority lists for three different classes of service. Workers' names could only be on one seniority list at a time. Jefferson asked that the names of these white trainmen be removed from the seniority lists of the engine foremen and yard helpers.[68] MoPac refused to do so, saying nothing more than that the lists furnished were correct and they would not be altered. No change was in order.[69]

Still another disagreement occurred over pillow service provided by brakemen to passengers on the trains. Previously, brakemen owned pillows that they would allow passengers to use on long trips. In a conference, the CTA and MoPac agreed upon the pay that brakemen would receive for this service. After this verbal agreement, MoPac sent a letter to the CTA on July 28, 1936, outlining the conditions for payment. The CTA discovered the compensation terms guaranteed in the letter were less than the pay MoPac promised in the conference.[70] The CTA wrote MoPac of their dissatisfaction on July 30 and again on August 7 after receiving no reply.[71] Finally, MoPac replied on August 11, still refusing to pay rear brakemen for furnishing passengers with pillow service.[72] Unsatisfied, the CTA requested a meeting with the general manager of MoPac.[73] Its request was ignored by MoPac, so it wrote again on September 28.[74] MoPac then arranged a meeting for October 9, but canceled it October 6.[75] Finally, a conference was held in San Antonio on October 27. In the end, the CTA never received additional compensation for their brakemen who provided pillow service.

During this struggle the CTA wrote letters twice to MoPac but received no response. MoPac's general manager canceled their meeting without rescheduling the conference until the CTA insisted. Its union members were forced to accept a compensation package that was unacceptable to them. After making multiple attempts to hold MoPac to its 1929 working agreement, and seeing 135 of their members fired in one day, it was logical for the CTA to accept the pay offered their brakemen for pillow service.[76]

By 1936, as the railroad industry was shrinking with the economy, keeping what few jobs were left was of ultimate importance to the CTA. The 1940s should have improved job availability for CTA members. If World War I increased the railroad's demand for black labor, World War II could have done the same. It did, but not to the extent that World War I boosted employment and wages in the railroad industry. An interview with a citizen of Kingsville revealed that black brakemen received a pay increase at some point during World War II.[77] This might indirectly imply that job availability for blacks increased. But the newspaper in Kingsville recorded that the pay increase was only due to a rise in the minimum wage.[78] The demand for labor on the railroad was not as high as it had been in World War I because there were other ways to transport goods and people.

As a result, in the 1940s the CTA was not often successful in its negotiations with MoPac. In July 1941 the black brakemen requested that MoPac porters in DeQuincy be paid the same as brakemen because they were loading and unloading freight and mail. Traditionally, porters were only responsible for loading and unloading passengers.[79] The practice of assigning additional duties was objectionable for two reasons. First, people performing work in the same class of service were not paid equally. This violated the CTA's 1929 working agreement with MoPac. Second, there was a rule that all porters must be neat and clean at all times. The Colored Trainmen of America argued that porters could not remain clean if they loaded and unloaded cars in their uniforms. In its response to the grievance, MoPac stated that porters in DeQuincy had always helped load and unload mail and it then declined to increase their pay.[80] In this response MoPac addressed none of the CTA's concerns. It openly refused to follow the working agreement with the CTA that required the highest pay for the highest class of service performed. Here MoPac also created an impossible situation for porters who were required to unload cars yet remain clean. This impossibility allowed the company to fire these men for cause at any time. The conflict was partially caused by the 1929 agreement that did not clearly define the duties of a brakeman or a porter. As a result, MoPac could claim that being a brakeman in DeQuincy required different duties than it did in Kingsville. In this instance, the 1929 agreement served as both blessing and curse.

The agreement had also fixed pay for brakemen based upon mileage traveled. This came back to haunt the CTA when, in 1942, it asked MoPac to pay brakemen for the time spent taking engines into the yard in Houston. MoPac responded by stating that these men were being paid for the two miles of the trip into the roundhouse. They would not obtain higher wages. This two-mile trip occupied one hour of time.[81] It was cheaper to have CTA brakemen do this duty than it was to pay members of the BRT by the hour to do it.

During the 1940s the Brotherhood of Railroad Trainmen obtained jobs as flagmen and brakemen on the MoPac. This work had always been done by blacks and BRT members had considered it black men's work. But a shrinking railroad economy forced them to take these positions in order to remain employed. In December 1946, the BRT negotiated with MoPac and were guaranteed some brakemen and flagmen positions for its members.[82] CTA Chairman W. H. Jefferson reminded MoPac that, according to the Railway Labor Act, which was made national law in the early 1930s, a carrier must give an organization thirty days' notice and set up a conference when jobs are taken away from that organization.[83] This was a futile effort on Jefferson's part. The BRT received some of the flagman and brakeman jobs. A shrinking railroad economy favored white employees over black employees.

Not only did whites have some "Negro jobs," they were paid more than blacks to do this same work. On January 15, 1946, MoPac and CTA met in Houston to discuss the issue. The trainmen proposed changes in pay for both brakemen and flagmen. The railway refused to consider the proposal until negotiations with other white brotherhoods were finalized. The CTA refused to wait, so a MoPac representative responded to the union in writing saying, "You stated that you were not agreeable to my suggestion, therefore, this is to advise you that your proposal for any change in rate, of pay, rules, or working conditions is denied."[84] By the 1940s the shrinking economy deprived the CTA of most of the bargaining power it had in the early 1920s. MoPac valued the black men only because they would work for less pay, making them an asset to an industry whose clientele was disappearing. By the late 1940s, it was fairly obvious that the CTA would not strike against the company to get better pay and working conditions. If it did, BRT members, also struggling in a degenerating rail industry, would now be willing to occupy any and all brakeman jobs. The CTA was virtually powerless in a time of labor surplus.

The railroad industry in the 1950s was marked by technological changes and further economic decline. Diesel engines were introduced to the industry and became widely used. CTA Grand President Jordan Jefferson wrote a column in every issue of the *Negro Railway Labor News*. For January and February 1950 he wrote, "The installation of diesels has hit us hard. Work for our trainmen and yardmen is down 38% as compared to last year. And the mechanical department has been cut 70%. Our railroad shops in Kingsville and DeQuincy are almost shut down completely. We now have brakemen on the extra board who have held regular jobs for the last ten years.[85]"

With these new engines, fewer men were required to operate a train. This necessitated more MoPac layoffs. The carrier also closed its accounting offices in Kingsville and the coach shop in 1958.[86] The railroad made deep personnel cuts in 1955 and attempted to consolidate its work forces in Houston in the same year.[87] Seniority lists compiled by the CTA during 1947, the first year diesel engines were employed on the Gulf Coastal Lines, show that there were 303 CTA brakemen; ten years later the seniority list only contained 182 brakemen—a reduction of almost half.

Very little correspondence occurred between MoPac and the Colored Trainmen of America in the 1950s. Few grievances were filed. CTA members were certainly losing their jobs, but they had no grounds to object. Their 1929 working agreement with MoPac allowed the carrier to eliminate any position due to natural attrition.[88]

Even further decline of railroad business occurred in the 1960s, hindering the economic progress of CTA members. When compared to the 1920s, 1968 marked a 60 percent decline in employment on the railroad including many black railroad workers in Kingsville. C. O. Barney stated that the black population there in 1928 was at least twice that of 1970.[89] In addition, use of other forms of transportation by consumers caused passenger service in Kingsville to be discontinued in 1966.[90] Furthermore, black railworkers were trapped in low-paying positions and were not promoted. When new machinery was placed on trains and in repair shops nationwide, management preferred to place the new and expensive machinery in the hands of whites, not blacks.[91] This led to further decline in the number of blacks employed by the railroad industry.

At the same time, major national events led to improvements for African Americans. By the 1960s schools were desegregated and the civil rights movement was at its peak. Consequently, blacks across the country had hope that they could achieve equal treatment in the workplace. Hopeful CTA members again attempted to propose a pay raise for brakemen in 1962.[92] MoPac again refused to consider these compensation matters until a national working agreement with the white brotherhoods was finalized. Awareness of the national political changes that occurred as a result of the civil rights movement moved the CTA to use this national settlement with white unions as a legal basis for their grievances with MoPac concerning equal pay and treatment.

A national railway strike in 1963 prompted the United States Congress to issue Public Law 88–108 forcing the embittered parties (rail carriers and white labor unions) into binding arbitration to resolve their differences. The resulting award of Special Adjustment Board #282, forcing rail carriers nationwide to succumb to some demands of the large railroad unions, could not be denied by either party. Normally, governmental mediation and arbitration results were not binding, but in this case, both the white brotherhoods and all rail carriers had to accept this arbitration award.[93]

CTA attempts to use this award to their advantage in negotiations was somewhat successful in the beginning. Black trainmen demanded pay and working conditions equal with that of the award. On May 25, 1964, MoPac announced in writing that it was prepared to deal with CTA grievances. Enclosed in this letter were copies of MoPac's new proposed agreement that gave more working rights to CTA members in Kingsville than those in DeQuincy. Also enclosed was a copy of a new work rule forcing the retirement of workers at age 65 instead of 70.[94] The CTA rejected both proposals and requested a meeting with MoPac's general manager to negotiate an agreement satisfactory to all CTA members.[95] The two parties conferred and conflicted over multiple issues. CTA Chairman Truett Tillmon stated that the proposal included nothing to protect the employees or to insure compliance by company officials. In light of these discrepancies, the CTA refused MoPac's proposal.[96]

MoPac then submitted another proposal to the CTA. It allowed for one CTA brakeman in every crew, in all classes of road service, and one CTA foreman and helper on yard engines doing yard transfer, beltline, or miscellaneous yard service.[97] The Colored Trainmen of America again refused MoPac's offer. It wanted two brakemen for all mainline service in Kingsville and DeQuincy.[98] MoPac's proposal excluded DeQuincy union members. MoPac responded by stating that the CTA's requests were unreasonable and that a guarantee of two black brakemen on all trains was not possible. MoPac then insisted that if any more negotiations were to take place the black trainmen must initiate them.[99] The CTA then wrote MoPac to remind the carrier that in failing to negotiate, it was refusing to uphold the guidelines of the award of Special Adjustment Board #282.

The CTA did not request another conference. CTA Grand President Tillmon wrote MoPac threatening to use the Special Adjustment Board #282 award to force it to negotiate.[100] Then he contacted CTA lawyers who arranged a meeting with MoPac on August 4, 1964.[101] After meeting with attorneys, the carrier submitted another proposal that again neglected black brakemen on the DeQuincy division.[102] Consequently, the CTA declined to accept it.[103] This refusal went without response from MoPac and the issue remained unresolved.

In the meantime, the CTA negotiated the details of a health and welfare group policy with Traveler's Insurance Group. Once completed, the CTA contacted MoPac to resume negotiations on five issues including a raise in pay, a health plan, improved pay for deadheading, a guaranteed extra board, and employee protection.[104] After receiving no reply, CTA Chairman Truett Tillmon wrote MoPac emphasizing that both should meet to resolve differences over the makeup of train crews. The CTA still wanted DeQuincy jobs protected and refused to sign any MoPac proposal that did not include it.[105] MoPac answered by reluctantly arranging a meeting in St. Louis, Missouri, January 11, 1965.[106]

At this meeting MoPac offered to increase vacation allowances, to increase pay $1.44 per day, and to add an expense allowance for train trips away from home. All of these were issued to whites in the Special Adjustment Board #282 award but up to this point had not previously been offered to the CTA. The Colored Trainmen of America requested that all of these new privileges be put in writing."[107] MoPac did refuse to grant it a health and welfare plan and the CTA asked them to reconsider this emphasizing that any final agreement must include such a plan.[108]

The CTA continued to write MoPac of its concerns over the inadequacies of all previously submitted MoPac agreement proposals. In a letter to MoPac's director of labor relations, the CTA summarized their contentions with prior proposals. It objected to the reduction of the CTA members working on train crews in the DeQuincy division, and it wanted a clearer definition of a "protected employee." The CTA opposed forced retirement at age 65 and asked that MoPac delay its decision on that issue. In this letter the black trainmen reminded MoPac of its obligation to uphold the Railway Labor Act and the award of Special Adjustment Board #282.[109]

MoPac's General Manager B. W. Smith responded, refuting points addressed by the CTA letter. In addition, he neglected to mention the health and welfare policy altogether.[110] Throughout this conflict MoPac attempted to stall the CTA. It offered some of the privileges it desired, but not others, and still others were left unmentioned. At times, MoPac representatives verbally granted guarantees that were never put in writing. The reason for this gamesmanship was revealed in a CTA letter dated March 11, 1965. The BRT had an agreement with MoPac that guaranteed that BRT brakemen worked the train runs out of DeQuincy and it could not promise an equal agreement to the CTA.[111] Rather than resolve its differences with the CTA, MoPac preferred to wait and hope that the black trainmen were impatient and frustrated enough to accept a working agreement that was less than what they desired.

MoPac finally responded offering an agreement that included a health and welfare plan.[112] This concession was designed to entice the CTA into signing a proposal that did not contain all they wanted. This new agreement forced brakemen to retire at age 65, did not include protection for DeQuincy brakemen, and did not clearly define a "protected employee."[113] CTA leaders refused to sign the agreement. They then contacted their attorney and submitted a complaint to the National Mediation Board.[114]

In conclusion, MoPac's interests revolved around profit, as do all private companies. The management of the carrier valued black workers because they would work for less pay, thereby increasing profits. As long as this was true, MoPac protected the employment of blacks to a degree but also knew they were trapped in one of the only industries that offered high pay to African Americans. Considering this, the CTA made important progress through its 1922 strike, 1929 working agreement, and privileges offered them in the 1960s. But, in the end, their success in negotiations with MoPac was very limited due to competition of the BRT, a shrinking railroad industry, and the resulting labor surplus in the industry.

## NOTES

1. Lisa Armitta Manheimer Neely, "The Value of a Handshake: The Controversy Surrounding the Location of the General Offices of the St. Louis, Brownsville and Mexico Railway" (master's thesis, Texas A&M University–Kingsville, 1994), 1–2.

2. Operating Agreement between Johnston Brothers and the St. Louis, Brownsville, and Mexico Railway, June 18, 1904, J. L. Allhands Collection, A 1963.14, Box 35, Folder 14, South Texas Archives (cited hereafter as STA), Texas A&M University–Kingsville.

3. Neely, "The Value of a Handshake," 3; Ben Wilson Jr., "Organization and Impact of the St. Louis, Brownsville, and Mexico Railroad" (master's thesis, Texas College of Arts & Industries, 1939), 36; J. L. Allhands, *Gringo Builders* (Dallas, Texas: privately printed, 1931), 85; James N. Krug, "The Kingsville Railroad Depot," *Journal of South Texas*, 8 (1995): 40–52.

4. Cecilia Aros Hunter and Leslie Gene Hunter, eds., *Historic Kingsville, Texas: Guide to the Original Townsites* (Kingsville: Kingsville Historical Development Board, 1994), 97; Ben Wilson Jr., "Organization and Impact of the St. Louis, Brownsville, and Mexico Railroad," 36.

5. Marcus Phillips, "Sketches of Early Days," Reference File: Marcus Phillips, STA; J. L. Allhands, *Railroad Stories* (Salado, Texas: Anson Jones Press), 70.

6. Neely, "The Value of a Handshake," 3. For additional information concerning the construction and operation of the St. Louis, Brownsville, and Mexico Railway, see the J. L. Allhands Collection, STA.

7. Neely, "The Value of a Handshake," 4–5; J. L. Allhands, *Uriah Lott* (San Antonio, Texas: Naylor, 1949), 136.

8. Annie Campbell Cornell, interview by Gene Brooks, June 10, 1989, interview 1989–26.13a and -b, typescript, South Texas Oral History and Folklore Collection, STA.

9. Woodie Hom Jr., interview by Gene Brooks, February 14, 1989, interview A1989, STA.

10. Howard W. Risher, *The Negro in the Railroad Industry* (Philadelphia: University of Pennsylvania Press, 1971), 1.

11. Annual Reports for St. Louis, Brownsville & Mexico Railroad to the Railroad Commission of State of Texas, 1918–1921, Record Group 455, Texas State Archives (cited hereafter as TSA), Austin, Texas.

12. Hunter and Hunter, eds., *Historical Kingsville*, 97.

13. Ibid.

14. Ibid, 98.

15. Annie Campbell Cornell, interview by Brooks.

16. Eric Arnesen, "'Like Banquo's Ghost, It Will Not Go Down': The Race Question and the American Railroad Brotherhoods, 1880–1920," *American Historical Review* 99, no. 5 (December 1994): 1609.

17. William Brophy, "The Black Texan, 1900–1950: A Quantitative History" (PhD diss., Vanderbilt University, 1974), 102.

18. Herbert R. Northup, *Organized Labor and the Negro* (New York: Periodicals Service Company, 1944), 49.

19. Risher, *The Negro in the Railroad Industry*, 38.

20. Ibid.

21. Alwyn Barr, *Black Texans: A History of African Americans in Texas 1528–1995*, 2nd ed. (Norman: University of Oklahoma Press, 1996), 150.

22. Arnesen, "'Like Banquo's Ghost,'" 1621.

23. Ray Marshall, *The Negro and Organized Labor* (New York: John Wiley, 1965), 92; Sterling D. Spero and Abram L. Harris, *The Black Worker: The Negro and the Labor Movement* (New York: Columbia University Press, 1931), 288.

24. Marshall, *The Negro and Organized Labor*, 243.

25. Horace R. Cayton and George S. Mitchell, *Black Workers and the New Unions* (Chapel Hill: University of North Carolina Press, 1939), 301.

26. Brophy, "The Black Texan," 154.

27. Evelyn Andrews, interview with Gene Brooks, July 6, 1989, interview 1989–26.21a and -b, typescript, South Texas Oral History Collection, STA.

28. Brophy, "The Black Texan," 159; Barr, *Black Texans*, 59–60.

29. Brophy, "The Black Texan," 156.

30. Colored Trainmen of America (cited hereafter as CTA) Constitution, April 6, 1918, CTA Papers, Metropolitan Research Center (cited hereafter as MRC), Houston Public Library.

31. Ibid.

32. Ibid., 139.

33. Neely, "The Value of a Handshake," 116.

34. Brophy, "The Black Texan," 97.

35. Arnesen, "'Like Banquo's Ghost,'" 1608.

36. Brophy, "The Black Texan," 152.

37. Charles Scott, interview by Dan Eggleston, July 28, 1970, typescript, Notes on the Black Community of Kingsville Collection, STA.

38. Arnesen, "'Like Banquo's Ghost,'" 1623.

39. *Kingsville Record*, October 16, 1963; Annual Reports of the St. Louis, Brownsville, and Mexico Railroad to the Commission of the State of Texas, 1918–1921, Record Group 455, TSA.

40. Ed Erard, interview by Dan Eggleston, August 13, 1970, typescript, Notes on the Black Community of Kingsville Collection, STA.

41. Ibid.

42. Ibid.

43. Ibid.

44. Ibid.

45. *Kingsville Record*, October 16, 1963.

46. Erard interview.

47. Ibid.

48. Cayton and Mitchell, *Black Workers and the New Unions*, 305.

49. Brophy, "The Black Texan," 97.

50. *Kingsville Record*, June 29, 1927.

51. C. O. Barney, interview by Dan Eggleston, July 2, 1970, typescript, Notes on the Black Community of Kingsville Collection, STA.

52. Agreement between the Colored Brakemen and the Management of Gulf Coast Lines, January 1, 1929, CTA Papers.

53. Ibid.

54. Ibid.

55. Ibid.

56. Ibid.

57. Risher, *The Negro in the Railroad Industry*, 46.

58. Barr, *Black Texans*, 151.

59. Brophy, "The Black Texan," 97.

60. Risher, *The Negro in the Railroad Industry*, 2–3.

61. George O. Coalson, "Kleberg County," *Handbook of Texas Online*, http://www.tshaonline.org/handbook/online/articles/KK/hck10.html.

62. Risher, *The Negro in the Railroad Industry*, 46.

63. Barney interview.

64. Willie Keno, interview by Dan Eggleston, July 9, 1970, typescript, Notes on the Black Community of Kingsville Collection, STA.

65. W. H. Jefferson to Superintendent G. C. Kennedy, January 5, 1936, CTA Papers.

66. Agreement between the Colored Brakemen and the Management of Gulf Coast Lines, January 1, 1929.

67. Gulf Coast Lines to W. H. Jefferson, January 15, 1936, CTA Papers.

68. W. H. Jefferson to Superintendent G. C. Kennedy, January 5, 1936, CTA Papers.

69. Gulf Coast Lines to W. H. Jefferson, January 15, 1936, CTA Papers.

70. L. A. David to W. H. Jefferson, July 28, 1936, CTA Papers.

71. Ibid., July 30, 1936, CTA Papers (MRC); L. A. David to W. H. Jefferson, August 7, 1936, CTA Papers.

72. W H. Jefferson to L. A. David, August 11, 1936, CTA papers.

73. Ibid., August 14, 1936, CTA Papers.

74. Ibid., September 28, 1936, CTA Papers.

75. L. A. David to W. H. Jefferson, October 2, 1936, CTA Papers; G. C. Kennedy to H. F. Gwin, October 6, 1936, CTA Papers.

76. L. A. David to W. H. Jefferson, October 3, 1936, CTA Papers; W. H. Jefferson to L. A. David, October 24, 1936, CTA Papers; L. A. David to W. H. Jefferson, October 31, 1936, CTA Papers.

77. Harry Murray, interview by Dan Eggleston, July 9, 1970, typescript, Notes on the Black Community of Kingsville Collection, STA.

78. *Kingsville Record*, February 27, 1941.

79. CTA General Chairman to A. B. Kelly, July 7, 1941, CTA Papers.

80. A. B. Kelly to W. H. Jefferson, July 10, 1941, CTA Papers.

81. Ibid., February 16, 1942, CTA Papers (MRC); CTA General Chairman to A. B. Kelly, February 6, 1942, CTA Papers.

82. Brotherhood of Railroad Trainmen (BRT) Working Agreement with MoPac, 1943, CTA Papers.

83. Jefferson to Gregory, December 15, 1943.

84. A. B. Simmons to Superintendent H. Johnson, August 29, 1944; H. E. Hall to Amos Hayes, January 19, 1946.

85. *New York Negro Railway Labor News*, January–February, 1950.

86. *Kingsville Record*, February 26 and July 2, 1958; for additional information concerning MoPac shops and general offices see Neely, "The Value of a Handshake."

87. *Kingsville Record*, October 18, 1972.

88. Risher, *The Negro in the Railroad Industry*, 14.

89. Barney interview.

90. *Kingsville Record*, January 5, 1966; for additional information about changes in railroad service, including passenger service to Kingsville, see James Krug, "The Kingsville Railroad Depot," *Journal of South Texas* 8 (1995): 40–52.

91. Cayton and Mitchell, *Black Workers*, 287.

92. B. W. Smith to H. C. Caraway, June 25, 1962; E. C. Thompson to Caraway, June 27, 1962; Caraway to B. Smith, July 2, 1962; Caraway to B. Smith, August 1, 1962.

93. Public Law 88–109, *U.S. Statutes at Large*, 77 (1963), 132–33; Special Board of Adjustment Established under Arbitration Board No. 282 between MoPac and the BRT, CTA Papers (MRC); Risher, *The Negro in the Railroad Industry*, 46.

94. B. Smith to T. V. Tillmon, May 25 1964.

95. Tillmon to B. Smith, May 30, 1964.

96. B. Smith to Tillmon, June 22, 1964.

97. lbid.

98. Tillmon to J. C. Love, July I5 1964.

99. D. J. Smith to Tillmon, July 17, 1964.

100. Tillmon to Missouri Pacific Railroad, July 22, 1964.

101. Tillmon to B. Smith, July 30, 1964.

102. Ibid.

103. B. Smith to Tillmon, August 6, 1964

104. Tillmon to B. Smith, November 19, 1964.

105. Ibid., December 4, 1964.

106. B. Smith to Tillmon, December 24, 1964.

107. Tillmon to B. Smith, January 26, 1965.

108. Ibid., January 29, 1965.

109. B. Smith to Tillmon, February 15, 1965.

110. Ibid., April 5, 1965.

111. Ibid., March 11, 1965.

112. Ibid., April 5, 1965.

113. Ibid.

114. Tillmon to B. Smith.

# Divided We Stand

## *Jim Crow Education in Victoria, Texas, 1901–1966*

EDWARD BYERLY[1]

IN 1849, BENJAMIN ROBERTS, A BLACK RESIDENT of Boston, Massachusetts, brought suit against the city's public school committee on grounds that his daughter, Sarah, had been denied equal access to public schooling because of her race. Sarah Roberts walked past no fewer than five primary schools on her way to the city's lone black school in 1849, and her father argued that the school committee's refusal to allow his daughter to attend a school closer to home violated state law. Famed abolitionist and future senator Charles Sumner argued Roberts's case before the Massachusetts Supreme Court, but the Court ruled against Sumner, finding that Sarah Roberts had not been denied access to public schooling as she was quite free to enroll in the city's schools for black children. In ruling against her, the Court effectively conceded to the school district power to classify students by race, religion, or national origin, and assign them to schools accordingly. In years to come, *Roberts v. the City of Boston* would be cited by state courts throughout the country, and in 1896 it served as principal test case in the *Plessy v. Ferguson* ruling that established the federal "separate but equal" standard.[2]

In Texas, lawmakers laid a foundation for public school segregation in the state constitution of 1876. Article seven, section seven stipulated that "[s]eparate schools shall be provided for the white and colored children, and impartial provision shall be made for both." Though the constitution required an impartial provision of resources among black and white schools, it did not expressly forbid black children from attending white schools. In order to establish a more concrete expression of segregation, in 1879 the state enacted a civil statute that specifically prohibited black and white children from attending the same school.[3] Thus by 1896, when the federal courts affirmed the separate but equal doctrine, Jim Crow school laws had been on the books in Texas for almost two decades. Up to that time, black schools typically had been administered as pay schools by humanitarian and religious organizations and were largely independent of public oversight.[4] That was certainly the case in Victoria, Texas, where members of the Palestine Baptist Church and the local chapter of the United Brothers of Friendship organized schools for black children in the years immediately after the Civil War. In 1898, two years after the *Plessy* decision, civic leaders in Victoria initiated a consolidation movement designed to create a city-wide public school district. The Victoria Independent School District (VISD) was born. The first board of trustees consisted of prominent citizens including J. M. Brownson (president), F. B. Lander (secretary), J. D. Mitchell, G. H. Hauschild, and C. S. Thurmond. State law placed both white and black schools under the board's administrative authority, meaning that it now assumed responsibility for overseeing a segregated school system.[5]

Located in the heart of a thriving agricultural region that catered especially to cattle ranching, Victoria was a city that relied heavily on black and Mexican residents for labor. Ranchers and local businessmen employed workers in a variety of different capacities, and it was critical that the new public school system mold young people into competent yet compliant workers. Shaping the community's black youth, however, posed special challenges. It had been more than thirty years since the end of slavery and a new generation of black Victorians was coming of age. To this new generation, slavery was a relic of the past, one they knew only through stories they heard told among their elders. Protocols including deference to whites were worth challenging as a growing sense of intellectual independence gave them strength. The new-found sense of intellectual independence, however, posed a threat to long-standing social order in the community, and among the city's white patriarchs, control of the school district's black students came at a critical time in the city's history. African American education was an issue that certainly concerned young Leopold Morris, editor of the *Victoria Advocate*. Purchased by George Henry French in 1901, the *Advocate* had served as a voice of stability in preserving the city's social order since 1846. Like many white southerners Morris feared that a literate black citizenry would bring a demise of southern society. In a March 1903 issue of the paper he used the words "frank" and "logical" to describe the views of South Carolina's notoriously bigoted congressman, Senator Benjamin "Pitchfork" Tillman. He quoted Tillman directly, writing, "[e]very man who can look beyond his nose can see that, with negroes constantly going to school, the increasing number of people who can read and write among the colored race will in time encroach upon and reach and overbalance our white men."[6]

Morris realized that black intellectual independence would lead to political empowerment, and he warned against that development. In August of 1903 he stated his own position with respect to the place of blacks in society. "The people of the South have no ill will against the negro. They oppose the potentiality of his bulk in local government because . . . he does not know, and but few of his kind ever can know, the ethics and import of a citizen's political duties. But if the negro will labor he will always find work and wages sufficient to make him the most independent and happiest of the labor classes in the world."[7] To men like Morris, African American education should channel students away from intellectual pursuits and into vocational programs to produce the kind of workforce that local employers needed. Toward this end, in 1901 the city's newly elected school board contracted to build the Victoria Colored School. Located on Convent Street a block east of the Palestine Baptist Church, the Victoria Colored School remained the center of black education in town until 1939. The school accommodated primary and secondary students, including secondary students bused to the city from outlying rural areas. To serve as principal of the new school, VISD hired a very capable African American administrator named Frederick W. Gross.

Born in Marshall, Texas, in 1861, Gross was an 1885 graduate of Bishop College. He had also studied at Wiley College, Fisk University, and the University of Chicago. After teaching nine years in East Texas, he arrived in Victoria in 1887, and two years later became principal at Brown School, one of four schools for black children then operating in Victoria County. He was a professional acquaintance of Booker T. Washington and was undoubtedly well versed in the economic independence argument put forward by Washington. But in contrast to Washington, Gross maintained an abiding commitment to intellectual enrichment through academic preparation. During his six years at the school he encouraged students to take literary classes and pursue college degrees. Under his leadership Victoria Colored School became a recognized institution among the black colleges of Texas, and as evidence of his ongoing personal commitment to academics, he completed a master of arts degree in 1902. Gross hired outstanding faculty to teach at the school, including the two men who would eventually succeed him as principals. In addition to his work as an educator, throughout his years in Victoria he remained active as grand secretary of the state chapter of the United Brothers of Friendship. In 1907, Gross accepted the presidency at Houston College[8] where he remained until his death in 1915. He became a nationally respected educator during his years in Houston, but Victoria remained his home. Members of his family had died and been buried there, and in 1915, F. W. Gross too was laid to rest in the section of Evergreen Cemetery that was for blacks.[9]

The population of Victoria County boomed during the first two decades of the twentieth century. From 1900 to 1910 the total population increased by nearly 10 percent, and the next decade by 22 percent. As the city's population grew, the school board moved quickly to meet the ever-growing demand for school facilities.[10] Central High School was built in 1902 as both a primary and secondary school for the city's white students. By 1910, crowding was a problem at the school, and the next year VISD opened Brownson and North Heights (later renamed Juan Linn) for white children in the primary grades. Six years later the school district expanded facilities for white students again when rancher John J. Welder donated twenty-five acres of land on North Street for the construction of Patti Welder High School. Central High School now became an intermediate school that was renamed Mitchell School in 1922. While the white population grew, the county's black population declined slightly during the first two decades of the twentieth century as a result of outward migration. District officials apparently saw no need for expansion of the Victoria Colored School, and the result was a general neglect of the school. Facilities were subpar and crowding occurred. The school building was considerably smaller than Central High School and much smaller than Patti Welder. The fact that it was accommodating students at both the primary and secondary levels created additional challenges for educators. To make matters worse, a growing interest in secondary education had prompted more parents in surrounding communities to begin sending their children to Victoria to go to school. By 1920, VISD had built a total of four schools for the white children of the community, while black students from throughout the area were attending classes under a single roof.

As difficult as conditions were for black children, they were initially even worse for Victoria's Mexican children. Despite the fact that state law defined colored children as "all persons of mixed blood, descended from negro ancestry," between 1906 and 1920, VISD used race as a basis for segregating Mexican children as well.[11] The practice of segregating Mexican students based on race had started in Seguin, Texas, in 1902 and spread quickly throughout the region. On September 20, 1906, VISD leased a house at 1005 South Bridge Street from C. L. Goehring for $100 a month and began using the facility as a school for Mexican children.[12] Though the school was never properly provided for and was almost certainly a safety hazard, the school district ultimately purchased the building, thereby establishing it permanently as the city's only public school for Mexican children. The facility was in no way equal to the district's other schools, but parents of Mexican children had an advantage over black parents in that they had an alternative to the public school. Mexican children also attended Guadalupe School, a free Catholic school for elementary students run by the Sisters of the Incarnate Word. Guadalupe originally served as a preparatory school for young Mexican girls wishing to enroll at Nazareth Academy, a parochial school in Victoria that had been training girls for the sisterhood since 1867. By the early 1900s, Guadalupe

School had been opened to boys as well, furnishing English language and basic educational skills necessary for transfer to St. Joseph's Catholic School for boys. Both Nazareth Academy and St. Joseph's cost money, however, and for this reason few Mexican families could afford to send their children to school beyond sixth grade. Students who demonstrated extraordinary potential might secure assistance to further their education, but a child in the classroom meant one less wage earner at home. Since most South Texas Mexican families needed the additional income, a significant percentage of children were forced to drop out of school due to economic necessity.[13]

The decade of the 1910s represented the golden age of agriculture in American history, and in Victoria this translated into a booming economy that very much shaped the city's labor demands and educational curriculum. But Victoria County continued to witness a black exodus during the war years as many black citizens found opportunities in larger cities, especially Houston. In 1900 blacks had constituted 28 percent of the county's population and contributed greatly to the local labor force. In 1910 the percentage dropped to 24 percent and by 1920 blacks constituted only 13 percent of the population. Despite the relative decline in population, the demand for skilled workers remained high and was reflected in the curriculum and management of the Victoria Colored School. In 1907 C. H. McGruder succeeded F. W. Gross as principal at the school. McGruder had arrived as a teacher at the school in 1902, and, more than his predecessor, he stressed the importance of an applied curriculum and especially the industrial arts.[14] A highly skilled carpenter himself, McGruder strictly enforced the district's policy, which required all young men to take courses in the industrial arts before graduation. Under his guidance, and no doubt to the delight of civic leaders, the Industrial Arts Department at the Victoria Colored School grew rapidly. By 1920, enrollment in the vocational programs was straining the school's ability to accommodate the student population. McGruder and others in the black community lobbied for additional funds in order to expand the Industrial Arts Department, but VISD officials were reluctant to bear the additional cost of construction. Rather than building a new facility for the vocational program, the school board adopted a plan that would inexpensively expand vocational facilities at the school while simultaneously relieving pressure building among Mexican parents to end racial segregation of their children.

On October 11, 1920, VISD announced that it would be closing the Mexican school permanently and that students at the school would henceforth be enrolling in the city's white schools. Instead of buying new materials for the Industrial Arts Department at Victoria Colored School, the board planned to dismantle the old Mexican school and turn the materials from the building over to McGruder. Black students would now build an industrial arts facility themselves. The plan would save the district the cost of materials and labor, and almost as important, it would furnish valuable experience to young black workers.[15] On the other hand, the decision to begin integrating Mexican children generated anxiety and even anger among many white parents. The integration initiative had actually started in 1916 when Carlos Delgado, an affluent Protestant citizen, petitioned the school board to allow his children to attend one of the city's public white schools. The board initially attempted to placate Delgado by proposing improvements at the Mexican school, but local influence prevailed, and the next year Delgado was allowed to enroll his sons in the white schools. In light of the concession made to Delgado, others came forth with similar demands—until 1920 when VISD finally elected to close the Mexican school altogether. The decision to integrate Mexican children angered many white parents who expressed fear that integration of Mexican children (whom they stereotyped as dirty and unsanitary) would expose their children to a wide variety of maladies. They further argued that in catering to Mexican students the district's curriculum would hold their children back thereby undermining the educational process. A movement to reinstate segregation briefly gained momentum in the city but ultimately failed. Still, segregationists gained important concessions in the form of a policy designed to protect white children from the supposed health risks of integration. Mexican children would be inspected regularly for contagious diseases including vermin and would be removed from school when circumstances warranted.

Though VISD policies were an affront to the Mexican community, they were nevertheless preferable to the previous system of segregation. Under these conditions, Mexican children would attend school with white children until the end of the decade.[16]

Unfortunately, for most Mexican children, integration brought little assurance of graduating from high school. On May 11, 1930, the *Victoria Advocate* announced the largest graduating class in Patti Welder High School's history. Of the seventy students listed in the announcement, Mary Trevino was the only graduating senior with a Hispanic surname.[17] Despite the attrition that was obviously taking place among Mexican children, VISD officials continued to explore ways to reinstate segregation. In 1932, School Superintendent Virgil Griffin read the school board a letter he had recently received from State Superintendent of Public Education S. M. N. Marrs. Griffin had earlier communicated to Marrs his fear that integrated classrooms were holding back Victoria's "American" children. He proposed segregation as a means of fixing the problem. Marrs's response to Virgil was brief and to the point. "The Attorney General and also the higher courts have held that Mexican children may be segregated from American children for pedagogical reasons but not on racial grounds." He went on to state, "I agree with you that children who are not English-speaking will retard the progress of the American children" and that "it would be a better organization for the non-English speaking children to be segregated."[18] Two years later, the school board directed Griffin to make a survey of the city's population "with the purpose of locating the homes of Mexican children, the ability of each child to speak the English language, and any other data to enable the school board to best make a program for the Mexican children and for the general welfare of the schools in Victoria as a whole."[19]

Griffin stepped down from his post at VISD in July of 1935, but his successor, Porter Garner, immediately implemented a plan designed to segregate Mexican children based on language. On January 2, 1936, Garner hired J. W. Edgar of Mirando City as the school district's new director of instruction, and under Garner's oversight, Edgar began the process of segregating Victoria's "Spanish-speaking" children. Fire had recently forced closure at Mitchell School, and when it reopened in the fall of 1936, Mitchell served as the home of the newly created Latin American Department for the instruction of Spanish-speaking children. Under the tutelage of Rebbie Robbins, first and second graders would now undergo a rigorous Americanization program designed to break down their Mexicanidad. Meanwhile, "American" children would attend Brownson and North Heights schools during first and second grade. White students would transfer to Mitchell School for third grade, at which time integration occurred.

Given the financial challenges faced by Mexican families, it is not surprising that few students moved into the higher grades. Indeed, the number of Hispanic surnames among students graduating from Mitchell, Victoria Junior High, and Patti Welder High School remained well below the proportion of Hispanics in the population as a whole.[20] Despite the scarcity of high school graduates, VISD's program received high marks from outside observers. In the summer of 1938, W. A. Stigler of the State Department of Education commended Rebbie Robbins as one of the outstanding teachers of Spanish-speaking children in the state: "I was very pleased to find on my visit to Victoria last spring the ideal conditions which exist there. . . . Spanish-speaking children were being afforded equal opportunities with the non-Spanish-speaking children, teaching facilities were adequate, all teachers were well-trained, and the teaching was as thorough as any I have witnessed."[21]

Stigler was not alone in his praise of VISD's program. Representatives of the League of United Latin American Citizens also spoke favorably of the district's handling of Spanish-speaking students. In the spring of 1939, the League's council secretary, James Tafolla Sr. of San Antonio, wrote to Porter Garner to express the council's appreciation for VISD and the opportunities it afforded Latin Americans: "In making the official report of our recent trip to Victoria, special reference was made to the school situation in that city. This report commended you highly on account of the able, just and impartial manner in which you handle the situation there. Our members were specially happy to learn that no discrimination exists there against our people, and a motion was made, seconded and adopted unanimously, to the effect that we write you a letter, thanking you for the fair, just and impartial service rendered to the people of our extraction in the educational field."[22]

In spite of Tafolla's praise, the completion rate among Mexican students remained low. In May of 1939, Patti Welder High School announced a graduating senior class of 110 students—Alfred Fernandez was the only senior with a Hispanic surname.[23] Six months later, Porter Garner would step down from his position as school superintendent in order to go into private business. Though graduation rates among Mexican students remained low, both the state of Texas and the leading Mexican American civil rights organization of the day had praised his policy. Perhaps more important, he could boast that a brighter day was on the horizon. Like students in Americanization programs throughout the Southwest, Victoria's Mexican children would now be indoctrinated with a sense of pride in the English language and a concurrent feeling of shame for their ancestral tongue. Within the black community, public education meant an opportunity to secure skills denied generations of ancestors. It consequently meant an opportunity to build and shape a proud identity. To members of the Mexican community, on the other hand, public education meant the loss of a once-proud ethnic identity. Many Mexican students would go on to serve in the armed forces and in the years after World War II would develop an even stronger sense of loyalty to a thoroughly homogeneous American ideal. As historian Anthony Quiroz has demonstrated, the postwar years would witness the rise in Victoria of a middle class that was as much American as Mexican. Certainly a foundation for that identity was laid by VISD in 1936.[24]

As Victoria's Mexican community struggled with segregation issues related to assimilation and Americanization, members of the black community faced a harsh form of segregation designed to accomplish racial exclusion. Combating this segregation required both discipline and tact. In February of 1933, a few months after the Supreme Court's *Nixon v. Condon* ruling seemingly had overturned the white primary in Texas, Dr. G. M. Wilkins addressed a letter to the *Victoria Advocate* concerning black participation in an upcoming election.[25] Dr. Wilkins was accommodating and even self-deprecating in his language, and though the deference he exhibited must have pained him (especially given the fact that he was a physician), he nevertheless flattered Leopold Morris in the hope of securing the paper's support for black voting rights. Wilkins wrote, "Practically every negro citizen in Victoria County has the greatest respect for you and your ability and we feel that your influence would go a long ways toward moulding public sentiment in favor of a weaker race which is striving to make good and substantial citizens in the community in which we live."[26]

Citing Democratic Party rules, Morris's response was all too predictable. "There is nothing that the *Advocate* or its editor can do in this case." More revealing than Morris's response is the tone of Wilkins's letter. It reveals the challenge that an educated black man faced in Jim Crow Victoria. Educated black men were scarce in the community, and when they spoke publicly they had to do so tactfully. It was critical to strike a balance between what needed to be said and what powerful men like Morris wanted to hear. Nobody knew this better than the man who served as principal at the Victoria Colored School from 1923–39.

Alonzo Daniel Sheffield was born October 12, 1884, in the Spring Creek community north of Victoria. His father, George Washington Sheffield, was a farmer and young A. D., as Alonzo Daniel was called, and his brothers proved to be very capable students. A. D. graduated from the Victoria Colored School and Bishop College in Marshall, Texas, before returning to Victoria County to teach. In 1923, he became principal at the Victoria Colored School and for the next sixteen years served as both a highly respected educator and a prominent citizen within the community.[27] Like his mentor, F. W. Gross, Sheffield was deeply committed to the intellectual development of both students and faculty. During summer sessions he himself had studied at the University of Colorado and Lewis Institute in Chicago. In February of 1922 he was largely responsible for organizing the Thirteenth Annual South Texas Colored Teachers Association Conference, which was held in Victoria, and two months later, he and his colleagues were instrumental in local planning for the National Health Fair, an event designed to promote greater awareness of health issues among black citizens.[28] Like most in the black community, Sheffield was concerned about the inequitable investment of resources in the public school system. As enrollments grew, teachers at Victoria Colored School found themselves handling unmanageable workloads, a situation made more despicable by the fact that salaries for black teachers were, on average, 36 percent lower than those paid to teachers in the district's white schools.[29]

Despite relative success in the area of academic preparation, in the summer of 1932 Sheffield received disappointing news. The Victoria Colored High School had failed to gain accreditation as a preparatory school for the state's public college. An anonymously written letter to the *Advocate* revealed a lack of qualified teachers, inadequate space, and an absence of science equipment as the reason for denying accreditation. Signed simply, "A Colored Citizen," the letter included a plea for assistance. "We are going to ask our citizens to do whatever is needed to place our school on the accredited list. In the face of the excellent schools here for the major group we feel it will be an easy matter to enlist the white people to aid in placing the Victoria Colored School on the accredited list of high schools. . . . [I]t is hardly possible for a negro school to advance farther than a majority of the leading white citizens permit."[30] The *Advocate* printed the letter, but it would take seven years and a generous federal grant before VISD would finally address the issues of crowding and deficient facilities.

One of the most galling reminders of the inferior status of black citizens (and one of the most powerful instruments used by whites to reinforce that status) was the name given to the school itself. White schools in the city had been named for prominent families including the Welders, Brownsons, and Mitchells. These individuals represented a distinguished past of which Victoria was proud. The black school, on the other hand, remained known as simply "The Victoria Colored School." It was a constant reminder that students and graduates were destined to occupy the lowest rung on Victoria's social ladder. In September of 1934, A. D. Sheffield proposed renaming the school

F. W. Gross School in honor of the school's first principal. Members of the black community immediately embraced the idea and began referring to the school by that name, but VISD would not recognize the change until the board officially approved it. Despite the seemingly innocuous nature of the proposal, those concerned with the changing status of blacks in Victoria apparently were not overly receptive to the idea. Segregation had to be more than a physical separation of the races; it had to be conceptual as well. The word "colored" in the name of the school was critical to achieving the conceptual segregation the white community sought. In the fall of 1935, nine faculty members at Gross School sent a petition to Porter Garner urging board action on the proposed name change. On January 2, 1936, the "petition was read and after some discussion a motion was made . . . and carried that the Colored School be known in the future as F. W. Gross School." Though the change had become official, the *Victoria Advocate* and VISD officials themselves continued to refer to the school as F. W. Gross Colored School.[31]

Though it seemed a minor detail, Sheffield had actually won a major victory. A badge of shame had been removed from the school, and students could now speak proudly of their school, especially when attending interscholastic events. But Sheffield knew that the school needed more than just a name change. By 1934, enrollment had swelled to numbers that rivaled the more spacious facilities at Patti Welder High School.[32] Especially burdensome was the growing number of rural students who were forced to attend Gross School because of an absence of black high schools in the surrounding area. Ignoring the needs at Gross, in 1935, VISD took advantage of Public Works Administration funding to launch two major construction projects that benefited the city's white children. In February, the school board announced it was beginning construction of a new 1,700-seat gymnasium to be located immediately east of Patti Welder High School. The gymnasium would double as an auditorium and would satisfy a variety of different needs within the community. The gymnasium opened the next September, and less than a month later the board announced approval of a second project, the construction of a new junior high school.[33] Two months later, fire forced closure of Mitchell School again, and the school district faced the additional expense of rebuilding that structure.

None of the construction projects benefited the black community directly. Students at Gross School continued to meet their classes in crowded classrooms and hold special events in the UBF Hall across the street from the school. Athletic practices and some competitions were held in a vacant lot across the street, and teacher salaries continued to lag behind those of white teachers. In the school year ending in 1931, teachers at Gross received on average $73.64 a month versus an average $134.05 for teachers at the white schools. At $60.00 per month, the district's custodian made almost as much as the average black teacher.[34] Though frustrated by the situation, A. D. Sheffield refrained from stirring the pot publicly. In January of 1936 he issued a polite appeal to the citizens ofVictoria County on behalf of the Gross School library. In order to expand the library's holdings he opened the facility to use by the general public in hope that the gesture would attract donors. Six weeks later he brought an Ethiopian prince to speak at Gross School. Sheffield was always mindful to invite white citizens to special events as such gestures were critical to the school's efforts to secure support from local patrons. The supreme irony was that in order to accommodate white visitors, Sheffield had to furnish white seating—thus on special occasions the segregated school, itself, became segregated.[35]

Problems at Gross were compounded further by overcrowding in elementary schools in the surrounding rural area. In 1937, as the Westside Colored School became overcrowded the school board's response was to begin transferring students from that school to Gross. While it was not uncommon for high school students to be bused to Gross, now elementary students were being transported as well. In April of 1937, A. B. Williams and a committee of parents from the Westside School addressed a letter to Superintendent Garner and the school board urging reconsideration of the decision and requesting expansion and another teacher at the school. After giving the matter some thought, on June 2, the school board instructed Garner to "write the committee and tell them the findings of the board were such that they felt that an addition to the Westside School was not needed at present."[36]

Two weeks later, school board president William Offer informed the board that he had begun making inquiries into the purchase of land directly east of Gross School for the purpose of making "necessary additions" at the school. On July 7, Porter Garner reported that the "deal for additional grounds" had been completed but that "people in that vicinity objected to the use of this property for a Negro school." Securing land elsewhere in the city would be equally difficult and costly, so as an alternative, the board inquired about the possibility of purchasing from the Palestine Baptist Church the vacant lot across the street to the west of Gross School. Acting as trustees for the church, A. D. Sheffield and O. W. Allen informed Garner and the school board that the congregation was not interested in selling the land.[37]

After years of procrastination and neglect, on February 1, 1938, VISD officials finally revealed a plan for addressing overcrowding and inadequate facilities at Gross. As part of a $125,000 school bond package that included construction of a new wing for Victoria Junior High and a new science building for Patti Welder High School, the district planned to add a study hall and assembly hall at Gross, as well as the installation of indoor restrooms.[38] Exactly how Sheffield and the black community reacted to the plan remains unclear, but dissatisfaction apparently rose from some quarter. Three weeks after the announcement, the *Victoria Advocate* ran a second notice announcing that if the school bond passed, the district would now be building a new African American school altogether. The $11,000 building would be located in a vacant area of town south of the railroad tracks on Depot Street and would house either the high school or the elementary school. The old Gross School would remain open under another name and would accommodate students in whichever grades were not relocated to the new school. On February 23, the bond passed overwhelmingly, but the next April the school board put all plans on hold in order to apply for federal Public Works Administration (PWA) matching funds. In September, Superintendent Garner received word that the PWA would supplement the local bond with an additional $102,150. The school district was now in a position to invest more generously in the new school. On March 17, 1939, architect Kai Leffland opened sealed bids for the construction of a new $66,000 black school. Ed Wagner, the city's most prominent contractor, won the bid, and construction began immediately.[39]

In June of 1939, VISD officials took stock of the facilities at the old Gross School. Special Supervisor D. D. Taylor presented the findings from an investigation of conditions at the school. The report revealed faculty members who had not yet completed bachelor's degrees, overcrowded classrooms, and a need for dictionaries, maps, and science lab equipment. Especially revealing was Taylor's assessment of the language curriculum at the school. Under Sheffield's administration, students were required to complete four years of language including two years of Spanish and two years of Latin. Taylor believed the language requirement to be excessive, noting that "a two-year language course is all that might be needed in any high school department." Failing to see the sense in teaching Latin, he recommended dropping it from the curriculum but he recommended retaining the two-year Spanish requirement. Thus instead of retaining the language that would have prepared students for college and careers in law or medicine, he recommended retaining the language that would best prepare them to communicate in the local labor force. For white students, on the other hand, the Latin requirement was apparently not excessive in the least. In fact at nearby Victoria Junior College, students could "proficiency out" of elementary Latin by completing two years of Latin in high school.[40]

Despite Taylor's recommendation, the dream of many in the black community was finally coming to fruition. Sadly, A. D. Sheffield himself would not be around to witness the groundbreaking. In February of 1939, Sheffield began experiencing intestinal bleeding and was forced to seek bed rest. He traveled to New Orleans where his brother Jesse was a physician, and it was there that Sheffield spent the remaining days of his life. He was admitted to Flint Goodridge Hospital in March and the diagnosis revealed stomach cancer in an advanced stage. He underwent surgery to remove a portion of his stomach, but on May 2, 1939, at the age of 54, A. D. Sheffield died. He had lived in Victoria his whole life, and the *Advocate* eulogized him as a man who had given both to the field of education and "to the civic affairs of the colored citizens of the city." He was laid to rest in Evergreen Cemetery in a grave just up the hill from his mentor, F. W. Gross.[41]

Despite Sheffield's untimely passing, construction of the new F. W. Gross School pushed forward rapidly. In early October, students began the process of moving books, desks, and chairs into the new facility. On December 5, one month after Porter Garner announced his resignation as school superintendent, the whole city was invited to the grand opening of the new school. The senior class of 1940 presented the school with a picture of A. D. Sheffield, which was hung in the front hall alongside that of C. H. McGruder and F. W. Gross.[42]

The *Advocate* boasted that the new school was "as modern as any in the entire city school system and gives Victoria one of the best negro schools in this section of the state."[43] To be sure, the facility was well provided for. Most notably, students now had more classrooms, a gymnasium, and a modern science lab. However, the *Advocate* announcement told only a portion of the story. The new school was located in a bushy, overgrown bottomland in the Guadalupe River flood plain. When the land around the school was cleared, workers found that the school sat atop an old dump site and commercial hog pens. Though the city had launched an extensive paving project in September of 1938, the roads south to the school were unpaved, and the city had no immediate plan for paving them. Thus the new Gross School was difficult to access in stormy weather, and the school grounds could be covered with standing water for extended periods of time. Making necessary improvements at the school would require leadership, and A. D. Sheffield's death meant the black community had lost a valued spokesman. The gap would soon be filled by a local physician.

Dr. C. A. Dudley was one of the most visible and respected men in all of Victoria. Born in Wascom, Texas, in 1894, he had come to Victoria to assume his brother's medical practice in 1923. In the years after America's entry into World War II, Dr. Dudley proved to be a talented organizer and prominent spokesman for civil rights. On January 17, 1940, he organized and agreed to chair the F.W. Gross Athletic Council. Originally organized as an athletic booster club, the council soon became involved in a variety of both school and civic activities. It began organizing fundraisers, borrowing money, and lobbying the city and school district for improvements at the school. The top priority was to put the school's grounds in order so that children could play and athletic teams could practice. Brush, garbage, and hog pens were removed from the premises and once the land was cleared, dirt was hauled in to fill, level, and raise the grounds around the school. The Athletic Council arranged with the city engineer to have concrete sidewalks laid out and gravel put down to make streets navigable during rainy weather. Wartime rationing hindered the process, but by 1946, the school grounds were greatly improved. A playground was in place and practice fields were much safer. Additionally, the council made contributions to a variety of different community causes including the Valley Orphanage and the NAACP Cemetery Fund.[44]

At a meeting on June 21, 1944, the Athletic Council voted to organize a Progressive Voters League in the city in order to promote political empowerment in the black community. The decision proved to be a momentous one, as it moved the Gross High School Athletic Council into the realm of political activism.[45] Dudley and fellow members of the Athletic Council would now become increasingly vocal in expressing their views concerning the discriminatory nature of life in the city and especially the public school system. They were quick to note that during a time of significant growth in the city, the school district had transformed Gross High School into a catchall for black students from throughout the area. Indeed large numbers of high school students from surrounding rural communities were being taken via bus to Gross, and the result was crowding that seemed to be getting worse by the year. In 1951, the Progressive Voters League took extraordinary action by placing its own candidate on the ballot for a seat on the school board. Charles R. Callis was a 1936 graduate of Gross High School who had studied under the tutelage of A. D.

Sheffield. After graduation he became a very successful real estate entrepreneur, and in April of 1951 Callis announced his candidacy for one of six vacant seats on the board. In a letter to the *Victoria Advocate*, Callis called for expanded school facilities for all students "irrespective of race or nationality."[46]

Also declaring his candidacy in 1951 was grocery store operator Ralph Molina, along with six white candidates. Apart from Callis, no other candidate issued an official statement of policy priorities. Instead, the white community moved to crush the candidacies of both Callis and Molina. The *Advocate* reminded readers that no law existed or court order had been issued requiring that minorities serve on school boards. Telephone drives were launched and Sunday church sermons rallied white voters to get out to the polls. The city did its part by posting a person to serve as a "peace officer" at the ballot box in order to prevent "loitering and marking of ballots by others." When the votes were tallied, Victoria had witnessed the largest turnout in a school board election in its history. With 1,418 votes cast, the total vote nearly doubled the previous high for a school board election; remarkably, it even surpassed the 1950 general election for the entire county by nearly 500 votes. Both Callis and Molina were routed in a landslide.[47]

Despite the disappointing setback, activists associated with the Progressive Voters League continued to push for greater educational opportunity. For many, the key to the crusade was eradication of the powerful stereotype that held that black Victorians constituted a servile, laboring class. For students who were academically inclined, this stereotype proved to be especially debilitating, as it meant the dream of attending college would likely go unrealized. Indeed Jim Crow's grip on education in Victoria was in no way limited to the primary and secondary schools. Opened by VISD in 1925, Victoria Junior College had for decades furnished white students with academic coursework that could be transferred to one of the state's four-year colleges. The school was initially housed within the confines of Patti Welder High School, but in September of 1926 VISD oversaw passage of a $70,000 bond issue that financed construction of a new junior college building. The two-story brick structure was located immediately adjacent to the high school, and for the next twenty-three years remained under the administrative authority of VISD.[48]

While state law mandated segregation of public schools for children, no such law existed for adults in institutions of higher learning. The state made separate universities available to blacks, but it did not expressly prohibit blacks from enrolling in white colleges and universities. The decision to exclude blacks from white colleges and universities was made and enforced by popularly elected governing boards that administered the institutions themselves. As long as Victoria Junior College was located on the Patti Welder High School campus, VISD officials could cite state law in justifying exclusion of blacks from Victoria College. Under the federal "separate but equal" doctrine, the district should have been forced to furnish a college for blacks in the community, but such a facility was never built. Indeed before 1949, with a few rare exceptions, the college had nothing to do with Victoria's black community. One of those rare occasions occurred in the spring of 1933, when college president V. L. Griffin announced that a series of cooking classes would be offered by the college. Leopold Morris of the *Advocate* explained the rationale behind these classes. "This is a worthy project, especially during these days of 'depression.' Many wealthy people are doing their own work because the colored cooks waste too much food. This class will give the cooks a chance to redeem their jobs or hold the jobs which they have. This class will be maintained to help cooks prepare menues [sic] which are given them by landladies. . . . We are requesting the white citizens to urge their cooks to attend."[49]

Clearly, when Victoria Junior College did offer classes to the black community, it was to reinforce the social status quo by emphasizing workforce skills, not academic preparation. If students wished to earn academic credit they would have to enroll at one of the state's black colleges and universities. And even when Victoria College included blacks, it maintained a rigid adherence to the Jim Crow tradition. The 1933 cooking class, for example, was offered not at the college, but at the Victoria Colored High School.

After more than twenty years under VISD's administrative oversight, in December of 1947, the citizens of Victoria County voted to create an independent junior college district. Members of the Victoria College's newly elected board of directors in turn took advantage of the expansive mood in the city to call for a new campus and new facilities for their college. The next April, trustees on the board voted to increase the college's tax rate and to put a $750,000 bond issue before voters for the purpose of buying land and initiating construction. In a hotly contested June election—an election that revealed a deep rift between rural and urban interests—supporters of the bond won a narrow victory. By the beginning of the 1949 school year, Victoria had a brand new junior college campus.[50]

With the junior college now removed from the high school premises, college officials found themselves confronting the segregation issue. An increasingly vocal and organized black community began demanding academic coursework opportunities for black students. A survey at Gross High School in the spring of 1949 revealed that twenty-six students at the school were interested in taking academic courses at Victoria Junior College. The question, they asked, was would the board of trustees allow them to enroll at the new campus? The answer came swiftly and would produce feelings of anger that haunt many to the present day. In August of 1949, President J. D. Moore and Dean John W. Stormont traveled across town to Gross High School to inform students and faculty that they were in the process of organizing the new colored branch of Victoria Junior College.[51]

The next month, as white students began enrolling at the college's new facility on the east end of town, black students began enrolling for classes in a hastily thrown together night school located at Gross High School. The *San Antonio Register* later described the Gross Branch as "no better than makeshift" and so it was.[52] Heavy daytime use at the school meant students were forced to take classes at night. Still more troublesome was the fact that the college offered only four academic courses at Gross: one each in English, education, history, and mathematics. For the next five years, the Gross Branch existed solely for the purpose of satisfying the Supreme Court's separate-but-equal clause with little concern for the needs of students. Black students seeking academic transfer credit could not even take a full course load at Victoria Junior College, and recent high school graduates began to see little point in enrolling at all. By September of 1953, enrollment at the Gross Branch had dropped to only fourteen students; all fourteen were Army veterans.[53]

The next May, the U.S. Supreme Court sent shockwaves throughout the South when it issued its ruling in the school segregation case of *Oliver Brown v. the Board of Education of Topeka, Kansas.* The Court ruled that "in the field of public education the doctrine of 'separate but equal' has no place. Separate educational facilities are inherently unequal."[54] In the coming months and years, segregated schools throughout the country began the slow and often painful process of dismantling their Jim Crow education policies. In Texas, the decision meant that the state's civil statute mandating segregation among public school children was no longer in force. The decision also meant that local Jim Crow practices would now encounter challenges. While the Court's decision prompted violence in Little Rock, Arkansas, the process of dismantling Victoria's segregated policy was peaceful.

In the aftermath of the *Brown* decision, Dr. G. M. Wilkins, who was now president of the local chapter of the NAACP, along with Progressive Voters League President Francis Williams Jr. and C. R. Callis, spearheaded an initiative to end segregation at the Victoria Junior College. On June 7, 1954, the three men accompanied Gross High School graduate Dorothy Mae Hobbs to the Victoria College campus where Hobbs applied for admission. Upon receiving the application, college officials informed Hobbs that her case would be taken up by the board of trustees at the next regularly scheduled meeting. A week later the board, citing the Fourteenth Amendment to the Constitution and the "tenets of Christianity," voted unanimously to close down the Gross branch. Victoria College began admitting black students on the main campus the next September. That fall, President Moore informed the *Advocate* that the college's enrollment might reach a record 700 students this year. The *Advocate* reported, "While on the subject, he said four Negroes are now enrolled in the day school at Victoria College under the new policy adopted by the board in June."[55]

With only four students enrolling, the breaking of the color barrier at the college created little protest either on campus or within the community. Integrating the public primary and secondary schools, on the other hand, presented a different set of challenges. Fortunately for the school board, the *Brown* decision came at a time when Victoria was experiencing unprecedented growth. The arrival of petrochemical companies in the Gulf Coast region resulted in a doubling of Victoria's population from 16,126 in 1950 to 33,047 in 1960, and the new arrivals settling in the north and east ends of town demanded schools for their children. In the midst of this economic boom, and shortly after the *Brown* decision, VISD officials announced plans to expand the school system by renovating one school and building two new facilities in the north and east ends of town. With construction of the new schools proceeding on schedule, on April 16, 1956, the school board announced its plans for desegregation. Initial desegregation would affect the first three grades of primary school. Black parents who wished to enroll their children in a school other than Gross would have from April 23 to April 27, 1956, to complete the registration process. If a parent did not register his or her child during open enrollment, the child would be required to attend Gross. Any black child who arrived in the city after open enrollment had ended would also be required to attend Gross. When open enrollment ended on April 27, little had changed. Of the 223 black children who enrolled, 164 remained at Gross. Those who elected to attend a previously all-white school included twenty-nine students at Hopkins and twenty at Juan Linn. Mitchell School enrolled only four black students, while newly constructed Shields, Primrose, and Mayfair Schools enrolled only one black student between them. In years to come, the enrollment at Hopkins and Juan Linn Schools would become increasingly Hispanic and black, while schools on the north end of town remained almost exclusively white. VISD would later expand its integration policy to include children in the upper grades including high school. In the early 1960s, the district began transferring black teachers from Gross to Patti Welder High School in order to gauge white reaction. By 1964, black students had the option of choosing which school they would like to attend. Most opted to remain at Gross School, which continued to function as an exclusively black high school until 1966.[56]

By the 1960s, African American and Hispanic residents of Victoria had made significant headway in their fight against Jim Crow education. Public schools were nominally integrated, and as Anthony Quiroz has documented, members of the Hispanic community had even secured election to the school board.[57] Quiroz's work is significant because it sheds light on the history of Victoria's Mexican American community, but the history of the African American community remains somewhat shrouded. Though sometimes controversial, men like F. W. Gross, A. D. Sheffield, C. A. Dudley, and C. R. Callis acted as powerful catalysts in unifying Victoria's black community and making it strong. But Victoria's educational priorities were never designed to reinforce the sense of ethnic pride necessary for building an African American historical tradition. Rather, the school district sought to bolster the local labor force by training blacks to be competent workers. The unfortunate reality is that neither VISD nor the Victoria Junior College did enough to prepare African American children for positions of leadership within the community. The tragic result is that today, the African American community has lost much of its historical identity. Gone to a large degree is a sense of appreciation for the sacrifices made by earlier generations. In 2007, young arsonists set fire to the school in South Victoria named for C. A. Dudley. Later that year the headstone atop Dudley's grave in Evergreen Cemetery toppled from its pedestal. Like so many headstones in the section of the cemetery once designated "colored," it tumbled to the ground as the result of a slumping foundation—and it remains lying face down to this day. Dudley was a man who gave of his time and resources to help make Victoria a better place, and his memory deserves more in the way of respect. On the other hand what better symbol of the educational legacy of "separate but equal"?

## NOTES

1. The author wishes to thank Bruce Glasrud for his valuable comments in helping prepare this paper for publication.

2. Leonard W. Levy and Harlan B. Philips, "The Roberts Case: Source of the 'Separate but Equal' Doctrine," *American Historical Review* 56 (April 1951): 510–18; Donald M. Jacobs, "The Nineteenth Century Struggle over Segregated Education in the Boston Schools," *The Journal of Negro Education* 39 (Winter 1970): 76–85; Douglas J. Ficker, "From Roberts to Plessy: Educational Segregation and the 'Separate but Equal' Doctrine," *The Journal of Negro History*, 84 (Autumn 1999): 301–14.

3. *The Revised Civil Statutes of the State of Texas*, 1879, art. 3709, states, "The children of the white and colored races shall be taught in separate schools; and in no case shall any school consisting partly of white and partly of colored children receive any aid from the free school fund" (532).

4. Pay schools were schools for which students paid a weekly fee. The standard cost in the years after the Civil War was five cents per week, and thus the schools were occasionally called "nickel-a-week" schools.

5. Mary Charles Baas, "History of Early Education in Victoria, Texas" (master's thesis, Southwest Texas State Teachers College, 1951), 23, 38.

6. *Victoria Advocate*, March 28, 1903.

7. *Victoria Advocate*, August 22, 1903. For a discussion of white views of black education in antebellum Texas see Michael R. Heintze, *Private Black Colleges in Texas, 1865–1954* (College Station: Texas A&M Press, 1985), 16–20.

8. Houston College was established as the Houston Academy by Antioch Baptist Church minister John Henry "Jack" Yates in 1885. Though it became known as Houston College, it operated as a primary-, secondary-, and industrial-education school. Located east of College Memorial Park Cemetery on Dallas Street, the school closed its doors in 1921. See Rutherford B .H. Yates Sr. and Paul L. Yates, *The Life and Efforts of Jack Yates* (Houston: Texas Southern University Press, 1985), 42–46, and Louis F. Aulbach, "Buffalo Bayou: An Echo of Houston's Wilderness Beginnings," an undated online article at http://users.hal-pc.org/-IfaBB34.html (accessed May 1, 2009).

9. Frederick W. Gross's achievements have been pieced together from a variety of sources. These include A. D. Sheffield, "History of Colored Education," *Victoria Advocate*, 88th Anniversary Edition, September 1934; the "Teacher" file in the Sydney Weisiger Collection at the Victoria Regional History Center, Victoria, Texas; *The Booker T. Washington Papers*, ed. Louis R. Harlan and Raymond Smock (Urbana: University of Illinois Press, 1981), vol. 11, 1911–1912, 342, http://www.historycooperative.org/btw/; and Robbie A. Parkman, *Victoria Schools 1824–1980* (Victoria, Texas: Victoria Independent School District, 1980), 80.

10. The total population of Victoria County was 13,678 in 1900. It increased to 14,990 in 1910. During that same period, the county's black population dropped from 3,787 to 3,600. See University of Virginia Library Historical Census Browser, http://fisher.lib.virginia.edu/collections/stats/histcensus/.

11. Revised *Civil Statutes of the State of Texas, 1879*, 532.

12. "Mexican School" file 186, Sydney Weisiger Collection.

13. For an excellent discussion of the educational challenges faced by Mexican families in South Texas see Mario T. Garcia, *Mexican Americans: Leadership, Ideology, and Identity, 1930–1960* (New Haven: Yale University Press, 1989), 62–83.

14. C. H. McGruder served as principal of the Victoria Colored School from 1907 until 1923 when he left Victoria to take an administrative position with the Houston chapter of the United Brothers of Friendship. He died from gall bladder complications in Houston in June of 1935. *Victoria Advocate*, June 12, 1935, 2.

15. Sheffield, "History of Colored Education"; Victoria Independent School District (VISD) School Board minutes, November 17 and December 14, 1920.

16. Anthony Quiroz, *Claiming Citizenship: Mexican Americans in Victoria, Texas* (College Station: Texas A&M University Press, 2005), 55–56; "Mexican School" file 186.

17. *Victoria Advocate*, May 11, 1930.

18. VISD School Board minutes, February 24, 1932.

19. Ibid., February 21, 1934.

20. In 1930, Mexicans constituted roughly 27 percent of the population of Victoria County. University of Virginia Library Historical Census Browser.

21. *Victoria Advocate*, August 18, 1938.

22. VISD School Board minutes, June 2, 1939.

23. *Victoria Advocate*, May 28, 1939.

24. Quiroz writes, "Culturally, the Mexican American community wished to maintain the Spanish language and Mexican traditions. But socially, economically, and politically, there were strong desires to accept, not the status quo, but the fundamental premises of society. . . . For Victoria's Mexican Americans, the only permissible avenues for protest involved options such as the ballot box and the lawsuit to gain acceptance as equal citizens. . . . Through the growth of a professional wing of the Mexican American middle class, Mexican Americans promoted themselves as equal citizens interested in the welfare of the general society as well as their own upward mobility" (*Claiming Citizenship*, xviii).

25. For a detailed discussion of *Nixon v. Condon* see Darlene Clark Hine, *Black Victory: The Rise and Fall of the White Primary in Texas* (Columbia: University of Missouri Press, 2003), 142–71.

26. *Victoria Advocate*, February 26, 1933.

27. Telephone interview with Sheffield's son, Alonzo Daniel Sheffield Jr., June 30, 2008 (cassette tape and transcript in the author's possession). See also "Teacher" file in the Sydney Weisiger Collection, and Sheffield, "History of Colored Education."

28. *Victoria Advocate*, February 22 and March 31, 1922.

29. During the 1923 school year, VISD paid the thirty-three teachers at its white schools $3,767 per year, or an average monthly salary per teacher of $114.15. The District paid $874.26 to the twelve teachers at the Victoria Colored School for an average monthly salary of $72.85. See the VISD School Board minutes, August 16, 1923.

30. *Victoria Advocate*, September 1, 1932.

31. VISD School Board minutes, January 2, 1936.

32. Enrollment by school in 1934 was as follows: Mitchell School, 590; Patty Welder High School, 400; Brownson School, 210; Victoria Colored High School, 395. *Victoria Advocate*, September 12, 1934.

33. *Victoria Advocate*, February 6 and October 1, 1935.

34. VISD School Board minutes, May 10, 1930.

35. *Victoria Advocate*, January 27 and March 5, 1936.

36. VISD School Board minutes, April 22 and June 2, 1937.

37. The congregation later built a new church edifice on land that VISD sought to purchase, but in 1937 the corner lot served as a playground for children. VISD School Board minutes June 14, July 7, and August 12, 1937.

38. *Victoria Advocate*, February 1, 1938. Gross was not the only school to have outdoor restroom facilities. Both Mitchell and Brownson schools also had outdoor restroom facilities that were scheduled to be moved indoors.

39. VISD School Board minutes, April 20 and May 5, 1938; *Victoria Advocate*, February 21 and September 18, 1938, and March 16, 1939.

40. VISD School Board minutes, June 2, 1939. A copy of the 1938–39 *Victoria Junior College Catalog* is preserved in the "1939" file of Charles Spurlin's Papers on the History of Victoria College, Victoria Regional History Center.

41. *Victoria Advocate*, May 3 and May 4, 1939.

42. *Victoria Advocate*, December 6, 1939.

43. *Victoria Advocate*, October 9, 1939.

44. Dudley's ambitious agenda led to conflict with Gross administrators and VISD officials. In the summer of 1941, the Athletic Council requested an accounting of how contributions to the school were being spent. Principal F. W. Carter, who was also a member of the council, assured Dudley that the district would furnish a report, but when Carter failed to deliver a satisfactory accounting, Dudley appealed directly to Superintendent J. H. Bankston. At a meeting with Dudley and Carter, Bankston assured the council that an acceptable report would be furnished, but to Dudley's dismay, future reports were sporadic and incomplete. Relations with the school district soured until September of 1944, when the Athletic Council voted to suspend sundry cash donations to the school altogether. After 1946, internal discord prompted the council to finally dissolve its ties to the high school. Dudley continued to work for the community, and in 1949 he realized one of his dreams when the black community celebrated the opening of George Washington Carver Center, a recreational park for blacks located on the south end of the city. Minutes of the F. W. Gross Athletic Council Meetings were published in John W. Huff Jr., *The History of the George Washington Carver Center* (Victoria, Texas: n.p., 1955).

45. Huff, *History of the George Washington Carver Center*, p. 54.

46. *Victoria Advocate*, April 1, 1951.

47. *Victoria Advocate*, April 8, 1951.

48. Charles Spurlin, *The Victoria College, 1925–2000: A Tradition of Excellence* (San Antonio, Texas: Historical Publishing Network, 1999), 7–14.

49. *Victoria Advocate*, March 17, 1933.

50. Spurlin, *Victoria College*, 50–65. The Board of Trustees included Web DeTar, Arvie Elliott, Joseph Wearden, Fred Proctor, Raymond Hill, C. P. Montier, and Winston Zirjacks.

51. *Victoria Advocate*, August 9 and August 11, 1949.

52. *San Antonio Register*, June 18, 1954.

53. *Victoria Advocate*, September 15, 1953.

54. Quoted in Richard Kluger, *Simple Justice: The History of Brown v. Board of Education and Black America's Struggle for Equality* (New York: Vintage Books, 1977), 707.

55. Victoria College Board minutes, June 14, 1954; *Victoria Advocate*, June 15 and September 14, 1954. Though the student body at Victoria College was integrated in 1954, the faculty was not integrated until 1983, when Agnes Jewett was hired as a counselor. See Spurlin, *The Victoria College*, 163.

56. *Victoria Advocate*, April 17 and April 28, 1956.

57. Manuel Velasco won election to the board in 1958; John Artero was elected in 1964. See Quiroz, *Claiming Citizenship*, 59–60.

# Maury Maverick and Racial Politics in San Antonio, Texas, 1938–1941

JUDITH KAAZ DOYLE

ON MAY 20, 1941, SAN ANTONIO MAYOR MAURY Maverick left a sick bed against doctor's orders and went to a greater San Antonio campaign rally at Hermann Sons Hall. The ailing Maverick was entering the final week in a tense runoff campaign for mayor. He expected few votes from San Antonio's east side, where most of the city's blacks lived. Somewhere out there, east of Hermann Sons Hall, a black racketeer was trying to defeat him. Why should the racketeer corral most of the black vote? Maverick could not understand these eastside people. Unlike blacks elsewhere, in his view they rejected his New Deal liberalism in favor of reactionary machine candidates. Such behavior, he thought, must stem from their political immaturity and his opponent's cleverness. In 1941, far from Washington and the national issues he enjoyed, Maury Maverick fought San Antonio's masters of local politics. The frustrations of this losing battle would soon drive him to racist campaign rhetoric that clashed with his historical reputation as an advanced southern liberal.[1]

By the time Maverick took part in this San Antonio showdown, the liberal legend surrounding his name had already taken root. Only six years earlier, in 1935, the thirty-nine-year-old Maverick had claimed his seat in the U.S. House of Representatives, and soon after he took "'a running broad jump onto the nation's front pages."[2] He certainly did not get there because of a pretty face. On the contrary, his protuberant greenish eyes and his unusually wide mouth gave him an unmistakably toadlike appearance. But this "Unbranded Bullfrog's" words and actions drew far more attention than his looks.[3] Determined to live up to his surname, with its connotations of independence and unpredictability, Maverick soon developed an outspoken, almost deliberately provocative political style. Both Maverick's natural speaking talents and his staunch defense of the right to free expression reinforced his candor.[4]

Maverick's liberal image did not spring solely from his colorful style. His actual positions on a wide range of issues proved that his reputation had substance. As tax collector of Bexar County—where San Antonio is located—Maverick had pushed for political reform and for a more vigorous relief policy in the early 1930s. From his congressional position he supported expanded work-relief programs and a minimum-wage law. He defended civil liberties against legislative attacks and loudly complained when the U.S. Supreme Court ruled against New Deal programs.[5]

Maverick deserved the reputation he earned in Congress, but the legend that surrounded him has obscured the real tensions he faced as a southern liberal. The most difficult internal struggle that Maverick and other pioneering southern liberals of his era waged was over race. A staunch champion of civil rights in the abstract, Maverick, nevertheless, had to cope with a regional legacy of irrational prejudices and traditions. Few of Maverick's nonsouthern contemporaries appreciated his personal battle over the issue. In fact, on the national level, there was little sense that Maverick's flamboyant liberalism had any flaws or inconsistencies.[6] Maverick's friendly biographer, Richard B. Henderson, noted in 1970 that "Maverick was often wrestling with himself" over this matter, but Henderson never fully described how the peculiar racial situation in San Antonio and Maverick's own paternalistic theories intensified this struggle.[7]

Maverick's identity as a *southern* liberal pressured him to confront the issue of race before he had fully worked out his own feelings. Ironically, circumstances thrust a southern identity upon him. His precongressional correspondence contains few indications of special concern for the South's regional problems. On the contrary, Maverick's early interests focused on national, international, and universal questions, and they remained preferred topics for him throughout his life.[8]

Maverick's primary regional ties, to the extent that he had any, were to the Southwest, not to the South. His hometown of San Antonio was not a deep South city, and Texas was not a deep South state. "The Great Southwest," Maverick wrote in the 1930s, "is the land of my fathers. The old South, on the other hand, seems to me to be the land of my forefathers, a strange and distant illusion."[9]

During Maverick's first two terms in office Franklin D. Roosevelt focused attention on the South as an economic problem and, incidentally, as an important cog in the Democratic New Deal coalition. The suggestions of such southern regionalists as Howard W. Odum and Herman C. Nixon enjoyed a sympathetic audience of new dealers in Washington. A wave of regionally oriented southerners like Aubrey W. Williams and Will W. Alexander found themselves working for the Roosevelt administration. By Maverick's second term he too had sensed the growing interest in the South as a region, and he made it the subject of several magazine articles. Many chapters of his autobiography, *A Maverick American*, published in 1937, dealt with southern topics.[10]

Maverick's "adoption" of the South and its problems yielded him good publicity. He was, according to many, the most liberal southerner on Capitol Hill. By emphasizing his southernness he grabbed the limelight from other liberal congressmen, but his new role as a regional representative forced him to confront that quintessentially southern problem—the issue of race. Because he was unprepared for this confrontation, the resulting inner conflict temporarily shattered Maverick's liberal idealism that all minorities and oppressed people would recognize the fairness of his policies and support him.

Some of Maverick's early thoughts on racial issues appear in his correspondence with Forrest Bailey, national director of the American Civil Liberties Union (ACLU) in the late 1920s. In 1928 Maverick presented his racial philosophy, which would remain basically unchanged until after World War II: "I do not believe in social equality oft [sic] the races, and act accordingly. I have my prejudices, which are mine. However, I should not deny a negro his civil liberties, and would go down the line to see that the Constitution is obeyed."[11] In

May of the next year Maverick further explained to Bailey: "Social equality comes with not economic equality but economic superiority. In other words, when the colored people have had more than enough of the world's goods, for a full generation, then they'll be equal."[12]

Almost a decade later, when Roosevelt's New Deal was in full swing, Maverick again stressed the economic component of America's racial problems in his autobiography: "The first thing to do about the question is to see the colored people eat, and have jobs. . . . If economic opportunities are fair, and the different races show restraint, other questions will work themselves out."[13] Thus according to Maverick economic progress must form the basis for general racial progress. Ideally blacks should first attain economic gains; only then could they expect political and social equality. Maverick advocated the protection of blacks' civil liberties, but his definition excluded the right to fully effective suffrage. Pressing for political and social equality would violate the restraint necessary to prevent a white backlash.

Maverick's economically oriented racial theories may have come from socialist publications that he read as a youth. Many American socialists of the early twentieth century believed that social equality for blacks would emerge as capitalism disappeared. The New Deal reformers that Maverick later met in Washington also shaped his racial ideas. New dealers emphasized economic causes and solutions to social problems. They thought that racism resulted from economic depression in the South, and their solutions consisted of attempts to reduce poverty among people of both races. This exciting task would then reduce race consciousness and foster unity. Maverick accepted this analysis because it reinforced his racial notions and his budding faith in regional planning.[14]

Whatever the sources of Maverick's racial theories, their content placed him within the mainstream of southern liberalism in the early 1930s. Like Maverick, many other southern liberals compromised between deeply ingrained racial prejudice and sincere desire for racial change by avoiding the controversial issues of political and social equality. Instead they concentrated on reducing the obvious hardships caused by low standards of living and unfair law enforcement.[15]

This philosophy had definite limitations, though it had advanced beyond the views of the previous generation. By 1937 Maverick was publicly advocating equal pay for equal work, opportunities for blacks to participate in organized labor, and assurances of equal access to jobs and education. But he made no firm commitment to the concept of social equality between the races. He relegated this issue to the comfortably distant future. Like many white reformers he did not recognize that social and economic inequality fed on each other. Maverick's unsympathetic dismissal of blacks' social goals drew little attention in the early 1930s, but it became increasingly unpalatable to black leaders as they grew more assertive in the early 1940s.[16]

Maverick's support of the white primary also flawed his racial liberalism. Maverick inherited his position on this issue from the southern progressives of the early twentieth century. In order to end manipulation of black votes, progressives in several southern states had established nominating elections that barred blacks from participation. They promoted these measures as replacements for undemocratic nominating conventions, but white primaries became de facto elections in the heavily Democratic South. These measures thus removed blacks from political participation and made their votes useless to corrupt politicians. Of course, white primaries effectively disfranchised blacks. But southern progressives did not see this as a real problem. Essentially paternalistic in their racial attitudes, they believed they could work politically to improve racial conditions better than blacks themselves could. In his support of the white primary Maverick revealed this same paternalism.[17]

The political situation of blacks in Maverick's hometown of San Antonio also influenced his position on the white primary. A strong machine had long operated in the city. Since the late 1910s San Antonio blacks had participated in city government through this machine. At that time a black man named Charles Bellinger became an aide to a prominent member of the machine. Bellinger realized that the city's black preachers were the key to an organized black vote. Working through these preachers Bellinger built up a strong bloc of black voters. In the 1930s Bellinger was reputedly able to deliver five thousand to eight thousand votes to the machine.[18]

This was a sizable bloc in a city noted for its political apathy. During the 1930s San Antonio's Mexican American population ranged from 35 to 40 percent of the total, and this impoverished group tended to refrain from organized political participation. The city's military, oil, and cattle interests often resided in the city only seasonally. When they were in town they seemed willing to let the professional politicians run the city. Bellinger's bloc of organized, reliable black voters made up as much as 25 percent of the total in some city and county elections, despite the fact that blacks made up only about 8 percent of the city's population. By mobilizing his bloc, Bellinger obtained benefits for the black community as well as protection for his own real estate and gambling interests.[19]

In a state that had largely disfranchised its black citizens, San Antonio blacks had to fight to protect the utility of their voting bloc. They conducted vigorous and largely successful "Pay Your Poll Tax" campaigns to overcome this particular obstacle to voting. Although such things are difficult to prove, it seems likely that Bellinger and other machine members at times provided poor blacks with funds to pay this impost, despite the illegality of such actions.[20]

The white Democratic primary posed more difficult problems, but certain factors worked in favor of the city's blacks. In the first place, the city's municipal elections were nonpartisan, so white primary directives did not apply to them. Second, during the 1920s the U.S. congressional district that included San Antonio contained one of the strongest Republican Party organizations in the state. In a real two-party situation the general election became an important contest, and blacks gained bargaining leverage. The city's blacks had lost this advantage by 1934, however. Intraparty squabbles, the death of popular Republican congressman Harry M. Wurzbach, and the redistricting that created the Twentieth Congressional District had, by that year, reduced the Republicans' power.[21]

Even without these circumstantial advantages, the black bloc itself, once it had been formed, had a self-preserving quality that tended to defeat the purposes of various white primary measures. During the stormy history of the white primary in Texas the institution sometimes developed loopholes as a result of imperfectly drawn legislation or successful court challenges. During such periods county Democratic party officials had the power to decide whether or not blacks should be allowed to vote in the Democratic primaries. Bexar County Democratic officials had fought over this question for years by the time Maverick entered politics. These officials, who were often members of the machine, at times decided that the utility of an organized black vote outweighed the ideological considerations of white supremacy. Thus blacks sometimes voted in nominally white Democratic primaries. The power of the bloc served to protect the black vote, and the machine earned the reputation of being an opponent of the white primary in spite of the self-serving nature of its opposition.[22]

As a liberal reformer, Maverick had belonged to the antimachine camp since his first involvement in Bexar County politics in 1929. Early on Maverick realized the significance of Bellinger's powerful black bloc and worked to support the white primary. In 1932 the white primary issue erupted in the middle of Maverick's campaign for renomination as the Democratic candidate for the position of county tax collector. Two months before the July primary, in its *Nixon v. Condon* decision, the U.S. Supreme Court had overturned the latest version of Texas's white primary that allowed the Democratic State Executive Committee to determine party membership qualifications. The party as a whole had reinstated the white primary at its annual convention in late May, but the Supreme Court's ruling cast enough doubt on the legality of the institution to encourage further challenges.[23]

On July 10, 1932, C. A. Booker, a black San Antonian represented by white machine lawyer Carl Wright Johnson, filed for an injunction to force party officials to allow him to vote in the July 23 primary. When the federal district court in San Antonio granted Booker's injunction the day before the primary, Maverick and a fellow reform candidate sprang into action to get the injunction overturned. They eventually succeeded, but not before about one thousand blacks voted in the primary on election day. The reformers, including Maverick, won anyway, but the whole affair permanently damaged Maverick's relationship with San Antonio blacks.[24] As one of Maverick's colleagues put it, "[Maverick] became a famous liberal. But one part of the liberal hegemony, the blacks, never forgave him for his midnight intervention in the *Booker* case. Maury, characteristically, never forgave them either—never forgave them for not forgiving him."[25] In 1934 Maverick again tried to get unenthusiastic county Democratic Party officials to enforce the state organization's white primary policy.[26]

Why did Maverick support the white primary so strongly? His biographer has indicated that Maverick's motive in these endeavors was purely practical; he wished to reduce the voting strength of his political opposition.[27] This explanation flies in the face of Maverick's lifelong dedication to civil rights and civil liberties. Surely the idealistic Maverick needed a better excuse than "practical politics" to justify involvement in an effort to abridge his fellow citizens' suffrage. Although Maverick never discussed his motives, his stand probably grew out of a conviction that, in their present economically depressed conditions, blacks would inevitably fall prey to the advances of corrupt politicians. For Maverick, the goal of clean elections and progressive government took precedence over political equality for blacks. As with social equality, political equality would come about at some future date when blacks had overcome their "political immaturity."

For whatever reason, Maverick supported the white primary, apparently until the U.S. Supreme Court ruled it unconstitutional in 1944. His support seriously affected his relationship with his black constituents at home, but it had surprisingly little impact on his national reputation as a racial liberal—at first. National-level racial reformers seemed either uninformed or unconcerned with Maverick's position on this issue until 1940.[28]

In spite of Maverick's position on social equality and the white primary, an aura of racial liberalism surrounded him during his two congressional terms. His concept of economic equality impressed blacks hard hit by the Great Depression. But more than anything else, Maverick's stand in favor of antilynching legislation marked him as an ultraliberal on racial issues. No southerner other than Maverick voted for the Gavagan Anti-Lynch Bill in 1937. Many southern liberals hesitated to endorse antilynching legislation because it aroused suspicions about federal intervention in local affairs. Maverick may have inherited some southern prejudices, but he had no qualms about a strong federal government. His solitary support made him an obvious target of praise by black racial reformers. But Maverick actually approached this legislation as a civil rights advocate rather than as a racial reformer. In a speech supporting the bill he presented it as a measure to protect the civil rights of both blacks and whites. He stressed that he was not supporting the bill in order to gain black votes.[29]

The immediate and sweeping praise Maverick received from black leaders for his antilynching stand embarrassed him. "I do not want colored people to run up to me with a red bandana handkerchief, singing 'Coming Through the Rye,'" he stated soon after the antilynching vote.[30] He then complained that antilynching legislation was "always approached in the slip-shod manner of degraded politics—catering to the Negro vote."[31] He did not want anyone to think that this had been his motive. He began to work on a general bill for federal enforcement of the entire Bill of Rights, subsuming the racial issue under this broader campaign.[32]

Three years later, in a moment of frustration over what he perceived as the ingratitude of racial reformers, black and white, Maverick implied that his stand on the antilynching bill had cost him his 1938 bid for congressional renomination. But this seems unlikely. Maverick earlier stated that there was little reaction to the vote in his district. Antilynching legislation evidently provoked little interest among his Bexar County constituents.[33]

Instead, Maverick's 1938 primary defeat resulted from more general causes. He faced a determined and well-financed campaign in which the San Antonio city machine played an important role. By 1938 the real control of the machine lay in the hands of three men. Tall, gray-haired, and dignified, Mayor Charles Kennon (C. K.) Quin furnished a full complement of legitimate and illegitimate patronage. Owen W. Kilday was a bushy-browed, hot-tempered son of Ireland from Uvalde County, Texas. He provided political acumen and influence among the city's numerous Catholics. In 1940 he became even more powerful as sheriff and chief dispenser of county jobs for Bexar County. Although Charles Bellinger had died two years earlier, the machine hoped that his son, Harvard-educated Valmo C. Bellinger, would be able to continue the black bloc tradition, at least in the city's nonpartisan municipal elections where the white primary did not apply.[34]

In 1938 Quin and Kilday moved the San Antonio machine against Maverick in the Democratic primary. Their goal was to replace him with Owen Kilday's brother, Paul Joseph Kilday. Vice President John Nance Garner, the crusty patriarch of Texas Democrats, apparently cooperated in this effort. Conservative interests in the state wanted Maverick out, and the nation's turn to the right in 1938 provided an appropriate atmosphere for that change. Mayor Quin helped remove him by padding the city payroll. Later investigation indicated that he may have paid as much as $3,000 of city funds to 400 extra city employees hired at election time.[35]

In the July 27 primary Kilday defeated Maverick by 493 votes out of 49,151 cast. Unless Maverick could somehow defeat Kilday in the general election, he would lose his congressional seat. Maverick and his friends toyed with the idea of an independent candidacy in the general election. Here success would depend on San Antonio black voters. Barred from the primary, they made up the largest group of unpledged voters in the district. Even though Maverick had denied that he expected or desired black votes in return for his stand on the antilynching bill, he evidently counted on some. He believed that with his liberal reputation he could break the pattern of black support for machine candidates.[36]

Maverick may have judged the situation correctly; he knew he could count on support from some national black leaders. Most Bexar County blacks were ambivalent about Maverick, but some indicated support. Many signatures on his petition for candidacy belonged to blacks. A columnist for the *San Antonio Register*, which was owned by Valmo Bellinger, even had kind words for Maverick after his primary defeat. The columnist reminded readers that Paul Kilday had attacked Maverick's antilynching vote during the primary campaign. Bellinger himself may have considered supporting Maverick. Certainly his inherited gambling empire would be safer with Maverick in Washington than with him unemployed and loose in San Antonio, a consideration that Bellinger's white cronies had seemingly overlooked.[37]

Maverick's independent campaign never materialized, however. The Texas secretary of state decided that his bid was illegal, since he had already run in the Democratic primary. This decision put an end to Maverick's 1938 congressional aspirations, but he did not retire from politics. Reasoning that further attempts to regain his congressional seat would fail as long as the San Antonio machine remained intact, Maverick turned to municipal politics. His new goal was to break the machine and to establish local support that would later enable him to return to Washington where he had friends and influence.[38]

A less energetic man might have paused before tackling San Antonio's established order; conditions there seemed to preclude quick and easy revisions. Maverick knew from previous experience that the city's apathetic voters were difficult to rouse. Although the city's commercial and financial groups were suffering under heavy taxes and offered potential support for reform, this conservative group shunned sweeping changes. These kinds of conditions had helped the machine maintain the status quo for decades.[39]

By entering city politics Maverick pitted himself against the Quin-Kilday-Bellinger triumvirate and challenged an entire political style. He had several handicaps in this contest. Whereas political theory had created many of Maverick's policies, practical politics dictated machine action. Maverick spoke out on issues; the machine dodged them or manufactured them. Maverick's primary goal was to establish progressive city government; the machine's goal was to stay in power. Maverick saw local affairs as specific examples of broader national issues. San Antonio's machine politicians were artists of local politics; they saw power as something accumulated from the bottom up and wielded from the top down, and they carefully maneuvered their reserves of power.

Maverick's principles and his national, rather than local, orientation were disadvantages in the San Antonio arena, but he soon received a lucky break. In December 1938 a grand jury indicted Mayor Quin for misapplication of public funds, citing as evidence San Antonio's July city payroll. Quin's primary campaign activities had caught up with him. Although Quin escaped the charges, some members of the machine dropped him as a mayoral candidate in 1939. For awhile this machine faction supported Theo M. Plummer, the city's tax commissioner, and even the police chief, Owen Kilday, originally joined the anti-Quin group. But Quin refused to bow out and announced his own candidacy and his own slate of commissioner candidates. Although Plummer eventually withdrew from the mayoral race, the incumbent commissioners stayed in. In addition, Leroy Jeffers, a friend of the Kildays but also the assistant district attorney who had prosecuted Quin, announced his mayoral candidacy and his slate of commissioner candidates. The machine had fallen into total disarray. Meanwhile, on February 2, 1939, Maverick had entered the fray by announcing his candidacy for mayor. He soon joined with a group of reform-minded commission candidates to form the Fusion ticket. The challenge to San Antonio's divided machine was on.[40]

Maverick started his mayoral campaign confident that he could collect a sizable portion of the black vote. His congressional fame as a racial liberal would help him; it gained him endorsements by black weekly newspapers in Houston, Dallas, and Waco.[41] He could also point to the encouragement he received from blacks during his stillborn 1938 independent campaign. But he failed to take into account the fact that support for him as a congressional candidate might not translate into support for him as a mayoral candidate.

As a congressional candidate Maverick stood for the New Deal, and San Antonio blacks had benefited from the New Deal. In 1935 blacks made up somewhere between 7 and 8 percent of the city's population, but they accounted for about 14 percent of the city's relief recipients. Despite complaints of discrimination in the administration of some specific programs, the city's blacks cautiously approved of New Deal efforts in general.[42]

In the 1939 mayoral campaign Maverick ran as a progressive municipal reformer rather than as a new dealer. This platform had much less appeal for the city's blacks. The machine had facilitated black political participation and had provided tangible benefits such as street paving, lighting, schools, police protection, and jobs. Reformers, including

Maverick, had reduced black political participation by supporting the white primary. Whatever their ultimate goals had been, the progressives had never improved black standards of living. As mayor, Maverick could neglect or roll back gains blacks had made under machine rule. Bellinger and his political aides emphasized the patronage benefits blacks had enjoyed under machine administrations and stressed that no one knew what Maverick would do as a local official.[43]

Despite the black community's caution, subtle changes that would enhance Maverick's chances for black support were taking place on the east side. Black political and civic organizations had appeared; some were tied to national groups. In the 1930s many of these national organizations maintained that the future of blacks lay with the forces of liberalism. Even if Charles Bellinger had lived, he would have been forced to deal with the increasing political diversity among San Antonio blacks. His death and Maverick's challenge simply accelerated this trend toward greater diversity.[44]

As a nationally known racial liberal, Maverick enjoyed support from some of the new black organizations. The Bexar County Educational League, a local group opposed to the machine, endorsed Maverick. The National Negro Congress (NNC) collected money for Maverick's campaign through its San Antonio branch, headed by George J. Sutton. The NNC's national office sent word of its official endorsement of Maverick to thousands of local blacks. Evidently even some elements of the normally nonpartisan National Association for the Advancement of Colored People (NAACP) considered endorsing Maverick, though the group finally decided to remain neutral.[45]

The support Maverick received from these nascent organizations held qualitative, not quantitative, significance. Even with the help they provided, Maverick ran behind Quin on the east side. On May 9 Maverick won the three-cornered mayoral contest, receiving almost 41 percent of the 44,873 votes cast. Quin, his closest opponent, got 33 percent of the citywide vote. Yet in the city's black precincts Maverick received only 35 percent of the vote. He never admitted that his share of the black vote was even this large; at the time and almost a year later Maverick asserted that he had only received 21 percent of the black vote. Yet the precinct returns from the black neighborhoods, as well as the estimates that San Antonio blacks forwarded to their national organizations, indicate that Maverick received more black votes than he had thought. Definite cracks had appeared in the black bloc; liberal black organizations helped deliver some votes for Maverick and the Fusion ticket. The machine no longer could claim the support of all but a few dissenting blacks. If he had worked with these new black organizations Maverick could have benefited from the changes in the black community.[46]

Maverick's analysis of the election, however, discouraged him from cultivating this support. He dwelt bitterly on the eastside results, still refusing to admit that blacks had supported him as much as they had. Considering his liberal record, he reasoned, blacks ought to have trusted him to advance the whole community's general interests. But local blacks actually had as much reason to distrust him as to trust him. Already predisposed to doubt the political maturity of blacks in general, Maverick evidently concluded that black San Antonians voted against him, not out of caution or rational choice, but rather because the machine bribed them or misled them and thus subverted the democratic process. Maverick's strategy toward the black community followed from this analysis. He had to destroy the machine in order to liberate the east side. He was unwilling to make direct appeals to blacks and therefore could do little to nurture the black support already committed to him.

As mayor, Maverick spent little time analyzing the local political scene, black or white. Relentless machine attacks diverted his attention. When free, Maverick chose to invest his time and energy making speeches and renewing Washington contacts in preparation for the 1940 presidential campaign. He administered the city's government efficiently but neglected local politics, as his relationship with San Antonio blacks showed.[47]

Maverick could have cultivated local black support at the beginning of his term. Tom Miller, then mayor of Austin, wrote that "if he uses a little judgment with the negroes he can make firm friends out of them" even though "they have been a little prejudice [sic] against him on account of some of his alleged past actions."[48] Surprisingly, even the Bellinger forces seemed friendly at first. An editorial in the *San Antonio Register* proclaimed that if Maverick kept his campaign promises to improve city health, sanitation, and recreational facilities, he would "certainly win undivided loyalty . . . and possibly gain even greater support from the Negroes than was accorded the late Mayors John Tobin and C. M. Chambers, behind whom the Race stood solidly."[49] Valmo Bellinger actually met with Maverick representatives in 1939, but no political agreements resulted. As long as Bellinger continued in the lottery business, he and Maverick had little basis for allegiance.[50]

Any black support Maverick received would have to come from sources other than those controlled by Bellinger. Unfortunately, Maverick failed to woo those sources and botched his public relations with blacks. An exasperated Elisha Thompson, vice-president of the San Antonio Negro Voters League, sent a hand-delivered message to get his attention; Thompson chided him for being elusive. Paul Johnson, a black college graduate, worked diligently to collect Maverick support within the NAACP, the Negro Chamber of Commerce, and the Negro Voters League, but when he wrote Maverick reporting his successes, Maverick replied with a vague note of thanks, expressing no interest in the details.[51]

Maverick took for granted the valuable support of the National Negro Congress. The NNC was founded under the leadership of John P. Davis in 1935 as an umbrella organization to coordinate the efforts of other black groups. It was one of the most militant black political organizations in America. Its members openly criticized New Deal policies that discriminated against blacks. Despite Maverick's somewhat gradualist racial philosophy, this organization consistently backed him with local and national resources. In 1939 the local NNC surveyed San Antonio blacks to see what public improvements they most desired. This local chapter sent Maverick the results soon after his election. Typically, Maverick was out of town, but John E. Babcock, the city's public relations director, assured the NNC that the city would take action. One year later a dissatisfied NNC committee appeared before the mayor and commissioners, claiming the city had done nothing.[52]

The NNC committee complained specifically that the city had failed to hire enough blacks, thus raising the important but touchy issue of patronage.[53] Maverick had always disapproved of political hiring, preferring, like any good progressive, civil service recruitment to assure competent, efficient public employees. But patronage was a deeply entrenched part of the San Antonio political scene, and it created problems for Maverick as mayor. The day after Maverick's victory, Dan Quill, San Antonio's postmaster and an astute political observer, said that "Maury has a very difficult task ahead of him, and the worst thing is some 3,000 workers he had and everyone of them without jobs, plus about 1,700 city employees, everyone of whom is going to do everything possible to keep his job."[54]

Blacks on the city payroll were, if possible, even more determined to maintain their positions than their white counterparts. Public employment had a special attraction for blacks and other racial minorities. Private industry seldom offered white-collar positions to blacks, so they anxiously sought those jobs in the public sector. In addition to economic security, these jobs provided symbolic evidence of racial progress. Blacks also wanted efficient city government, but unlike Maverick, they had racial goals as well. The situation held great potential for creating misunderstandings on both sides.[55]

During Maverick's administration the number of blacks on the city payroll increased from thirty-one to ninety-one, but the number holding white-collar positions declined. While the Maverick administration hired black garbage collectors, janitors, and maids, it removed black health inspectors, librarians, and nurses. In doing so, Maverick angered the most politically active elements in the black community. C. H. M. Furlow, secretary of the Negro Voters League, lost his position as food inspector. Pearl Arzolia Thompson, a police department employee, was also fired after having held white-collar city positions for twelve years. As a result, she became an implacable and active foe of the Maverick administration. Even George J. Sutton, the local NNC president and a Maverick supporter, protested the removal of a nurse from the Negro clinic. Maverick replied that the nurse was incompetent and promised to replace her, yet the number of Negro city nurses dropped from three to one during the Maverick administration. Maverick's civil service reforms in the police department prevented blacks from entering the force for almost two years. Remaining black workers also experienced salary cuts.[56] Despite Valmo Bellinger's biases, his words provide a summary of the dismay many blacks must have felt toward the Maverick administration by 1940: "Maverick is determined not to see a Negro in any leading capacity. . . . [He] 'has made brave and courageous speeches in the South and over the country for civil rights and for economic justice to the Negro, but here in San Antonio he hasn't done a goddam thing for Negroes that they didn't receive and to a much greater extent under Quin or Tobin.'"[57]

Maverick had indeed often urged increased economic opportunities for blacks, and his administration did hire large numbers of them to serve in menial jobs. But the assignment of white-collar jobs presented complex problems. In his campaign Maverick had promised efficient government and removal of political appointees from the payroll. The police and health departments, where many blacks held white-collar jobs, were the specific targets of reform.[58] Many of these people lost their jobs as the Maverick administration made changes. If Maverick made efforts to hire blacks to replace those who had been fired, these efforts were not vigorous enough to satisfy even those who, like the members of the NNC, already supported him. He certainly did not win over hostile or uncommitted blacks with his hiring policies. On the contrary, the results of Maverick's efficiency drive confirmed suspicions that his progressive reform would backfire against the black community.

Maverick brushed off local blacks' criticisms of his public relations and patronage policies because he believed he had little chance of winning black votes anyway. By 1940 frustrated local blacks evidently appealed to their national organizations to get Maverick's attention. In an ironic twist, national black leaders found themselves trying to explain San Antonio's black citizens to their own mayor. In January Maverick received a letter from William Pickens, national director of branches of the NAACP, who assured Maverick that more San Antonio blacks supported him than it might appear. In a phrase that must have infuriated the reform-minded Maverick, he explained that San Antonio blacks "do not dare sometimes to turn the old machine loose, lest the new machine fail and leave them high and dry."[59] A few months later, after Maverick's actions had further disillusioned even his national supporters, John Davis, secretary of the NNC, felt compelled to remind Maverick that not all San Antonio blacks were "gamblers, racketeers, and voters whose votes were at the disposal of the highest bidder."[60]

In early 1940 Maverick's national black critics grew louder. They questioned not only his judgment but also his commitment to racial reform. In March 1940, for instance, Maverick went to Washington, DC, to testify before a House subcommittee on behalf of an impeccably liberal cause—the abolition of the poll tax. Although he argued the right cause, his line of reasoning dismayed more militant racial reformers. Maverick virtually endorsed the white primary when he claimed that it would prevent Negro domination even if the poll tax were abolished. His main concern, he told the subcommittee, was to enfranchise the poor white man, not the black man. This pragmatic approach infuriated John Davis. Soon after Maverick testified, Davis wrote a caustic letter of disapproval. Several other blacks objected to Maverick's testimony, and some of his northern friends also demurred. At the same time the southern press attacked him for his position on the poll tax itself.[61]

Caught in the classic crossfire so often aimed at southern liberals, Maverick protested loudly. In April 1940 Maverick spoke on the poll tax before the second general meeting of the Southern Conference for Human Welfare, an organization that had been formed in 1938 to combat the South's economic problems and its disregard for the civil rights of both blacks and whites. In martyred tones Maverick chided blacks and northern liberals for their impatience. He thought he deserved his liberal credentials and willingly took abuse from southern conservatives, but criticism from other liberals disturbed him. He had not changed, he said, yet now fellow liberals acted as if he were a turncoat. Though Maverick continued to oppose the poll tax, his enthusiasm for the cause waned appreciably.[62]

In fact, the rising tides of racial liberalism had swamped Maverick. The atmosphere of the nation was changing, but Maverick had not modified his basic attitudes in over a decade. Now economic equality was no longer enough. Political and social equality had also become goals. The acceleration of the movement left Maverick and other southern liberals struggling with their prejudices; they were dangerously close to lashing out at what they believed was the source of their confusion—the black race. Maverick himself recognized this danger. The bitter example of Tom Watson haunted him. But he vowed he would "never go the Tom Watson way"; he would not turn upon those he felt had betrayed him. Yet he defensively challenged blacks to make the first move toward improved race relations in the South, advising them to "free themselves from political domination of any machine or party, and when they vote, vote for those who stand for better living conditions for the Negro people, and don't support those who flatter, cajole, promise, and extend temporary political or financial benefits."[63]

Maverick's own interpretation of the local situation had reinforced his prejudices about blacks' political abilities. He did not believe that blacks were politically mature. He would not uphold their right to political equality until they proved themselves worthy by "properly" exercising the limited rights they already held.

Unfortunately for Maverick, events in the spring of 1940 kept the white primary issue alive. In May the NAACP launched a statewide fund-raising drive to finance a legal challenge to Texas's white primary. Prominent black San Antonians, including Valmo Bellinger, participated in the effort, and it received ample publicity in the *San Antonio Register*. In his official capacity Maverick could do little to aid or to hinder the NAACP effort. But his earlier stand put his black supporters in a difficult position during the campaign, especially since the machine had often opposed the white primary.[64] San Antonio blacks chafed under the white primary's limitations, but they felt secure in their ability to affect San Antonio's "nonpartisan" municipal elections.

Maverick and the commissioners shattered this security in November 1940 when they submitted a proposal for a new city charter.[65] In the handling of this issue Maverick's strong dedication to progressive municipal reform once again overwhelmed his tenuous commitment to racial liberalism. In his 1939 campaign Maverick had advocated charter revisions in order to reduce the machine's ability to dominate city elections. The machine had long ago subverted the supposedly incorruptible commission form of government. To correct this problem Maverick wanted the city to adopt a council-manager plan in which an elected council appointed a professional, disinterested administrator to manage city affairs.[66] As a general theory of municipal government the council-manager plan contained nothing inimical to black political participation. Maverick's handling of the reform, however, and the specific provisions of the plan offered to the voters in 1940, outraged the black community. Maverick failed to appoint any blacks to the committee drafting the reform, and when his black supporters pointed out this oversight, he still took no action.[67] More important was the fact that portions of the committee's plan threatened to curtail black political influence.

Because of the apathy of San Antonio's white population, the organized black bloc had for years carried disproportionate weight in the citywide commissioners' elections. Although the at-large nature of these elections made the victory of a black candidate for mayor or commissioner very unlikely, the black community had been able to use its bloc to bargain with the white machine for racial benefits. In the new plan, however, the committee proposed to replace the election of at-large commissioner candidates with candidates chosen from eleven geographically based councilman districts. Such a change would have prevented a black bloc from operating as a swing vote in the mayoral and the commissioners' races. On the other hand, single-member districts usually enhance the possibilities of black office-holding. But the council districts the committee proposed divided the black community, gerrymandering it out of the opportunity to affect any council race.[68] In short, the new plan would have reduced the blacks' former advantages without replacing them with any new opportunities.

If Maverick had been as fearlessly dedicated to racial reform as he was to many other controversial issues, he might have tried to influence the charter committee to create at least one predominantly black district. Not only would this have been seen as a stunningly liberal move, but it might have garnered a political payoff. If properly constructed, single-member council districts could have given the reformers a big bargaining chip in the black community. The machine, after all, had never offered blacks a chance for elected office.

But Maverick exercised no such liberal leadership. The committee's plan promised to achieve his major goal of breaking the machine's hold over municipal politics by splitting the black vote so the machine could gain nothing through "unprincipled" attempts to win black votes. The plan, however, created a situation in which no political candidate, machine or otherwise, could gain much by courting blacks. In other words, the destruction of black political power was, for Maverick, an acceptable solution to the "irresponsible" use of such power. He endorsed the plan as written, though he did not vigorously campaign for it.[69]

The black community reacted immediately to the charter proposal. Coming so late in the year the election took everyone by surprise. For San Antonio blacks 1940 was an off year, since municipal elections normally occurred in odd-numbered years. Many blacks had probably failed to pay their poll taxes, even though a year earlier the far-sighted editor of the *San Antonio Register* had warned that a special election might occur.[70] Because of the short period between the announcement of the plan and the election, the campaign took on a tone of desperation.

The effort to defeat the charter united the black community. Robert (Bob) Sullivan, former Maverick supporter and head of the Bexar County Educational League, cochaired the Colored Anti-City Manager committee with Valmo Bellinger. Black ministers opposed the plan from their pulpits. The lists of speakers at the Anti-City Manager rallies included the names of the leaders of "Santone" society. Key members of the NAACP, the Negro Voters League, and the Negro Chamber of Commerce opposed the plan. Only the loyal, long-suffering G. J. Sutton supported the plan, and even he had "little to say" about it.[71]

The Anti-City Manager forces won, eliciting a nearly unanimous vote against the plan among blacks on the east side.[72] An editorial in the *San Antonio Register* claimed the election demonstrated that "when confronted by a common danger, the Negroes of San Antonio can, and will, present a determined united front against any inroads that might threaten their civil and economic security."[73] Many San Antonio blacks saw the charter as a threat to the effectiveness of their municipal suffrage. Although some blacks probably excused Maverick from complete responsibility for the plan, the whole affair appears to have had his blessing.

For Maverick the eastside results of the special election confirmed the pessimistic conclusions that he had drawn after the 1939 election—the machine dominated San Antonio's black voters. Certainly machine politicians had exploited the issue, and on the surface the unity of the black vote recalled past triumphs of machine manipulation. But many blacks had opposed the plan in a rational exercise of political choice. Maverick, however, believed blacks to be incapable of such rationality, and he prepared for his 1941 reelection campaign expecting little black support.

Maverick again faced C. K. Quin as his major opponent in 1941. Moreover, during Maverick's two years in office, Owen Kilday had entrenched himself as county sheriff. In addition, a change in state law required San Antonio city officials to receive a majority, rather than a plurality, of votes. With the machine reunited, no split would aid Maverick. If the machine regained power through winning the mayor's office too, all of Maverick's new reforms would disappear, forcing any later challenges to start from scratch. Maverick had no time to play tug-of-war with a city machine, for memories in the nation's capital were short. To return to Congress and to regain his privileged position in national politics, he had to destroy the machine completely.

Maverick decided to run on his excellent administrative record. As a progressive reformer he had secured much-needed improvements in the police and health departments and had rationalized tax collection. He had erected new tourist attractions in the city and had made a dent in the city's vice and gambling industries.[74] Yet Maverick had made political mistakes, and the machine focused on these mistakes to augment their campaign promises of more patronage jobs for blacks. Maverick had left town too often, running off to make controversial speeches or to visit his Washington friends. Maverick was a "red"; had he not upheld the Communists' right to use the Municipal Auditorium? At black and Mexican American rallies, the anti-Mavericks chipped away at the mayor's image as a racial reformer, reminding audiences of their exclusion from city jobs and promising changes.[75]

Maverick's record contained few items that he could use to counter the racially oriented appeals. He had worked for the city as a unit, not for individual groups. He complained about the anti-Mavericks' special appeals. "You would think Kilday was a carpetbagger from the North down here just after the Civil war, attempting to raise the colored people against the whites," Maverick declared after Owen Kilday reminded blacks of certain deteriorations in their patronage benefits.[76] Yet Maverick's opponents easily dragged him away from his record and into the quicksand of special-interest politics.

Meanwhile, the machine recognized changes in San Antonio's black political structure and quickly adapted. The anti-Mavericks exploited the remnants of Valmo Bellinger's eastside influence, but they also branched out, collecting support through the black Bexar County Civic Association. The Reverend O. S. Wilkinson and J. W. ("Pops") Hemmings, who had lost his city job as director of the Negro Recreation Department, headed this new organization. It contained black voters who disliked Maverick but shied away from the disreputable Bellinger forces. Maverick had missed his opportunities to consolidate such support.[77]

The May 13 election results discouraged the Maverick forces. The race between Maverick and Quin was close, and the presence of four minor mayoral candidates on the ballot meant that no one received a majority. Quin received a plurality, with 17,435 votes to Maverick's 16,202. Maverick lost much of the westside Mexican American vote he had received in 1939. As he expected, he lost heavily on the east side, but, once again, blacks had not voted as a bloc. In fact, more blacks voted for Maverick in 1941 than in 1939. He received 35 to 45 percent in some precincts.[78] But Maverick, facing a tough runoff against

Quin, searched wildly for a scapegoat. In his eyes San Antonio blacks had rejected him even though he embodied the New Deal liberalism that he believed was the true salvation for blacks all over the country. Maverick's disappointment and views of black voting habits kept him from acknowledging their increased support. What he interpreted as blacks' loyalty to the machine once again proved to Maverick that the city's blacks could not discern their own best interests. But this time Maverick contemplated this "fact" in the heat and desperation of a campaign that would determine his long-term political future. He had to win the election and break the machine so that he could eventually return to Washington as a champion of the people.

In his mind a group of irresponsible blacks stood between him and his cherished goals. He had fought his prejudices and had made concessions on racial issues. Having earned the praise of racial reformers in the 1930s, he thought his painful struggles were over. But now it seemed to him that blacks' demands were insatiable. He could never satisfy them, so why should he continue to try? Why should he treat these black people with careful consideration when they were about to ruin his election chances? Perhaps he could still win if he could somehow arouse white San Antonians. And so, at some point during the hectic days before the runoff election, Maverick decided to discard all efforts to maintain a liberal stance on race. Instead, he appealed to whites only. Frustration with San Antonio blacks made his demagoguery ring true, and he began to sound more and more like Tom Watson.

"If it hadn't been for the Negro vote, the complete greater San Antonio ticket would have been reelected in the city's primary election," Maverick lashed out at a Denver Heights rally three days after the first vote. "Valmo Bellinger, son of the late Charles Bellinger, is Quin's chief supporter."[79] Maverick declared that he no longer cared whether he got any black votes or not; he was "tired of petting Negroes!"[80]

Sick and desperate, Maverick began the final week of campaigning by addressing an audience at Hermann Sons Hall on May 20. He raised the specter of Negro domination at which he himself had scoffed in the past: "If Quin goes into the city hall, Bellinger will be the most important man there. . . . Even your cook would be more important than you. We can't afford to have San Antonio dominated by the colored race."[81]

Shocked black supporters of Maverick immediately protested, reminding Maverick that their hundreds of votes contributed to keeping him in the race. Leading black ministers jointly condemned all forms of racketeering in an effort to refute Maverick's contention that Valmo Bellinger controlled all blacks. The Bexar County Civic Association disclaimed any ties to Bellinger. But Maverick continued to vent his frustrations until the runoff election on May 27.[82]

Amazingly, Maverick's tirades had only a slight effect on the black vote. Maverick's share of the vote in the black precincts dropped from almost 38 percent in the first election to 36 percent in the runoff . Maverick's scorned black supporters were loyal indeed. But his demagoguery gained him no white support either. The final tally gave Quin 20,982 votes to Maverick's 19,799. By doing virtually nothing, or at least nothing in public, Quin had gained bits of support throughout the city with a nice chunk from the Mexican American west side. Maverick never broke the machine and never held elected public office again, though within months he returned to Washington as a wartime administrator.

Maverick probably never recognized how his challenge to the machine affected San Antonio's black political development. During the time of his involvement in city politics, several changes had occurred in the black community. First, no one succeeded Charles Bellinger after his death, and Valmo Bellinger never could deliver a black bloc vote in the face of a real challenge. The closest Bellinger came to victory was in 1939, but even then the black bloc was starting to fall apart as black turnout, freed from the discipline imposed by Charles Bellinger, declined.[83] More important, significant segments of the black community that did vote escaped Valmo Bellinger's control. Valmo Bellinger probably was not as good a politician as his father had been, but he also faced a changed black community.

In a way the black bloc vote destroyed itself. By voting as a bloc, San Antonio blacks received political experience and knowledge of government operations. Their political power shielded them from the kinds of intimidation that kept so many other southern blacks from developing alternate political tactics. The black bloc vote brought improved schools where black children learned to read and to interpret current events. Many of the black community's new clubs, political and otherwise, had affiliations with national organizations. Through these groups San Antonio blacks learned how blacks all over the country felt about various issues and people. The city's black voters became more independent and their political environment became more complex.[84]

At the very time that San Antonio blacks were developing independent political viewpoints, Maury Maverick arrived to challenge the San Antonio machine. His challenge actually forced the disintegration of the black bloc vote. Confusion resulted within the black community when it received conflicting political advice about Maverick. The machine counseled blacks to oppose him, yet national black organizations supported him even as they sternly urged him to continue his evolution as a racial liberal. Maverick's challenge forced cracks in the bloc in 1939, and by 1941 one could no longer call it a bloc, though Maverick himself did. The machine would retain some influence in the black community for years to come, but its control would never again be as monolithic as it had been in the legendary days of Charles Bellinger.[85]

Logically Maverick, had he recognized them, could have exploited these changes more effectively than he did. After all, his liberal reputation had caused some of them. But he was more interested in questions of national policy than in the characteristics of his own constituents, and he missed the discontinuities between national and local politics. When Maverick entered municipal politics, he considered San Antonio blacks to be just a small subset of American blacks who should automatically favor the New Deal and the type of racial liberalism that he had been advocating for years. After all, many national black leaders had endorsed him. But San Antonio blacks had their own standards, and their expectations were higher than those of most southern blacks. Maverick never really took this local variation into account.

Even if Maverick had been more in touch with his black constituents' demands, his racial prejudices curbed his efforts to gain black votes. Maverick suffered from acute ambivalence in his attitude toward black political support. He was willing to accept, and at first even expected, the votes of San Antonio's partially enfranchised black citizens. He had, after all, actively supported economic equality for all races, and he had voted for antilynching legislation. Yet he had no firm commitment to uphold black political rights. At bottom, he felt that blacks could not be trusted to make rational political decisions in their own best interests. In 1939 Maverick was at least superficially willing to be proved wrong about blacks' political abilities, but the only evidence that he would accept was a wholehearted, unequivocal vote for him. When this failed to materialize, he minimized the black support that he did have and reverted to his original position by lumping all blacks together and viewing them as political puppets manipulated by an unscrupulous machine. As a result, he gave up any attempt to win black votes, partly because he felt such attempts would be doomed to failure and partly because he was disgusted at the idea of opportunistically appealing to such "unworthy" voters.

This attitude led the liberal "Texas Firebrand" into seemingly uncharacteristic behavior during his tenure as mayor. He upheld the white primary even though it deprived blacks of an effective franchise. He instituted progressive civil service reforms at the expense of the already painfully small group of black white-collar workers in the city. He stood back while the all-white charter committee that he had selected attempted to gerrymander blacks out of a voice in city affairs. And in 1941 he stooped to racial demagoguery in an attempt to gain votes.

This turned out to be the low point in Maverick's attitude toward blacks, however. Once out of elected office, Maverick's racial theories, which had been static for so long, began to evolve once again. By the time of his death in 1954 he had developed a more consistently liberal attitude toward blacks.

One of the touchiest aspects of the issue of political equality disappeared from the realm of controversy in 1944 when the U.S. Supreme Court ruled the white primary illegal. However Maverick reacted to this decision at first, by 1952 he was willing to accept black voters as an integral component in the Texas liberal coalition. In fact, he chastised Adlai E. Stevenson's campaign workers for failing to recognize their importance. He even reached some kind of *modus vivendi* with Valmo Bellinger. In a 1952 letter to Walter White he praised a speech that Bellinger had made at a Democratic party meeting that they had both attended.[86]

Maverick's position on social equality also changed, perhaps in part because of his new perception of blacks as political allies. In 1952 he wrote noted southern liberal Virginia Durr, describing the racially integrated political buffets that he had begun hosting in his home. He staunchly opposed racial segregation at political fund-raising affairs during the 1952 presidential campaign.[87]

Maverick had at last taken the southern liberal's final step. His prolonged hesitancy to follow the black civil rights movement to its logical conclusion is a poignant testimony to the durability of southern racism. After all, Maverick fought fearlessly for civil rights throughout his adult life. In the case of blacks, he balked, not out of timidity or even political pragmatism, but rather because since childhood he had absorbed the idea that white people should treat black people with benevolent paternalism. It took almost an entire lifetime for him to admit the mistakenness of this attitude.

## NOTES

1. *San Antonio Light*, May 21, 1941, Scrapbook 4K122, Maury Maverick Sr. Papers (cited hereafter as MMP), Barker Texas History Center, University of Texas, Austin.

2. J. August Wolf, quoted in Richard B. Henderson, *Maury Maverick: A Political Biography* (Austin: University of Texas Press, 1970), 65.

3. The nickname appears in "Unbranded Bullfrog," *Time*, May 22, 1939, 22.

4. Henderson, *Maury Maverick*, 66, 74, 89–90; Stuart L. Weiss, "Maury Maverick and the Liberal Bloc," *Journal of American History* 57 (March 1971), 881–82, 892–95.

5. Henderson, *Maury Maverick*, 51–53, 78, 90–93; Mary Maverick McMillan Fisher, "San Antonio 1: The Hoover Era," in Robert C. Cotner et al., *Texas Cities and the Great Depression* (Austin: Texas Memorial Museum, 1973), 66; Maury Maverick, *A Maverick American* (New York: Covici-Friede, 1937), 337–41.

6. The pro-Maverick bias of the eastern press tended to obscure certain ambiguities in Maverick's racial beliefs and to strengthen his reputation as a racial liberal. See Weiss, "Maury Maverick and the Liberal Bloc," 892, 886. Heywood Broun, "A Sock for Garner," *New Republic* 99 (May 24, 1939), 72, and Charles Curtis Munz, "Gunning for Maverick," *Nation* 149 (December 16, 1939), 673–74, provide examples of press reinforcement of Maverick's image.

7. Henderson, *Maury Maverick*, 60 (quotation). Harvard Sitkoff presents a similar picture in *A New Deal for Blacks: The Emergence of Civil Rights as a National Issue*, vol. 1, *The Depression Decade* (New York: Oxford University Press, 1978), 112, 124, 131—32, 136, 289–90. Weiss also portrays Maverick as thoroughly liberal. See Weiss, "Maury Maverick and the Liberal Bloc," 880–95.

8. Henderson's biography, *Maury Maverick*, amply details Maverick's fascination with national and international issues. See also the recollections of Malcolm Bardwell, a former employee and political associate, in his interview with Dorothy Pierce, October 17, 1968, transcript pp. 4–5, Lyndon Baines Johnson Library (cited hereafter as LBJ Library), Austin, Texas.

9. Maverick, *A Maverick American*, 224.

10. Franklin D. Roosevelt, "A Message to the Conference on Economic Conditions of the South," July 4, 1933, in Samuel L Rosenman, comp., *The Public Papers and Addresses of Franklin D. Roosevelt*, v01.7, *The Continuing Struggle for Liberalism* (New York: Russell and Russell, 1938), 421; Sitkoff, *A New Deal for Blacks*, 128–30; Morton Sosna, *In Search of the Silent South: Southern Liberals and the Race Issue* (New York: Columbia University Press, 1977), 60–65; Maury Maverick, "The South Is Rising," *Nation* 142 (June 17, 1936), 770–72; Maverick, *A Maverick American*, 19–20, 26–27, 33–34.

11. Maverick to Forrest Bailey, October 29, 1928, Box 21.45, MMP.

12. Ibid., May 14, 1929, MMP.

13. Maverick, A Maverick American, 272.

14. Ibid., 58; James R. Green, *Grass-Roots Socialism: Radical Movements in the Southwest, 1895–1943* (Baton Rouge: Louisiana State University Press, 1978), 32, 96; John B. Kirby, *Black Americans in the Roosevelt Era: Liberalism and Race* (Knoxville, Tennessee: University of Tennessee Press, 1980), 92–93 passim.

15. Sosna, *In Search of the Silent South*, 18–19, 40, 63, 89, 120, 136–37 passim. See Charles W. Eagles, *Jonathan Daniels and Race Relations: The Evolution of a Southern Liberal* (Knoxville, Tennessee: University of Tennessee Press, 1982), 21–23, for an example of a similar type of limited southern liberalism in the early 1930s.

16. Maverick, *A Maverick American*, 222, 265–73; Maverick, address to International House students, February 1938, typescript, Box 21.60, MMP; Kirby, *Black Americans in the Roosevelt Era*, 94–95; Sitkoff, *A New Deal for Blacks*, 298.

17. C. Vann Woodward, *The Strange Career of Jim Crow*, 2nd ed. (New York: Oxford University Press, 1966), 84–85; Dewey W. Grantham, *Southern Progressivism: The Reconciliation of Progress and Tradition* (Knoxville, Tennessee: University of Tennessee Press, 1983), 112–21.

18. Owen P. White, "Machine Made," *Colliers*, September 18, 1937, 32, 35; Neil Gary Sapper, "Survey of the History, 1930–1954" (PhD diss., Texas Tech University, 1972), 68.

19. U.S. Bureau of the Census, *Fifteenth Census of the United States, 1930: Population*, vol. 3, pt. 2 (Washington: Government Printing Office, 1932), 1009; Audrey Granneberg, "Maury Maverick's San Antonio," *Survey Graphic: Magazine of Social Interpretation* 28 (July 1939), 423; Green Peyton, *San Antonio: City in the Sun* (New York: Kessinger Publishing, 1946), 75–76, 178–79, 181–83; White, "Machine Made," 32, 35.

20. *San Antonio Express*, December 21, 1938; Ralph J. Bunche, *The Political Status of the Negro in the Age of FDR*, ed. Dewey W. Grantham (Chicago: University of Chicago Press, 1973), 131.

21. Roger M. Olien, *From Token to Triumph: The Texas Republicans since 1920* (Dallas: Southern Methodist University Press, 1982), 30–31; "Don Politico," *San Antonio Light*, August 28, 1938, Scrapbook 4K149, MMP; Henderson, *Maury Maverick*, 61.

22. Darlene Clark Hine, *Black Victory: The Rise and Fall of the White Primary in Texas* (Millwood, New York: KTO Press, 1979), 47–48.

23. Ibid., 110, 124, 152; *Nixon v. Condon* et al., 286 U.S. 73 (1932).

24. Hine, *Black Victory*, 152–53; Nowlin Randolph, *The Citizens League Will Win Again* (San Antonio, Texas: Marjorie McGehee Randolph, 1973), 33–36; Sapper, "Survey of the History," 29–30, 38. Sapper estimates that as many as three thousand blacks voted in the election.

25. Randolph, *Citizens League*, 36.

26. Richard B. Henderson, "The Political Philosophy of Maury Maverick Sr. with Respect to Civil Liberties" (PhD diss., University of Maryland, 1960), 242; Hine, *Black Victory*, 157.

27. Henderson, "Political Philosophy of Maury Maverick," 242.

28. *Smith v. Allwright, Election Judge, et al.*, 321 U.S. 649 (1944).

29. *Charleston* (SC) *News and Courier*, December 21, 1939, Scrapbook 4K121, MMP; *Philadelphia Independent*, July 31, 1938, Scrapbook 4K149; Sitkoff, *A New Deal for Blacks*, 290; Eagles, *Jonathan Daniels and Race Relations*, 34, 57; Jacquelyn Dowd Hall, *Revolt Against Chivalry: Jessie Daniel Ames and the Women's Campaign against Lynching* (New York: Columbia University Press, 1979), 243; 75th Cong., 1st sess., *Congressional Record*, April 15, 1937, 3536–37

30. Maverick, *A Maverick American*, 272.

31. Ibid., 18.

32. Ibid., 18–19; Maverick to H. L. Mencken, May 23, 1938, Box 21.45, MMP.

33. Maverick, an address to the Southern Conference for Human Welfare, Chattanooga, Tennessee, April 16, 1940, typescript, Box 21.62, MMP; Maverick, address to International House students, February 1938. For evidence of San Antonians' real if somewhat grudging tolerance toward an earlier antilynching proposal, see Olien, *From Token to Triumph*, 33–34.

34. Peyton, *San Antonio*, 180–82, 186–88; Bunche, *Political Status of the Negro*, 465–66.

35. Peyton, *San Antonio*, 187; Broun, "A Sock for Garner," 72; George Norris Green, *The Establishment in Texas Politics: The Primitive Years, 1938–1957* (Norman: University of Oklahoma Press, 1979), 15–44; Granneberg, "Maury Maverick's San Antonio," 426.

36. Henderson, *Maury Maverick*, 180; "Don Politico," *San Antonio Light*, August 28, 1938, Scrapbook 4K149, MMP.

37. John P. Davis to Maverick, March 11, 1940, Box 2L25, MMP; *San Antonio Light*, "Don Politico," August 28, 1938, Scrapbook 4K149, MMP; J. W. Aitch, "T'id Bits from the Weekly News," *San Antonio Register*, July 29, 1938. Aitch heavily qualifies his praise for Maverick, however.

38. Henderson, *Maury Maverick*, 185. Maverick never explicitly stated that he wished to return to Washington, but both his friends and enemies assumed that a return was his ultimate goal, and he was always careful to leave his options open. See the *San Antonio Light*, December 30, 1938, Scrapbook 4K120, MMP; Tom Miller to Lyndon Johnson, May 11, 1939, papers of Lyndon B. Johnson as Congressman, Box 5, folder "Miller, Tom," LBJ Library; typescript of article from the *Capitol Daily*, June 6, 1930, folder "Maury Maverick," LBJ Library; Maverick, draft and revisions of radio speech for station WOAI, San Antonio, February 10, 1939, Box 2L61, MMP.

39. Granneberg, "Maury Maverick's San Antonio," 425–26; Peyton, *San Antonio*, 175–79.

40. Granneberg, "Maury Maverick's San Antonio," 426; *San Antonio Express*, February 11, March 15, 1939; "Don Politico," *San Antonio Light*, February 23, 1939, Scrapbook 4K120, MMP; *San Antonio Express*, March 3, 1939; *San Antonio Light*, February 3, 1939, Scrapbook 4K120, MMP.

41. Sapper, "Survey of the History," 43.

42. Lyndon Gayle Knippa, "San Antonio 2: The Early New Deal," in Cotner, *Texas Cities and the Great Depression*, 7; Julia Kirk Blackwelder, *Women of the Depression: Caste and Culture in San Antonio, 1929–1939* (College Station, Texas: Texas A&M University Press, 1984), 120–23; *San Antonio Express*, January 26, 1939.

43. White, "Machine Made," 35. Bunche also notes benefits received by San Antonio blacks, but, understandably, considering his own liberalism, his analysis minimizes the extent to which these benefits resulted from machine activities. See Bunche, *Political Status of the Negro*, 465; Editorial, San Antonio Register, May 5, 1939.

44. Sitkoff, *A New Deal for Blacks*, 332–34.

45. Bunche, *Political Status of the Negro*, 70; John P. Davis to Maverick, March 11, 1940, Box 2L25, MMP. A *San Antonio Register* editorial lavishly praised the NAACP's nonpartisan position. Presumably the threat of a Maverick endorsement provoked this response. Editorial, *San Antonio Register*, March 31, 1939.

46. The final vote citywide was Maury Maverick—18,375, C. K. Quin—14,874, LeRoy Jeffers—11,503, Maude Pridgen Butler—65, Charles E. Hummel—45, S. M. Esler—11. *San Antonio Express*, May 10, 1939. My calculations indicate that Maverick received approximately 35 percent of the vote in the black precincts. Both Walter White and John P. Davis thought that Maverick got 35 to 40 percent of the black vote in 1939. Ralph Bunche also thought Maverick got as much as 30 percent. But Maverick himself consistently maintained that he received only 21 percent of the black vote in this election. See John P. Davis to Maverick, with Maverick's marginal comments, March 11, 1940, and Walter White to Maverick, June 17, 1939, both in Box 2L25, MMP; Bunche, *Political Status of the Negro*, 131; Maverick, address to the Southern Conference for Human Welfare.

47. Henderson, *Maury Maverick*, 196–97, 203–208; *San Antonio Light*, May 28, 1941, Scrapbook 4K122, MMP; Maverick, draft of radio speech for station KTSA, San Antonio, July 22, 1940, Box 2L62, MMP. By 1940 Maverick was drawing criticism for his trips away from San Antonio. See the draft of Maverick's speech before the regular meeting of the City Commission of the City of San Antonio, "San Antonio's Connection with the Federal Government and the Future of the City," March 14, 1940, Box 2L61, MMP.

48. Tom Miller to Lyndon Johnson.

49. Editorial, *San Antonio Register*, June 2, 1939.

50. Sapper, "Survey of the History," 70.

51. Elisha Thompson to Maverick, August 12, 1939, Box 2L24, MMP; two undated letters, Paul Johnson to Maverick and Maverick to Paul Johnson, April 18, 1940, both in Box 2L25, MMP.

52. Office memo, John E. Babcock to city departments, July 28, 1939, Box 2L24, MMP; *San Antonio Register*, August 4, 1939; *San Antonio Register*, August 16, 1940.

53. *San Antonio Register*, August 16, 1940.

54. Dan Quill to Lyndon Johnson, May 10, 1939, Box 31, folder "Quill, Dan," LBJ Library.

55. Harold F. Gosnell, *Negro Politicians: The Rise of Negro Politics in Chicago* (Chicago: University of Chicago Press, 1935), 163–64.

56. Bunche, *Political Status of the Negro*, 562–63; filing reference to a let-

ter from Elisha Thompson to Maverick, June 7, 1940, Box 2L25, MMP; A. W. Jackson, *A Sure Foundation* (Houston: privately printed, 1938), 103; Robert L. Whitfield, Robert (Bob) Sullivan, Mrs. J. M. E. Lee, and F. R. Lee to Floyd McGown, May 7, 1940, Box 2L25, MMP; filing reference to a letter from G. J. Sutton to Maverick, July 15, 1939, Box 2L24, MMP; *San Antonio Register*, April 25, 1941.

57. Quoted in Bunche, *Political Status of the Negro*, 562–63.

58. Maverick, draft of radio speech for station WOAI, San Antonio, February 10, 1939.

59. William Pickens to Maverick, January 3, 1940, Box 2L25, MMP.

60. John P. Davis to Maverick, March 11, 1940, Box 2L25, MMP.

61. Maverick, address to the Southern Conference for Human Welfare, April 16, 1940; John P. Davis to Maverick, March 11, 1940, Box 2L25, MMP. Maverick's actual testimony was not published, but what he said may be reconstructed using these sources.

62. Thomas A. Krueger, *And Promises to Keep: The Southern Conference for Human Welfare, 1938–1948* (Nashville: Vanderbilt University Press, 1967), 20–21, 53, 57; Maverick, address to the Southern Conference for Human Welfare, April 16, 1940; Maverick to Crawford Peffer, April 22, 1940, Box 2L25, MMP.

63. Maverick, address to the Southern Conference for Human Welfare.

64. Front-page articles on the white primary battle appear frequently in the *San Antonio Register* from June 1940 through May 1941. See especially June 28, 1940, and February 7, 1941. Also see "Broad Fight for Vote Launched by NAACP," *Crisis* 47 (May 1940):149–50; Carter W. Wesley, "Texans Seek Right to Vote," *Crisis* 47 (October 1940), 312–13, 322.

65. *San Antonio Express*, November 7, 1940.

66. Maverick, draft of radio speech, "Fusion vs. Confusion," for station WOAI, San Antonio, May 3, 1939, Box 2L61, MMP. For other examples of corrupted commission-led cities see Bradley Robert Rice, *Progressive Cities: The Commission Government Movement in America, 1901–1920* (Austin: University of Texas Press, 1977), 96–99.

67. List of the Advisory Committee to Draft the City Manager Charter, n.d., Box 2L75, MMP; filing reference to a letter from G. J. Sutton to Maverick, February 26, 1940, Box 2L25, MMP.

68. Chandler Davidson and George Korbel, "At-Large Elections and Minority Group Representation: A Reexamination of Historical and Contemporary Evidence," in Chandler Davidson, ed., *Minority Vote Dilution* (Washington, D.C., 1984), 65–79; editorial, *San Antonio Register*, December 13, 1940.

69. *San Antonio Express*, November 7, 1940. John A. Booth and David R. Johnson, "Power and Progress in San Antonio Politics, 1836–1970," in David R. Johnson, John A. Booth, and Richard J. Harris, eds., *The Politics of San Antonio: Community, Progress, & Power* (Lincoln: University of Nebraska Press, 1983), 19, suggest that Maverick may have actually wanted the charter plan to be defeated. Whether or not this was the case, he was intimately associated with the plan and had to bear the burden of its political unpopularity in the black community.

70. Editorial, *San Antonio Register*, December 29, 1939.

71. *San Antonio Register*, November 29, 1940, December 13, 1940 (quotation). "Santone" is a term San Antonio blacks used to refer to themselves. The *San Antonio Register* frequently used it.

72. Ibid., December 20, 1940.

73. Editorial, ibid., December 27, 1940.

74. Henderson, *Maury Maverick*, 226; San Antonio *Light*, June 1, 1941, Scrapbook 4K123, MMP; *San Antonio Express*, April 30, 1941, Scrapbook 4K122, MMP.

75. Much of the content of Quin's campaign can be deduced from Maverick's reactions to it. See *San Antonio Express*, May 1, 1941, Scrapbook 4K121; and ibid., May 9, 1941, Scrapbook 4K122, both in MMP.

76. *San Antonio Light*, May 10, 1941, Scrapbook 4K122, MMP.

77. "Don Politico," *San Antonio Light*, May 4, 1941, 4K122, MMP

78. The minor candidates received the following votes citywide: Norman Brock—1,104, W. B. Ling—317, Bob Mcnefee—506, and H. L. Summerville—230. *San Antonio Express*, May 14, 1941, Scrapbook 4K122, MMP.

79. *San Antonio Light*, May 17, 1941, Scrapbook 4K122, MMP.

80. *San Antonio Register*, May 23, 1941.

81. *San Antonio Light*, May 21, 1941, Scrapbook 4K122, MMP (quotation); *San Antonio Express*, May 21, 1941, MMP.

82 "Don Politico," *San Antonio Light*, May 22, 1941, MMP.

83. In 1939, 5,580 blacks registered to vote. Ralph Bunche estimated that approximately half of these actually voted. Bunche, *Political Status of the Negro*, 466. In 1939 the total vote reported in the fifteen precincts that I have identified as predominantly black was 3,118. Although these precincts contained a small admixture of white voters, they also excluded the votes of blacks scattered throughout other parts of the city. It seems fairly safe to conclude that black turnout was somewhere between 2,500 and 3,000 in 1939, or considerably lower than estimates for elections earlier in the 1930s. This decreased black turnout should not he read as a sign that San Antonio blacks were sinking into political inactivity. They were adjusting to a power vacuum caused by Charles Bellinger's death. See note 85 below.

84. V. O. Key Jr. notes the long-term results of black political participation: "In localities that have accepted Negro Voting for many years . . . Negroes seem to manifest less solidarity than in those areas where the right to vote is less firmly established. They divide in the manner of whites." See his *Southern Politics in State and Nation* (New York: Knopf, 1949), 649.

85. For example, in 1946 Valmo Bellinger ended up supporting the liberal, antigambling reformer Homer Rainey for governor against the wishes of the machine. This was the only way he could maintain the fiction of control over the black vote, since San Antonio blacks overwhelmingly supported Rainey. See Donald S. Strong, "The Rise of Negro Voting in Texas," *American Political Science Review*, 42 (June 1948), 510–22; see 520. The influence of Maverick's black ally George J. Sutton rose over the years. In 1948 a coalition of blacks and Mexican Americans, working against the machine and Bellinger, elected Sutton to a school board position. In 1972 Sutton became a state representative from Bexar County. See Sapper, "Survey of the History," 167; John L. Davis, *San Antonio: A Historical Portrait* (Austin: Encino Press, 1978), 41. See Robert A. Goldberg, "Racial Change on the Southern Periphery: The Case of San Antonio, Texas, 1960–1965," *Journal of Southern History*, 49 (August 1983): 349–74, for evidence of the durability of the Sutton-Bellinger rivalry for the allegiance of the black voter.

86. Maverick to Adlai E. Stevenson, telegram, September 1, 1951, Box 2L40, MMP; Maverick to Walter White, December 15, 1952, Box 2L41, MMP.

87. Maverick to Virginia Durr, November 19, 1952, Box 2L41, MMP; Maverick to India Edwards, September 3, 1952, Box 2L40, MMP.

# The Houston Eagles and the End of the Negro Leagues

ROB FINK

AFRICAN AMERICAN BASEBALL IN TEXAS HAD a brief but vibrant history. From the unaffiliated semiprofessional teams that existed around the state to the Texas-Oklahoma-Louisiana League, baseball remained a constant aspect of African American life in Texas. In 1949, black professional baseball came to Texas in the form of the Houston Eagles of the Negro American League (NAL). The Eagles' arrival came as part of a last-ditch effort by owners of black teams to compete with the then-integrating Major League clubs. Given the state's role in the creation of the first black league by Rube Foster, and the rise of prominent players including Willie Wells and "Smokey" Joe Williams, it is perhaps fitting that Texas played a role in the end of African American baseball. Indeed in many ways the story of the Houston Eagles offers closure for both a league and an era.

In the years after World War II, baseball experienced wide-spread popularity around the country. Major League players like Ted Williams and Joe DiMaggio returned from combat, and their return to baseball rekindled America's love of the game. Black baseball too saw a brief resurgence after the war. Players such as Max Manning of the Newark Eagles returned from the armed forces, while others, like Willie Wells, returned from Latin America. In Texas, black baseball got caught up in the same postwar excitement. Owing to an absence of players and fans, many of Texas' black semiprofessional teams had folded during the war, but African American baseball never completely died and the postwar years witnessed a revival. In 1945, the Negro National League and Negro American League held a North-South All-Star Game in Houston featuring such stars as Josh Gibson, "Cool Papa" Bell, and Roy Campanella.[1]

So popular was the All-Star Game that fans in Texas began calling for the return of black professional baseball to the state. One sports writer for the *Houston Informer* declared that because Houston had "the largest black population in the South according to ratio," it stood to reason that black baseball would succeed in the city if someone of ability and experience would step forward to assume a role of leadership.[2] According to the reporter, the once-prominent Houston Black Buffaloes had failed because the team's owners had lacked experience (they were unable to manage the team's finances and were inept at generating public interest).[3] Thus by extension, if an experienced, competent person organized a black team in Houston, it would almost certainly be successful.

Two years later, baseball changed forever when Branch Rickey and the Brooklyn Dodgers took the first major step toward desegregating Major League Baseball. On April 15, 1947, a former All-American athlete at the University of California, Los Angeles, named Jackie Robinson took the field for the Brooklyn Dodgers in a game against the Boston Braves. As an African American, Robinson gained off-field notoriety for his role in integrating the major leagues, but his on-field heroics were equally striking. He helped lead Brooklyn to numerous National League pennants and one World Series Championship. He won the Rookie of the Year award in 1947, as well as the Most Valuable Player award in 1951.

When Robinson broke the color barrier he paved the way for other black players to follow. Larry Doby of the Newark Eagles joined the Cleveland Indians later in the 1947 season. The next year, more African Americans entered the major leagues as owners scrambled to tap into the vast reservoir of Negro league talent. Like Robinson, many of these players excelled in the majors. Don Newcombe and Satchel Paige both won Rookie of the Year awards. Roy Campanella, a former student of Biz Mackey, won two National League Most Valuable Player awards for the Dodgers. Their success drew a wealth of support as African American fans turned out by the thousands to watch their heroes compete.

While integration proved profitable for Major League Baseball, the

Negro leagues suffered irreparable damage. Fans now preferred to attend the games of the integrated professional teams as opposed to those of the all-black leagues. When the Brooklyn Dodgers played a spring training series with the Fort Worth Cats (a member of the white Texas League), over eleven thousand fans, half of them black, came from all over the state to watch the games.[4] As fan support shifted away from African American baseball, so did press coverage. The black newspapers continued to write of the exploits of black Major Leaguers while virtually ignoring the all-black teams.

The loss of talent, fans, and newspaper coverage acted as a death sentence for the Negro leagues. The Newark Eagles saw their yearly attendance drop from one hundred twenty thousand in 1946 to fifty-seven thousand in 1948. After two years of declining attendance the Negro National League folded its operations taking many teams down with it. As professional black baseball struggled to survive, the Negro American League attempted to salvage operations by absorbing the stronger teams from the defunct league to make one big league. Tired of losing money, at the end of the 1948 season, Effa and Abe Manley, owners of the Newark Eagles, sold their club to W. H. Young, a prominent black Memphis businessman who saw an opportunity for the club in Houston.[5] Hoping to capitalize on the city's large African American population (more than eighty thousand people) as well as on the absence of a major league club in the market area, Young relocated the franchise to Texas.[6]

With high hopes the Houston Eagles joined the Western Division of the Negro American League in 1949. From a business perspective the team and the city seemed to be a good fit. The city welcomed the Eagles with great optimism and many looked to Houston as the salvation of black baseball. Unfortunately, the club could not escape the infatuation with major league baseball that was sweeping through African American communities throughout the country. In an attempt to reclaim fans and reduce operating expenses the NAL began experimenting with new ideas. For example, the league only scheduled games on weekends, which helped keep salaries down while also offering greater assurance of higher gate receipts. For their part the Eagles tried to boost attendance by playing all home games at night.[7]

Unfortunately, the Eagles never made much of an impact in the NAL. When the team held its first spring training camp in Hot Springs, Arkansas, problems seemed to plague the franchise from the start. Early on, pitcher Max Manning held out for more money and failed to report to camp. To make matters worse, the team's two brightest prospects, pitcher Leon Day and third baseman Ray Dandridge, forced Young to sell their contracts when they too refused to join the team.[8] The close of spring training failed to bring much relief. The Eagles lost their opening series by dropping both games of a double header to the Birmingham Black Barons by scores of 4–1 and 4–3. Playing on a muddy, rain-soaked field in Birmingham, the Eagles gave the series away by committing numerous errors.[9]

After their season-opening losses to the Black Barons, the Eagles returned to Houston for a home opening stand with the Memphis Red Sox. Despite the team's early problems, baseball fever swept the city, prompting the *Informer* to proclaim Houston "one of the greatest Negro League baseball towns in the country."[10] Enthusiasm for baseball, according to the *Informer*, came from the large number of immigrants who arrived in the city from rural America during the Great Depression and war years. For these fans, baseball gained its place in America as "the national pastime" by being a "clean sport" that "affords recreation for folk in all walks of life, from the most menial and common of laborers to the highest professionals."[11]

The Eagles brought a talented corps of players with them to Houston. Managed by Reuben Jones, the team fielded such players as Bob Harvey and Johnny Davis, two of the best hitters in the league. Shortstop "Curly" Williams was called by his manager the next Jackie Robinson, while catcher Leon Ruffin was an experienced veteran who had played in the league longer than any other current catcher.[12] Unfortunately, the citizens of Houston knew nothing about these players, and once the initial excitement wore off, the team struggled to find players with local fan appeal.

Ironically, the biggest opening-day attraction was not an Eagles player, but rather the player/manager of the Red Sox. Texan Willie Wells no longer had the skills he exhibited as a young man playing in Austin, but his name still had incredible drawing power. Playing second base alongside his shortstop son, Willie Wells Jr., Wells and the Red Sox offered fans the opportunity to see the first father-son combination in professional baseball history.[13]

The home opener witnessed much fanfare and ceremony. Playing at Buffalo Stadium, the white Texas League park, Dr. John Davis, a local black doctor named Man of the Year by the *Houston Informer*, threw out the first pitch, and Roscoe Cavitt, executive secretary of the Houston Chamber of Commerce, spoke to the crowd.[14] The pregame excitement carried into the early innings of the game when, with two outs and runners on second and third, the Eagles attempted a bold double steal. Jimmy Wilks, the Eagle's runner on second, got caught in a rundown while the runner on third, Andrew Peterson, broke for the plate. Wilks was tagged out, and an argument ensued between one of the Red Sox players and an umpire known as "Roughhouse" over whether Peterson had crossed the plate before the tag.[15] The umpire resolved the situation by allowing the run and ejecting the Red Sox player. Unfortunately, Houston was unable to score any more runs and lost the game 6–1.

The next weekend the Eagles won their first series, defeating the Kansas City Monarchs two games to one. After dropping the first game to the Monarchs 3–2, Houston came back to win the second and third games. In the bottom of the eighth inning in the second game, Eagles outfielder Johnny Davis hit a homerun to give the Eagles a 2–0 victory, and in the third game, Davis hit another homerun and Johnny Williams scored the winning run in the seventh inning. The victory prompted the *Informer* to predict optimistically, albeit prematurely, "[t]he Eagles are definitely on the rise for pennant contention."[16]

In the coming weeks the Eagles were able to address some of their players' personnel issues, and as they did their lineup became more formidable. Most significantly, ace pitcher Max Manning finally came to terms on a contract and reported to the team. The twenty-nine-year-old right-hander had posted a record of nineteen wins and three losses in 1946 and the team desperately sought his services. In an effort to bolster his defense and give the Eagles more local appeal, Young also signed Curley Andrews, a veteran infielder from Houston.[17]

Despite the changes, Houston struggled during the first six weeks of the season to maintain a .500 winning percentage. By the middle of June, the team was in next to last place in the Western Division.[18] Still more troublesome, the people of Houston were having trouble identifying with the team. Team executives had assumed that fans would identify with the Eagles based on their illustrious history in New Jersey. In Newark, the Eagles had fielded such stars as Larry Doby, Don Newcombe, and Montey Irvin, all of whom went on to play Major League Baseball. It was players more so than the team, however, that brought out fans, and the apparent disinterest in the Eagles caused the *Informer* to ask: "Are the Eagles a semipro outfit?" And, "why aren't more local players on the team?"[19] It didn't help that the Eagles had an early-season scheduling conflict that forced them out of town for a multiweek road trip. The team was gone for an unexpectedly long period of time and the absence further prevented fans from bonding with them.[20]

Despite many disappointments, the Eagles did experience some bright spots in their inaugural season. By June, Curly Williams was in fourth place in the NAL batting race with an average of .364.[21] On June 18 and 19 of 1949, the team swept a series with the Cleveland Buckeyes. In the seventh inning of the first game, Boo Wilson hit an inside-the-park home run for the Eagles. That same game Johnny Davis hit a home run out of the park, while also pitching a complete game shutout to win 4–0.[22]

On June 26, the Eagles and the Chicago American Giants opened a six-game series in Chicago. Most of the games were played in Chicago, but the two teams also traveled to smaller cities in an effort to publicize the league and draw more fans to the games. The Eagles counted on the bat of their first baseman Johnny Williams to carry the team,[23] but unfortunately they lost the series five games to one.[24] Spending so much time on the road, the team now began to experience severe financial shortages. W. H. Young addressed the problem by selling the contract of pitcher Jonas Games to the Philadelphia Stars.[25]

Upon finally returning to Houston, Young hoped to change his luck (as well as increase ticket sales) by holding a fan appreciation day. Scheduled around a doubleheader with the Philadelphia Stars, the team sponsored a parade, hired a band to play music between innings, and gave out prizes to the fans. Also, the players received gifts from representatives of the city.[26] In the end, the increased effort brought little in the way of change. The Eagles lost the series and with it the support of the *Informer*. Newspaper coverage now became almost caustic, as reporters lashed out at players, treating them as if they were highly paid superstars. "Johnny Davis's bat has wilted. Of all things Tuesday night, he had the audacity to strike out when he knows his public expects him to knock one over the left field fence every time he comes to bat."[27]

The Eagles finished the first half of the 1949 season in last place. Reuben Jones retired as manager at the break, citing old age as the cause.[28] Hoping to see improvement both on the field and in the box office, Young now hired the former player/manager of the Houston Black Buffaloes, Roy "Red" Parnell, as his new field manager. In order to generate enthusiasm the team also began hyping right fielder Johnny Davis, who led the NAL in home runs, as one of the league's rising stars.

Unfortunately, the second half of the season proved no different than the first. Houston continued to lose, holding firm to its position in the division cellar. Meanwhile, the accomplishments of African Americans in Major League Baseball continued to garner more attention in the local press than the Eagles. As the 1949 season drew to a close, Young fired Parnell and promoted catcher Leon Ruffin to interim manager. In an effort to end the season on a positive note, Ruffin revamped his lineup, playing those players who clearly exhibited a "will to win."[29] None of the changes made a significant difference, however, as the Eagles continued to lose.

The 1949 season brought economic loss to both the Negro American League and the Houston Eagles. Every team in the league saw its attendance decline steadily. In Chicago, the American Giants, once the most profitable team in black baseball, averaged only three thousand fans per game (this, while playing their home games in 48,000-seat Comiskey Park).[30] Even the annual East-West All-Star game ceased to be successful. Jimmie Blair, a writer for the Negro Associated Press, attributed the problem to the fact that Major League Baseball had now signed the best players away from Negro teams. Following the Brooklyn model, each Major League club now had extensive scouting systems and training programs in place. For black baseball to survive, Blair believed it would have to follow Major League Baseball's example.[31]

Effa Manley, former owner of the Newark Eagles, issued her own statement to the Negro Associated Press concerning the situation of African American baseball. She prophetically predicted that unless black teams found a way to begin attracting fans, the Negro leagues might disappear altogether. She placed much of the burden on the black press, which she felt needed to begin promoting the Negro American League more forcefully. But she also believed that the teams needed to do more to assure a caliber of play that would keep fans interested.[32] Despite Manley's gloomy synopsis and the disappointing 1949 season, some fans did find positive things to say about the Eagles. For example, Chick Solomon, an old-time black baseball player who called himself a student of the game, called Eagles outfielder Jimmy Wilks the "best defensive center fielder in baseball today."[33] Not just in black baseball, he said, but in "baseball period."[34]

Still, fan interest continued to decline. As the Baltimore Elite Giants and Chicago American Giants squared off in the Negro World Series, last-place Houston played its own postseason game. Unfortunately, a game between the Eagles and the New Orleans Creoles failed to attract much attention. The main selling point was the Creoles' female second baseman, Tony Stone.[35] The degree to which fan loyalty had shifted to Major League clubs became especially apparent in November 1949 when Jackie Robinson took an all-star team of black major and minor leaguers on a barnstorming tour of the country. Accompanied by Larry Doby, Roy Campanella, and Don Newcombe, Robinson's team faced a team of all-stars from the Negro American League in Houston.[36] While the Houston Eagles typically drew a few hundred fans to their games, several thousand fans sat through the cold rain to cheer on Robinson's team to a 6–2 victory.[37]

The NAL held a two-day meeting in Chicago in February of 1950 to make plans for the upcoming season. Rumors circulated that the league had plans to restructure by eliminating the Philadelphia Stars, Baltimore Elite Giants, and New York Cubans be-cause of poor play and weak ticket sales. Owners in the Western Division felt dissatisfied with a ten-team league and believed the best solution was to eliminate the three Eastern Division teams. The proposal failed when it came up for vote, but the fact that it came to a vote at all demonstrated the tenuous position of the NAL.[38] Some league changes did occur at the meeting. For example, team representatives approved a transfer of ownership for the Memphis Red Sox. League members voted out Dr. W. S. Martin who had owned the Red Sox since 1928. In his place they selected Martin's brother, Dr. B. B. Martin, MD, who received the franchise. Though the franchise had a new owner, W. S. Martin still maintained ownership of Martin Stadium in Memphis as well as trademark privileges for the team's name.[39]

The Houston Eagles also made off-season changes. W. H. Young brought Red Parnell back as manager, and Leon Ruffin returned to his position behind the plate. Houston also sold its best pitcher, Rufus Lewis, to the Brooklyn Dodgers, and brought in Bob Turner, recently released by the Boston Braves, to serve as an assistant coach and catcher. To fill Lewis's spot, the Eagles signed eighteen-year-old left-handed pitcher John Wesley Odell.[40] They also held an open tryout in Houston on March 25 in an attempt to attract local players and give the Eagles a stronger local drawing power.[41]

The team opened its second season with much fanfare against the Chicago American Giants on April 15, 1950. Red Parnell declared his team to be in excellent shape and ready to bring the pennant to Houston.[42] The *Houston Informer*, on the other hand, voiced some apprehension. The biggest concern was the question of how to keep the "big league and white minor" teams from raiding the Eagles' roster.[43] But Parnell refused to let the player issue bother him. When asked if his players would be ready for opening day he boasted that he "wasn't planning to drop any games this season, least of all his opening game."[44] He went on to add, "I want to put Houston back on the baseball map again. And with the type of youngsters and seasoned veterans I have this year, I don't believe we'll be anybody's pushover . . . I promise Houston fans that if they'll give me their support, they'll get a team they can be proud of."[45]

On the field, the Eagles started the season on a positive note. Playing the opening series in Galveston to take advantage of the island city's large stadium, the Eagles defeated the American Giants 15–9 in the opening game. In the sixth inning, the Eagles sent a total of twelve men to the plate and scored nine runs. Though successful on the field, it looked from the start as though the team's financial woes would continue in year two. Only five hundred people came out to the game, leaving most of the stadium's several thousand seats empty.[46]

On May 14, the Eagles returned to Houston for a series with the Cleveland Buckeyes. To kick off the series, Houston Mayor Oscar F. Holcombe threw out the first pitch and a Marine Corps unit performed during the pregame ceremony. The first game witnessed the return of Rufus Lewis, the pitcher whose contract the Eagles had sold to Brooklyn the previous year. Lewis returned to Houston after failing to make the team and pitched the first game of the day/night doubleheader.[47] The Eagles took the series by winning two out of three games. After the series Parnell issued a challenge to the fans, saying, "[t] he boys are hustling to display wares that will mean a trip upstairs, but the fans must turn out and help maintain a proving ground for these future stars. I am sure they won't let their youth down."[48]

Despite early successes on the field, ominous clouds lay on the league's horizon. W. H. Young was finally forced to admit that, due to poor attendance, he had suffered heavy financial losses during the 1949 season.[49] He reassured readers of the *Informer*, however, that there was no need to worry. He said, "We had some things to straighten out. All is well as we open up the year and I know the citizens of Houston will give their own manager Red Parnell a welcome return to his home by good attendance of the games played by a team that we spent plenty on to make Houston proud of."[50]

Other teams in the Negro American League were experiencing the same problem. In fact every team opened to small crowds. In Chicago, only two thousand fans came out to watch the Chicago American Giants face Houston in Comiskey Park, while across town on the same day, forty thousand people saw the New York Giants and Hank Thompson, formerly of the Kansas City Monarchs, defeat the Chicago Cubs. The same thing happened in New York. Six thousand spectators came to the Polo Grounds to watch the New York Cubans play the Indianapolis Clowns, while fifty-four thousand people packed Yankee Stadium to watch a game between the Yankees and the Cleveland Indians, who featured Larry Doby and Satchel Paige.[51]

As the Eagles prepared to face the Birmingham Black Barons, rumors began to circulate that Young was considering relocating the Eagles back to New Jersey. Newark's franchise in the white International League had moved to Springfield, leaving the city without a team. With the Eagles struggling financially in Houston, Newark officials invited Young to bring the team back to New Jersey. Young, however, turned down the offer and again assured Eagles fans that the team was happy in Houston, and he had no intention of leaving.[52]

As the preseason pick to win the Western Division, the Eagles played much better baseball in 1950. Unfortunately, by the end of the first half of the season, they found themselves in third place in the division. The team drew sparse crowds, as Houston's African American community found little reason to support a Negro American League team.[53] When the first half of the season ended, few in Houston even noticed that the Indianapolis Clowns and Kansas City Monarchs had won the first half of the season in their respective divisions. In the *Informer*, major league box scores and stories continued to dominate the sports page, while the Eagles received little coverage whatsoever. In fact, the paper covered the local black softball league more than it covered the Eagles. The exploits of such teams as the Grand Prize Pale Drys and the Houston Cotton Clubbers appeared weekly in the paper, while the Eagles received scant consideration if they were mentioned at all. The lack of press coverage underscored a declining national interest in Negro professional baseball. The fact that the softball teams consisted of local residents while the Eagles were a group of unknowns certainly helps explain the lack of interest on the part of the black press. Add to that the Eagles' disappointing record and it becomes apparent why the *Informer* lost interest in the Eagles.

And as the press lost interest, the Eagles and other NAL teams lost money. The NAL tried a variety of gimmicks to attract fans to the ballpark. In Chicago, the American Giants attempted to compete with the Cubs and White Sox by signing two white players, Lou Chirban, a pitcher, and Louis Clarizion, an outfielder. William Little, the owner of the American Giants, called the players' signing an "experiment."[54] Since the major league teams were increasing their attendance by signing black players, Little hoped to attract white fans to his games by signing white players.[55] To his dismay, the idea never caught on.

Houston, which started the season playing well, began to drop rapidly in the standings. By the middle of July, the Eagles record stood at seventeen wins and nineteen losses, and they had fallen to fourth in the Western Division.[56] The absence of press coverage only served to make matters worse. After the Eagles started the second half of the season by dropping their first five games, the *Informer* published no articles on the team until the end of August. Instead, the paper gave front-page coverage to such stories as Lewis Theater's victory over the Playboy's Sport Shop in the city black softball league championship.[57] Not until the East-West All-Star game in late August did the *Informer* even bother to mention the Eagles. Outfielder Bob Harvey joined Eagle teammates pitcher Jehosie Herd and infielder Curly Williams as NAL All-Stars. Just before the game, league officials learned they had lost their best player, Elston Howard, to the New York Yankees. Howard had been one of the NAL's biggest draws, and his departure further reduced the already dwindling pool of talent. To illustrate just how bad the talent situation had become, the ace of Houston's pitching staff, Jehosie Herd, made the All-Star team with a record of only six wins and eight losses.[58]

With the exception of the East-West Game, by August football had pushed the Eagles and baseball completely off the sports page. Without any fan support or newspaper coverage, the Eagles limped unnoticed through the remainder of their season. They finished in a disappointing last place, with a second-half record of only five wins and seventeen losses.[59]

After the season ended, the *Houston Informer's* sports page declared, "Negro Baseball on the Ropes."[60] The article claimed that black baseball faced a knockout without the help of the fans. Calling the Negro leagues a potential training ground for African American players hoping to play Major League Baseball, the paper issued a plea on behalf of black baseball. The major problem was low attendance at Negro American League games. The Chicago American Giants' games at Comiskey Park drew less than five thousand people a game. Rumors circulated that the Baltimore Elite Giants, the 1949 champions, were now planning to fold. The Cleveland Buckeyes had already folded, and the Philadelphia Stars paid Satchel Paige one thousand dollars a game in a last-ditch effort to bail out that faltering franchise. The Negro American League also faced problems concerning scheduling, the use of stadiums, and constantly rising operating costs. If the teams failed to address these problems, the paper predicted that black baseball would not survive.[61]

To add insult to injury, four thousand fans turned out in Houston to watch Jackie Robinson's All-Stars play the Indianapolis Clowns in an exhibition game.[62] For the second year in a row, the Houston Eagles lost money. Despite W. H. Young's assertion that the Eagles were happy in Houston, the owner decided to relocate the team to New Orleans after the 1950 season. The Eagles' management hoped New Orleans might save the team from financial ruin. Unfortunately, the Eagles continued to lose money and the franchise folded after the 1951 season.[63] The loss of the Houston Eagles marked the end of professional black baseball in Texas. The Eagles took with them the legacy of the Texas-Oklahoma-Louisiana League as well as prominent players like Willie Wells and "Smokey" Joe Williams. In the years after World War II Americans began lashing out against racial segregation in the armed forces, public education, and public transportation. The assault on segregation paved the way for sweeping changes in American society, but ironically, the assault also spelled doom for one of the most beloved and successful African American institutions. The passing of black professional baseball meant that an era had come to a close, not only in Texas but in the United States more generally.

## NOTES

1. *Houston Informer*, October 6, 1945.

2. Ibid., March 22, 1947.

3. Ibid.

4. Ibid., April 20, 1948.

5. Mark Ribowsky, *A Complete History of the Negro Leagues*, 1884–1935 (Secaucus, New Jersey: Citadel Press, 1995), 306.

6. U.S. Bureau of the Census, *Statistical Abstract of the United States, 1950* (Washington, D.C.: Government Printing Office, 1960), 55.

7. *Houston Informer*, March 26, 1949.

8. *Dallas Express*, March 25, 1949.

9. *Houston Informer*, April 30, 1949.

10. Ibid., May 7, 1949.

11. Ibid.

12. Ibid.

13. Ibid.

14. Ibid., May 14, 1949.

15. Ibid.

16. Ibid., May 21, 1949.

17. Ibid., May 28, 1949.

18. Ibid., June 11, 1949.

19. Ibid.

20. *Dallas Express*, May 28, 1949.

21. *Houston Informer*, June 11, 1949.

22. Ibid., June 25, 1949.

23. Ibid.

24. Ibid., July 2, 1949.

25. *Dallas Express*, June 11, 1949.

26. *Houston Informer*, July 2, 1949.

27. Ibid., July 9, 1949.

28. *Dallas Express*, July 22, 1949.

29. *Houston Informer*, August 20, 1949.

30. *San Antonio Register*, July 8, 1949.

31. *Houston Informer*, September 3, 1949.

32. *Dallas Express*, July 2, 1949.

33. *Houston Informer*, September 10, 1949.

34. Ibid.

35. Ibid., September 17, 1949.

36. Ibid., October 22, 1949.

37. Ibid., November 5, 1949.

38. Ibid., February 18, 1950.

39. Ibid.

40. *Dallas Express*, April 1, 1950.

41. *Houston Informer*, March 18, 1949.

42. Ibid., April 15, 1950.

43. Ibid.

44. Ibid.

45. Ibid.

46. Ibid., April 29, 1950.

47. Ibid., May 13, 1950.

48. Ibid.

49. Ibid.

50. Ibid.

51. Ibid.

52. Ibid., May 20, 1950.

53. Ibid., June 10, 1950.

54. Ibid., July 8, 1950.

55. Ibid.

56. Ibid., July 15, 1950.

57. Ibid., July 29, 1950.

58. Ibid., August 12, 1950.

59. Ibid., September 9, 1950.

60. Ibid., September 16, 1950.

61. Ibid.

62. Ibid., October 28, 1950.

63. *Pittsburgh Courier*, January 12, 1952.

# Corpus Christi's Galvan Ballroom

## *Music and Multiculturalism in the 1950s*

DAVID LOUZON

RELATIVELY FEW OF CORPUS CHRISTI'S MORE historically important cultural landmarks remain intact today. North Beach, which once teemed with arcades and pedestrian traffic, the municipal fishing pier, the saltwater swimming pool, and the Ferris wheel are gone or so altered that they no longer hold the same significance. One exception to this dearth of historical sites, however, is Corpus Christi's Galvan Ballroom. Built in 1950 by Rafael Galvan Sr., the ballroom represents a Mexican American family's contribution to the city's culture in the post-World War II era and it serves as an example of multiculturalism within the city.

During its early years, the Galvan Ballroom, like similar establishments in urban areas of the South, transcended legal restrictions on segregation and provided Corpus Christi residents with opportunities for a limited mixture of race, ethnicity, and class. The ballroom fostered the growth of a multicultural community in three ways. First, it provided a meeting place for Hispanics, blacks, and Anglos. Second, the Galvan Orchestra, comprised of Rafael Galvan's four sons, provided a repertoire of African American-influenced jazz and swing, music that promoted cultural pluralism and tolerance between Corpus Christi's various racial and ethnic groups. Finally, the ballroom showcased major bands of differing races and nationalities, which bestowed on South Texas music lovers a broader spectrum of multicultural entertainment.[1]

These three elements provided a catalyst for cultural exchange. Historian Louis Erenberg observed the centrality of black musicians within "the lives of white fans, how jazz clubs became interracial settings, and how the black musicians stood as bohemian alternatives to a narrowing middle-class world."[2] The example of the Galvan Ballroom strongly suggests that Erenberg's theory held true in Corpus Christi. The ballroom and the African American-inspired music played there accelerated Corpus Christi's ability to transition from legal segregation to multicultural acceptance. The music itself played just as important a role. Jazz and swing, according to historian Anthony Macias, resisted "social segregation and highbrow reification by fostering contact and comprehension, as well as musical and physical expression, in public spaces."[3] As one of those public spaces, the Galvan Ballroom allowed Anglo-American and Mexican American audiences to hear African American music, to see professional black musicians, and to experience and appreciate a small segment of black culture.

Married in 1919, Rafael Galvan Sr. and his wife Virginia reared a large and close-knit family. They had five girls—Beatrice, Rosa, Patty, Mamie, and Virginia—and four boys—Ralph, Sammy, Eddie, and Bobby.[4] A career police officer and long-time businessman, Galvan knew the importance of keeping his nine children busy after school. In the early 1930s, he hired Bernabe Alvarado, a local music instructor, to walk his young children home and provide them with music lessons.[5] For three hours each evening, therefore, Alvarado tutored the Galvan children.[6] Many years later, youngest son Bobby remembered these lessons vividly and best summed up their effect by noting that he and his siblings became "fanatics about music." They practiced and performed together regularly as a family. They played at home, in school, at social gatherings, and at local clubs. Sammy and Ralph even performed while serving in the military during World War II.[7]

As young musicians, the Galvan brothers enjoyed many opportunities to share their talent. Starting in their early teens, Ralph and Eddie played at area nightspots and at events with the locally renowned Jake Stephens Orchestra. However, one December evening in 1946 while playing at the popular Riviera Club, Stephens notified his band members they would have to play longer hours for less money than their current $65 a week salary. Consequently, Ralph and Eddie gave two weeks' notice. That night, the two brothers returned home and reluctantly informed their father what had transpired. According to Ralph, the eldest son, their father supported their decision, telling his boys he had anticipated the day they would need to form their own orchestra. He said, "Money was not a problem," and he bought them all the necessary equipment and a complete library of musical arrangements.[8]

On January 27, 1947, the fifteen-piece Ralph Galvan Orchestra, the largest orchestra in Corpus Christi at the time, performed its first engagement at the Corpus Christi Civic Center. Playing for the Mardi Soir, a Hispanic ladies' club, the orchestra's repertoire included both American and Latin American music. This occasion was just the beginning. The Galvan Orchestra later played all over South Texas for high school dances, proms, private clubs, and public dances. According to Ralph Galvan, that January evening in 1947 represented a "culmination of his [father's] dream to keep his family together" in Corpus Christi.[9]

Three years later, Galvan Sr., who owned numerous rental properties in the area including homes, a grocery store, restaurant, pharmacy, a movie house, and the Laguna Fish and Oyster Company, decided to open a ballroom to provide a permanent venue for his sons. Aware of their ability and growing popularity, and worried that another band might lure them away from South Texas, the ballroom secured their commitment to Corpus Christi and to their large family. No longer would they have to work for someone else in possibly distant locales. "Mr. Galvan wanted his sons to be good musicians, but not necessarily to leave with a traveling orchestra," recalled local jazz musician Eddie Olivares.[10] However, the ballroom's opening was significant to more than just the Galvan family. It provided a lasting contribution to the city of Corpus Christi as well.

The Galvan Ballroom opened March 2, 1950, with a performance by the Galvan Orchestra.[11] This represented a dream come true for the family.[12] One month later, on March 30, the ballroom's grand opening featured nationally known musician Tommy Dorsey—the "Sentimental Gentlemen of Swing—and his equally famous orchestra."[13] The place filled quickly, Ralph Galvan recalled, even to the point where they had to turn hundreds of customers away. Those lucky enough to gain entry enjoyed an evening of fabulous music, and Galvan estimated that the audience was comprised of a fifty-fifty split between Mexican and Anglo-Americans.[14]

According to Eddie Olivares, "without a doubt, the Galvan Ballrocm was one of the most well-known ballrooms for big band music."[15] But the local paper, the *Corpus Christi Caller*, made only passing reference to the opening, even though it debuted with both the Galvan Orchestra and Tommy Dorsey.[16] On April 2, 1950, a small article appeared mentioning the upcoming appearance of Gene Krupa. The article mentioned the ballroom's grand opening with Tommy Dorsey, but focused attention on the fact that limited space had forced the Galvans to turn hundreds of customers away.[17] The *Caller's* uneven coverage suggested that either shoddy reporting or racial bias existed within the editorial staff of the local paper.

The Galvan Ballroom quickly developed into an important social spot for Hispanic, Anglo, and even black residents of Corpus Christi. It accommodated private gatherings like social club dances, wedding receptions, and *quinceaneras*, and public activities like dancing on Sunday nights. During the Sunday night dances, the Galvan Orchestra or other local bands played primarily American music, but the ballroom also hosted big name Mexican and Tejano bands—a veritable multicultural pallet of music. Though not open to African American patrons, black bands did perform for guests at the ballroom and African American groups could rent the ballroom for black-only events.

Louis Erenberg's two books, *Steppin' Out* and *Swinging the Dream*, provide important context for an examination of the Galvan Ballroom. *Steppin' Out* examines nightlife culture in New York City. Erenberg demonstrates how the various elements of music and location (that is, cabarets, ballrooms, restaurants, and theaters) "fit together and helped to create a 20th century popular culture with norms acceptable for a large and diverse audience."[18] He argues that a real revolution occurred in 1912 when dancing changed following the introduction of more and more African American-inspired dances. During the early years of the new century, Erenberg maintains, Anglo Americans "began to reevaluate the role of blacks in entertainment, adapting more of black music and dance for their own."[19] No longer centered on specific steps and conformity, dancing, instead, focused on rhythm. Where chaperones and parents had traditionally monitored private dances closely, young people of the 1920s experienced more personal independence and social freedom.[20]

Erenberg's second work, *Swinging the Dream*, takes the reader from the 1920s to the 1950s, discussing the rise of swing and the importance of African American-inspired music such as jazz. According to Erenberg, music and dance portrayed the "cultural and gender crisis of the day." Of course, the Great Depression provided the crisis. The introduction of swing and the jitterbug, Erenberg maintains, mirrored society's struggle with the depression and subsequent mobilization for war.[21] Music, he suggests, provided people with an opportunity to break away from a "depersonalized and restrictive modern world."[22]

Erenberg's thesis appears to reflect the history of the Galvan Ballroom. The four Galvan brothers found inspiration in the rising stars of the 1920s and 1930s. They lived for swing and jazz. Through their performances at the Galvan Ballroom, the brothers shared their passion for music and gave a little bit of African American-influenced culture and New York City nightlife to Corpus Christi at a difficult and tumultuous time in our nation's history.

However, limits still existed. Changes in taste and in racial attitudes did not occur overnight, but gradually. Racism, especially in the South, provided one of the main obstacles to mainstream acceptance of certain types of music such as jazz and rock and roll. For some Americans, jazz and rock and roll appeared too "African" in nature since many of the leading musicians were either black or sounded like they were.[23] Limits set by racism and racially motivated attitudes still existed in the music world, but not for long.

Duke Ellington's performance at the Galvan Ballroom provides an example of the limits and triumphs of multiculturalism. One of the most prominent black bandleaders of his day, Edward "Duke" Ellington not only led, but also composed and arranged the music for his nationally celebrated orchestra. Erenberg observed, "Ellington showed white and black America that black artists could meet white standards," even playing at annual Carnegie Hall concerts.[24] On Valentine's eve of 1952, Ellington played to a sold-out audience of 650 people at the Galvan Ballroom, with about 80 percent of those in attendance Anglo-Americans and the rest Mexican Americans. At a cost of $3 a person for admission, Ellington's performance provided a once-in-a-lifetime opportunity for many Corpus Christians to enjoy a national music sensation.[25]

Ellington's visit to Corpus Christi offers both a glance into the city's history, and a demonstration of the uniqueness of one Corpus Christi nightspot. The Galvan Ballroom was unique because it was owned and operated by Mexican Americans yet showcased African American musicians and music to mixed Anglo and Mexican American audiences. According to both Ralph and Bobby Galvan, the ballroom brought everyone together, regardless of race, to experience two of the things they loved most, music and dancing.[26]

Interestingly, the *Corpus Christi Caller*, the *Corpus Christi Caller-Times*, and the *Robstown Record* failed to run a single article concerning Ellington's Valentines Day concert. The front pages mentioned the local Tarpon Rodeo and covered various musical engagements, though most pertained to Del Mar College and local high school bands.[27] It appears that one of the most popular African American musicians playing in a Hispanic-owned ballroom just was not newsworthy. The omission was startling for two reasons: First, the Galvans had advertised the engagement the preceding week in the paper, so the media certainly was aware of the event. Second, the *Corpus Christi Caller* reported on February 15 that San Antonio police fined Ellington in the early morning of the 14th while he socialized at an Alamo City club. Though he denied the allegations, he paid a $5 fine for drinking after hours.[28]

While the Galvans welcomed everyone to use their ballroom, segregation rules still applied.[29] Blacks could not attend the Duke's performance alongside Anglo patrons, and a second "black only" concert did not occur. During the 1950s, the majority of Corpus Christi's small black population probably could not have afforded the price of tickets.[30] Yet Galvan Sr. did allow black patrons and African American organizations to rent the facility for private functions. According to Ralph Galvan, the ballroom offered the only large facility in and around Corpus Christi open to them.[31] Mamie Galvan recalled one incident when a newly formed black social club, wishing to host its first ball, asked Galvan Sr. if he would allow them to rent the facility.

Galvan responded, "There is a segregation law, but that law does not apply to my ballroom. This is my property." The ballroom hosted the social club's first event at a time when most non-black-owned establishments in the city would not have even considered it.[32] The ballroom also featured African American musicians, and the impact of their jazz and ragtime repertoires brought blacks into the spotlight as "purveyors of the new music" to Anglo and Mexican American audiences.[33] Intermingling of the races, on the other hand, was not an option for all South Texans. At least for blacks, the law and regional custom required that businessmen adhere to segregation.

Today, one can easily find a place in Corpus Christi to listen or dance to a wide variety of music. Of course, going out today differs from the experiences of the 1950s. The music, the locations, and the makeup of the population have all changed. Most of the original locations no longer exist or have undergone so many alterations they are now unrecognizable. One of the biggest differences nowadays is whom one might expect to meet at one of these locations. While discrimination still exists, people can patronize any establishment they choose. Fifty years ago, that was not the case. If you were Hispanic or African American, segregation limited your choices. According to one local paper, "blacks and Mexican Americans were still excluded from restaurants, movie theaters, and other public facilities in the 1940s. The fight for acceptance and desegregation continued through the 1950s and 1960s."[34] In May 1954, the Supreme Court reversed *Plessy v. Ferguson* and Corpus Christi schools desegregated by 1955, but many private places resisted integration.[35] Nonetheless, some Corpus Christi residents exhibited a willingness to "let blacks eat in restaurants, stay in hotels, use public swimming pools, see movies, go bowling, play golf, and buy houses wherever they chose."[36] Not until the

1960s and 1970s, however, did the struggle to eliminate segregation achieve much success within the city.

Duke Ellington's Valentine's Day performance at the Galvan Ballroom demonstrated the hardships that accompanied legal segregation. Ralph Galvan recalled that Ellington roomed in San Antonio and had to charter a private bus for transportation because Corpus Christi lacked accommodations for blacks.[37] Ellington normally rented Pullman rail cars to avoid such complications, using them for not only traveling, but also for lodging and dining.[38]

Blacks did not face segregation alone. Mexican and Mexican Americans, especially those from lower income brackets, faced discrimination within the city. The apparent lack of interest by the local papers offers a glimpse into racial conditions in Corpus Christi midway through the twentieth century. The federal Census of 1950 listed Corpus Christi's population at 108,287. Of that number, the Spanish surname population composed a little over half with 58,939 and the African American population stood at 7,101.[39] If there was such a large Hispanic population, why did the newspaper not provide more coverage? Despite the local media's bias, the Galvans offered Corpus Christi residents a place where people could intermingle if they chose. The ballroom, just like Erenberg's cabaret, "relaxed boundaries between the sexes, between audiences and performers, between ethnic groups and Protestants, between black culture and whites."[40]

Within Corpus Christi's small African American community, the segregation laws were a constant reminder of their second-class status. Restrictive covenants and prejudicial Anglo-American landowners, for example, forced the city's black population into several isolated communities. On the north side of Corpus Christi (at the northwest corner of the intersection of what later became Highway 181 and Interstate 37) sat the region known as "The Cuts" or "Cut."[41] Corpus Christi blacks lived, operated businesses, and found diversions inside the Cut. Clubs like the Down Beat, In & Out Club, Hoot Club, Skylark Terrace, Club Alabam, and Cotton Club were all located in the Cut.[42] Local as well as big-name black musicians played in these establishments—primarily to African American audiences but with an occasional Anglo-American or Hispanic in attendance. The clubs in the Cut played African American music, mostly what one longtime black resident referred to as "rhythm and blues."[43]

According to Bobby and Eddie Galvan, after playing at an event they would drive over to the Cut to clubs like the Down Beat and the Cotton Club to "jam" with fellow musicians. Eddie Galvan recalled, "Ethnic backgrounds played no role." It was at these informal gatherings that the Galvans really learned to play jazz.[44] "All of the musicians met there. They'd stay open, especially on Saturday night, and there'd be jam sessions," recalled Bobby Galvan.[45] African American local Jimmie Tryon remembered that local bands played after hours, but so too did famous visiting musicians who gathered in the Cut after performances at the Corpus Christi Civic Center, in San Antonio, or in Houston.[46]

West of the Cut, along what later became the Crosstown Expressway, the Galvan Ballroom hosted a variety of events. Saturday nights usually found the ballroom rented out for private functions. Private social clubs like the Lords and Ladies, the Privateers Dance Club, and the Revelieres, as well as Mexican American clubs such as the United Married Couples Club, the Mr. and Mrs. Social Club, and the Hi-Fairness Girls Club were frequent patrons. Also, the Galvan Ballroom offered a venue for the black sorority and fraternity clubs of the community such as the Alpha Kappa Alpha.[47] At other times, individuals rented the ballroom for wedding receptions, *quinceaneras*, proms, and other social events.

The Galvans also opened their ballroom to the community for special events at no cost. According to one teacher from the old Northside Junior High School, Galvan made the ballroom available for student dances at no cost.[48] Mamie Galvan also recalled that her father hosted, at no charge, the annual Policeman's Ball and Sammy Galvan remembered the tradition lasted for many years.[49] Galvan Sr. offered the ballroom to all civic, veterans, and church organizations, to the American GI Forum, and to public schools to raise money for their various needs.[50]

While the renters' wishes dictated the ballroom setup on Saturday nights, Sunday nights were different. Public dancing took priority on

Sunday nights. The simple layout of the ballroom offered rows of tables and chairs lining one wall, but chairs only on the opposite side.[51] Along the back wall, the young men stood, summoning the courage to ask young women to dance. "We were teen-agers when the ballroom opened. We girls would sit at a long table facing the dance floor, and our mothers sat across the ballroom from us but kept an eye on us," recalled Irma Grande in a *Corpus Christi Caller-Times* interview of residents.[52] During the 1950s, Hispanic culture mandated that a chaperone accompany a young woman to public functions. The chaperone served, according to historian Vicky Ruiz, to protect both the young girl and her family's place within the community.[53] In accordance with an age-old borderland tradition, "courting" took place in a courtyard and in full sight of adults. Chaperonage acted as a "traditional instrument of social control" and a "manifestation of familial oligarchy whereby elders attempted to dictate the activities of youth for the sake of family honor."[54] Much to the chagrin of the young people, a large gathering of ever-watchful mothers lined the right wall of the Galvan Ballroom with their daughters, requiring the young men to approach the young women (rather than vice versa) with their request for a dance.

Not only did singles attend public dances, married couples did as well. Both Willie and Anita Rivera recalled attending dances at the ballroom early on in their marriage. To them, the ballroom provided a "neighborly" place where people knew each other. The Riveras also remembered that the ballroom provided a safe location where they never witnessed a fight.[55]

Low cost offered another incentive for people to go. Women attended free of charge, while single men and couples paid only a small admission.[56] There were other sorts of entertainment available to Corpus Christi residents, but according to the Riveras, the Galvan ballroom was popular with "Spanish people" and close to home.[57] During the post-World War II years, close to home meant saving money and gas. However, Ralph Galvan recalled that the majority of patrons still arrived in automobiles.[58]

Social-cultural historians have long been interested in the significance of dance halls. Ballrooms offered their patrons new forms of entertainment and an avenue for socializing not available at home or work. They also allowed for interaction of different races, classes, and cultures in a way not always acceptable under the public eye.[59] According to music historian Charlie Gillett, "the initial reaction of society [to such interaction] was generally disapproving, which served to reinforce whatever rebellious feelings existed among the adolescents, thereby contributing to an identity and a style until, by the early fifties, adolescents really seemed to consider themselves a 'new breed' of some culture."[60] The youth of the fifties stretched the established social norms to create their own identity through music and dance.

The impact of cultural change among the youth provided new challenges for their families. In her work on Mexican American women, Vicki Ruiz argues that against their parents' wishes, some young people strove to fit in with or assimilate into mainstream American culture. While some rebelled against tradition or attempted to "circumvent traditional standards," many also accepted the limits placed on them by their families. When discussing the limits of the Hispanic tradition of chaperonage, one interviewee in Ruiz' book recalled, "I could care less as long as I danced."[61] In her analysis, Ruiz found that in all cases where young women recalled breaking with tradition or "circumvented chaperonage," they worked full-time outside of the house. Women who found employment realized more liberation, took greater risks, and were more likely to challenge familiar norms.[62] Ballrooms, consequently, played a role in the conflict between the older, more traditional Mexican culture and the new North American culture. In Corpus Christi, this change occurred in bars, nightclubs, and dancehalls throughout the city.

Music on Sunday nights at the Galvan Ballroom included popular American songs played by the Galvan Orchestra, Latin bands, and bands from Mexico and Laredo.[63] According to Eddie Olivares, swing and jitterbug, both very popular at the time, influenced the music and dance forms. While Latin or Hispanic bands did perform, American music such as big band, jazz, and swing dominated the ballroom.[64] Music and dancing changed continually with new styles and moves. Jazz and ragtime introduced dancers to a "heightened bodily expression and intimacy with their partners."[65] African American musical influences also emphasized individuality and an invitation to participate instead of watch.[66]

Swing music plays an important role in correctly placing the Galvan Ballroom within its proper historical context. John Rublowsky's *Popular Music* traces the origins of jazz, discusses its earliest forms and its transition to big band and swing, and ends with its influence on rock and roll. Rublowsky argues that "jazz represents a synthesis, a coming together of various musical strains."[67] The term *jazz* first came into use in 1915 in the title of *Brown's Dixieland Jass* [sic] *Band*, but probably originated in pre-Civil War era plantation culture.[68] Its use expanded to the rest of America around 1917 with the closing of Storyville—New Orleans's notorious "red light" district. Fearful of its amoral distractions, the U.S. Navy pushed for the closure of Storyville, which consequently threw numerous African American musicians out of work.[69] These displaced musicians traveled the country in search of employment, and many ended up working in the North. By the end of the 1920s, big band music appeared, but its organization and arrangement stripped jazz of its original spontaneity. Rublowsky argues, "the big band demanded orchestral arrangements written out in advance that were carefully rehearsed before the performance. Bands such as those led by Fletcher Henderson and Duke Ellington incorporated not only talented musicians, but also artful arrangers who could masterly arrange the role of each instrument."[70] Swing became the new sound of these big bands and it rose to great popularity in the 1930s. The Galvan Orchestra and its ballroom offered swing music and both benefited from the style's widespread popularity.

By the 1940s, the more traditional improvisational jazz returned with a stronger rhythm section, "with the pulse that took the drummer's foot off the bass pedal," creating the new sound of bop.[71] The return of traditional jazz coincided with the rise of country-western music. According to Rublowsky, jazz represented a "merger of white country singing with Negro rhythm and blues, which led to rock-n-roll."[72] Jazz also facilitated the merger of several separate cultures.

African American influences within mainstream American music encouraged contact and familiarity between the cultures, which eventually led to acceptance. At least in the field of music (and subsequently dance), certain aspects of African American cultural expression became more widely acceptable. Because the Galvan Orchestra played jazz and swing, it participated in this important transition in Corpus Christi.

A closer examination of jazz in Texas also reveals a strong connection to East Texas. David Oliphant argues in *Texan Jazz* that Texas musicians played in all major jazz cities throughout the nation. While Texas possessed no single city that can claim credit for major jazz developments (like New Orleans or New York City), Texans still made a significant contribution to the genre. The music they played contained a unique regional style.[73] Early Texans also played a valuable role in the development and spread of jazz. Black Texans like Scott Joplin, Ferdinand "Jelly Roll" Morton, Henry "Rag Time Texas" Thomas, "Blind Lemon" Jefferson, and Sippie Wallace gave their audiences a taste of music that reflected African American culture. The Galvans gave these early Texas jazz and blues legends a voice in Corpus Christi by playing their music and the music inspired by them, providing the city an avenue for cultural pluralism not always possible at home or in the workplace.

An examination of more traditional sources of Mexican and Mexican American music demonstrates that the musical repertoire of the Galvan Ballroom (and especially the Galvan Orchestra) did not always fit convenient stereotypes. Manuel Pena's *Musica Tejana: The Cultural Economy of Artistic Transformation* maintains that the Saturday night dances "contained a number of distinctive features that marked them strongly as ethnic *mejicoamerican* celebrations. A deeply felt sense of sociability was present," and these dances fostered a sense of community. While Pena sees music as a clash of cultures or "cultural economics" and Tejano music as a form of resistance, none of the interviewees for this work harbored such notions while discussing their experiences performing or dancing at the Galvan Ballroom."[74] That is not to say that they did not see the Galvan Ballroom as a place of strengthening their sense of ethnic pride and community. On the contrary, one couple, Willie and Anita Rivera, attended the Galvan Ballroom because of safety and familiarity, and its primarily "Hispanic location."[75]

Pena's theory concerning the use of music by an "aspiring class of an upwardly mobile group espousing an ideology of acculturation or more precisely, biculturation" fits the Galvans' situation more closely. The *Orquesta Tejana*, which emerged with a style modeled off the famous big swing bands of the era, represented this acculturationist influence most clearly.[76]

Ralph Galvan experienced some of the same musical roots through his contact with the Jake Stephens Orchestra. At the time, "Jake Stephens' band was the 'big' band in the area." While Anglo-Americans led most bands in Corpus Christi, they used Hispanic musicians because, according to Olivares, Hispanics played best. Local jazz musician Beto Garcia also emphasized the contribution of Hispanic musicians stating, "most top jazz musicians in Texas were Mexicans . . . We got our [musical] roots from across the border."[77] Within the larger well-known bands, younger musicians seized the opportunity to learn from the professionals. The bands played all around Corpus Christ and the surrounding area. Sometimes, younger Hispanic musicians played for country clubs or other private clubs that according to Olivares, did not necessarily "want Hispanic bands," but were willing to accept bands that included Hispanic musicians.[78] According to Bobby Galvan, "In the music field you were not judged by your color, you were judged by your ability."[79]

While listings in a local telephone directory are not all encompassing, a perusal through the 1951 Corpus Christi directory found Galvan's establishment the only listing under "Ballrooms." Listings under "Dancing" provided three additional places: Club Frontier, The Round Top, and Salon Las Delicias, while listings under "Cafes," yielded none. An additional seventeen entries appeared under "Recreational Parlors," though none of the entries specifically mentioned the availability of dancing.[80] Other places existed in Corpus Christi for dancing, but it appears the Galvan Ballroom was the only one appropriate for big events. On certain evenings, the Civic Center and the Plaza Hotel offered music and dancing for Corpus Christi residents.

Dinner clubs like the Riviera and the Trocadero showcased bands and dancing, while the Carpenter's Hall, the Driscoll Hotel, and the American Legion Hall accommodated private functions. The Corpus Christi Naval Base had an Officers' Club, Non-Commissioned Officers' Club, and Enlisted Club, all hosting live bands on weekends, as did bases in Kingsville, Victoria, and Beeville.[81] And of course, the Cut also hosted a large number of entertainment hotspots.

The one thing that set the Galvan Ballroom apart from the others, Eddie Olivares recalls, was that the Galvans brought in "big name bands which hardly any other place did." This statement needs a little clarification. The Galvan Ballroom—one of the largest dance halls in the city—offered the physical space needed for large performances that many other clubs did not have. Additionally, while the Galvan Ballroom (as well as other clubs) hosted big-name bands for private events, the Galvans also hosted them for public performances.[82] Overall, this access to big-name entertainers provided one of the single most important contributions to the city. The brothers' talent, especially Ralph's ability with the trumpet, brought them into contact with other well-known bands and with influential people in the music industry. The Galvans used these connections to share music and culture with their hometown in a way others were unwilling or unable to emulate.

Traveling and performing with other big name bands and musicians brought the Galvan brothers not only national attention, but access to artists that may never have considered Corpus Christi as a potential venue. During the 1930s and 1940s, Eddie Olivares recalled, "people were hungry for jazz music."[83] Olivares and Beto Garcia proved this statement with their founding of the Texas Jazz Festival—a tradition started in 1955. During the next five years the audience expanded, the festival's informal performances outgrew the local college facilities at Del Mar, and it moved to larger locations.[84] The Jazz Festival provided an annual taste of jazz music to the city, but the Galvan Ballroom provided weekly exposure.

While the music or composition of some bands encouraged an intermingling of races more than others, in 1950s Corpus Christi, most residents were not quite ready. In his discussion of the music scene in

Los Angeles during the 1950s, Anthony Macias interviewed several Hispanic patrons who regularly danced with African Americans, but noted the interaction was restricted to the dance floor.[85] Neither the Riveras nor Gilbert Garcia recalled intermingling of blacks and Hispanics during their visits to the Galvan Ballroom, although Garcia assumed the presence of Anglo-Americans.[86] Ralph and Bobby Galvan both recalled that on Sunday nights in particular one could expect to find both Anglo-American and Hispanic dancers crowded together.[87]

Even the Galvan Ballroom building itself, located at 1632 Agnes Street, featured a multicultural mixture of architecture. Galvan Sr. commissioned his son Ralph to tell the architect, E. E. Hammond, just what he wanted. With a facade replicating the famous Lichtenstein Building (one of the city's finest shopping establishments), and a ballroom and stage patterned after the Balinese Ballroom in Galveston, Texas, the Galvan Ballroom drew wide attention.[88] A place of beauty, both Eddie Olivares and Gilbert Garcia remember the impact of its elegance. "The most beautiful thing was the chandelier hanging over the dance floor," recalled Gilbert Garcia.[89] The revolving chandelier with four spotlights, was custom-made and predated the reflective balls commonly used today.[90] The chandelier still hangs above the dance floor today.

Because of the perception that the ballroom was located in the "rougher" side of town, some Anglos and Hispanics inevitably stayed away.[91] According to Ralph Galvan, the U.S. Navy even placed it off limits. Nevertheless, patrons still came in large numbers, drawn by the music, the dancing, and the friendly atmosphere. Galvan Sr. considered the location important and told his son, Ralph, "this is the part of the town where I made my money, and this is the part of town where some of my friends are." That part of town stretched down to the Cut. He knew the people in the area, and while most were black, he considered many of them friends.[92]

Trouble rarely—if ever—arose at the ballroom, and Ralph Galvan recalled there was neither violence nor fights. Of course, close community ties and the fact that Galvan Sr.'s long-time police friends frequently stopped by probably helped keep the ballroom violence-free. Frank Dolan, one of Galvan's friends from the police department, oversaw security.[93] One Corpus Christi resident, Robert Puente recalled, "The ballroom was the place you could go and enjoy yourself and not have to worry that somebody would try to harm you."[94]

To understand the Galvan Ballroom and its impact on Corpus Christi, one also must know its history. Yet the ballroom's history began before its grand opening in 1950. Instead, it began with the dream of one post-World War II Mexican American family who sought to make a difference in the lives of their children, friends, and the larger community in Corpus Christi. A study of the Galvan Ballroom during its early years demonstrates that it contributed to the creation of a vibrant interracial community. It offered a physical meeting place for all Corpus Christi residents—regardless of color—and because the Galvans played African American-inspired music such as jazz and swing, the ballroom provided the city with an opportunity to experience an important facet of black culture. Using their music and the ballroom, the Galvans provided a catalyst for cultural exchange. Finally, by drawing in major bands of various races, ethnicities, and nationalities, the ballroom provided Corpus Christi with a broader spectrum of interracial entertainment. That legacy continues today not only with the ballroom, but also within the rich cultural history of the "City by the Bay."

## NOTES

1. Not much in the way of written sources concerning the Galvan Ballroom exists. The newspapers provided a few articles pertaining to either the ballroom or the bands it hosted. But the general lack of newspaper references may be due to the lack of an index, compounded by the absence of dates. Interviews provided only estimated dates and even the photographic archives, of which two exist, seldom yielded more than "circa 1950s." The final possibility, the one the author believes most likely, is that the Anglo-operated newspapers did not consider Hispanic events newsworthy. To prove or disprove this theory would require a much more thorough reading of the local 1950s newspapers. Therefore, interviews of the Galvan brothers, Ralph and Bobbie, provide the basis for most of this discussion. Both played in

the Galvan Orchestra at the Galvan Ballroom and at times managed it. Two local jazz musicians, Eddie Olivarez (also a professor at Texas A&M–Corpus Christi) and Alberto "Beto" Garcia provided insight into jazz and the Corpus Christi music scenes. Finally, interviews of several ballroom patrons not directly related to the Galvans provided added perspective on the role of the ballroom in the community.

2. Lewis A. Erenberg, *Swingin' the Dream: Big Band Jazz and the Rebirth of American Culture* (Chicago: University of Chicago Press, 1998), 235.

3. Anthony Macias, "Bringing Music to the People: Race, Urban Culture, and Municipal Politics in Postwar Los Angeles," *American Quarterly* 56, no. 3 (September 2004), 712.

4. Galvan Sr.'s first wife died before his marriage to Virginia. Beatrice and Rosa Galvan both came from his first marriage, but Virginia reared all nine children as her own.

5. Ralph Galvan, interview by the author, February 3, 2006.

6. Sammy Galvan, Galvan brothers interview by Tara Walter, KED-TV, March 20, 1998.

7. Bobby Galvan, interview by the author, March 3, 2006; Eddie Galvan and Sammy Galvan, Galvan brothers interview. Sammy Galvan recalled many occasions when he and his brother found other pastimes for their afternoons than practicing music. Erenberg, *Swingin' the Dream*, 181–82, 184. Big band music and jazz did not influence just American culture at home; it played a large international role through America's war efforts. Wartime combined the best of depression-era music with a sense of national pride and purpose. Like many other big band musicians who enlisted or were drafted into the armed services, both Ralph and Sammy Galvan joined the Army. Not surprisingly, each military corps had its own swing-inspired band, and some bands were led by the top swing band leaders themselves, such as Glenn Miller. The bandleaders who did not join the services directly entertained soldiers through USO tours, bond rallies, and concerts at bases and hospitals.

8. Ralph Galvan, author's interview of February 3.

9. Ibid., interview by KED-TV; ibid., interview by the author, April 19, 2006.

10. Eddie Olivarez, interview by the author, February 20, 2006.

11. Ralph Galvan, author's interview of February 3.

12. Ibid., KED-TV interview.

13. *Corpus Christi Caller*, March 29, 1950, p. 7.

14. Ralph Galvan, author's interview of February 3.

15. Olivarez interview.

16. *Corpus Christi Caller-Times*, March 31, 1950, 2, April 14–16, 1950; Galvan Family Papers, Collection 118, Special Collections and Archives Division, Mary and Jeff Bell Library, Texas A&M–Corpus Christi, Corpus Christi, Texas, 118–125.

17. There was no follow-up on the subsequent Krupa concert.

18. Lewis A. Erenberg, *Steppin' Out: New York Nightlife and the Transformation of American Culture, 1890–1930* (Chicago: University of Chicago Press, 1981), 150.

19. Ibid., xiv.

20. Ibid., 153–54, 156.

21. Erenberg, *Swingin' the Dream*, xii-xiii, 37–38.

22. Ibid., 52.

23. Charlie Gillett, *The Sound of The City: The Rise of Rock and Roll* (New York: Outerbridge and Dienstfrey, 1970), 21.

24. Erenberg, *Swinging the Dream*, 9, 101.

25. Ralph Galvan, author's interview of April 19; Jan Weaver, "The Day Duke Ellington Came to Town," *South Texas Informer & Business Journal*, August 1999, 3. This informative article, written by a Texas A&M–Corpus Christi archivist, is the only mention I have found of Duke Ellington's Corpus Christi appearance. It incorporates the recollections of Ralph Galvan.

26. Ralph Galvan, author's interview of February 3; Bobby Galvan, author's interview.

27. *Corpus Christi Caller-Times*, February 14–17, 1952; *Robstown Record*, February 21, 1952.

28. *Corpus Christi Caller-Times*, February 15, 1952.

29. According to one contemporary source, blacks were "barred from hotels and restaurants, required to sit in the rear of busses, denied most opportunities for skilled employment, [and] restricted to substandard housing and to all but Negro elementary and high schools." Arthur D. Morse, "When

Negroes Entered a Texas School," *Harpers Magazine*, September 1954, 47. A review of the 1958 City Ordinances revealed no specific city laws prohibiting blacks from intermingling with white patrons; however, on December 12, 1964, the City of Corpus Christi passed an ordinance specifically prohibiting persons and businesses from discriminating and withholding services based on "race, color, or ethnic origin" (Corpus Christi, Texas, Public Amusement Places [1964] 67–1, 7421).

30. Ralph Galvan, interview by the author, December 5, 2006.

31. Ibid, KED-TV interview.

32. Ibid., author's interview of February 3; Mamie Galvan, interview by the author, March 7, 2006.

33. Erenberg, *Steppin' Out*, 152. The U.S. Supreme Court did not revoke most segregation laws until 1964. C. Vann Woodward, *The Strange Career of Jim Crow*, 2nd rev. ed. (London: Oxford University Press, 1966), 181. Woodward wrote that the "Civil Rights Act of July 1964 aimed at racial discrimination in public accommodation, public schools, labor unions, employment, and economic activity."

34. Danny Goddard, "City Populated by Diverse Ethnic Groups 450 Years," *Corpus Christi Caller: Consolidation of the Corpus Christi Free Press and Sunday Morning Ledger: Centennial Journey* (Corpus Christi Caller-Times, 1983), 99–100.

35. Jimmie Tryon, interview by the author, April 24, 2006. Tryon, a black man and a native of Corpus Christi, recalled going to Cunningham High School in 1955 as opposed to the all-black Cole High School that blacks had previously been limited to attending.

36. Goddard, "City Populated by Diverse Ethnic Groups," 99–100.

37. Ralph Galvan, author's interview of February 3.

38. Erenberg, *Swingin' the Dream*, 114.

39. Harley L. Browning and S. Dale McLemore, *A Statistical Profile of the Spanish-Surname Population of Texas*, Population Series 1 (Austin: Bureau of Business Research, University of Texas, 1964), 2–3, 15. Not until 1950 did the U.S. Census Bureau attempt to distinguish Spanish-speaking and Spanish-surnamed individuals from the category of the white population. Bureau of the Census, *1950 Census of Population*, vol. 2, *Characteristics of the*

*Population*, part 43: Texas (Washington, D.C.: U.S. Government Printing Office, 1952), Table 4, 42–110 and Table 34, 43–100.

40. Erenberg, *Steppin' Out*, xiii.

41. Cindy Tumiel, "H. Boyd Hall Led Fight on Segregation," *Corpus Christi Caller . . . Centennial Journey*, 53. According to Woodward, restrictive housing contracts, which were private agreements, were one of the most effective ways to segregate home ownership. It was a practice overruled by the U.S. Supreme Court in 1948, it but "made relatively little impression on actual structure of segregated housing" (*The Strange Career of Jim Crow*, 101, 140–41).

42. Jenny Strasburg, "Jazz Giants: Northside Nightclubs Hosted Kings of Swing," *Corpus Christi Caller-Times*, February 16, 1998. Also available from the *Caller-Times* at http://web.caller.com/newsarch/news10599.html, 1, 3–4.

43. Jimmie Tryon interview.

44. Bobbie Galvan and Eddie Galvan, KED-TV interview.

45. Strasburg, "Jazz Giants," 3.

46. Jimmie Tryon interview.

47. Ralph Galvan, author's interview of February 3.

48. Florence A. Adam, "Strictly Ballroom," interview in *Corpus Christi Caller- Times*, August 7, 1997, People, 6.

49. Mamie Galvan interview; Sammy Galvan, Galvan brothers interview.

50. Ralph Galvan, author's interviews of February 3 and December 5.

51. Ralph Galvan, author's interview of February 3. A review of photos taken at the Galvan Ballroom in the 1950s confirmed this. Doc McGregor Photo Collection, Corpus Christi Museum of Science and History, Corpus Christi, Texas.

52. Irma Grande, "Strictly Ballroom," interview in *Corpus Christi Caller-Times*, August 7, 1997, People, 6

53. Vicki Ruiz, *From Out of the Shadows: Mexican Women in Twentieth-Century America* (New York: Oxford University Press, 1998), 63.

54. Ibid., 51–52.

55. Guillermo "Willie" and Anita Rivera, interview by the author, February 13, 2006.

56. Ralph Galvan, author's interview of February 3.

57. Willie and Anita Rivera interview of February 13.

58. Ralph Galvan, author's interview of April 19.

59. Erenberg, xi.

60. Gillett, 18.

61. Ruiz, 59.

62. Ibid., 63.

63. Ralph Galvan, author's interview of February 3.

64. Olivarez interview.

65. Erenberg, 153–54.

66. Charles Keil, *Urban Blues* (Chicago: University of Chicago Press, 1966), 39.

67. John Rublowsky, *Popular Music* (New York: Basic Books 1967), 64.

68. Ibid., 64–65.

69. Ibid., 74. Originally a primarily African American area of New Orleans, Storyville came to be known as a place of pleasure, music, cabarets, and prostitution. It was also where many black musicians developed their roots as well as earning a living.

70. Ibid., 76–77.

71. Ibid., 78.

72. Ibid., 93.

73. David Oliphant, *Texan Jazz* (Austin: University of Texas Press, 1996), 2–5.

74. Manuel Pena, *Musica Tejana: The Cultural Economy of Artistic Transformation* (College Station: Texas A&M University Press, 1999), 9, 15–16.

75. Willie and Anita Rivera interview of February 13; Ralph Galvan, author's interview of February 3; Bobby Galvan interview.

76. Pena, 118.

77. Olivarez interview; Alberto "Beto" Garcia, interview by the author, March 7, 2006.

78. Olivarez interview.

79. Bobby Galvan interview.

80. *Corpus Christi Telephone Directory*, Southwestern Bell Telephone Company, 1951. The category "restaurants" did not exist; the heading was "Cafes."

81. Olivarez interview.

82. Ralph Galvan, author's interview of April 19.

83. Olivarez interview.

84. "Beto" Garcia interview. Today the jazz festival, held at Heritage Park, still lives.

85. Macias, 705.

86. Willie and Anita Rivera and Gilbert Garcia, interview by the author, March 20, 2006.

87. Ralph Galvan, author's interview of February 3; Bobbie Galvan interview.

88. Ralph Galvan, author's interview of February 3. Construction on the ballroom was begun in August 1949 by O. J. Beck and Sons and was completed in 1950. The building has the Streamline Moderne look of the late 1930s through the 1950s, demonstrating a form of post-depression exuberance and great potential; it is a building in motion. Art Deco architecture was "a statement of twentieth-century modernity and technological progress," but it was also a period in transition. Streamline Moderne used new, modern materials, made new use of old materials, and adopted innovative lighting. See Carla Breeze, *American Art Deco: Architecture and Regionalism* (New York: Norton, 2003), 9, 16–17, and David Gebhard, *The National Trust Guide to Art Deco in America* (New York: John Wiley, 1996). The total cost for construction of the Ballroom, at $150,000.35, was a sizeable investment for a single family in postwar America. The Corpus Christi National Bank turned down the loan twice due to its risky nature before Galvan Sr. secured a $60,000 loan from the local First Savings and Loan. He procured the remainder of the financing in small notes, using much of his rental property as collateral. Galvan Sr. paid off the loan in only three years (interview with Ralph Galvan, December 5, 2006).

89. Olivarez interview; Gilbert Garcia, interview.

90. Ralph Galvan, author's interview of April 19.

91. Olivarez interview.

92. Ralph Galvan, author's interview of April 19.

93. Ibid., February 3.

94. Robert Puente, "Strictly Ballroom," interview in *Corpus Christi Caller-Times*, August 7, 1997, People, 6.

# Racial Change on the Southern Periphery

## *The Case of San Antonio, Texas, 1960–1965*

ROBERT A. GOLDBERG

THE BLACK DRIVE FOR CIVIL RIGHTS HAS BEEN the most studied and closely observed social movement in American history. Television brought the movement into the American living room and fixed attention on the issues of the conflict. Journalists inundated readers with information about civil rights activists and personalities. Participants in the movement supplemented these sources with published accounts of their experiences. Those who sympathized with the movement wrote "histories with a message." In their wake came scholars who studied the tactics of civil rights organizations, traced presidential decision making, and constructed indices measuring the degree of integration success and failure.[1]

Despite this plethora of material the movement remains only partially explored. Television cameras and scholarly studies have focused selectively on the civil rights struggle in the deep South where segregation was most vigorously defended and violence was an all-too-frequently chosen instrument of resistance. But what occurred in the towns and cities outside the deep South? Television reporters rarely recorded events in the "quieter" communities of Virginia, Tennessee, Kentucky, Missouri, and Texas. The upper South and border states with their smaller black populations and their less rigid caste systems did not attract prominent activists or detachments of journalists. Outside the media spotlight, these areas remained distant from northern public opinion and presidential concern. On the southern periphery, where the infection of bigotry was less virulent, integration movements operated in isolation and under different conditions. What was the black experience in these border communities? How did government and established community groups react to the black challenge?

San Antonio, Texas, was one of the quiet communities of the southern periphery. It captured national attention only briefly as the first southern city to integrate its lunch counters in 1960. In 1965 its city council passed an ordinance integrating all public accommodations. These beginning and ending points are clearly marked, yet the process of integration remains unexamined. A case study of the San Antonio integration effort provides an important opportunity to investigate a neglected facet of the civil rights movement in its least publicized environment. Unlike the deep South, the finished portrait of the San Antonio situation is without sharp contrasts. The line between right and wrong, heroes and villains, is not obvious. The San Antonio example also sheds light on the relationship between minorities. Included in the San Antonio equation were not only blacks and whites but a large Mexican American population.

San Antonio, with a population in 1960 of almost 588 thousand, was the third largest city in Texas. Primarily a distribution and collection point for South Texas, the city had no significant industrial plants. Since World War II government spending and employment have been responsible for a significant share of San Antonio's income. The community sheltered five army and air force bases, and jobs in the public sector were held by just over 16 percent of the working population. Tourism, too, played a critical role in the local economy. Only 41,605 blacks resided in the city, constituting 7 percent of the population. The number of blacks in San Antonio had increased by 12,876 since 1950, but they had barely maintained their percentage of the population. While the United States census did not differentiate Mexican Americans as a separate population category, it was estimated that they formed approximately 40 percent of the city's inhabitants.[2]

San Antonio like every other southern community in the early 1950s followed the color line. The city had never passed a segregation ordinance, but custom and the police department enforced a racial separation that proved as binding. Blacks and whites patronized their respective municipal parks and playgrounds, rest rooms, drinking fountains, hotels, restaurants, and schools. Where segregation proved unwieldy, as in public transportation or motion picture theaters, blacks were expected to retreat to the back of the bus or to "nigger heaven." Housing in most of San Antonio was unavailable to blacks, and they were restricted to an overcrowded and decaying eastside neighborhood. Blacks were economically depressed, with nearly 70 percent employed in semiskilled, unskilled, or domestic-service jobs.[3]

Segregation was woven into the fabric of San Antonio life, but it did not elicit violence or impassioned defenses. San Antonio did not spawn a White Citizens' Council or a Ku Klux Klan movement. From the point of view of the majority of whites, segregation was simply a style of interaction that had been accepted from the past without thought and had continued into the present without protest. Whites were oblivious to the black situation in San Antonio and obeyed segregation signs as they would traffic lights. Attorney and later city councilman Jack H. Kaufman recalled, "I didn't really quite grasp . . . the extent of the problem. . . . I didn't like the system as it was. . . . I felt embarrassed by the system as it was, but I had too many other things to occupy my time. It was just not a problem that had presented itself to me:"[4]

Blacks in San Antonio opposed racial segregation and inequality, but the moderate racial climate tempered their opposition. Harry Burns, a leader of the local branch of the National Association for the Advancement of Colored People (NAACP), characterized San Antonio as "heaven on earth" when compared to other southern cities.[5]

Joseph Scott, a black schoolteacher, agreed: "San Antonio was not a city that dictated a Martin Luther King. San Antonio was a mildly discriminatory city. No pressure had been brought on blacks by whites . . . . It was not a Birmingham, it wasn't a Deep South City."[6] The Reverend Samuel H. James said, "There was never a hard racial feeling; there was never this bitterness in San Antonio."[7]

A variety of factors combined to moderate the racial atmosphere in San Antonio. Most obviously, the black community was quite small (just 7 percent of the population). Whites did not perceive blacks as having the numerical base, and thus the potential power to mount an effective challenge to their political, economic, social, or racial status. White contacts with blacks were kept to a minimum because blacks lived almost exclusively on the east side of town. A significant Mexican American population also obscured the dividing line of color. The Mexican Americans were considered nonwhite and were subjected to social and economic discrimination. Yet, they enjoyed civil rights, had access to public accommodations, and were recognized as a legitimate constituency by the local political structure. Mexican Americans, then, blurred the "us-them" perception of racial conflict, weakened a strict segregationist orientation based on color inferiority, and deflected prejudice and attention away from blacks. The five military bases located in and around San Antonio also lessened the noxiousness of segregation. During the 1950s the military integrated its units and its on-base schools, stores, and recreational facilities, and it provided working models of an interracial society. Finally, though most religious leaders remained silent about the racial situation in the 1950s, some chose to chip away at the community consensus and prepare the ground for racial peace and cooperation. In particular, the Catholic church under the leadership of Archbishop Robert Emmet Lucey condemned color prejudice and acted to remove barriers between parishioners of the different races. Before the U.S. Supreme Court decision in *Brown v. Board of Education*, Archbishop Lucey announced on April 5, 1954, that all of San Antonio's parochial schools and the two Catholic colleges would be integrated. The Reverend C. Don Baugh, director of the San Antonio Council of Churches, agitated among his fellow clergymen for an end to black second-class citizenship. A small but vocal group of liberal Protestant ministers similarly stressed that true Christians were color-blind.[8]

Especially important in explaining the absence of racial tension and rigidity were the actions of the city government. In the 1950s and 1960s the Good Government League (GGL), a bipartisan coalition of business and financial leaders, dominated municipal political and governmental decision making. The GGL and its members in government promised to administer San Antonio honestly and efficiently while fostering economic growth in an environment free of conflict. This program required the GGL to seek support from all the city's diverse constituencies. Thus, the organization allocated positions to Mexican Americans on its electoral tickets, consulted with black leaders about candidates and policy, and maintained close ties to and even counted as members representatives of the media and liberal church groups.[9]

The desire for economic development and community tranquility generated a government strategy of gradualism and the avoidance of confrontation in the face of minority efforts to effect change. Demands for reform had to be guided, and the pace and style had to be directed and controlled. Decision makers evaded controversy until pressured to react, often failed to acknowledge the existence of pressure, and in the end delivered just the minimum response necessary. Expediency far outweighed justice or morality as the rationale for change. Still, racial conditions were ameliorated, the sphere of minority rights expanded, and violence never enveloped San Antonio. The effectiveness of this approach in stifling black or white resistance is obvious.[10]

Thus, while much of the South delayed or resisted the civil rights movement, San Antonio pursued a policy of gradual progress and boasted that it was "the most liberal city in the region." In 1954 prodded by an NAACP lawsuit, the city council passed an ordinance desegregating municipal parks, golf courses, and tennis courts but maintaining the racial barrier in swimming pools. In 1956, again with NAACP prompting, the city desegregated its swimming pools, buses, railroad stations, and all activities in municipal buildings. Unlike many southern communities, San Antonio accepted the Supreme Court's *Brown* decision quite calmly. A school desegregation plan was inaugurated in the fall of 1955 in ten schools for the first, second, seventh, and tenth grades—the lowest grades in each educational level. The junior colleges were integrated as well. This gradual approach effectively eliminated de jure segregation by 1960. The city proceeded with its plan despite an NAACP demand for immediate school integration.[11]

City officials presented each of these actions as business decisions made in terms of costs and benefits and unmarred by value judgments. Racial change was depicted as inevitable, and the deliberate nature of these adjustments made them easily acceptable to San Antonians. Further, strong support from the newspapers, clergy, influential whites, and the traditional black leadership accompanied every shift in the system of segregation. A determined and united government backed by local opinion makers acted to silence those opposed to the relaxation of racial barriers. Similarly, the policy of gradualism and control undercut black activists who sought to accelerate the pace of desegregation. The government's strategy, said the Reverend Claude Black, was "to give it to you and not give it to you. It is a pattern that has made it most difficult to develop the kind of unity that you need in the black community in order to develop the opposition. Any time you give people in desperate conditions a glimmer of hope, you defuse them."[12]

San Antonio's benign segregation and controlled racial progress became less tolerable to a small but influential segment of the black community in the late 1950s. In cities like San Antonio the gap between racial reality and the dream of equality was perceived as especially wide. On the one hand, there was an absence of racial animosity, and advances had been made toward desegregation; on the other hand, there were daily reminders of the blacks' second-class status in public accommodations, jobs, and housing. The Reverend Black recalled, "San Antonio did not have that raw racist expression, but you did not have either the dignity of being a person, a citizen of the community. . . . It was not difficult for a black person to develop inwardly a tremendous amount of hostility towards the community."[13] For such individuals events in Montgomery, Little Rock, and other deep South cities created a mood of impatience with the pace of racial change and a suspicion of white motives and commitment. Spurred on by these distant events, black men and women rejected passive roles and moved to rectify a racial situation that had become unacceptable.[14]

On February 1, 1960, four black college students in Greensboro, North Carolina, sat down at a segregated lunch counter and refused to leave when they were denied service. This simple act of protest ignited a chain reaction against segregation as blacks throughout the South adopted the sit-in tactic to secure equal treatment.[15] Three groups in San Antonio were especially tuned to the news from Greensboro and other southern communities. The owners and managers of San Antonio's downtown stores with lunch counters agreed not to serve blacks who attempted to break the color barrier. The sit-in demonstrations affected the timing but not the desegregation plans of the local chapter of the NAACP. The organization had announced plans to integrate downtown eating facilities on January 1, 1960. Thus, with the support of the chapter's leadership, Mary Andrews, a freshman at Our Lady of the Lake College and president of the NAACP's Youth Group, sent letters on March 7 to six stores asking that they serve blacks at their lunch counters. Black ministers followed these letters with visits to the targeted stores, but they set no deadline for compliance.

Concurrent with these activities, the Reverend C. Don Baugh, executive director of the San Antonio Council of Churches and a member of the GGL, approached Mayor J. Edwin Kuykendall and suggested that the city government assume leadership and inaugurate an official program of desegregation. Such an effort, he believed, would spare the city the strife enveloping the rest of the South. Calling desegregation a moral issue, the mayor proposed instead that church leaders resolve the question while keeping government officials informed during all stages of the process. Baugh then approached representatives of the city's major religious groups and the president of the Chamber of Commerce and convened a series of meetings to find a solution to the potentially volatile situation. The lunch-counter operators were then consulted. Baugh did not invite blacks to participate in these discussions nor did he inform them of the deliberations.[16]

The NAACP briefly took the initiative on March 13 by sponsoring an antisegregation rally. Over 1,500 people cheered activists Harry Burns and the Reverend Black, who announced that demonstrations against the lunch-counter operators would commence on March 17 if store policies did not change. Baugh, pressed by the NAACP's action, summoned his committee and the lunch-counter operators to a meeting on March 15 that was closed to blacks and the press. Looking back, Baugh now regrets excluding them: "This was paternalism. The white man was once again needing to see what he was willing to give the black person. At the time, I didn't see it."[17]

Economic considerations dominated the discussion in the all-day meeting. The businessmen feared integration would lead to white economic reprisals, while resistance could provoke violence and a subsequent loss in revenue. Moral suasion and appeals to the Bible and the Constitution did little to sway the businessmen. The economic rebuttal of the representative from Sears, Roebuck and Company was more persuasive. The San Antonio Sears store had quietly integrated its lunch counters in the 1950s and had suffered no decline in white patronage. Conversely, business had fallen off between 45 and 60 percent in the southern stores of the chain that had experienced demonstrations. City government officials undercut further those contemplating continued opposition. Chief of Police George Bichsell told reporters that the police would not interfere with sit-in demonstrators unless they created a disturbance. City Attorney Carlos C. Cadena clarified Bichsell's remarks by declaring that a sit-in demonstration would not be considered a breach of the peace.[18]

The store owners finally agreed to serve blacks at lunch counters but demanded several safeguards. To defuse a potential white counter-reaction, the businessmen asked the Catholic, Jewish, and Protestant clergymen present to mobilize the religious community in support of integration. Subsequently, Baugh wrote to all San Antonio ministers, rabbis, and priests requesting them to speak from their pulpits and "cooperate by commending the businessmen for their vision and action and ask your congregation to show their appreciation by continued patronage and in every other means of assurance."[19] In addition, the businessmen wanted reassurances from San Antonio's blacks that they would not inundate the lunch counters but would move slowly and exercise their new right in a nonobtrusive manner. To execute this agreement Baugh called four black representatives to the conference, the Reverend Samuel H. James, the Reverend P. L. Wood, realtor Samuel J. Davis, and mortician James Taylor. These men were the traditional leaders of the black community, who had often served as intermediaries with the city's white establishment. All were members, though not officers, of the NAACP, nor were they activists or individually instrumental in rallying blacks against lunch-counter segregation. At least two participated in GGL activities. The blacks approved the businessmen's conditions, and James and Wood signed a press statement issued by the clergy outlining the agreement. The news was learned by the people of the eastside ghetto through the black owned and edited *San Antonio Register*, an NAACP-sponsored meeting, and letters sent home with schoolchildren.[20]

On March 16, without fanfare or disturbance, four blacks were served at previously segregated eating facilities. Except for a few cancelled charge accounts and hostile telephone calls the change in store policy went unnoticed. The *San Antonio Express* joined other opinion makers in voicing its support for integration: "We are confident that everyone concerned in the present situation has come this far in good faith. It is incumbent upon us all to see that this good faith approach is allowed to continue."[21] Thus, San Antonio basked in the national spotlight as the first major southern city to integrate its lunch counters.[22]

Three days after the lunch-counter desegregation, blacks and whites attended a banquet to celebrate the city's nonviolent step toward racial equality. The mood was self-congratulatory and optimistic. The Reverend Samuel H. James expressed the thoughts of many in describing the lunch-counter victory as "just an opening wedge" and announcing that hotels, restaurants, and other public accommodations were to be the next targets.[23] These words seemed to be substantiated with the creation of the San Antonio Interracial Committee the next month. Growing from the efforts of the Baugh group, the Interracial Committee was a permanent organization designed to mobilize public opinion against segregation. Choosing to assail discrimination with a strategy least likely to generate white antagonism or disturbances, the committee planned to visit businessmen and attempt to convince them to integrate their facilities voluntarily. Forty whites and ten blacks, all well connected politically, socially, and economically with their respective communities, initially agreed to serve. Although not an official city agency, the committee received the endorsement of and was in continuous informal contact with government leaders.[24]

Expectations of rapid progress toward a racially open city soon foundered against the reality of opposition, apathy, and weaknesses within the integration effort. Joske's of Texas, the leading department store in San Antonio, had during the lunch-counter negotiations requested a thirty-day grace period to consult with its parent company about racial policy. After the period elapsed the store announced that its basement cafe, which it considered analogous to a lunch counter, would be integrated but that its two more exclusive restaurants would remain closed to blacks. Asking blacks to be patient and to accept the compromise, Executive Vice-President J. H. Morse declared that the store would desegregate only when there was a "change in community custom and practice in all public restaurants throughout our city."[25] The NAACP rejected this offer and on April 23 began sit-in demonstrations at the store's restaurants. On the first day approximately fifty protesters were refused service, and the restaurant was closed to all customers. The next day and for the next week store guards permitted only whites to enter the restaurants. Blacks countered by standing in the doorways and blocking customer traffic. Supplementing their activities was a "I-have-quit-Joske's" boycott campaign. On May 3 a pushing and slapping incident involving a black protester and a white customer seeking to enter one of the restaurants led the store management to close all eating facilities indefinitely. Integration of the Joske's restaurants finally occurred in the late summer after a series of meetings with the Interracial Committee and scores of letters from black and white churches.[26]

Joske's had succumbed, but the victory was pyrrhic. The confrontation consumed considerable time and energy and sapped the integration movement of the momentum generated during the lunch-counter desegregation. Further, it concentrated attention exclusively on one store when nearly every restaurant in San Antonio remained closed to blacks. Those who considered Joske's the trendsetter among commercial establishments in the city were discouraged when their domino theory of desegregation was not substantiated. The integration of Joske's, concluded the Reverend Baugh, "brought a final lethargy that almost buried all future efforts and motivations for desegregation. In fact, many in the community expressed the judgment that we had now solved all our problems in the area of human rights in San Antonio."[27]

In order to effect changes in law or policy, vehicles of protest like the NAACP must be able to apply negative or positive inducements when bargaining with community decision makers. The NAACP's initial bargaining efforts in the form of the March 13 rally and the threatened demonstrations sparked the drive to desegregate the lunch counters. Yet, the organization was quickly outmaneuvered. No NAACP representative was invited to participate in the negotiations, and the organization received no recognition for its role in the desegregation campaign. The NAACP did not regain the momentum of the Joske's demonstrations, and many black San Antonians doubted that it even commanded the resources of the black community. There were no mass sit-ins, stand-ins, or picketing efforts. White faces were as evident as black ones in the demonstrations. Black financial pressure was minimal. A minority of the minority group appeared to be generating the commotion.

The NAACP's failure to generate a grass-roots protest movement stemmed from several factors. Racial moderation and gradual progress had created apathy among the majority of blacks. Although backed by the churches and on occasion given use of the pulpit for appeals, the NAACP could not convert a general sense of approval and appreciation into active participation in a mass movement. This lack of commitment was even noticeable among the young, who were the shock troops of the civil rights campaign. Especially revealing was a newspaper interview with six black high school students. Sixteen-year-old Lillian Amy Clark summed up their mood: "As teenager citizens, we are proud to know that we are living in a community that is brave enough to put into action the democracy we read about, sing about, and pledge allegiance to."[28] This failure to generate enthusiasm was also evident in NAACP membership figures. From a peak of approximately 2,500 in the mid-1950s, membership had fallen to 297 at the beginning of 1959. Much of this decline can be attributed to the 1956 lawsuit of the attorney general of Texas to enjoin the NAACP from operating in the state. Although this move was defeated in 1960, the *San Antonio Register* was still attempting two years later to convince blacks that the NAACP was not an illegal organization.[29]

Lacking a broad base of support, NAACP leaders had no incentive to modify their organization's traditional style of agitation. Rather than massing protesters in direct-action drives, NAACP agitation usually meant sending small delegations to the city council's chambers or legal challenges through the court system. The 1960 lunch-counter desegregation rally was a rare departure from this pattern. As a result of this continuous cycle of black apathy and detached NAACP leadership, the organization obtained a reputation in the eastside community as elitist. With a relatively small membership and lacking a legitimate claim to be the representative of the black population, the NAACP offered white decision makers few incentives to bargain.[30]

Internal dissension also blunted the NAACP's effectiveness by disrupting harmony, hampering coordination, and engendering personal animosities. Conflicts rooted in philosophical differences and personal ambitions eroded its strength. Contested elections for leadership posts in the early 1960s stood in stark contrast to the 1950s, when the nominating committee's selections were rubber-stamped by the membership. The *San Antonio Register* advised members after the 1960 elections, "The ranks should be closed and all hands should get together for continued progress. . . . There is much that remains to be done. It can be done—with all working and fighting—TOGETHER, for a common goal."[31] Again in 1962 the *Register* editorialized, "There is steadily growing, among the crusaders, ill-concealed jealousy. The important thing should be getting the job done, not who did it."[32]

The existence of an alternative black leadership group completed the wall of isolation that separated the NAACP from white decision makers and from the people of the eastside ghetto. The NAACP activists—Harry Burns, the Reverend Black, and George J. Sutton—appealed to blacks with a style of leadership that openly challenged city officials. To whites these men were "professional Negroes" with "chips on their shoulders"[33] who "drew their support from being against the rest of the community: being saviors and protectors of their followers from the community."[34] To interpret the mood of black San Antonio, government leaders approached instead a traditional and unofficial elite for advice and assistance. Whites considered such black establishment figures as Valmo Bellinger, editor of the *San Antonio Register*, the Reverend Samuel H. James, schoolteacher Joseph Scott, realtor Samuel J. Davis, and mortician James Taylor "reasonable and easy men to work with."[35] Through their GGL connections these men represented black interests and exerted influence that in turn generated power and respect within the ghetto. While they agreed with the NAACP activists as to the ultimate end of integration, they rejected direct action in favor of behind-the-scenes bargaining.

From 1960 to 1962 the members of both black groups perceived their actions as being complementary. The activists were credited with creating a "crisis" and focusing attention on segregation while the traditional leaders (and the Reverend Baugh as well) used the threat and reality of demonstrations as levers in behind-the-scenes negotiations. For a time leadership styles became indistinguishable, with the activists tempering their tactics and taking a more conciliatory stance. This period of cooperation, however, proved short-lived because the debate over means resurfaced and fostered resentment between the two factions.[36]

One major element in the San Antonio political, economic, and social equation missing from the desegregation effort was the Mexican American community. A small band of Mexican Americans supported and participated in civil rights activities, but the majority of Hispanics, their leaders, and their organizations remained silent. Mexican Americans with their distinct history, religion, and cultural heritage did not feel a common identity with blacks. "Our roots are different; explained Dr. Jose San Martin, a dentist. "Our problems have been different, our solutions have been different. Therefore our philosophy is different."[37] Antipathy, not unity, existed between blacks and Hispanics. A mid-1960s study measuring social distance found that San Antonio's Mexican Americans were more prejudiced toward blacks than were Hispanics in Los Angeles and Bakersfield, California. Thirty-five percent of the Mexican Americans in the San Antonio bar-rio considered it distasteful to eat with blacks; 65 percent, to dance with blacks; and 89 percent, to intermarry with them. According to sociologists Leo Grebler, Joan W. Moore, and Ralph C. Guzman, "There is really no substantial reason, apart from claims of some spokesmen, to expect Mexican Americans to be particularly tolerant toward Negroes. The Mexican tradition is not one of tolerance."[38] Further, public accommodations in San Antonio had been open to Mexican Americans since the 1940s, and the black civil rights movement in the 1960s provoked no sense of shared grievances. Economic discrimination, which affected both minorities, actually generated more conflict because of perceived and actual competition for jobs and housing. "Sometimes," said NAACP leader Harry Burns, "we feel that they are our oppressors. . . . They try stepping on our heads to get ahead."[39] Claude Black summed up his community's opinion: "It's like having a brother violate some right of yours. You can hate the brother much more than you would the outsider because you expected more from the brother." [40]

Integration efforts proceeded along several different fronts following the Joske's demonstrations. In early 1961 integrationists redirected their protest against segregation in San Antonio's motion picture theaters. Theater operators admitted blacks only through a "colored" entrance and required them to sit in the balcony. One theater excluded blacks entirely. In the 1950s intermittent picketing against this policy had proved unsuccessful. On February 12, 1961, Students for Civil Liberties, an organization that drew members from the six local colleges, reopened the issue with a stand-in at the downtown Majestic Theater. Led by Leonei Jabier Castillo and Perfecto Villarreal, twenty-five white and brown students each paired with a black would attempt to buy tickets at the main entrance. When the blacks were refused admittance the pair would move to the end of the line and renew the process. For three hours the students tied up business in an orderly action that produced no arrests and no breakthroughs. The stand-in was repeated again in February, twice in March, once in June, and once in July.[41]

The stand-ins disrupted business but failed in themselves to move theater management. However, like the NAACP-sponsored rally that sparked the lunch-counter desegregation, the protest did focus attention on the issue. Demonstrators gave bargaining power to the Interracial Committee, which negotiated secretly with the theaters for integration. Nearly a year after the first stand-in the Majestic Theater agreed to a trial desegregation. In December 1961 mixed groups of blacks and whites were allowed to buy tickets and sit anywhere in the theater. Since no public outcry was registered all restrictions on the seating of blacks in the theaters were dropped on January 1, 1962. The city's other twenty-seven theaters accepted the change shortly thereafter.[42]

The Interracial Committee acted as the principal representative of the integration campaign during this period. Organized after the lunch-counter desegregation, the committee enlisted prominent white, black, and brown citizens to enlarge further the sphere of civil rights. Without publicity, the committee sent delegations to restaurants, hotels, and movie theaters to convince businessmen to integrate voluntarily. Such men as Rabbi David Jacobson, the Reverend Baugh, Dr. Jose San Martin, Samuel J. Davis, the Reverend Emerson Marcee, and William Donoughue approached reluctant businessmen with civic, moral, and economic arguments while emphasizing the threats of demonstrations and violence. After nearly a year of such activities the committee's tally of integrated establishments comprised only twelve restaurants and lunch counters. Five other restaurants had agreed to serve blacks in military uniform. According to one member many community leaders belonged to the Interracial Committee, but "most would not attend meetings, much less accept any real responsibility."[43] Moreover, the committee, having grown to eighty-two members organized into five subgroupings, proved to be organizationally ineffective and "floundered structurally."[44] In 1961 and 1962 a revamped committee under new leadership added the city's movie theaters and twenty-five more restaurants to those already integrated. Major downtown hotels had also begun to desegregate gradually, and by the end of 1962 they rented rooms without regard to race.[45]

The results of these integration efforts in the two and a half years following the lunch-counter desegregation were mixed. The city continued to make racial progress without engendering animosity or violence. Integrationists had opened the movie theaters and the large downtown hotels. Inroads had been made against restaurant segregation. Yet the campaign suffered from a lack of coordination and focus. Integrationists had attacked their targets with too little community support and too few resources. Government officials had remained mute during the period, abdicating their roles as leaders and educators. The white press reported news about desegregation without editorial comment. Thus, the integrationists had created neither a sense of need nor a self-generating cycle of change. Black activists once more lost patience with the pace of progress and a desegregation program that failed to identify integrated businesses or to ensure compliance with voluntary pledges. Even traditional black leader Valmo Bellinger complained on August 24, 1962, in a *Register* editorial that San Antonio "lags very noticeably behind some of Texas' notoriously 'rebel' cities."[46] On October 19, 1962, he wrote, "efforts should and must be renewed to erase the remaining problems—and there are certainly more than a few."[47] Again, the activists in the NAACP were to be the catalysts for change in San Antonio's racial environment.

On October 23, 1962, NAACP president Harry Burns wrote Mayor Walter W. McAllister asking the city council to pass an ordinance outlawing discrimination in public accommodations. The slow pace of voluntary integration, recent reports that black civil servants had refused transfer to San Antonio because of its discriminatory practices, and the enactment of a desegregation law in El Paso, Texas, prompted the appeal. The mayor, instead of opening hearings on the proposal or even placing it on the council agenda, polled the body's members informally. "The majority opinion, at least," he concluded, "was that we were stepping out of bounds as a government agency to direct the policy of private business."[48] Burns persisted and brought the proposed ordinance before the city council on February 13. The Reverend Black, Father Sherrill Smith, and Mexican American businessman Joseph Guerra appeared with Burns and spoke in support of a measure that would impose a maximum fine of $200 on any merchant who discriminated on the basis of race, religion, or color. McAllister referred the ordinance to City Attorney Crawford B. Reeder to ascertain its constitutionality and promised council consideration pending the decision.[49]

Two weeks later, without referring to Reeder's findings, the council again rejected the NAACP proposal. McAllister, speaking for the council, expressed sympathy for black aspirations but opposed the coercion of white businessmen as the means to integration. City officials counseled patience and favored continuing the voluntary approach to desegregation because it was the one least likely to spark resistance or violence. With municipal elections scheduled for April 2, political considerations were also important. The GGL and the city council had no intention of injecting a potentially explosive issue into the campaign.[50]

The council had refused to consider the NAACP proposal, but it was nevertheless under pressure on the matter. NAACP-sponsored demonstrations could disrupt the community. Several members of the Interracial Committee had stressed the need for the city council to assume a more active role in the public accommodations campaign and to revive the stalled voluntary desegregation effort. Reports of the presence in San Antonio of a Black Muslim organizer and circulation of copies of the newspaper *Muhammed Speaks* provided government leaders with additional reasons to assume control of the situation. Thus, the council paired its denial of the NAACP request with the appointment of a committee composed of its liberal GGL members to study the question and to recommend a course of action. The subsequent victory of the complete GGL slate on April 2 not only enabled the committee to start its work but also was interpreted as a mandate for the council's consideration of the segregation problem.[51]

The city council's refusal to consider an ordinance outlawing segregation naturally angered black activists. George J. Sutton threatened to organize an appeal to President John Fitzgerald Kennedy asking for federal economic retaliation if the council did not pass the ordinance: "The blood," he told the council, "will be on your hands."[52] Rev. Black called the establishment of the committee "a delaying action." He continued, "It was studied 100 years ago and brought forth the Emancipation Proclamation." He believed that "all that is under discussion now is a 'remnant of slavery.'"[53] To this day Harry Burns denounces McAllister as a"die-hard," and Black labels him an "old time vicious racist."[54] McAllister did and does believe that whites, blacks, and Mexican Americans are inherently different both mentally and physically. "People of racial extraction," he declared, "all have certain particular characteristics. They don't all have the same characteristics."[55] Though he counted no blacks or Mexican Americans among his close friends, McAllister was not a Governor George Corley Wallace or a Sheriff James "Jim" Gardner Clark Jr. His racial philosophy was flexible and subordinate to his primary goal of fostering the continuous commercial development of San Antonio. Boosting San Antonio's economy required an environment free of racial conflict and violence. Integration was for McAllister "the expedient thing to do, it was anticipating the future."[56] The great majority of San Antonio's blacks and its traditional leadership greeted the council's decision with silence.[57]

The report of the three-person committee, presented to the council on May 29, 1963, was an unequivocal brief for the integration of public accommodations in San Antonio. Citing the city's special obligation to all Americans and to foreign military personnel training at the local bases, and its role as the caretaker of the Alamo (the shrine of Texas liberty), the committee called for an immediate end to the "denial of complete individual freedom by the practice of discrimination." Moreover, unresolved racial conflicts threatened to cloud San Antonio's economic future. Progress had been made in many areas, the report continued. The schools, municipal recreation facilities, public transportation, theaters, and lunch counters had all been integrated. It was now time to move forward again and complete the task. The report recommended against a city ordinance as the means to integration and in favor of an accelerated voluntary desegregation program conducted under city government auspices. Further delay, the committee warned, "represents a potential hazard to the welfare of the people of San Antonio."[58]

The council accepted the report unanimously and moved quickly to implement its recommendations. On June 5 the council created a Committee on Desegregation headed by GGL member and television station owner James M. Gaines. Gaines, in consultation with governmental officials, businessmen, and blacks, named a committee consisting of the "movers and shakers of the community."[59] The committee included such prominent San Antonians as Colonel Bernard Justine Horner, publisher of the *San Antonio Light*; Conway C. Craig, publisher of the *San Antonio Express;* Jack H. Morse, executive vice-president of Joske's Department Store; Bob Roth, president of a television station; former city councilman Dr. Jose San Martin; Gilbert Lang, president of Frost Brothers; and businessman Henry Catto, chairman of the Interracial Committee. Traditional leaders Valmo Bellinger, James Taylor, and Everett Jennings represented the black community, and NAACP activists were either ignored or refused to serve. With unsurpassed credentials in the GGL, the media, and business and financial circles these opinion makers could exert persuasive pressure in the city. These men could and did call upon other members of the elite for support. Later in June, fifty-three leaders of the city's financial, governmental, and social establishments signed a public announcement published in all San Antonio newspapers that declared: "Desegregation of publicly-used facilities is no longer a matter for debate. It must become a universal and immediate reality if San Antonio is to avoid the regrettable events of other cities across the face of the United States of America."[60] Voluntary desegregation also received the endorsements of San Antonio's newspapers, the Chamber of Commerce, the Bexar County Democratic Party, Texas governor John Bowden Connally, and seventeen leading churchmen representing Protestant, Catholic, and Jewish congregations. Resistance to such a formidable display of power and unity would prove difficult.[61]

The committee planned a vigorous one-month campaign and symbolically chose the Fourth of July as its target date for desegregation. Integration pledge cards were sent to all hotels, motels, restaurants, and other places of public accommodation. Merchants who failed to return their cards were visited by teams comprised of businessmen and clergy. As before, integration advocates found that arguments based on morality or justice did little to move the reluctant. Once again, hesitant businessmen were persuaded that they would not be alone in their shift of policy and that failure to integrate could provoke demonstrations and violence. Integrationists also contended that desegregation was necessary to prevent federal intervention in San Antonio. This threat was given substance when President Kennedy's Commission on Equal Opportunity in the Armed Forces released a report recommending "that 'off limits' declarations be made for those civilian establishments refusing to desegregate." It further asserted, "Should all other efforts fail, the Services must consider a curtailment or termination of activities at certain military installations."[62] Throughout the month the committee generated its own momentum with a carefully planned series of releases to radio, television, and the press. A bandwagon effect was created. The constantly growing, published tally of integrated businesses and the steady stream of supporting editorials and endorsements produced a sense of urgency and inevitability.[63]

Black leaders divided over the voluntary desegregation campaign. Accommodationists such as the Reverend Samuel H. James, the Reverend P. S. Wilkinson, and teacher Joseph Scott lauded the city council's plan as the quickest and least disruptive approach to the integration of San Antonio. "Our people desire desegregation now," maintained committee member James Taylor. "Just how it comes and who gets the credit is not important."[64] Seventeen prominent blacks, one-third of whom were ministers, offered to help the council reach its goal. Valmo Bellinger, also a committee member, put the *San Antonio Register* behind the effort. NAACP activists Claude Black, George J. Sutton, and Harry Burns rejected the voluntary approach. The city's program was merely another example of white paternalism that robbed blacks of a sense of their own ability to effect change in their lives. The Reverend Black labeled the city council's campaign "a delaying action lacking in understanding of the Negro citizen's needs."[65] "They were making the decisions," he later said. "They were giving the privilege. We didn't want a privilege, we wanted a right. They were holding the power in their own hands."[66] The NAACP therefore continued to agitate for an ordinance and began picketing city council sessions to generate support in the black community. "Many instances," recalled Black, "when we went to the city council we knew we couldn't win. But the task was to create enough disturbance that we could come back to the black community and it would pull them together."[67] But, with desegregation occurring through the city's programs and the *Register* closed to the activists, the majority of blacks remained uninvolved. City Hall picketers never numbered more than twenty-two. Isolated from the eastside ghetto, the demonstrators were condemned by the white press as "the agitation wing" of the NAACP, given to making "intemperate and abusive charges."[68] If the activists weren't sufficient to frighten white businessmen, reports again circulated of Black Muslim activity in San Antonio.[69]

Integrationists had made obvious progress by the Fourth of July. Nearly two-thirds of all hotels, motels, restaurants, and other places of public accommodations had agreed to desegregate. These businesses accounted for nearly 95 percent of all hotel rooms, 90 percent of all motel rooms, and 90 percent of all restaurant meals served in San Antonio. Businessmen who had not returned their pledge cards were subsequently contacted, and by July 11, 95 percent of all places of public accommodation had integrated. Three months later only twenty-six restaurants and five motels had refused to participate in the voluntary program. Most of these businesses would soon succumb to public pressure or the personal intervention of Mayor McAllister. A *San Antonio Register* editorial titled "THIS IS GRATIFYING" probably voiced the black mood in commending the city council's work "in the field of human rights and equality." [70] Even the Reverend Black conceded that "It was more successful than we wanted it to be."[71] Committee Chairman James Gaines, arguing that "the tremendous momentum developed must not be permitted to be dissipated," recommended that the city create new committees to combat prejudice and discrimination in employment and housing.[72] Inequality in these areas, however, aroused the opposition of diverse groups and proved more difficult to eradicate. Content with the hiring of four blacks to teach in schools with previously all-white staffs, the employment of the first black bus driver, and the integration of a housing development near one of the military bases, the city allowed its committees to become inactive.[73]

Spurred by scattered reports of violations of the desegregation pledge, NAACP activists continued to urge the adoption of an ordinance. Their requests rebuffed, the blacks again picketed the city council in August 1963. The climax of their efforts occurred on October 3, when George J. Sutton confronted an embarrassed city council with a 1941 law that revoked the license of any place of public accommodation refusing service "to anyone because of his citizenship in any Latin American Republic of the Western Hemisphere or merely because of his racial origin from one of these Republics:"[74] Sutton asked that the ordinance be amended so that the protection afforded Mexican Americans be extended now to blacks. The council delayed action until November 14, when it again denied the NAACP's petition. In a four-page statement Mayor McAllister recounted the progress made through the voluntary program and asserted that an ordinance was no longer necessary. Moreover, passage of such a law would result in "the destruction of the advances already made."[75] The mayor did not elaborate on his statement. A week later the NAACP organized its last demonstration on the issue. It greeted visiting President Kennedy with picket signs reading: "SEGREGATED CITY RECEIVES FED. SUPPORT" and "Rights not favors."[76] Security precautions and a tight itinerary prevented the blacks from delivering a message to the president before his departure for Dallas.[77]

In 1965 the GGL responded to the lobbying efforts of members Valmo Bellinger, Joseph Scott, and James Taylor and nominated the Reverend Samuel H. James as its first black candidate for the city council. James, a moderate black leader and supporter of the city's voluntary desegregation program, attributed the selection to his longtime record of cooperation with white decision makers: "They knew me."[78] Mayor McAllister told the press, "We realized the Negroes needed representation on the council. Let's face it. The Negroes haven't been treated fairly, they've been discriminated against. But that day is past."[79] Despite activists' dismissal of James as "a token," he polled nearly double the vote of his closest rival and became the first black to win a seat on the council of a major Texas city.[80]

The San Antonio council now judged the time propitious to enact the long-requested antidiscrimination ordinance. Councilman James, not the NAACP, received the credit for proposing the measure and guiding it through the legislative process. To eradicate the last pockets of segregation in public accommodations the council, on November 11, 1965, unanimously approved Ordinance 33863, which fined any businessman who denied service on the basis of race, color, or religion. The law, coming over two years after the voluntary desegregation program and five years after it was initially proposed, had lost all but symbolic meaning. "It was passed," said Councilman Jack Kaufman, "and it was a ho-hum thing. . . . It won't make anybody mad. . . . It was a nothing."[81] A disillusioned Claude Black declared, "It didn't matter anymore."[82]

The image of the civil rights movement as a bloody confrontation between nonviolent blacks and racist whites is not applicable to San Antonio. Racial progress was the product of a series of interactions among diverse local groups, each of which played a necessary but not all-sufficient role in the desegregation process. NAACP activists, white liberals, and the black establishment worked toward the same end but differed over the speed and manner of integration. The NAACP generated the "crisis" that dramatically drew attention to the problem. Yet, lacking support in the black community and suffering from internal weaknesses, it was more an observer of the negotiations than a participant, and it was used as a negotiating threat by white liberals and traditional black leaders. To bring change in 1960 and 1963, liberals such as Baugh and Gaines manipulated government and business fears of NAACP-sponsored demonstrations. Concurrently, black leaders used their power base in the eastside ghetto and their long-established connections with the white establishment as levers to achieve reform. They cooperated with the voluntary desegregation program and claimed it as their victory. Thus, they witnessed civil rights advances, and they also withstood challenges to their positions and increased their prestige in government and the community.

San Antonio city officials were the subjects of much of the pressure for reform. Authorities publicly ignored the issue and preferred a quiet, voluntary approach engineered by members of the clergy and GGL. Peace and prosperity, not racial justice, were the city's goals. When demonstrations threatened this program, integration then became an acceptable price for continued stability. Once the course of action was approved, city leaders moved unequivocally to summon the resources of opinion makers in business, the churches, and the media. The goal was achieved according to the city's plan and timetable. The rapidity and decisiveness of the action made dissent unrealistic.

In many deep South communities the events of desegregation changed the lives of ordinary black and white citizens. However, San Antonio's leaders acted on their constituents' behalf and did not mobilize grassroots activity. Only the NAACP attempted to rally the support of the larger black community. But the organization's elitist image and the apathy produced by San Antonio's moderate racial climate smothered the effort. White opposition, tempered by the small black population and the gradual nature of racial change, was always overestimated. For Mexican Americans the struggle for black civil rights had no meaning, and prejudice and economic competition heightened the barrier between the two minorities. Those few Hispanics who did join the protests did so as individuals and had no organizational support. Though Mexican Americans were unsympathetic to the blacks, there is no evidence to suggest that blacks would have welcomed their involvement.

By the middle of 1963 San Antonio had virtually eliminated discrimination in public accommodations. Racial distinctions in theaters, restaurants, and hotels had ended. San Antonio had advanced far beyond communities in the deep South and had anticipated by one year the Civil Rights Act of 1964. White liberals and traditional black leaders congratulated themselves and their city upon the ease of the racial transformation. Black activists, however, were more ambivalent and considered the means as important as the end. The desegregation campaign in San Antonio was a history of racial progress and black failure. Much of the black community had remained passive during the struggle, and the

NAACP was largely impotent. White decision makers organized and directed the vehicles of racial change. Civil rights had been granted, not won. Rather than emerging from the period united and determined to press for further reforms, blacks remained divided and complacent. "To have done it the way we had wanted it done," remarked activist William Donoughue, "would have been a demonstration of power and strength. And power and strength are the only common denominators understood in this community."[83]

The San Antonio pattern of voluntary desegregation, with its features of racial cooperation, belated but effective government action, and minimal black agitation and white resistance, was duplicated in nearly all the major cities of Texas. Governor Connally and other state officials advocated the voluntary approach as the most reasonable means of remedying racial inequality in public accommodations and of forestalling federal intervention. "I intend," said the governor, "to see that we live up to our responsibility. But in our own Texas way."[84] City officials all over the state chose the "Texas way" of planned reform and were able to steer their communities through the racial turmoil of the early 1960s. By late 1963 Abilene, Amarillo, Austin, Corpus Christi, Dallas, Fort Worth, Galveston, Houston, and Lubbock had joined San Antonio in voluntarily desegregating public accommodations. EI Paso was the only major city to desegregate by statute. In only a few communities, such as Marshall in East Texas, was the deep South experience duplicated. Whether the San Antonio pattern of racial change represented the situation on the southern periphery and thus differed substantially from events in communities of the deep South is a matter for further research.[85]

## NOTES

1. For example, see Carl M. Brauer, *John F. Kennedy and the Second Reconstruction* (New York: Columbia University Press, 1977); William H. Chafe, *Civilities and Civil Rights: Greensboro, North Carolina and the Black Struggle for Freedom* (New York: Oxford University Press, 1980); John M.

Ehle Jr., *The Free Men* (New York: Harper and Row, 1965); David J. Garrow, *Protest at Selma: Martin Luther King, Jr., and the Voting Rights Act of 1965* (New Haven, Connecticut: Yale University Press, 1978); James A. Geschwender, ed., *The Black Revolt: The Civil Rights Movement, Ghetto Uprisings, and Separatism* (Englewood Cliffs, New Jersey: Prentice-Hall, 1971); Martin Luther King Jr., *Stride Toward Freedom: The Montgomery Story* (New York: Harper and Row, 1958); King, *Why We Can't Wait* (New York: New American Library, 1964); Anthony J. Lewis, *Portrait of a Decade: The Second American Revolution* (New York: Random House, 1964); Louis E. Lomax, *The Negro Revolt* (New York: Harper and Row, 1962); Anthony R. Oberschall, *Social Conflict and Social Movements* (Englewood Cliffs, New Jersey: Prentice-Hall, 1973), 204–41; Frances F. Piven and Richard A. Cloward, *Poor People's Movements: Why They Succeed, How They Fail* (New York: Knopf, 1977); Charles E. Silberman, *Crisis in Black and White* (New York: Random House, 1964); Alan F. Westin, ed., *Freedom Now! The Civil-Rights Struggle in America* (New York: Basic Books, 1964). Research for this article was funded in part by the Faculty Development Committee, College of Humanities, University of Utah. The author would like to thank Larry R. Gerlach, Ronald G. Coleman, and Susan Kralick-Goldberg for their valuable comments.

2. T. N. Picnot, *An Economic and Industrial Survey of San Antonio, Texas* (n.p.: n.p., 1942), 108–109; Richard C. Jones, "San Antonio's Spatial Economic structure from the Mid-1950s to the Present," unpublished manuscript in the author's possession, 1980, 4, 5, 16; U.S. Bureau of the Census, *Eighteenth Census of the United States* (cited hereafter as *Eighteenth Census*), vol. 1: *Population*, part 45: Texas (Washington, D.C.: Government Printing Office, 1963), 107, 123, 414; U.S. Bureau of the Census, *Seventeenth Census of the United States* (cited hereafter as *Seventeenth Census*), vol. 2: *Population*, part 43: Texas (Washington, D.C.: Government Printing Office, 1952), 94, 103; L. Tucker Gibson Jr. and Robert R. Ashcroft, "Political Organizations in a Nonpartisan Election System" (unpublished manuscript in the author's possession, 1977), 9.

3. Frederic A. Bruton, "Desegregation in San Antonio" (master's thesis, Trinity University, 1971), 3–4; interview with the Reverend Claude Black, San Antonio, April 18, 1980; interview with Harry

Burns, San Antonio, April 19, 1980; interview with the Reverend Emerson Marcee, San Antonio, March 29, 1980; *Seventeenth Census*, vol. 2, part 43, 129, 131; *Eighteenth Census*, v01.1, part 45, 420, 442; interview with Rabbi David Jacobson, San Antonio, May 9, 1980.

4. Jacobson interview; interview with Jack Kaufman, San Antonio, June 6, 1980.

5. Burns interview.

6. Interview with Joseph Scott, San Antonio, May 3, 1980.

7. Interview with the Reverend Samuel H. James, San Antonio, May 2, 1980.

8. C. Don Baugh, "A Report Covering the Effects of Desegregating San Antonio, Texas, through the Voluntary Process, 1953–60" (unpublished manuscript in the author's possession, 1964), 5; *San Antonio Register*, April 16, 1954; J. Kenneth Morland, *Lunch-Counter Desegregation in Corpus Christi, Galveston, and San Antonio, Texas* (Atlanta, Georgia: Randolph-Macon Woman's College, 1960), 6, 10; Bruton, "Desegregation in San Antonio," 19; Jacobson interview; Black interview; Burns interview; Kaufman interview; interview with José San Martin, San Antonio, May 30, 1980; interview with the Reverend C. Don Baugh, San Antonio, May 14, 1980. See Thomas F. Pettigrew and M. Richard Cramer, "The Demography of Desegregation," *Journal of Social Issues* 15, no. 4 (1959): 61–71, for a study of desegregation in five border states including Texas.

9. Luther L. Sanders, "Non Partisanship: Its Use as a Campaign Appeal in San Antonio" (master's thesis, St. Mary's University, 1974): 47–60; John A. Booth and David R. Johnson, "Elites and Urban Development in San Antonio: Charter Change as a Means of Elite Control, 1885–1975" (unpublished manuscript in the author's possession, 1978), 35–41; Gibson and Ashcroft, "Political Organizations," 3–6; San Martin interview; interview with Walter W. McAllister, San Antonio, May 19, 1980; Baugh interview; interview with Valmo Bellinger, San Antonio, April 19, 1980.

10. Black interview; Burns interview; interview with Albert Pena, San Antonio, May 23, 1980; Chafe, *Civilities and Civil Rights*, 5–7, 211–12.

11. Marcee interview; Baugh, "Report," 6, 8; Bruton, "Desegregation in San Antonio," 10, 32–33, 39, 43–45, 54, 58–59; *San Antonio Register*, June 17, September 16, 1955; March 30, 1956; September 13, 1958; quotation from McAllister and Jacobson interviews.

12. Black interview. On public attitudes and desegregation see Elaine O. McNeil, "Policy-Makers and the Public," *Southwestern Social Science Quarterly*, 39 (September 1958): 95–99.

13. Black interview.

14. Ibid.; Burns interview.

15. Chafe, *Civilities and Civil Rights*, 115–17; Morland, *Lunch-Counter Desegregation*, 6–7; *San Antonio Register*, January1, February 19, March 4, 11, 1960; *New York Times*, March 20, 1960, 1, 48.

16. Baugh, "Report," 9–11. The Reverend Baugh believed that his membership in the Good Government League (GGL) gave him a measure of influence with the mayor and the city council. Black activist William Donoughue suggested an even closer relationship between Baugh and the San Antonio Council of Churches on the one hand and the GGL and the city government on the other: "We are talking about the same people." Baugh interview; interview with William Donoughue, San Antonio, May 8, 1980.

17. *New York Times*, March 14, 1960; *San Antonio Register*, March 18, 1960; *San Antonio Express*, March 14, 1960; Baugh, "Report," 12–14; Baugh interview (quotation).

18. Baugh interview; *San Antonio Express*, March 14, 15, 16, 1960; Baugh, "Report," 12–17; Morland, *Lunch-Counter Desegregation*, 7–8; Jacobson interview.

19. Morland, *Lunch-Counter Desegregation*, appendix B (includes Baugh letter).

20. Ibid., 7–8; Baugh, "Report," 16–17; *San Antonio Express*, March 16, 1960; *San Antonio Register*, March 18, 1960; *New York Times*, March 20, 1960, 1.

21. *San Antonio Express*, March 17, 1960.

22. Ibid., March 16, 17, 23, 1960; *San Antonio Register*, March 18, 25, 1960; Baugh, "Report," 4; *New York Times*, March 17, 1960, 37; March 20, 1960, 1, 48; Morland, *Lunch-Counter Desegregation*, 8.

23. *New York Times*, March 20, 1960, 1, 48 (quotation).

24. *San Antonio Register*, April 22, 1960; *San Antonio Light*, April 15, 1960; Morland, *Lunch-Counter Desegregation*, 9–10; Baugh, "Report," 7–10, 22.

25. *San Antonio Register*, April 15, 1960.

26. Ibid., April 15, 22, 29, May 6, 13, June 17, July 29, 1960; *San Antonio Express*, April 16, 24, 29, 30, May 1, 4, 6, 12, 1960; *San Antonio Light*, May 4, 1960; James interview; Baugh interview; Jacobson interview; Baugh, "Report," 13–14.

27. Baugh, "Report," 14.

28. *San Antonio Express*, May 12, 1963.

29. Baugh interview; Black interview; Marcee interview; Donoughue interview; James interview; Bellinger interview; Burns interview; *San Antonio Register*, September 28, 1956; January 9, 1959; February 10, September 8, 1961; June 8, 22, September 7, October 5, 1962; May 3, 17, 1963; Bruton, "Desegregation in San Antonio," 66. The paralysis of the San Antonio NAACP is revealed in a letter sent by Mrs. S. A. Robinson to NAACP national membership secretary Lucille Black: "From the year of the Court Injunction here nobody had collected and sent my dues. I had been wanting to send it to you at your office there in New York while we were inactive here. I didn't know how to do so and keep out of trouble." Robinson to Black, January 31, 1960, Group III, Series A, San Antonio, Texas Branch, National Association for the Advancement of Colored People Records (Manuscript Division, Library of Congress, Washington, D.C.).

30. Black interview; Bellinger interview.

31. *San Antonio Register*, December 30, 1960.

32. Burns interview; *San Antonio Register*, July 15, August 26, December 30, 1960; December 1, 1961; January 26, April 13, June 29, July 13 (quotation), November 30, December 21, 1962; February 8, 1963.

33. Baugh interview.

34. Kaufman interview.

35. McAllister interview.

36. Black interview; James interview; Bellinger interview; Donoughue interview; Scott interview; Baugh interview; Burns interview; Kaufman interview. For more on styles of leadership in other black communities see Chafe, *Civilities and Civil Rights*, 27–28; Lewis M. Killian and Charles U. Smith, "Negro Protest Leaders in a Southern Community," *Social Forces*, 38 (March 1960): 253–57; Harold W. Pfautz, "The Power Structure of the Negro Sub-Community: A Case Study and Comparative View," *Phylon* 23 (Summer 1962): 156–66; Jack L. Walker, "Protest and Negotiation: A Case Study of Negro Leadership in Atlanta, Georgia," *Midwest Journal of Political Science*, 7 (May 1963): 99–124.

37. San Martin interview. See note 40 below for sources on the general attitude of the Mexican American community toward blacks.

38. Leo Grebler, Joan W. Moore, Ralph C. Guzman, et al., *The Mexican-American People: The Nation's Second Largest Minority* (New York: Free Press, 1970), 394.

39. Burns interview.

40. Black interview. For the relationship between blacks and Mexican Americans see Pena interview, Marcee interview, Bellinger interview, San Martin interview; Grebler et al., *Mexican-American People*, 393; Scott interview; Burns interview; Jacobson interview; Kaufman interview; Black interview; Leonel J. Castillo, "Inter-Minority Relations," in John H. Burma, ed., *Mexican Americans in the United States: A Reader* (Cambridge, Massachusetts: HarperCollins, 1970), 63–72; and Alphonso Pinkney, "Prejudice Toward Mexican and Negro Americans: A Comparison," ibid., 73–80.

41. Bruton, "Desegregation in San Antonio," 27, 73, 74; Pena interview; Baugh interview; Donoughue interview; *San Antonio Express*, February 11, 12, 13, 27, March 13, 27, June 12, July 23, 1961; *San Antonio Register*, December 4, 11, 1959; February 17, 24, March 10, July 28, 1961.

42. Baugh, "Report," 19–20; *San Antonio Express*, August 9, 1961.

43. Baugh, "Report," 9.

44. Ibid., 11.

45. Marcee interview; San Martin interview; Baugh interview; Donoughue interview; Jacobson interview; Baugh, "Report," 8, 9, 11, 12, 14–19, 22.

46. Black interview; Baugh interview; Donoughue interview; Burns interview; Bellinger interview; Baugh, "Report," 11; *San Antonio Express*, February 13, 27, March 13, 27, June 12, July 28, August 9, 1961; *San Antonio Register*, August 24, 1962.

47. *San Antonio Register*, October 19, 1962.

48. Ibid., March 8, 1963.

49. Burns interview; *San Antonio Register*, June 22, October 26, November 2, 1962; February 22, March 8, 1963; *San Antonio Express*, February 14, 16, March 4, 1963; Council of the City of San Antonio, Minutes of the Proceedings (cited hereafter as City Council Minutes), GG, February 13, 1963, 587, San Antonio City Hall.

50. Kaufman interview; McAllister interview; City Council Minutes, GG, February 27, 1963, 604–605; *San Antonio Express*, February 14, 27, 28, March 1, 1963; *San Antonio Register*, March 8, 1963.

51. Kaufman interview; McAllister interview; *San Antonio Light*, January 18, 1963; *San Antonio Register*, March 8, 1963; *San Antonio Express*, January 18, 19, February 13, 14, April 3, 1963; City Council Minutes, GG, February 27, 1963, 605.

52. *San Antonio Express*, February 28, 1963.

53. Ibid.

54. Burns interview; Black interview.

55. McAllister interview.

56. Ibid.

57. *San Antonio Express*, February 28, 1963; Pena interview; Black interview; Burns interview; Baugh interview; Kaufman interview; McAllister interview; Jacobson interview.

58. City Council Minutes, HH, May 29, 1963, 46.

59. Baugh interview.

60. *San Antonio Register*, June 28, 1963; *New York Times*, July 13, 1963, 51.

61. City Council Minutes, HH, June 19, 1963, 81; Baugh, "Report," 22; Kaufman interview; *San Antonio Express*, May 30, June 4, 6, 28, 29,

1963; *San Antonio Light*, June 28, 1963; *San Antonio Register*, June 7, 1963; *San Antonio City Directory*, 1963 (Dallas: R. L. Polk, 1964).

62. City Council Minutes, HH, July 3, 1963, 99.

63. Kaufman interview; San Martin interview; Baugh interview; *San Antonio Express*, June 13, 15, 19, 22, 27, 29, 1963; City Council Minutes, HH, July 3, 1963, 99; Baugh, "Report," 22–24.

64. *San Antonio Register*, June 7, 1963.

65. *San Antonio Express*, May 30, 1963.

66. Black interview.

67. Ibid.

68. *San Antonio Express*, June 21, 1963.

69. *San Antonio Register*, May 31, June 21, 1963; *San Antonio Express*, May 30, June 1, 7, 13, 14, 15, 17, 18, 20, 21, 22, 26, 27, 1963; City Council Minutes, HH, May 29, June 5, 19, 1963; Black interview; Burns interview; Kaufman interview.

70. Baugh, "Report," 24; *San Antonio Express*, July 4, 14, 1963; City Council Minutes, HH, July 3,1963, 98–100; Baugh interview; Kaufman interview; *San Antonio Register*, July 5, 19 (quotation), 1963.

71. Black interview.

72. *San Antonio Express*, July 14, 1963.

73. *San Antonio Express*, July 14, August 1, September 19, October 16, 17, 1963; *New York Times*, July 14, 1963, 51; *San Antonio Register*, September 6, 20, 1963; City Council Minutes, HH, July 24, 31, 1963, 123–24, 139; Black interview; Kaufman interview; Baugh interview; *San Antonio Light*, September 4, 19, 1963; C. Don Baugh, "Progress Report," November 14, 1963, in City Council Minutes, HH.

74. *San Antonio Express*, July 30, 31, August 4, 8, 19, 25, 29, October 3, 4, 11, 16, 17, 1963; *San Antonio Light*, July 31, September 30, 1963; *San Antonio Register*, August 30, September 6, October 18, 1963; City Council Minutes, HH, August 28, October 3, November 14, 1963, 174, 208, 244.

75. *San Antonio Express*, November 15, 1963; City Council Minutes, HH, November 14, 1963, 245.

76. *San Antonio Express*, November 22, 1963.

77. Ibid.

78. James interview.

79. *San Antonio Express*, March 19, 1965.

80. *San Antonio Register*, March 19, 26, April 9, 1965; *San Antonio Express*, March 19, 1965; Scott interview; James interview; McAllister interview; San Martin interview; Pena interview.

81. Kaufman interview; City Council Minutes, II, November 11, 1965, 580.

82. *San Antonio Express*, October 29, November 5, 11, 12, 1965; San Antonio Register, November 12, 1965; Ordinance Book of the City of San Antonio, RR, July 8, 1965–December 30, 1965, 775–77 (San Antonio City Hall); James interview; McAllister interview; Kaufman interview; Black interview.

83. Donoughue interview.

84. Quoted in Artis Hill, "Jim Crowism in Several Areas of Twentieth-Century Texas Life Relative to the Negro: Transportation, Eating and Lodging Places, Public Parks and Movie Theaters" (master's thesis, Abilene Christian College, 1969), 63.

85. Ibid., 40–95; Morland, *Lunch-Counter Desegregation*, 1–21; *New York Times*, March 9, p. 19; March 11, p. 15; March 26, p. 10; March 27, p. E8; March 30, p. 25; April 2, p. 21; April 6, p. 27; May 1, p. E6; August 26, p. 9; September 13, 1960, p. 34; July 28, pp. 1, 9; July 30, 1961, p. 56; *San Antonio Express*, March 5, 27, April 3, August 26, 1960; June 30, 1963; *San Antonio Register*, June 21, August 2, 1963.

# "A Pearl of Great Price"

## *Socio-Literary Activism in the Life and Writings of Olga Samples Davis*

JEANETTE NYDA PASSTY

REGIONAL VERSE IS RARELY A SOUGHT-AFTER commodity in the literary marketplace; nevertheless, *A Time To Be Born*, by African American poet, playwright, educator, and social activist Olga Samples Davis, appeared in four editions. *Palo Alto Review* founding editor Ellen Shull has lauded Davis's poems as "packaged exuberance," "black pearls," finding in the works themselves "joy, laughter, soul, goodness, beauty, peace . . . faith, hope, love."

This study seeks to explore biocritically—on both the physical and metaphysical planes—Davis's poems; her one-act play, *Artemisia* (1993); and her collaborative, multimedia, multi-ethnic art exhibit, *Ageless Women, Timeless Stories* (1997), a celebration of sixteen unsung regional feminist archetypes.

No study of Davis is complete unless it includes a biographical perspective. Davis's mother, Browning McKinney Samples, was widowed early, but she taught her children, Olga, Carlotta, and Ronald, the value of education by pursuing it for herself and imparting it to others. From her mother Davis also received a "deep spiritual base, and that was the foundation of [her] existence." Beginning in their earliest childhood, Davis and her sister were taught the "Mamaisms" that reminded them daily "who [they] were, and *Whose* [they] were" (that is, the Lord's).

Davis's lifelong "Walk of Faith," which is matrilineal, has borne fruit, not only in what she terms the "sometimes encoded spirituality" in her paintings and poems, but in her social activism as well. Soup kitchens, homeless shelters, battered women's centers, impoverished public schools, and nursing homes are among the "list of one hundred agencies" Davis and the St. Philip's College students she teaches have benefited with their volunteer efforts.

But it was a 1989 pilgrimage to the African motherland—to Gambia, Ghana, the Ivory Coast, Liberia, Senegal, and Sierra Leone—and especially to "the village of Juffure, where Binta Kinte, Alex Haley's precious African relative, lives," and to the slave castles on the Senegalese island of Goree, that caused Davis to hear "all those spirits . . . calling out" to her.

This biocritical journey will venture into all of the above, so as to evoke the life, explore the works, and thereby celebrate the social and literary achievements of Olga Samples Davis.

It is seven o'clock on the morning of Tuesday, November 7, 1995. The staff from KLRU-TV in Austin is already on the set as the four poets arrive. They will be taping the third of three segments of a program called *Poetry Aloud*. After hours of preparation and rehearsal, the poets will read in a simulated coffee house, to musical accompaniment, before a live audience; each reading will be prefaced by a statement of the poet's personal aesthetic. At 5 P.M., Naomi Shihab Nye, her sensitive face helmeted by glossy brown hair gathered into a ponytail at the base of her neck, leads off the program: "You have to pause to hear a poem, truly. To write a poem, you pause. To read a poem, you pause. And I think that our lives are such at the end of this century that we need more pause. I think that's what poetry can give us."[1]

Nye's reading of a poem that transmutes a colorful holiday parade through the streets of downtown San Antonio into a sequence of metaphysical metaphors meets with warm applause from her audience.

Susan Bright, blonde and fair—with glittering eyes, flushed cheeks, and feminist fire—then pays tribute to Mary Wollstonecraft and Mary Shelley. Enthusiastically applauded in her turn, she yields the spotlight to the Byronic black curls, bronze skin, latino voice, and impish multicultural humor of Jesse Cardona, whose "muscles are monolingual,"[2] and whose trip into the *panaderia for pan dulce* is a retrospective rite of passage back into his chicano youth, for himself and for his delighted audience.

In regal purple headdress and dashiki, with eye-catching earrings, caramel complexion, immutable presence and grace, Olga Samples Davis arrives next on stage. Her reading is the longest and the most sensual; her audience becomes progressively more involved in the undulating rhythms of her voice—and the eloquent gestures of her arms—until it is transformed into her chorus, chanting the refrains to her poems. Her rapport with each individual in the studio grows into a paradigm of mutual adoration as she invites them to "Come . . . let me bathe you / in the waters of my love." This is a scene that has been repeated many times in the course of Davis's long and flamboyant career in South Central Texas. It is perhaps as much due to her personal charisma as to her seemingly magical power over words that her slender paperback collection of poems and prose anecdotes, *A Time To Be Born*, is still sought after in its fourth edition. "Like you must breathe," she tells her enraptured audience, "I must write."[3] "I try to pass on history, love, wisdom," she explained to the author of this paper on another occasion. "If I can practice with you and you with me a politics of inclusion, good people will rise to the top like cream. Nobody wins in hate, ignorance, meanness. Nobody wins in those negativities. . . . We all have talents and treasures . . . to share."[4]

Promulgating these views, in person and in print, is the Alpha and the Omega[5] of her artistry, and her message has drawn a warm response from her reviewers: "Davis's poetry is a call to action for those who love life. . . . Her spirit is riveting," applauds Gemeral Berry Jr.[6] "Her works speak to a new generation of African Americans who live in the twentieth century. . . . She talks the tale and the emotions of today's people connecting to the past so beautifully," exults Voris Brumfield.[7] "Clearly inspired by real people and events, the characters that populate the pages of this little book are audacious and authentic, gritty and genuine, generally memorable, and obviously very black. . . . [Yet] the work has meaning beyond ethnicity, and the mind behind the work clearly has alacrity, vitality, humor, and compassion," writes Andrew B. Preslar.[8] Professor Ellen Shull views Davis's poems as "black pearls" and exults: "Oh, the music. The rhythm . . . these gems . . . demand the voice speak, sing out the words."[9]

In exploring the provenance of these "black pearls," it is a biocritical imperative to examine Davis's life, with emphasis on her pilgrimage to Africa. The family history of Olga Stephanie "Ouija" Samples Davis is both intriguing and intricate. Her mother, Browning, was the daughter of the Reverend Robert Carson McKinney, a graduate of Gammon Theological Seminary, and his wife, Louvenia, a graduate of Clark College. The couple's passion for history, language, and literature determined the names of their six surviving children: Ulysses, Signorina, Browning, Tennyson, Valeda, and Theodora. Two other children of the family died in infancy or in early childhood.[10]

Davis's father, Eugene Samples, had been married to three other women prior to marrying Browning. All three divorces were amicable, and each of his ex-wives—Zenobia, Matty, and Paula—had been given her own home by Eugene, along with sufficient property to guarantee her and her children financial security. Eugene had, moreover, an uncontrollable compulsion to feed the hungry, shelter the homeless, and provide generous support for the local clergy.[11] He was much older than Browning McKinney, still in her early twenties, when she came to work for him as a barber. At the time, Eugene owned an all-black hotel, restaurant, and barber shop in St. Paul Square, near the Union Pacific Railroad Station.[12] Although these businesses had numerous patrons, and Eugene, assisted by Browning, worked "an endless job,"[13] Davis recalls, "I guess, by that point, he was basically poor. [He] died when I was five, and it was really a tragedy. My mother didn't speak much in those days. She was a very young widow with three small children."[14]

Eugene Samples was fabled among black San Antonians of his day for his countless benevolences, but there was a negative side to him as well. At Olga's birth, on March 13, 1949, in an old hospital on the east side of San Antonio, her father made no secret of his bitter disappointment: "I was supposed to be a boy—my father wanted one—and here I was, a girl. His was an iron fist that had no velvet glove."[15] She attended kindergarten at the parochial school down the street, St. Peter Claver;[16] first grade at nearby Cuney Elementary; and second through sixth grades at Fannin Elementary, "which was also right around the corner and was integrated." Since Davis and her older sister, Carlotta, were "the only little chocolate chips in class," their teacher, Mrs. Arnold, "explained about us to our classmates by telling that story about 'God's oven.'" Davis asserts that Mrs. Arnold was "actually nice; she was doing the best she could" in a teaching situation that was new to her.[17] From the seventh through the ninth grades, Davis enjoyed Emerson Junior High, but it was because she was compelled to take the bus to far-away Jefferson High, the public college-preparatory high school African Americans were permitted to attend, that she became a writer: "That meant leaving at 5 A.M., catching three busses, traveling through downtown; that's when I really became a writer. On those long bus rides, you've got to entertain yourself. And those other people on the bus gave me a lot of information, only they didn't know it. [After Carlotta graduated, I was] riding the bus alone my senior year. [It was] that quiet time, that sacred time. It was the aha! moment, the come-to-Jesus moment, the thank-you-Jesus moment."[18]

After high school, Davis began college at Hampton Institute in Hampton, Virginia. Orientation the first semester required students to immerse themselves in religion. This was intended to give them "a sense of how greatness really was a part of each individual. Silence in chapel made it possible to discover this from the music and the meaning. . . . [The experiences we had there] were really exercises and lectures on greatness, duty, responsibility. Home and church had taught us these things; home came to us through these teachings; they were from the same community of hearts."[19]

Davis transferred from Hampton Institute to the University of Texas at Austin, where she earned a BA in fine arts. The experience robbed her of her naiveté but not of her idealism. At the time, "We African Americans were an anomaly there."[20] Surrounded as she was by icy indifference and fiery hostility, Davis remembers: "There wasn't a day when I didn't cry. But I learned to fight, became a woman's woman. . . . I went to work, class, home, work, class, home. . . . I responded to that environment in accordance with my life-long training: Hold on just a little bit longer, and everything will be all right. . . . Hey, there's an Amazing Grace out there. I wasn't going to let them make me a statistic in the column, 'Couldn't Perform.' On the way to that morning class, I'd be walking, crying, and singing every survival song I knew. I couldn't be weak. If you're weak, people will come in, set up housekeeping in the name of failure, jump on your one good nerve."[21]

In *A Time To Be Born*, Davis's negative experiences at UT–Austin are apparently recreated in a dialogue titled "The Element," in which an instructor draws a usually loquacious student aside from her classmates and renders her speechless by referring to her "element" as "Nigras" and demanding to know, "Just what do you people WANT?" While in Olga's retelling of the event, the student, smiling "one of those smiles," uses a phallic symbol—"one of my best pens"—to vanquish the boorish professor, it is probable that her victory was fantasized rather than factual.[22]

Physically, the community where Davis was raised and from which she received her "survival skills"—her sense of purpose and strength of character—was dominated by its graveyard, actually a succession of nine graveyards, which are, as Davis puts it, "so present in our neighborhood."[23] While residents of the area would stroll or bike along the dirt and gravel paths among the tombstones and mausoleums, these also served as an ever-present reminder to both young and old of the transience of earthly existence and the importance of putting "God first, others second, myself last."[24]

Although Davis, her older sister Carlotta, and her younger brother Ronald grew up without a father, every adult member of their close-knit, church-centered community took an intense, personal interest in their upbringing: "When I was a child, the whole community raised you and had permission to beat your butt if you were out of line, so you had five hundred mothers."[25] Any member of the congregation could and would openly call your attention to your faults—"You're lying like a rug," a sister of the church would tell you freely. "I can see by your face that you're just lying like a rug."[26] Children in the community were preached to incessantly: "Each child in this community was like a small baby bird who had to be taught repetitively until it learned to use its little feet and little wings. Each child received little sermonettes at home, little sermonettes at church from those who loved the child. All the adults of that community wanted the same thing for all the children of that community—success. But success was defined as being a good human being, doing right by others, treating them in a respectful, loving way, serving others, serving God, following the Ten Commandments, living the beatitudes."[27]

Davis perceives the oral tradition as the most significant factor in the ability of the African people to endure the vicissitudes of history. Talking, chanting, and singing made it possible for the captives to survive the Middle Passage. This survival skill, transplanted to her eastside San Antonio neighborhood, where books were in short supply,[28] was routinely practiced by whole families at the supper table; as the meal progressed, the children were called upon to recite Bible verses from memory and to comment on them.

It was also practiced on the front porch after supper, where family narratives and other stories were told. Perhaps most significant, churches of all denominations maintained an "open door policy" by which age-related activities—for youth, for adults, for seniors—were available to all comers, regardless of religious affiliation. Whether at a home church, or traveling the "Chitlin Circuit" in groups to other black churches—for safety—participants enjoyed opportunities to dance, sing, meet in disciplined bodies that adhered to the strictest parliamentary procedure, and practice composition and oration publicly and with intense seriousness. There would be, for example, "Bible competitions between groups . . . in performing the Twenty-third Psalm. We trained as a group in choral oration during which we would have to find new and different ways to articulate that psalm. Twenty-five people would be divided into five groups—broken up chorally—taught discipline, teamwork, [elocution], rhythm, memorization. [Moreover,] we had to write at church and at home. All this we did at my home, and it was done in other homes, too."[29]

Small wonder that, buoyed up by the "center" she had found in this "community of hearts," Olga Stephanie Samples floated safely through the storms of racism that threatened her undergraduate career at UT–Austin, carried her diploma home in triumph in 1973, and set her sights on a master's degree in higher education from the University of Texas at San Antonio, which she successfully completed in 1976. Subsequently, she accepted an instructorship at a small, historically black college in the neighborhood of her birth, and set out to fulfill her matrilineal potential. "Sister Girl / Got it honestly" she writes in the first poem in *A Time To Be Born* (the first poem she chose to read in the KLRU broadcast), and she goes on to enumerate these among many other traits of "Sister Girl" and her foremothers:

*Mustard seed faith*
*Wildcat spirit*
*Wholesale humor*
*Gift for gab. . . .*

*She was*
*Fighter quick*
*Mother wit strong. . . .*

*Sister Girl got it . . .*
*Got it honestly*
*From her mother*
*Her mother's mother*
*And then some.*

*It was her heritage.*[30]

Davis has an extraordinary gift for depicting the intimate and personal so that it resonates in every loving human heart, evoking the private, the personal, *and* the universal. Because another of Davis's poems (the last one she read at KLRU), "The Knot I Tie,"[31] never explicitly states that her mother is "the knot I tie when I'm at the end of the rope / and gotta hang on," each auditor or reader of the poem may call up an image of the beloved friend or relative who uplifts the soul being menaced by life's "sea of living storms."[32]

Davis's eloquent dedication to Browning Samples of her collaborative, multimedia, multiethnic art exhibit, *Ageless Women, Timeless Stories*, staged at St. Philip's College with photographer Casey Lieberman and painter Terry Gay Puckett in March 1997, constitutes a lasting tribute to the mother who, she said, provided "the foundation of my existence."[33] Here, as elsewhere in her life and writings, Davis oscillates between the sublimely inspirational and the outrageously humorous, saluting her mother on a poster at the entrance to the exhibition—along with her collaborators' mothers, Ida Levy Scharff and Alice Maltsberger Puckett—for "fine wisdom, great courage . . . magnificent beauty of mind and heart," but then playfully displaying an eye-catching cluster of twenty-five often outrageous "Mamaisms" on a wall of the exhibit itself, including "Don't let your mouth write a check your body can't cash," "Whatever won't kill you is bound to make you strong," and "I'm only beating you 'cause I love you."[34]

Visually, Davis and her mother appear to be antitheses: the mother is petite and self-effacing; the daughter is amply proportioned and theatrical. Yet there can be no doubt that Browning's determined evolution from widowed pink-collar worker to school teacher to college professor rendered her her daughter's role model.[35] "You are," writes Davis to her mother in "The Knot I Tie," my "star in a sky of darkness."[36]

Among Davis's many artistic pursuits are music and liturgical dance, which have been a significant influence on her poetry.[37] Moreover, her involvement in the theater as playwright, producer, and director has been perennial. As of 1991 (the only date for which an estimate is available), she had close to one hundred amateur and professional productions in the greater Austin-San Antonio area and elsewhere, to her credit.[38] Performance of Davis's one-act play *Artemisia* (1993), celebrating the life of Dr. Artemisia Bowden, the friend and correspondent of Mary McLeod Bethune who, with Bishop James Steptoe Johnson, founded St. Philip's College, became an annual ritual on that campus. Over the years, Davis has also pursued abstract painting—"My works, each one with a design that contained my encoded spirituality, sold for some nice money, which I donated to my campus ministry."[39] The field of interior design, in which both Davis and her late husband, Clinton Davis, earned over one hundred hours of credit, became not only a way of maintaining marital togetherness, but a serious artistic endeavor.

It is tempting to try to envision Davis's life as a series of concentric circles—or, perhaps more accurately, as concentric spheres of the ivory sort that can rotate independently of one another. At the center would be her mother's constant and luminous admonition to love and serve "God first, others second, self last."[40] Embellishing each would be incised patterns wrought by her lifelong achievements in the fine arts, including speech, which is the academic discipline she taught at a college where she was universally revered by her students and is now professor emeritus.

At times, her method of transforming her students into facile communicators seemed to give her affinities with Paulo Freire,[41] since it involved her and those she instructed in the politics of how this society deals with issues of marginalization, alienation, human suffering, and human needs. "It's very political," she observes, "when you insist on your students doing community service, insist that your students be responsible to the community, insist that they follow Mary McLeod Bethune's injunction that we 'Leave no one behind.'"[42] In partial fulfillment of the requirements of her courses, Professor Davis's students were required to become social activists, at least for a time. For decades, Davis maintained a list of one hundred agencies and other organizations that serve the impoverished, the battered, the ill, the elderly, and the otherwise underprivileged and abandoned of our troubled society. Having a child-care concern or a work-schedule conflict did not exempt a student from this requirement, since there would always be "some agency that's open twenty-four hours that needs volunteers to answer the phone and will let them bring along their children."[43] When Davis's students presented their speeches based on this field experience to her and their classmates, she observed, "the results were often enough to make you cry."[44] In 1991, a student related this incident to the author of this study: "I was feeling very sad and very sorry for myself, because I had recently moved to San Antonio and was going to be all alone on Christmas Day. I took my trouble to Ms. Davis, and she invited me to spend the day with her at a shelter for the homeless, where she and I served meals to people far less fortunate than we were. It was the best Christmas I'd ever had!"[45]

It is obvious that the concentric-spheres model for Davis's life and career is somewhat inadequate. One can alternatively consider her life as a kind of spectrum of goodness, a continuum of colors brilliant and beautiful, extending from here to heaven; or, in accordance with a celebrated mathematical model, as a kind of "Hilbert Hotel," in which an infinite number of guests are happily housed in an infinite number of rooms, but there will always be accommodations for one more welcome guest.

Wandering back down a corridor into one of those rooms, among Davis's past experiences, one finds her August 1989 trip to Africa, the pilgrimage that Davis herself has characterized as "the catalyst" that empowered her to write *A Time To Be Born*. A Judeo-Christian framework for the book is provided by Ecclesiastes 3:1–11, "To everything there is a season," and its poems are arranged into sections appropriately titled "A Time To Be Born," "A Time To Die," "A Time To Laugh." Nevertheless, the experiential "grains of sand" that engendered what Ellen Shull perceived as poetic "black pearls" were the direct result of her visit to African motherland. In the course of this pilgrimage, Davis, the only lay person in a party of African American Methodist clergy,[47] "got the blessing, the 'sending forth,' the benediction, the Alpha and the Omega, so [she] could . . . move on with the book."[48] In Ghana, Davis learned a vital lesson by watching how "the people rowed canoes hollowed out from trees. They rowed . . . knowing how to maneuver, knowing the tides. They went fishing on giant waves, made by humongous cargo ships, and they were singing as if life were nothing but celebration, but that is faith. There were three stories [sic] high waves [yet] people came back alive and with fish."[49]

On the island of Goree, Davis relived the atrocities of the past, grieved, honored her ancestors, and then let go of her grief and anger:

> There are hundreds of slave castles. They're made of stone. They'll last longer than we. Their architecture reflects French, Spanish, and English colonial influences. The most beautiful slave castles were in Ghana. . . . The slave castle in Goree was more of a holding cell for exporting, and the shackles were intact; they were *so* intact. The administrators were on the upper levels, living their rich lives; the slaves were below. I was just so in awe with that moment in time. You're just there. It takes over time. It's a presence and physicality that is so overwhelming, but it's more. You notice shackles on the wall, blood staining the floors and walls that cannot be washed away, but it's a presence because of some soul that has passed through those portals. Grown men sat on steps and cried. It just took over. Before we knew it, we were just crying and shaking. I called names aloud and threw flowers into the sea.
>
> When I made that moment for myself, that's when it hit: There was a round hole in the wall; it was a narrow portal, just large enough to push a human being through [along a plank and into a ship]. If one chose to fall—since they were chained together—all would fall.[50]

While in Africa, following the injunction of poet Sara Teasdale, Davis also sold, or rather traded, all she had "for loveliness," bartering virtually every possession in her suitcase—her clothes and shoes—for African wood carvings from a lepers' colony.[51]

All these experiences opened "the floodgates / of healing waters" for Davis, whose vignette, "Rightful Name," and poem, "In the Gambia," commemorate the pilgrimage that enabled her to draw inspiration directly from Binta Kinte:

> *Binta's presence and*
> *lessons of queenliness*
> *have an esteemed place in this heart.*
> *And often, when her face comes*
> *to mind,*

*my soul laughs*
*aloud*
*in empowered song.*[52]

Renewed by all that she saw and experienced in the homeland, Davis returned to America and composed poems that, as she expresses it, "celebrate both joy and sorrow."[53]

Toni Morrison prefaces her 1993 Nobel Prize acceptance speech with the story of the elderly blind woman famed for her wisdom who was asked whether a bird held by a youth was alive or dead. Knowing full well that if she said, "Alive," the youth could crush it in his hand, but if she said, "Dead," the youth could release the bird and it would instantly fly away, the old woman sagely replied, "It's in your hands." Likewise, the reputation of South Texas poet and social activist Olga Samples Davis now rests with you, the readers of the first scholarly article ever published on her life and work.

## NOTES

1. In *Poetry Aloud*, Program 3, VHS, directed by Jess Doutery, KLRU-TV, Austin, Texas, 1995.

2. Jess Doutery, in *Poetry Aloud.*

3. Olga Samples Davis, in *Poetry Aloud.* See also Davis, "In the Water of My Love," in *A Time to Be Born*, 4th ed. (San Antonio, Texas: St. Mary's University/Pecan Grove Press, 1991), 56–57.

4. Davis, interviews by the author, April 3–4, 1997; August 19, 21, 1997; October 16, 1997 (cited hereafter as "Interviews").

5. "The Alpha and the Omega" is the title of a love poem in *Time to Be Born*, 44–45.

6. Gemeral Berry Jr., review quoted in *Time to Be Born*, n. pag.

7. Voris Brumfield, review quoted in *Time to Be Born*, n. pag.

8. Andrew B. Preslar, review of *Time to Be Born*, in *Review of Texas Books* 7, no. 2 (Summer 1992): n. pag.

9. Ellen Shull, introduction to *Time to Be Born*, vi.

10. Their names are unknown to the present generation of the family.

11. Eugene Samples was particularly instrumental in fostering the career of the late Reverend Claude Black, a prominent eastside clergyman, providing him with, among other aids to his ministry, a place adjacent to one of Samples's business establishments where he could preach (Interviews).

12. The station was later refurbished and renamed the Amtrak Robert Thompson Transit Station.

13. Interviews.

14. Ibid.

15. Ibid.

16. Jeanette Nyda Passty, in "'The Lion Writes Her Story': How Nettie Patricia Brooks Hinton Took Washington and Then the World" (paper delivered at the Morehead State University Wilma E. Grote Symposium for the Advancement of Women, November 8, 1996), expands the study, presented a month before at the Sixth Annual American Women Writers Of Color Conference, of how "African American school children in San Antonio, Texas, learned not only . . . to write history, but to make history from the Catholic nuns who founded St. Peter Claver Academy" (ii).

17. Jade Snow Wong includes an account of her grade school teacher's using the identical story in the identical manner, in *Fifth Chinese Daughter* (New York: Harper & Row, 1950; rpt. Seattle: University of Washington Press, 1989).

18. Interviews.

19. Ibid.

20. See also N. P. Brooks Hinton's experience, as recounted in Passty, "The Lion": "If you know you're going into a situation like UT, you develop an attitude, 'I have something else I'm here for.' You can't become embittered" (7).

21. Interviews.

22. *Time to Be Born*, 46–47.

23. Interviews.

24. Ibid. This is one of the "Mamaisms" referred to in note 34, below.

25. Interviews.

26. Ibid.

27. Ibid.

28. Passty, in "The Lion," 8, explains how Nettie Patricia Brooks Hinton single-handedly desegregated the San Antonio Public Library System in 1960. Prior to that, as Davis recalled in the interviews, "the only library open to blacks was the Carver," where holdings were limited.

29. Interviews.

30. *Time to Be Born*, 15, lines 1–6, 10–12, and 16–21.

31. Ibid., 36–37.

32. Ibid., 37, line 34.

33. The exhibition was at St. Philip's College, March 1–31, 1997.

34. Davis's collection, "100 Mamaisms," ultimately evolved into *Things My Mama Told Me* (Colorado Springs, Colorado: Waterbrook Press, 2004).

35. Browning McKinney earned her BS in medical records librarianship from Incarnate Word College in 1965 and her MEd from Our Lady of the Lake University in 1972, after which she completed several additional graduate hours. She served successively as a reading teacher at Navarro Elementary School, a reading and English teacher at Emerson Middle School, and coordinator of a Title III educational improvement project at St. Philip's College. At her retirement, she was an associate professor and reading specialist at St. Philip's.

36. *Time to Be Born*, 37, line 33.

37. Interviews.

38. Gloria Hernandez, "Olga Samples Davis Publishes First Book," *St. Philip's Update*, July 17, 1991, 3.

39. In every one of her paintings, Davis has abstracted or otherwise disguised or concealed the letters WGATAP, i.e., "With God, All Things Are Possible."

40. Interviews. This is one of the "Mamaisms," cited in note 34 above.

41. Anna Flanagan, "English Educators Remember Paulo Freire," *Council Chronicle* (National Council of Teachers of English) 7, no. 1 (September 1997): 1, 6, discusses "Freire's contention that education is inherently political, and all teachers are politicians."

42. Interviews.

43. Ibid.

44. Ibid.

45. Quoted in a letter from Jeanette Passty to Ernest Spikes Jr., October 18, 1991, 2.

46. Quoted from "In the Gambia," *Time to Be Born*, 73, lines 121–24.

47. Thanks to Audrey L. Mosley and Sherry Rollins, the author of this paper was able to locate the memorandum from Rev. Richard R. Hicks, dated November 30, 1988, publicizing the trip, inviting United Methodist ministers, and providing a tentative itinerary. Also made available by Mosley and Rollins were the relevant flights, dates, a passenger manifest, and a letter dated June 12, 1989, from Davis's pastor, Rev. Robert E. Felder, praising her as "a superb choice," and promising to provide financial support for her trip.

48. Interviews.

49. Ibid.

50. Ibid.

51. Ibid.

52. "Rightful Name," *Time to Be Born*, 68–70; "In the Gambia," ibid, 74.

53. Interviews.

# Blacks in South Texas

## *Selected Bibliography*

BRUCE A. GLASRUD

Armstrong, Ira E. "A Historical Study of Public Elementary Schools in San Antonio, Texas with Special Emphasis on Elementary Schools for Negroes from 1910 to 1940." Master's thesis, Prairie View State Normal and Industrial College, 1941.

Bailey, Herbert J. "Charles Bellinger and Jim Crow in San Antonio, Texas, 1905–1937." *South Texas Studies* 4 (1993): 75–88.

Baker, T. Lindsay. "How to Use the W.P.A. Slave Narratives in Museum/Historic Site Interpretation." In Hutcheson, *Viewing the Past through Different Lenses*, 59–64.

Barr, Alwyn. "African American Reconstruction in Brazoria County." In Hutcheson, *Viewing the Past through Different Lenses*, 24–28.

———. "Reconstruction Change and Continuity in Brazoria County, Texas." *Houston Review* 18 (1996): 114–23.

Beall, Jonathan A. "The Military Occupation of the Lower Rio Grande Valley, 1865–1866." *Journal of South Texas* 16, no. 2 (2003): 195–236.

Black, Claude W., Jr. *Grandpa Was a Preacher: A Letter to My Grandson.* Bloomington, Indiana: AuthorHouse, 2007.

Borrer, Jennifer. "The Colored Trainmen of America: Kingsville Black Labor and the Railroads." *Journal of South Texas* 11 (1998): 74–103.

Brawner, Anne. "Guadalupe College: A Case History in Negro Higher Education, 1884–1936." Master's thesis, Southwest Texas State University, 1980.

Byerly, Edward. "Divided We Stand: Jim Crow Education in Victoria, Texas, 1901–1966." *South Texas Studies* 19 (2008–09): 1–32.

Campbell, Randolph B. "Nueces County." In *Grass-Roots Reconstruction in Texas, 1865–1880*, 193–219. Baton Rouge: Louisiana State University Press, 1997.

———. "Reconstruction in Colorado County, Texas, 1865–1876." *Nesbitt Memorial Library Journal* 5 (1995): 3–30.

———. "Reconstruction in Nueces County, 1865–1876." *Houston Review* 16 (Fall 1994): 3–26.

———. "The Slave Family in Antebellum Texas." *Victoria College Social Sciences Symposium*, 1988: 1–28.

———. "Slavery in Texas, 1821–1865: A Brief Overview, with Emphasis on the Lower Brazos River Valley." In Hutcheson, *Viewing the Past through Different Lenses*, 17–23.

Christian, Garna L. *Black Soldiers in Jim Crow Texas, 1899–1917*. College Station: Texas A&M University Press, 1995.

———. "The Brownsville Raid's 168th Man: The Court-Martial of Corporal Knowles." *Southwestern Historical Quarterly* 93 (1989): 45–59.

Crouch, Barry A. "The Freedmen's Bureau in Colorado County Texas, 1865–1869." *Nesbitt Memorial Library Journal* 5 (1995): 71–105.

———. "The Freedmen's Bureau in Colorado County Texas, 1865–1869, Part 2." *Nesbitt Memorial Library Journal* 7 (1997): 147–75.

———. "The Freedmen's Bureau in Colorado County Texas, 1865–1869, Part 3." *Nesbitt Memorial Library Journal* 8 (1998): 3–32.

Davis, Olga Samples. *Things My Mama Told Me*. Colorado Springs, Colorado: WaterBrook Press, 2004.

———. *A Time To Be Born*. San Antonio, Texas: Pecan Grove Press, 1991.

Doyle, Judith Kaaz. "An Ironic Crusade: Maury Maverick, San Antonio Politics, and the Black Political Machine, 1938–1941." Master's report, University of Texas at Austin, 1982.

———. "Maury Maverick and Racial Politics in San Antonio, Texas, 1938–1941." *Journal of Southern History* 53, no. 2 (May 1987): 194–224.

Fink, Rob. "The Houston Eagles and the End of the Negro Leagues." *South Texas Studies* 14 (2003): 98–113.

Fitzgerald, Dorothy. "Black History." In *Colorado County Chronicles*, compiled by Colorado County Historical Commission, 1:423–61. Austin, Texas: Nortex Press, 1986.

Fowler, Fred M., Jr. "The Original *San Antonio Register*, 1931–1978." Master's thesis, University of Texas at San Antonio, 1982.

Franklin, Antoinette V. *In the Mist of Struggle: Stands a Woman*. Bloomington, Indiana: AuthorHouse, 2005.

Glasrud, Bruce A. "Black Texas Improvement Efforts, 1879–1929: Migration, Separatism, Nationalism." *Journal of South Texas* 14 (2001): 159–69.

Glasrud, Bruce A., and Paul H. Carlson, eds. *Slavery to Integration: Black Americans in West Texas.* Abilene: State House Press, 2007.

Glasrud, Bruce A., and Archie P. McDonald, eds. *Blacks in East Texas History: Selections from the "East Texas Historical Journal."* College Station: Texas A&M University Press, 2008.

Glasrud, Bruce A., and Merline Pitre, eds. *Black Women in Texas History.* College Station: Texas A&M University Press, 2008.

Glasrud, Bruce A., and James M. Smallwood, eds. *The African American Experience in Texas: An Anthology.* Lubbock: Texas Tech University Press, 2007.

Glass, Olive Jewell. "Beyond the Dream: A Celebration of Black History: Discovering the Past, Understanding the Future." *Nesbitt Memorial Library Journal* 8 (1998): 181–82.

Goldberg, Robert A. "Racial Change on the Southern Periphery: The Case of San Antonio, Texas, 1960–1965." *Journal of Southern History* 49 (1983): 349–74.

Gonzalez, Jorge O. "The Black Experience in Laredo: 1755–1919." Master's thesis, Laredo State University, 1986.

Gower, Patricia E. "Unintended Consequences: The San Antonio Pecan Shellers' Strike of 1938." *Journal of South Texas* 17, no. 2 (2004): 88–103.

Harper, Bradly C. "The Frederick Douglass School and Early Black Education in Kingsville, Texas, 1909–1969." *Journal of South Texas* 6 (1993): 80–88.

Harris, Jamie L. Walker. *African Americans in Wilson County, Texas: 1860–1885.* Las Vegas, Nevada: LynBrook Books, 2006.

Hayes, Bonni C. "Fleming, Arizona." *Handbook of Texas Online.* http://www.tshaonline.org/handbook/online/articles/FF/fflmw.html.

Howell, Kenneth W. "Just Southwest of Dixie: Reconstruction in South Texas, 1865–1876." *Journal of South Texas* 16, no. 1 (2003): 45–64.

———. "The Untold Story of Reconstruction in South Texas, 1865–1876." *South Texas Studies* 14 (2003): 16–30.

Hutcheson, Barry, ed. *Viewing the Past through Different Lenses: The African American Legacy in the Lower Brazos Valley.* Austin: Texas Parks and Wildlife Department, 2000.

Jenkins, Rachel. "Vann Settlement, Texas." *Handbook of Texas Online.* http://www.tshaonline.org/handbook/online/articles/VV/hrv34.html.

Jones, Marie Beth. *Peach Point Plantation: The First 150 Years.* Waco, Texas: Texian Press, 1982.

Jordan, Edna. *Black Tracks to Texas: Solomon Melvin Coles—From Slave to Educator*. Corpus Christi, Texas: Golden Banner Press, 1977.

———. "Black Tracks to Texas." *Nueces County Historical Commission* 2, no. 1 (November 1989): 7–19.

Knight, Larry P. "Defending the Unnecessary: Slavery in San Antonio in the 1850s." *Journal of South Texas* 15, no. 1 (2002): 57–72.

Lane, Ann J. *The Brownsville Affair: National Crisis and Black Reaction*. Port Washington, New York: Kennikat Press, 1971.

Leiker, James N. *Racial Borders: Black Soldiers along the Rio Grande*. College Station: Texas A&M University Press, 2002.

Louzon, David. "Corpus Christi's Galvan Ballroom: Music and Multiculturalism in the 1950s." *Journal of South Texas* 20, no. 2 (Fall 2007): 213–36.

Lucko, Paul M. "Haller, Nathan H." *Handbook of Texas Online*.

http://www.tshaonline.org/handbook/online/articles/HH/fhafr.html.

Margraves, Nina Benware. "The Jaybird Democratic Association of Fort Bend County: A White Man's Union." Master's thesis, University of Houston, 1955.

Mason, Kenneth. *African Americans and Race Relations in San Antonio, Texas, 1867–1937*. New York: Garland Publishing, 1998.

Massey, Sarah R. "After Emancipation: Cologne, Texas." *Journal of South Texas* 20, no. 2 (Fall 2007): 184–196.

———, ed. *Black Cowboys of Texas*. College Station: Texas A&M University Press, 2000. See chapters on Peter Martin, Henrietta Williams Foster ("Aunt Rittie"), Ben Kinchlow, George McDow, Louis Power, and Richard "Bubba" Walker.

———. "Black Cowboys: Wrangling the Numbers." *Journal of South Texas* 17, no. 1 (2004): 15–30.

McQueen, Clyde. "South Texas." In *Black Churches in Texas: A Guide to Historic Congregations*, 190–211, 230–31. College Station: Texas A&M University Press, 2000.

Moneyhon, Carl H. "George T. Ruby and the Politics of Expediency in Texas." In *Southern Black Leaders in the Reconstruction Era*, edited by Howard N. Rabinowitz, 363–92. Urbana: University of Illinois Press, 1982.

Moore, Moses N., Jr., and Yolanda Y. Smith. "Solomon M. Coles: The First Black Student Officially Enrolled in Yale Divinity School." *Spectrum*, Winter 2007, 6–7.

Moore, Moses N., Jr., and Yolanda Y. Smith. "Solomon M. Coles: Preacher, Teacher, and Former Slave—The First Black Student Officially Enrolled in Yale Divinity School." http://www.yale.edu/divinity/storm/Coles.

Norris, Clarence Windzell, Jr. "St. Philip's College: A Case Study of a Historically Black Two Year College." PhD diss., University of Southern California, 1975.

Palm, Reba W. "Protestant Churches and Slavery in Matagorda County." *East Texas Historical Journal* 14, no. 1 (1976): 3–8.

———. "Slavery in Microcosm: Matagorda County, Texas." Master's thesis, Texas A&I University, 1971.

Passty, Jeanette Nyda. "'A Pearl of Great Price': Socio-Literary Activism in the Life and Writings of Olga Samples Davis." *South Texas Studies* 11 (2000): 65–82.

Petrovich, Alisa V. "The Jacksons of Brazoria County: The Life, the Myth, and the Impact of a Plantation Family." *East Texas Historical Journal* 36, no. 2 (1998): 42–49.

Pierce, Walter. "The Brownsville Raid: A Historiographical Assessment." In *Studies in Brownsville History*, edited by Milo Kearney (323–26). Brownsville, Texas: Pan American University, 1986.

Pitre, Merline. "Different Strokes for Different Folks." In Hutcheson, *Viewing the Past through Different Lenses*: 17–23.

———. "George T. Ruby: The Party Loyalist." In *Through Many Dangers Toils and Snares: Black Leadership in Texas, 1868–1900*, 166–73, 238–40. Austin, Texas: Eakin Press, 1985.

———. "Ruby, George Thompson," *Handbook of Texas Online*.http://www.tshaonline.org/handbook/online/articles/RR/fru2.html

Pruett, Jakie, and Everett B. Cole, eds. *As We Lived: Stories by Black Storytellers*. Burnett, Texas: Eakin Press, 1982.

Rives, Mary Jean. "Charles Andrews, Barber and Civic Leader." *Journal of South Texas* 9 (1996): 102–108.

Santos, Adolfo. "Explaining African-American, Hispanic, and White Vote Choices When the Candidates Are African-American, Hispanic, and White: The Case from the 2002 Texas Midterm Elections." *South Texas Studies* 15 (2004): 94–115.

Smallwood, James M. *The Feud That Wasn't: The Taylor Ring, Bill Sutton, John Wesley Hardin, and Violence in Texas*. College Station: Texas A&M University Press, 2008.

———. "G. T. Ruby: Galveston's Black Carpetbagger in Reconstruction Texas." *Houston Review* 5 (Winter 1983): 24–33.

———. "Sutton-Taylor: A Feud?" *South Texas Studies* 16 (2005): 1–27.

Stein, Bill. "Colorado County Black High School Football." *Nesbitt Memorial Library Journal* 8 (1998): 161–80.

———. "The Slave Revolt Revisited." *Nesbitt Memorial Library Journal* 1 (1991): 317–18.

Stein, Bill, ed. "The Slave Narratives of Colorado County." *Nesbitt Memorial Library Journal* 3 (1993): 3–32.

Thomas, Gates. "South Texas Negro Work-Songs: Collected and Uncollected." In *Rainbow in the Morning*, edited by J. Frank Dobie, 154–80. TFS 5. Austin: Texas Folklore Society, 1926.

Thomas, Matt. *Hopping on the Border: The Life Story of a Bellboy*. San Antonio: Naylor, 1951.

Thompson, Jerry D. "The Ku Klux Klan: Hooded Bigots at Laredo." In *Laredo: A Pictorial History*, chap. 26. Norfolk, Virginia: Donning, 1986.

Weaver, John D. *The Brownsville Raid*. New York: W. W. Norton, 1973.

Williams, Jerelyne Castleberry. *The Brackenridge Colored School: San Antonio, Texas, 1899–1936*. Bloomington, Indiana: AuthorHouse, 2006.

Wolff, Henry, Jr. "Madame Blackley: Seer of South Texas." In *Folklore: In All of Us, In All We Do*, edited by Kenneth L. Untiedt, 95–105. TFS 63. Denton: University of North Texas Press, 2006.

Wood, Rue. "The Forging of the African American Community in Corpus Christi, Texas, 1865–1900." *Journal of South Texas* 12 (1999): 34–75.

Woods, Randall B. "George T. Ruby: A Black Militant in the White Business Community." *Red River Valley Historical Review* 1 (1974): 269–80.

Yelderman, Pauline. *The Jay Bird Democratic Association of Fort Bend County: A White Man's Union*. Waco, Texas: Texian Press, 1979.

———. "Jaybird-Woodpecker War." *Handbook of Texas Online* http://www.tshaonline.org/handbook/online/articles/JJ/wfj1.html.

Young, Frederick Douglas. *From These Roots: Cologne—One Hundred Years, 1870–1970*. Houston: Texas Southern University, 1973.

# Contributors

**Jennifer Borrer** earned a master's degree from Texas A&M University–Kingsville. She teaches at Callahan High School.

**Edward Byerly** is associate professor of history and geography at Victoria College in Victoria, Texas. He is also coeditor of *South Texas Studies* and has researched and written on topics related to both history and geography. His article, "The Politics of Topographic Mapping: J. D. Whitney, C. F. Hoffman, and the California State Geological Survey, 1860–1874," won the Doyce Nunis Prize awarded by the Historical Society of Southern California in 2001. He holds a PhD in history from Arizona State University and an MA in human geography from Western Illinois University.

**Judith Kaaz Doyle** received a PhD in history from the University of Texas at Austin; her doctoral dissertation was entitled "Out of Step: Maury Maverick and the Politics of the Depression and the New Deal."

**Rob Fink** is an assistant professor of educational studies at Hardin-Simmons University in Abilene, Texas. He is the coauthor of *Love Unbounded: The Influence of First Baptist Church on Abilene, Texas* with his wife Tiffany Fink. He also wrote *Playing in Shadows: Texas and Negro League Baseball.* Fink holds a PhD in history from Texas Tech University.

**Bruce A. Glasrud** is a professor emeritus of history at California State University, East Bay, and a retired dean of the School of Arts and Sciences, Sul Ross State University. He now lives in Seguin, Texas. Glasrud specializes in the history of African Americans in the south and west.

**Robert A. Goldberg** is professor of history and director of the Obert C. and Grace A. Tanner Humanities Center at the University of Utah. A specialist in U.S. social history, Goldberg received his PhD from the University of Wisconsin at Madison; he has published eight books including *Hooded Empire, Grassroots Resistance, and Enemies Within.*

**Kenneth W. Howell** earned his PhD in history from Texas A&M University–College Station. An assistant professor of history at Prairie View A&M, Howell has several publications that focus on the history of Texas and the old South, including *Henderson County, Texas, 1846–1861: An Antebellum History; Texas Confederate, Reconstruction Governor: James Webb Throckmorton; Beyond Myth and Legend: A Narrative History of Texas; and Seventh Star of the Confederacy: Texas During the Civil War.* Currently, Howell is editing a book on violence in Texas during the Reconstruction era.

**Larry P. Knight**'s love of history began in part when he was an "army brat" in Germany. He had no access to television, so he resorted to reading and fell in love with biographies. He earned his bachelor's and master's degrees at what was Southwest Texas State University and his PhD at Texas A&M University. He has taught history at the college level since 1980. Concurrently, he practices his other profession—he is an emergency room RN.

**Rebecca A. Kosary** received her PhD in history from Texas A&M University–College Station. She is an assistant professor of history and the director of African American studies at Texas Lutheran University in Seguin, Texas, where she has taught since 2000.

**David Louzon** received a master's degree in history from Texas A&M University–Corpus Christi. Louzon now lives in San Antonio, Texas, with his family. He conducted his research into the Galvan Ballroom while finishing his master's degree.

**Sara R. Massey** retired from the University of Texas Institute of Texan Cultures at San Antonio where she was a developer of educational materials and Web sites concerning Texas history. She has received a national award for her curriculum project, *The Other Cowboys*. She is the editor of *Black Cowboys of Texas*, which won the T. R. Fehrenbach Book Award, the coauthor of *Turn of the Century Photographs: San Diego, Texas*, and editor of *Texas Women on the Cattle Trails*, which won the Liz Carpenter book award. She now lives on the Gulf Coast of Texas where she is writing a series of biographies, *Spirited Women of Texas*, for students in elementary schools.

**Jeanette Nyda Mendelssohn Passty** is an associate professor of English at St. Philip's College in San Antonio, Texas. She received that college's 2003–2004 Teaching Excellence Award as well as the 2003 NISOD Medallion for Excellence in Teaching and Leadership from the University of Texas at Austin. She was a contributor to *American Women Writers: A Critical Reference Guide from Colonial Times to the Present*, and author of an American Library Association Outstanding Academic Book of 1988–89, *Eros and Androgyny: The Legacy of Rose Macaulay*. The most recent of her numerous creative works, scholarly papers, and published articles—coauthored with research chemist William C. Davis—is "Creating the Spark: A Journey with Henry Ford, George Washington Carver, Wernher von Braun, and Rosalyn Yalow."

**Janice L. Sumler-Edmond** is a professor of history at Huston-Tillotson University in Austin, Texas, where she teaches U.S. history, African American history, and constitutional history and law. She holds both PhD and the JD degrees. Sumler-Edmond's book *The Secret Trust of Aspasia Cruvellier Mirault: the Life and Trials of a Free Woman of Color in Antebellum Georgia* was published by the University of Arkansas Press in 2008.

**Cary D. Wintz** is a professor of history at Texas Southern University, where he has taught since 1971. Wintz is the author/editor of nearly twenty books, including *Black Culture and the Harlem Renaissance, Harlem Speaks,* and *the Encyclopedia of the Harlem Renaissance*. He is coauthor on the last three editions of *Texas: The Lone Star State* and has written and published about African Americans in Texas.

**Rue Wood** has been an instructor of history at Indian Hills Community College in Ottumwa, Iowa, for the past ten years—four years as an adjunct and the past six years as a full-time instructor. She holds BA degrees in history and sociology from the University of Texas at San Antonio and an MA in history and politics from Texas A&M University–Kingsville.

# Permissions

Glasrud, Bruce A. "The African American Experience in South Texas: An Overview." *Journal of South Texas* 22, no. 2 (2009): 113–132. Reprinted by permission of the author and courtesy South Texas Historical Association. Revised and expanded.

Knight, Larry P. "Defending the Unnecessary: Slavery in San Antonio in the 1850s." *Journal of South Texas* 15, no.1 (2002): 57–72. Reprinted by permission of the author and courtesy South Texas Historical Association.

Howell, Kenneth W. "Just Southwest of Dixie: Reconstruction in South Texas, 1865–1876." *Journal of South Texas* 16, no. 1 (2003): 45–64. Reprinted by permission of the author and courtesy South Texas Historical Association.

Kosary, Rebecca A. "'Wantonly Maltreated and Slain, Simply Because They Are Free': Racial Violence During Reconstruction in South Texas." Printed by permission of the author.

Massey, Sara R. "After Emancipation: Cologne, Texas." *Journal of South Texas* 20, no. 2 (Fall 2007): 184–197. Reprinted by permission of the author and courtesy South Texas Historical Association.

Wood, Rue. "The Forging of the African American Community in Corpus Christi, Texas, 1865–1900." *Journal of South Texas* 12 (1999): 34–75. Reprinted by permission of the author and courtesy South Texas Historical Association.

Sumler-Edmond, Janice L. "Lola and Leon Houck v. the Southern Pacific Railway Company." Printed by permission of the author.

Borrer, Jennifer. "The Colored Trainmen of America: Kingsville Black Labor and the Railroads." *Journal of South Texas* 11 (1998): 74–

103. Reprinted by permission of the author and courtesy South Texas Historical Association.

Byerly, Edward. "Divided We Stand: Jim Crow Education in Victoria, Texas, 1901–1966." *South Texas Studies* 19 (2008–2009): 1–32. Reprinted by permission of the author and courtesy Victoria College South Texas Studies.

Doyle, Judith Kaaz. "Racial Politics in San Antonio, Texas, 1939–1941." *Journal of Southern History* 53, no. 2 (May 1987): 194–224. Copyright (1987) by the Southern Historical Association. Reprinted by permission of the editor, and courtesy the author, Judith Kaaz Doyle.

Fink, Rob. "The Houston Eagles and the End of the Negro Leagues." In *Playing in Shadows*. Lubbock: Texas Tech University Press, 2010. Reprinted by permission of the author and courtesy Texas Tech University Press. Originally published in *South Texas Studies*, reprinted by permission.

Louzon, David. "Corpus Christi's Galvan Ballroom: Music and Multiculturalism in the 1950s." *Journal of South Texas* 20, no. 2 (Fall 2007): 213–236. Reprinted by permission of the author and courtesy South Texas Historical Association.

Goldberg, Robert A. "Racial Change on the Southern Periphery: The Case of San Antonio, Texas, 1960–1965." *Journal of Southern History* 49 (1983): 349–374. Copyright (1983) by the Southern Historical Association. Reprinted by permission of the Editor, and courtesy the author, Robert A. Goldberg.

Passty, Jeanette Nyda. "'A Pearl of Great Price': Socio-Literary Activism in the Life and Writings of Olga Samples Davis." *South Texas Studies* 11 (2000): 65–82. Reprinted by permission of the author and courtesy Victoria College South Texas Studies. Minor editorial changes.

# Index

*Perspectives on South Texas, Sponsored by Texas A&M University–Kingsville*

*Nesting Birds of a Tropical Frontier: The Lower Rio Grande Valley of Texas*, Timothy Brush

*White-Tailed Deer Habitat: Ecology and Management on Rangelands*, Timothy Fulbright and J. Alfonso Ortega-S

*A Kiñeno Remembers: From the King Ranch to the White House*, Lauro F. Cavazos

*Texas Quails: Ecology and Management*, Leonard A. Brennan

*Ecologia y Manejo de Venado Con Blanca*, Timothy Fulbright and J. Alfonso Ortega-S.

*Petra's Legacy The South Texas Ranching Empire of Petra Vela and Mifflin Kenedy*, Jane Clements Monday and Frances Brannen Vick